Vitamin B12 deficiency in clinical pra
"Doctor, you gave me my life back!"

Dr Joseph Chandy (Kayyalackakom)

Medical Practitioner 1966-2015 (49 years)

in the National Health Service, UK

Written in collaboration with Hugo Minney Ph.D.

Chief Executive – B12 Deficiency Support Group

Published by Amazon, UK

ISBN 9781090400819 – black & white edition

ISBN 9781096782919 – colour edition

Editor: Margaret Greenhalgh

Illustrations: Hugo Minney unless otherwise attributed

Cover Design by Hugo Minney. Drawings of a human being (by Mikael Häggström used with permission), nerve axon, DNA and RNA, adapted from the Wikimedia Foundation web sites (including Wikipedia and Wikimedia Commons) under the Creative Commons Attribution/Share-Alike License.

This book is produced as a non-profitmaking educational venture. The cover price reflects production costs only. If you wish to make a donation to the B12d charity, please do so via the web page http://www.b12d.org/donate

The hymn of self-dedication

I, the Lord of sea and sky,
I have heard my people cry.
All who dwell in dark and sin my hand will save.
I, who made the stars of night,
I will make their darkness bright.
Who will bear my light to them?
Whom shall I send?

Here I am, Lord. Is it I, Lord?
I have heard you calling in the night.
I will go, Lord, if you lead me.
I will hold your people in my heart.

I, the Lord of snow and rain,
I have borne my people's pain.
I have wept for love of them.
They turn away.

I will break their hearts of stone,
Give them hearts for love alone.
I will speak my word to them.
Whom shall I send?

I, the Lord of wind of flame,
I will tend the poor and lame.
I will set a feast for them.
My hand will save.

Finest bread I will provide
'Til their hearts be satisfied.
I will give my life to them.
Whom shall I send?

From Dan Schutte's hymn *Here I am, Lord* © 1981 Daniel L. Schutte and New Dawn Music – based on Isaiah 6 and 1 Samuel 3.

Table of Contents

List of Tables

List of Figures

All figures drawn and © by the author (Hugo Minney) unless otherwise attributed

Patient brief case studies

List of Charts

Charts prepared by the authors (Dr Chandy and Hugo Minney) from patient data at Shinwell Medical Practice

List of Boxes

Recommendation to readers by Professor David Smith

Dr Joseph Chandy, a practicing doctor for almost 50 years, has written a fascinating and important book. Some 20 years after starting to practice, Dr Chandy came across a patient with vitamin B12 deficiency who presented with neurological symptoms, but without the characteristic changes in blood cells. In the subsequent 30 years, he dedicated himself in General Practice to identifying and treating patients who had insufficiency of B12. The book vividly describes this very human story and the challenges he faced from the authorities who were reluctant to admit that he was making the correct diagnoses. The authorities behaved very badly in prioritising the 'rule book' over the clinical symptoms. The book shines throughout with Dr Chandy's devotion to the well-being of the patient and it should be read by all GPs, in training and those with experience. Medical scientists should also read the book since Dr Chandy ranges across several areas of medicine where much more research is needed. The book is very readable and full of helpful practical information. If the regulatory authorities read the book, it could lead to an improvement in an unsatisfactory aspect of the current practice of medicine.

Professor A. David Smith FMedSci
Professor Emeritus of Pharmacology
Department of Pharmacology
University of Oxford
Founding Director, Oxford Project to Investigate Memory and Ageing (OPTIMA)
Founding Director, MRC Anatomical Neuropharmacology Unit

Dedication

God's will be done. Shortly after I started working in the NHS, I was responsible for a programme to bring quality improvement to many places, including a small GP practice in a little known part of north-east England, in Horden. There I made the most unlikely encounter, with a GP who had held firm to his belief in the importance of vitamin B12, in spite of numerous attempts to silence him – legends that would one day be put in a book.

I was intrigued. This doctor said that modern medicine isn't always for good, that we're forgetting some of the old-fashioned truths, and – most radical of all – that a simple nutritional deficiency could be responsible for a whole range of illnesses and syndromes that had elaborate descriptions and were named after this famous doctor or that famous researcher.

I already knew that many of the "new ideas" being promoted in the NHS, most of the good ones anyway, were recycled from 70 years of NHS history, and Dr Chandy certainly needed help. At first my job was to do the analysis and reporting for the Primary Care Trust (PCT), which showed that Dr Chandy and the Shinwell Medical Practice were complying with the restrictions imposed on his Practice. However, my closeness to the figures showed me that B12 deficiency is a significant reality, and that B12-replacement therapy (by oral tablets and by injections) did appear to remit the symptoms in many hundreds of patients, far more than could be explained simply by a placebo effect, and I was hooked.

Dr Chandy was destined to remind us, all of us, of the beautiful simplicity of God's world and the paths He has chosen for each of us. My part was to join this journey 25 years after it was started; to bring rigour and analysis to the treatment of patient after patient; and ultimately to write down Dr Chandy's vast knowledge and compare it with the published scientific and medical literature. I don't think I chose to be a part: it just came about.

I commend this book as probably the most definitive guide to B12 deficiency. It is based on nearly 40 years of personal observations in patients whose health Dr Chandy has been responsible for, not on an episodic basis, but for their whole lives from youth through adulthood and into old age.

Hugo Minney, Ph.D.

Preface

In 1981, I encountered my first case of vitamin B12 deficiency without macrocytosis. This dramatic discovery led me to a persistent and lifelong interest in the role played by this essential micronutrient in the human body. Over the next three decades, I discovered that B12 deficiency is far more prevalent in the population than the current paradigm suggests. As I delved deeper into the subject and the story unfolded, I found that many conditions not recognised as B12 deficiency nevertheless responded well to B12 supplementation, to the extent of complete remission from symptoms of many diseases considered incurable.

The journey has not been easy. I encountered strong resistance and inflexible views about how treatments in medicine should be made. It is not easy to overturn entrenched opinion but I could not deny the overwhelming evidence before my eyes: vitamin B12 therapy can cure many conditions and saves lives! Despite many setbacks in getting my discoveries acknowledged, I have drawn encouragement from the appreciation of my patients, the support of some receptive members of the medical profession in both Britain and India, and the many enquiries which have poured in to me from sufferers and doctors all over the world.

The effects of untreated B12 deficiency are devastating and can cause untold human suffering. I came to the medical profession out of a commitment to help my fellow human beings. This book is written to alleviate that suffering by sharing the extensive experience of B12 deficiency that I acquired over many years as a General Practitioner in the north-east of England. It is my fervent wish that this knowledge will help to guide future treatment and research in this crucial area, and help to eradicate the widespread ignorance of the condition and its frequent misdiagnosis.

The investigation of vitamin B12 deficiency has been not only a fulfilling clinical experience but also an intense spiritual journey.

I have the greatest respect for all faiths but in my personal life I have always felt guided, sustained and strengthened by my own particular Christian faith. Without this guidance, I would not have had the clarity of vision to recognise the symptoms of vitamin B12 deficiency, nor the courage to adhere to my convictions in the face of opposition. For this reason, I have thought it appropriate to include in this book references to events in my life of particular spiritual significance to me, and quotations from the Bible and other Christian texts which have inspired me.

Dr Joseph Chandy (Kayyalackakom),

Horden, County Durham, United Kingdom, 1 May 2019

Acknowledgements

In researching and writing this book I am deeply indebted to my family, GP and nurse colleagues and all the staff and patients of Shinwell Medical Practice, Horden, County Durham, UK. A very special thankyou goes to Hugo Minney for his invaluable contribution to the B12 cause since he joined the Shinwell Medical team.

I would like particularly to thank the late Ernie Bostwick and Betty his dear wife, the late Colin and Norma Reynolds, Susan Peacock, Ann Peel, Margaret Greenhalgh and Leanne Walker (née Chandy) for their various devoted contributions to my work and this book.

I also gratefully acknowledge the support and interest of all those in all walks of life who have supported my work by responding helpfully to submissions, inviting me to speak at conferences and providing evidence by testimony. I have greatly appreciated their encouragement. In particular, I wish to thank Professor A. David Smith, Emeritus Professor of Pharmacology, University of Oxford, for allowing me to reproduce (in Chapter 2) his letter of 29 November 2013 supporting my work, the Executive Chairman of the Pernicious Anaemia Society Martyn Hooper MBE who has asked us to speak at the Society's conferences, and the author Sally Pacholok who has mentioned my work in her book *Could it be B12? An Epidemic of Misdiagnoses* and invited me to write the foreword for the second edition.

May I also express my deep gratitude to the people of Horden and Peterlee, County Durham, UK, to the B12 Deficiency Support Group and its executive committee officers, and to all those kind people who have made generous donations since the charity and website were established.

Author's Note

The information in this book is based on the knowledge and experience of the vital importance of vitamin B12 for human health gained over 40 years of clinical practice as a General Practitioner (family doctor), including 34 years of administering vitamin B12 therapy. It also draws on extensive research on vitamin B12 conducted by other experts. The aim of the book is to provide information for the public and clinicians alike in the hope of raising awareness of the widespread effects of vitamin B12 deficiency and how it may be treated. All patients whose names and photographs appear in this book have given full written consent for their data to appear in the hope that their experiences may help others. The recommendations given here are based on sound medical experience but are not intended as a replacement for advice from a health professional. We would always encourage patients to seek such advice, in order especially to rule out alternative diagnoses. The author cannot be held responsible for a patient's failure to seek professional health advice.

The list below summarises the key points made in this book:

- Vitamin B12 is a vital micronutrient, ranking in our view only after oxygen and water in the list of molecules essential for health.

- Vitamin B12 deficiency is common in the general population and can manifest at any age. Its prevalence is generally under-recognised. We found a prevalence of 18% in a medical practice population of 5,760 patients in 2015.

- Vitamin B12 is crucial for many body systems; the deficiency manifests in an array of different symptoms in different people.

- Pernicious anaemia is only one manifestation of vitamin B12 deficiency. In our view it is a late stage of vitamin B12 deficiency and may be preventable. Many B12-deficient patients do not have the symptoms of pernicious anaemia but have other symptoms.

- Contrary to accepted belief, the presenting symptoms are frequently neurological or neuropsychiatric and only rarely haematological.

- Many people are suffering severely and unnecessarily because of lack of recognition of this condition. Prompt treatment is essential to prevent irreversible neurological damage leading to patients becoming wheelchair-bound.

- Neuropsychiatric symptoms such as depression, anxiety, other psychological disorders and even psychosis, are common in vitamin B12 deficiency and there is evidence that the condition may contribute to the onset of dementia.

- Guidelines on how to diagnose the varied symptoms are severely lacking.

- The serum B12 test in common use has been shown to be unreliable as a stand-alone marker and commonly accepted thresholds for B12 deficiency are questionable.

- "Subtle" vitamin B12 deficiency is particularly difficult to diagnose but has the potential to deteriorate to a severe deficiency very quickly.

- Causes of B12 deficiency include genetic disorders of B12 absorption, insufficient dietary intake, any gastrointestinal illness (especially atrophic gastritis) or surgery, use of antacid medications and proton-pump inhibitors, and alcoholism.

- Vitamin B12 is necessary for several important metabolic processes and contributes to DNA synthesis through its interaction with folate. If these processes are disrupted due to lack of vitamin B12, serious illnesses can result, such as cardiovascular diseases and even cancer.

- Like folic acid, vitamin B12 is especially important during pregnancy to ensure a healthy child. Deficiency can lead to severe birth defects.

- Based on our experience over many years, we drew up and implemented a **Protocol for excluding B12 deficiency (Megaloblastic anaemia, pernicious anaemia) from adult and child presentation** in cooperation with the local Primary Care Trust which is given at the end of this book (see Appendix 1).

- Vitamin B12 deficiency is linked to autoimmune illnesses and can lead to Autoimmune Polyglandular Syndrome (APS). Another life-threatening illness, hypoadrenalism, is common in vitamin B12-deficient patients. As this is another under-recognised illness in which we developed some expertise, we also drew up a Protocol for diagnosis which is included at the end of this book (see Appendix 2).

- Vitamin B12 is non-toxic (even at very high doses) and cheap compared with many medications. Therapy with vitamin B12 would result in huge savings to the NHS. It will cure, in contrast to the symptom-modifying (often expensive) medicines that are frequently used to treat conditions which are in reality vitamin B12 deficiency.

Introduction

This book is about vitamin B12 deficiency. This is an old illness – documented cases appear to go back nearly 200 years – and yet it is forgotten in the modern age of scientific medicine and pharmaceuticals.

The greatest discovery of the last century in medicine was the discovery of penicillin and that it can eradicate, as well as prevent, life-threatening bacterial infection.

The most fascinating and far-reaching clinical discovery that I and my patients have encountered in our Practice over 34 years (from 1981 to 2015) is how a simple, harmless and cheap B12 vitamin can not only cure but also prevent a wide spectrum of diseases affecting each and every part of the human body and mind. Vitamin B12 is so important that we would rank it as the third most vital element, after oxygen and water, for sustaining human life:

Table i-1 The order of importance of components vital to life

Physiologist's View	Our View
1. Oxygen	1. Oxygen
2. Water	2. Water
3. Salt	3. Vitamin B12
4. Potassium	4. Cortisol
	5. Salt
	6. Potassium

Over more than three decades, I diagnosed, treated and followed up patients suffering from B12 deficiency at my medical practice in Horden, County Durham, collating data, auditing it and widely sharing this evidence-based knowledge. This has resulted in 100% patient satisfaction and there are around 300 testimonies to confirm it.

Based on this experience, this book presents new data, new findings and new understanding. The story must be told, and it is underpinned by evidence. Every case study, graph and table in this book tells the same story. It has been said that "the plural of anecdotes is not data" but can we really deny the overwhelming evidence of over 1,000 anecdotes concerning patients whom the author has cared for as General Practitioner (GP - family doctor), with illnesses all pointing towards a single underlying cause?

Towards a new paradigm

It is our contention that the current paradigm which allows a diagnosis of vitamin B12 deficiency ONLY when macrocytosis and Intrinsic Factor (IF) antibodies are present needs to be changed. This paradigm is, in our view, based on limited understanding and pre-war clinical situations which, because of nutritional improvements, no longer apply. The modern-day presentation is different and diagnosis needs to take into account signs and symptoms which may be present even when macrocytosis and IF antibodies are not. More details of this much-needed crucial shift in diagnosis patterns are given in Chapter 2, and a new Protocol and guidelines for diagnosis and treatment are given in Chapter 3 and Appendix 1.

To quote another medical pioneer, Dr F. Batmanghelidj, MD:

"As an example, the understanding was that the Earth was flat. The new understanding is that the Earth is round...Adoption of a fundamentally significant new paradigm in the science of medicine is more difficult, even if the outcome is highly desirable and desperately needed by society."

Your Body's Many Cries for Water (Batmanghelidj, 2008)

I came to Horden/Peterlee to practice as a General Practitioner (GP) in 1970, and from that time saw a fruitful rapport between doctors and administrators working until 1997. Since then, in the last 20 years, the very sanctity of the holistic whole-person clinical care has been questioned and undermined systematically by NHS medical directors.

In the case of B12 deficiency, the lack of a holistic view has led to misdiagnosis or no diagnosis at all, resulting in serious irreversible damage to patients as well as distress and disappointment to their family members and dedicated carers. Conditions can deteriorate rapidly, with patients becoming housebound, wheelchair/crutches-dependent and without hope of recovery, if the autonomy of the GP is constrained in this way.

In order to put the discoveries that I and my patients have made into context, this introduction gives (in Part 1) some autobiographical detail and explains how I first encountered the extensive effects of B12 deficiency. Part 2 describes the difficulties I had (and still have) in getting the findings accepted, and Part 3 describes our continued efforts to propagate the knowledge and our Patient-Safe Protocol. Then follow nine chapters, each dedicated to a particular set of vitamin B12 deficiency-related illnesses or a condition. Each describes our experience, with examples, and suggests treatments based on this experience. All patients named and/or photographed in this book have given their consent to publication (and many video testimonials can be found on the B12 Deficiency Support Group website: www.b12d.org). Other data are presented anonymously.

Part 1: Dr Joseph Chandy: journey to discovery

Formative years

I was born Joseph Alexander ("Chandy") Kayyalackakom on 16 January 1941, in Kerala, south India. During the postwar period my parents were based in Thiruvananthapuram/Trivandrum, the capital of Kerala, lately known as "God's own country". I spent my formative years in this beautiful countryside.

Each day I could hear conversations between family and friends about the ongoing difficulties everyone was facing due to the long-term damage the Second World War had caused: disease, death and famine throughout the country.

During the same period, the independence struggle was gaining momentum and heartbreaking stories of human suffering could be heard from every part of the Indian continent, causing further sadness and concern. On 15 August 1947, to everyone's joy and surprise, we heard the much-awaited declaration that at long last our nation was independent, after 100 years of British rule. I was six years old and felt as though at long last my dream was beginning to come true. Unfortunately, my and the whole nation's joy was short-lived.

Months later on a calm quiet evening, the whole family was startled by the loud cry of many thousands marching through the main street and an inconsolable crowd weeping, beating their chests and lamenting as they came to know of the brutal assassination of Mahatma Gandhi, who was and still is the father of our nation. The entire crowd was repeatedly crying out "Who will answer for the blood of Mahatma Gandhi, who will answer for the blood of Mahatma Gandhi?" Hearing the people cry I began sobbing; I was inconsolable.

This incident had a lasting impact on my relationship with my fellow human beings, especially my patients after I qualified as a Medical Practitioner in 1965. I have always remembered Mahatma Gandhi's words: "Mine may today be a voice in the wilderness, but it will be heard when all other voices are silenced, if it is the voice of truth" (Kumarappa, 1951).

Medical training and first prophetic message

I and the whole family were excited when I received the letter of admission to the Kerala Medical College.

Soon the day came to say "goodbye" to my parents, brothers and sisters and move away from my home town to the capital city. Looking me in the eyes, my father said (knowing that in six years' time I would be a qualified medical doctor): "I am blessed with 12 children, six boys and six girls, will one of you one day make a valuable contribution to humanity?"

I hope and pray that I have not disappointed my dear father who is watching over me from his heavenly home. I also believe that the Father God will greet me, and invite me with open arms into his heavenly kingdom as a "good and faithful servant" after an earthly life of service for 50 years (1965-2015).

Encounter with B12 deficiency

In 1965 I qualified (MBBS in medicine) from Trivandrum Medical College, Kerala University (India). The following year I did my house physician's training under the supervision of a professor of medicine. Here I first encountered the effects of B12 deficiency.

In this city there were many Hindu Brahmin families who had been strict vegetarians all their lives. I noticed that some women between the ages of 20 and 30 presented in my outpatient clinic with a particular set of symptoms. Comparatively these women were quite fair in their complexion. All appeared pale, tired-looking and lacking in energy. They complained of aches and pains, headaches and dizziness. Having excluded other possible conditions, I was rather puzzled by these patients.

I sought my professor's guidance. His immediate advice was to give them weekly deep intramuscular (IM) liver extract injections which were painful. Eight weeks later, when they returned to the outpatient clinic, they appeared healthy and energetic and their pale faces had become pink and shiny.

I can recollect being intrigued and asking the professor how the liver extract could cause this remarkable transformation. My boss smiled and told me about the simple and life-saving discovery made by George Minot and William Murphy of the US regarding the "Liver Diet" in 1926.[1] This discovery was accidental. While having lunch they gave their bleeding dog some leftover liver. A few days later they noticed that the dog's bleeding had ceased. The two excited physicians decided to try the effect on chronically sick American soldiers. To everyone's amazement, all these soldiers fully recovered. It was not until 1948, however, that the B12 molecule was officially isolated by Edward L. Rickes, Norman G. Brink, Frank R. Koniuszy, Thomas R. Wood and Karl Folkers in the US (Rickes et al., 1948b) and E. Lester Smith and F. Parker in the UK (Smith, 1948).

During this period, I was inspired by the unique British welfare state system and the formation of the state-funded National Health Service (NHS) in 1948, providing "cradle-to-grave" medical care for all UK subjects, rich and not so rich. This welfare system had become the envy of the world.

I decided to leave for the UK. When I sought my parents' permission to leave, they asked me: "Why not practice in Kerala instead?" I gave two reasons:

- If I became an NHS doctor in England, I would not have to charge consultation fees from the rich or the not-so-well-off patients.
- In the UK I would be able to practice unhindered. The promise given by the then health minister, Aneurin Bevan, to the medical profession on 3 July 1948 had greatly influenced me: "My job is to give you all the facilities, resources, and help I can and then to leave you alone as professional men and women to use your skill and judgement without hindrance. Let us try to develop a partnership from now on" (Bevan, 1948).

An unexpected prophetic message

On the night of 26/27 August 1966 I was travelling for the first time outside Kerala State; I was not at all used to airports or flights. In the 1960s the foreign exchange reserve of India was minimal so the maximum amount of money I was allowed to take with me was a mere three British pounds.

My aunt, who lived in Chennai, drove me to the airport, gave me a few instructions and led me to the international departures lounge. While I was settling down in the lounge, to my surprise, an announcement came across, "Dr Joseph Chandy, please come to the travel desk". I was not expecting this added stress. I was anxious as to what it could be.

I walked towards the counter and joined the line. As the line began to move forward I noticed a respectable-looking senior gentleman moving forward, not in the line but on my left-hand side. Out of courtesy I asked him whether he would like to go in front of me. He responded "No, I will wait here," and asked me whether I was Dr Joseph Chandy. I said "yes".

Soon I reached the counter. The staff asked me whether I was prepared to give my seat to a family of five so that all of them could be seated in one row. I agreed, turned around and walked towards where I had been sitting in the lounge. To my surprise the senior gentleman was patiently standing at the same spot where he had said he would wait for me. I politely acknowledged his presence and

---

[1] George R. Minot, George H. Whipple and William P. Murphy were awarded the Nobel Prize for Physiology & Medicine in 1934 "for their discoveries concerning liver therapy in cases of anaemia" ("George R. Minot - Facts". NobelPrize.org. Nobel Media AB 2019. Sat. 9 Feb 2019. https://www.nobelprize.org/prizes/medicine/1934/minot/facts/.) See also Minot and Murphy (1926, 1983); NobelPrize.org (2016).

stood silent; he then began to speak: "I have an important message for you; listen to me, one day your discovery/work and your name will be spread all over the world". He repeated the same message once more. I was totally bewildered.

I responded by saying, "Sir, I am in fact nobody, just a recently qualified doctor from Kerala setting off to the UK for higher studies and then hoping to return to Kerala to serve my local community".

The gentleman kindly reminded me of what he had said earlier, "the important message". Confused, I asked him who he was. He replied that he was the Professor of Neurosurgery at Vellore Medical College not far from Chennai. Only then did I realise that he was in fact the world-renowned Professor Jacob Chandy (my namesake).[2] What a privilege I thought, although still very confused. As he walked away, I returned to my seat. I felt almost as if I was dreaming. I looked again around the whole departure lounge; nowhere could I locate the mystery professor. Soon the announcement to the British Airways flight to London was relayed.

First reported case of B12 deficiency without macrocytosis

So in 1966 I came to the UK and worked in paediatrics at teaching hospitals up to registrar level, passing my Diploma in Child Health (DCH) in 1969. Interestingly, at this time I came across a case of a rare condition, Waardenburg Syndrome, which presents as a tuft of white grey hair on the scalp of a newborn baby. There was previously no known cause for it. We now believe that this is a rare case of B12 deficiency causing vitiligo affecting hair follicles. (The baby was at the time of writing a teenager and still had the white tuft. Both mother and son have B12 deficiency and receive monthly B12 injections.)

This interest in maintaining the health of each person right from an early age continued after I became a GP. I had moved to the north-east to take up a post as a GP in a medical practice of 3,500 patients in Horden/Peterlee, County Durham.

It was by destiny that, ten years later, on 3 November 1981, I stumbled on my very first reported case of B12 deficiency with neuropsychiatric signs and symptoms, without macrocytosis (large immature red cells)[3] and without IF antibody being present. How this came about is described below.

One of my first assignments as a GP in 1970 was a call-out in the middle of the night to deliver a baby as the midwife could not get there. This event turned out to have momentous consequences for my future interest in vitamin B12.

Some time after the birth, the baby's mother, Glenise Mason, came to my surgery suffering from anaemia. Her blood test showed microcytosis (small red blood cells), indicative of iron-deficiency anaemia, so I treated her in the normal way with an iron supplement. Her condition improved but the anaemia did not completely clear up and she presented at regular intervals over the next ten

---

[2] Professor Jacob Chandy (1910-2007) established India's first Department of Neurosurgery in 1949 at Christian Medical College, Vellore (Abraham, 2007).

[3] Macrocytosis, or enlarged red blood cells with a volume > 97 µl, occur where the red blood cells have not fully matured and are rounded rather than doughnut-shaped. This means they have a smaller surface area- to-volume ratio and cannot carry as much oxygen so the patient is tired all the time.

years with recurrent anaemia. Her persistent symptoms included extreme fatigue, low mood, breathlessness and weakness.

It was not until 1981 that it suddenly struck me that she had a similar look to that of the Hindu Brahmin women I used to treat successfully with the liver extract injection in India. I then thought of testing for B12 deficiency. At the time, such a suggestion was unheard of because Glenise did not have what were then considered the classic and only signs of vitamin B12 deficiency: macrocytosis and IF antibody. These are the signs of pernicious anaemia which were considered the only manifestation of vitamin B12 deficiency (a view which still lingers on today). I had great difficulty convincing the haematologist at the laboratory that the B12 test needed to be done, but eventually he relented. To our astonishment, the result came back of 185 nanograms per litre (ng/L) blood serum B12 – a level which clearly indicated deficiency. The result allowed me to make an immediate diagnosis and commence B12-replacement therapy by injection. The diagnosis was confirmed when symptoms receded, and Glenise returned to her normal active life.

This experience was a revelation, for it overturned accepted dogma and opened up an entirely new line of clinical enquiry: if B12 deficiency could occur without macrocytosis and IF antibody, then what other symptoms might it lead to? I realised that the implications were vast.

Link between vitamin B12 and folic acid absorption

As if this was not a dramatic enough discovery in itself, other important but previously unknown aspects of vitamin B12 deficiency began to emerge. The first was the link between vitamin B12 and folate. In the 1980s, the importance of folate was less well known so I did not think of supplementing Glenise with folic acid. Nevertheless, her blood test results showed that as her B12 blood levels rose, so did her levels of folate despite the lack of folate supplementation.

This revealed, crucially, that folic acid availability to the body is very dependent on the B12 status (see Table i-2). Note how closely both B12 (which was being injected) and folate (which was not being supplemented) availability in the blood serum follow the same pattern. Both rise to replete levels when B12 injections are given, and both fall rapidly (far more rapidly than the textbooks would have you expect) when injections are withdrawn. (Injections were withdrawn on various occasions because of Primary Care Trust (PCT) embargoes on treatment described below.)

Table i-2 Relationship between B12 and folate levels in blood serum measurements

Test	*Dates of injections*									
	03/11/81 [1]	17/2/92	25/3/94	13/2/02	14/3/02 [2]	7/1/04 [3]	9/6/04	11/1/05	21/4/06	25/6/09 [4]
Blood serum B12 (200-900) ng/L	185	775	>2000	731	904	257	628	1443	1664	639
Blood folate (8-20)	2.8	14.3	>20	18.6	15.2	4.7	9.7	7.5	7.6	5.1
TSH		0.90	0.98			0.97		0.53		
Haemoglobin g/dl	10.3	15.5	8.3	12.0				12.6		
Mean Corpuscular Volume (MCV) fL	79	89.6		89.4		88.1				

[1] injections started 1mg/ml every 1 month;

[2] 14/3/2002 injections ceased after this date due to Easington PCT embargo;

[3] 7/1/2004 injections recommenced due to lifting of Easington PCT embargo on existing patients;

[4] 14/3/2007 injections ceased due to County Durham & Darlington PCT embargo (embargo lifted 10/2/11).

See also Charts in Chapter 5

Folic acid absorption and utilisation seem to be almost entirely dependent on optimum availability of B12 in the circulation. The pattern in the table above is reinforced by many more patient observations. In this case, the patient's folate levels responded to her B12 supplements even though there is no evidence that her dietary intake changed and 28 years of medical records show that she received B12 replacement but no folic acid or folate supplements. During each embargo period (see Table i-1 above - when B12 was not permitted to be given), her folic acid levels steadily dropped, and during B12 supplementation the blood levels of folate rose again (See also Chapter 5, Chart 5-1 which refers to the same patient).

Genetic predisposition

The second important aspect was that predisposition to B12 deficiency was inherited. In 1996, Glenise's daughter, the very baby I had delivered, attended my surgery aged 26 manifesting similar symptoms without macrocytosis. Treatment was commenced, and this patient also recovered. In both cases I did not rely on the presence of macrocytosis and/or the positive IF antibody to be present in order to arrive at the diagnosis of B12 deficiency. This shows that the gene transcription defect is passed down from one generation to the next (see further examples in Chapter 5).

The above two cases led me to consider *the very first reported case of B12 deficiency without macrocytosis;* until then, macrocytosis was required before the doctor would even consider B12 deficiency. We now know that B12 deficiency can be easily diagnosed from symptoms, and confirmed with the most basic empirical test: if supplementing with B12 relieves the symptoms, and failure to supplement or subsequent withdrawal causes the symptoms to return, then this is positive confirmation of the putative diagnosis.

My interest in vitamin B12 was kindled from that time on. As I began to research B12 deficiency I was surprised at the echoes down the centuries. Compare for instance these descriptions of symptoms:

> *"Lightheaded, felt faint, dizziness, pins & needles, numb sensation in limbs, tired, sallow complexion, numbness & shooting pain down left leg, loss of grip."* (Chandy in Glenise Mason's clinical notes recorded 1981).

and James S. Combe reporting in 1824 the first medical description of a patient likely to be suffering from B12 deficiency -

> *"His face, lips and whole extent ... were of a deadly pale colour ... languid; he complained of much weakness"* (Combe, 1824).

With this new understanding, despite the difficulties described below, over the next thirty years I was able to treat many patients who were suffering from B12 deficiency but whose blood test results did not show macrocytosis or IF antibody.

Referral to secondary care (hospital consultant)

However, whenever secondary care (hospital endocrinology consultant, for example) referral was clinically felt necessary, in consultation with the patient and/or the family member, I made the referral promptly.

Patient choice is embedded in the NHS Constitution. There have been patients who felt that they had confidence in me and did not wish to be referred to secondary care, especially since other patients with the same symptoms had been into hospital and as a result had been left with no treatment and repeatedly called back for "observation" whilst they deteriorated.

I knew that I could confidently and safely diagnose and treat my patients but where the patient has required this, I have respected patient choice. By adopting the primary care protocols, my experience and specialist knowledge in many areas of general medicine steadily improved over many years. This resulted in my being able to diagnose and treat successfully many patients who were misdiagnosed or did not have a credible proven diagnosis, even when the misdiagnosis was made in secondary care.

Part 2: Ups and downs

My Pathway of Care and Information for Patients

Anyone who knows the UK NHS will know that the only certainty is change. In 2000, the NHS was restructured into Primary Care Trusts (PCTs), each responsible for an average population of around 100,000. Horden/Peterlee, where I worked, was included in the Easington PCT. (Following a national restructure between 2004-06, PCTs were eventually abolished in 2013.)

I had been successfully prescribing B12 supplementation since that first case in 1981, but in March 2002 Easington PCT delivered a blanket ban stopping me from making diagnoses of B12 deficiency.

This naturally affected a lot of patients whose symptoms immediately returned once the B12 in their system (from supplements) had gone. I recorded symptoms at intervals for hundreds of patients, including an extensive patient survey, so demonstrating to Easington PCT that the treatment should be reinstated. In July 2006, Easington PCT accepted my case studies and my **Pathway of Care and Information for Patients**, and reinstated the diagnosis and treatment of patients with B12 deficiency. The Pathway (which became the **Protocol** – see Appendix 1) was based on a highly detailed study of vitamin B12-deficient patients and vitamin B12 therapy. It was developed jointly with Easington PCT and overseen by Dr Jonathan Wallis, Consultant Haematologist at the Freeman Hospital, Newcastle-upon-Tyne.

Although the Pathway of Care was revised with agreement from the PCT a number of times, my difficulties did not end there. In what follows I describe a number of instances where my assessment of the most appropriate care for patients was rejected by the health authorities. For a second time, my B12 treatment was stopped and the Protocol rescinded.

Referral to NCAA

On 2 September 2004 (eight months after reinstatement of the treatment pathway), the Chief Executive of the PCT wrote to me: "I am concerned both to secure the safety of patients and to safeguard your professional reputation as a doctor who has given outstanding service to his local community for over 30 years…However, I think we are at the stage that if you do not feel able to undertake a research project and you wish to continue your present line of treatment, then the only way I see of ensuring both patient safety and your professional good standing is to get advice from the NCAA".[4]

The meeting with the NCAA was scheduled for October 2004. I requested whether I could bring a GP colleague, or if not, then the Chair of the B12 Deficiency Patient Participation Group (a lay person). The answer was "no" to both requests. I had three weeks to prepare my defence. I knew from past experience that it was likely that false allegations and misinformation would be presented to the panel during a pre-meeting. I realised my situation was quite serious. I did not have any influential colleagues I could approach for my defence. I felt in this dark moment that the only friend I had was my Lord.

Every Friday evening after surgery I entered the chapel, knelt and prayed, often with tearful eyes. At the end of my prayer, lasting one hour, my Lord prompted me in my spirit to pick up any Holy Bible I could find. To my amazement, on each Friday evening the same page was opened from different Bibles and the reading was exactly the same:

---

[4] The National Clinical Assessment Authority (NCAA), renamed the National Clinical Assessment Service (NCAS) in 2005, works to resolve concerns about the practice of doctors, dentists and pharmacists. See http://www.ncas.nhs.uk/about-ncas/

I came home and remained silent until evening prayer time. Towards the end I opened the Bible the fourth time; my eyes led me straight to Psalm 23 verse 4 (King James Version):

"Yea, though I walk through the valley of the shadow of death, I will fear no evil: for thou art with me, thy rod and thy staff they comfort me".

The following day the NCAA meeting was scheduled for the afternoon. My morning surgery was quite busy. At 11.30 am the supervisor telephoned and said that an important senior doctor wanted to see me immediately as the matter was urgent. The supervisor told him that I still had patients. "Never mind the patients, I want to see him now," the visitor said. As it was lunchtime I asked the supervisor to have some tea and snacks ready. Within minutes the senior doctor was brought into my room. I stood up and respectfully asked him to be seated. He declined. I offered him some tea and snacks. He again declined and began saying, "I have come to warn you that if you promise to me now that from today you will not diagnose any case of vitamin B12 deficiency and will totally withdraw the B12 treatment regime you have been giving to all B12 deficiency patients since 1981, your job and your family will be safe and secure". I fell to the chair and began to shed tears. Suddenly the crucifixion of Jesus came into my spirit. I responded to the visitor (senior doctor) as I had prayed the night before, with Psalm 23 verse 4. The senior doctor began trembling and asked me "will I be your rod and staff?" I replied, "yes, you will be my rod and staff"; he turned around and left the room.

On 26 October at 3 pm, following a pre-meeting where my case would have been discussed, the PCT Chief Executive's secretary invited me into the boardroom. Almost for one hour they discussed not only the B12 controversy but all the past resolved issues. When I was asked to respond, I remained silent as I was commanded by the "word" I had received on the consecutive Fridays. To everyone's surprise the senior doctor who came to warn me stood up and spoke on my behalf. On all counts he justified my actions. He challenged the panel and asked them whether any one of them had read my study/observational analysis (which had been widely shared as per GMC guidelines); no one answered "yes". The senior doctor declared: "I read it last night; let me tell you, there is a gold nugget in his work. His protocol for B12d is not only safe: it saves lives". One by one they all left the boardroom except for the senior doctor and myself.

Rejection of my B12 deficiency work

In April 2006, six PCTs were merged to form a single PCT (the County Durham and Darlington PCT) covering a patient population of 600,000. The newly appointed Chair and the all-powerful medical director of the new PCT were fully aware of the existence of the former Easington PCT Approved Pathway of Care for B12 deficiency dated 3 July 2006.

Eight months later, on 14 March 2007, this officially approved Pathway of Care was unilaterality rescinded without any prior notice or consultation, or evidence being provided to support the decision. During the same period, an influential senior GP asked to see me urgently. When I questioned him the reason for the urgency of his visit, he replied: "[The new medical director] has already made up his mind to discredit your B12 deficiency study [approved by the former PCT]". What was more, he said, following Professor Mike Pringle's Investigation/Review (see below), the medical director would find reasons to suspend me and refer me to the General Medical Council (GMC).

I was in a state of shock. Fully realising the seriousness of the situation, my only remaining hope was to blindly trust in my Lord and Saviour. (All along, since I stumbled on the very first case of B12 deficiency without macrocytosis I had dedicated my work to my Lord Jesus.)

As I left home next day for the crucial meeting with the PCT, I decided not to tell my wife the threat we were under. On my way, I decided to step into the church to pray as a last resort. It was a rather cold, dark winter evening. I did not switch the light on at the church as I would be leaving soon. The parish priest thought a burglar had forced his way in to the church! I apologised for giving him a fright. I told him the reason I was there, seeking our Lord's protection in this critical situation. Both of us knelt and prayed for a few minutes.

The moment I stepped out of the church my mobile rang. It was my son Paul from India. I briefly told him what was happening. He understood the gravity of the situation. Without any hesitation, Paul, with confidence in our Lord Jesus, declared: "Dad, you are an overcomer. Dad, you are an overcomer. Dad, you are an overcomer."

As I walked into the surgery, to my surprise a priest and a gentleman were waiting to see me without a prior appointment. The supervisor told me the Irish gentleman had seen the BBC programme *Inside Out* about B12 deficiency[5] and had flown across to see me. I could not turn them away. They were satisfied with the consultation and the advice given for long-term wellbeing. At that point, I told them about the senior doctor waiting next door and what his agenda was. They were shocked by what they heard and prayed for me and reassured me.

After a few minutes, I invited the senior GP into my room. He told me bluntly that it was in my and the Practice's best interests for me to resign immediately and hand over the Practice to my remaining colleagues. Then I told him about my spiritual encounter with the parish priest and

---

[5] The BBC documentary *Inside Out*, featuring an interview with Dr Chandy, was broadcast on 31 October 2006. (Jackson, 2006)

prophetic message given by my son Paul. The senior doctor repeated again what awaited me if I did not follow his advice. I politely told him he could leave.

The effects on patients of the sudden withdrawal of B12 treatment through the rescinding of the officially approved Pathway of Care in March 2007 were dramatic, and we documented them.

We know that without B12, B12-deficient patients deteriorate steadily. However, when a patient receives B12-replacement therapy and then suffers a catastrophic withdrawal, the patient appears to deteriorate almost to the point they would have reached had they not received B12: deterioration after withdrawal is rapid. Many patients suffered and, sadly, one young mother developed double pneumonia and died. The number of patients suffering concurrently seems too much of a coincidence for us not to connect this death with the withdrawal of her regular replacement B12 injections for eighteen months, her immune system having thereby been compromised. This observation differs markedly from the proposed slow reduction in blood levels suggested earlier (Chanarin, 1979, 1980, 1982), and indicates how little we understand about the different efficiencies of different people to manage B12 in the body.

Independent academic review recommendations

At the same time as instituting this latest sanction on diagnosing B12 deficiency, County Durham and Darlington PCT brought in an NHS auditor: Professor Mike Pringle (of Nottingham University and PRIMIS)[6] was appointed to scrutinise my B12 diagnoses and treatment and ensure that it met NHS standards of care.

Professor Pringle audited all of the patients identified by the Practice as exhibiting B12 deficiency and who had been receiving B12 supplements before the latest sanction – approximately 600 people. His team carried out a very detailed audit, interviewed patients, and met the patients as a group. The team applied their clinical knowledge as well as the interviews with patients to verify the patient information recorded and the changes that the Practice observed. The team concluded (in its report entitled *Vitamin B12 prescribing in the Shinwell Practice, Horden, County Durham*, dated 31 August 2007) that:

- The B12 protocol and actions in the Practice highlighted several important findings with regard to diagnosis and treatment of B12 deficiency. They observed that patients did feel a genuine benefit and this could not be attributed to a placebo effect.

- The PCT should provide extra ring-fenced funding to set up special dedicated B12 clinics to continue to provide this effective treatment.

- The PCT were to assist the Practice with audits, and support the Practice to provide data and share patients with independent researchers.

Following the advice of Professor Pringle, Shinwell Medical Centre was asked to participate in three research proposals backed by Manchester University and London University and the Durham and

---

[6] Professor Mike Pringle CBE FRCGP was President of the Royal College of General Practitioners (RCGP) 2012–2015. PRIMIS is a University of Nottingham specialist organisation which provides advice on the capture, management, extraction and analysis of primary care data.

Sedgefield Research Body. Despite Professor Pringle's recommendations above, County Durham and Darlington PCT did not permit the Practice to be involved nor allow the Practice to advise patients of this research so they could apply independently.

After Professor Pringle's report was published, the ban on prescribing B12 was lifted but I was asked to keep meticulous records (which I had done anyway) and to submit them to the PCT every month.

Consequences of misdiagnosis

B12 deficiency is not understood, and as a result, is often not diagnosed. We believe it is widespread, and patients may be diagnosed as suffering from a range of other conditions (such as those listed below) whereas the root condition may be B12 deficiency (this list is not exhaustive):

- Adrenoleucodystrophy (ALD)
- Adrenal leucomyopathy
- Adrenal fatigue
- Chronic fatigue syndrome (CFS)
- Depression/anxiety neurosis
- Fibromyalgia (FM)
- Functional dysphagia (swallowing difficulties)
- Inappropriate behaviour which could lead to a Functional Behaviour Assessment
- Functional paraparesis
- Functional movement disorder
- Functional neurological disorder
- Functional paralysis
- Hereditary spastic paraparesis
- Hysterical paralysis
- Idiopathic disturbance of gait
- Multiple sclerosis (MS)
- Munchausen syndrome by proxy
- Myalgic encephalomyelitis (ME)
- Psychosis
- Stiff person syndrome
- Semantic dementia

These patients are then prescribed lifelong toxic symptom-modifying and symptom-subduing medications, with a long list of harmful side effects.

We show here that robust clinically-based evidence has been presented by doctors and researchers (including the author), based on live patients, and has been offered to the responsible medical establishment time after time.

Unfortunately, representations from my local MP and patient representatives have been ignored repeatedly and there has been no willing or enthusiastic engagement. Transparent discussion is needed, to be followed by an action plan.

It does not take a medical genius to work out that with the deficiency-related presentation such as vitamin B12 deficiency or hypoadrenalism, it is unethical and clinically unsafe to carry out a placebo trial and deprive patients of safe treatment that could relieve their suffering. For example, if someone is suffering severe dehydration, it is not ethical to deprive them of water in order to see if they die more quickly. Unfortunately, during two separate periods of more than 15 months, our patients have been subjected to enforced withdrawal of B12 replacement.

This action by the PCT caused untold suffering to many, including the tragic and untimely death described above of a 41-year-old mother in May 2010 who was previously eligible and receiving parenteral vitamin B12 every month, and whose symptoms had abated. Many other helpless patients have developed irreversible physical, neurological and psychological damage. It makes me wonder if someone is profiting from this life-destroying agenda to obstruct the totally harmless replacement therapy, when a deficiency is clinically established. How would Aneurin Bevan respond if he returned and became aware of this deliberate destruction of human life by the same people who had given an oath to protect and preserve life when they signed up to be NHS doctors?

These two periods of enforced withdrawal of treatment demonstrate what would have happened had a placebo trial taken place. They demonstrate that there is no further need for placebo trials, that the withdrawal of this vital substance, this vitamin, causes the patient to relapse to their former symptoms. In short, it demonstrates that B12 deficiency is a real nutritional problem, and not in the imagination.

Establishing patient-safe ranges and guidelines at two levels

If B12 deficiency is to be diagnosed from blood results, then some 'normal' ranges for the substances under test need to be established.

The most usual range accepted as 'normal' for serum B12 (B12 measurable in the blood) is 200 to 900 ng/L in the UK. There is some suspicion that this is actually the range of accuracy for the test equipment, and serves no biological function; 'normal' ranges are different in different parts of the UK, and appear to be different in different countries, and eminent researchers have called into question the accuracy of the current version of the blood test (Carmel & Agrawal, 2012; Hamilton et al., 2006; Nexo & Hoffmann-Lücke, 2011). Some hospitals in Japan use a higher reference range of 500-1300 ng/L.

There are instances where the long-established patient-safe ranges are altered in such a way that the level at which the deficiency can be diagnosed and treatment commenced is delayed indefinitely. As previously stated, this causes untold misery and often irreversible damage to patients' health and wellbeing. This is occurring with the following blood tests: B12, folic acid, ferritin, TSH, T4, T3, uric acid, cortisol, ACTH and antibodies, to name but a few.

Vitamin B12 deficiency, undiagnosed and untreated, can quickly lead to Subacute Combined Degeneration of the spinal cord (SACD). SACD was first identified over a hundred years ago (Russell et al., 1900), and is likely to be an early description of Multiple Sclerosis (MS). Prompt vitamin B12-replacement therapy reverses all the signs and symptoms of deficiency, including the neurological manifestations (Roessler & Wolff, 2017; see also Scalabrino, 2001) – and in our clinical experience, we have observed partial or complete remission from MS symptoms on a permanent basis. MS should be considered a description of the symptoms, and not the final diagnosis (see Chapter 6). It gives no clues as to the course of treatment, whereas vitamin B12 deficiency is much more specific and helpful.

Several of the previously listed misdiagnosed diseases can be prevented by preventative treatment from the beginning of life and at the pregnancy stage of the mother. For example, the mother should be screened for vitamin B12 deficiency, rather than wait until her child develops syndromes or diseases as infant, teenager or adult, which may by then be untreatable.

It is our belief that the NHS should try to proactively overcome diseases such as dementia and cancer by giving the human embryo the best possible chance. Mothers could begin with vitamin B12 supplementation as soon as a pregnancy is planned (see Chapter 5).

The topsy-turvy world of Patient Care Protocols

Some of the difficulties derive, in our view, from the diagnostic method which does not allow for a "whole person" approach.

For example, a patient presents with tiredness, anxiety, low mood and headaches. The clinician is required to use a standardised Patient Health Questionnaire (PHQ 9 form), completed by the patient. If he or she has scored high, the diagnosis of depression is required. The patient accepts the prescription for an antidepressant, which is followed by further mandatory reviews (which will earn more money for a GP practice). Because of the ubiquity of the PHQ 9, the patient's personal history, family history, and the possibility of other conditions such as a nutritional deficiency are not considered or explored with the patient.

Similarly, many of the syndromes listed above can represent other conditions such as underactive thyroid, B12 deficiency, ferritinaemia, or hypoadrenalism. However, diagnosis of these conditions does not attract achievement points for practice (QOF); the GP's autonomy as clinician is being eroded because of conflict of interest.

Misdiagnoses made predominantly by secondary-care clinicians (hospital doctors) include CFS, ME, FM, MS, functional paralysis, etc. These are perfect descriptions of symptoms, but it is a smoke-and-mirror effect. Following commencement of toxic symptom-modifying or symptom-subduing medications, every one of these unfortunate patients is being referred to nurse-led no-return clinics, to modify the symptoms, with no expectation of treatment or recovery.

We therefore explore the challenges, and propose a Protocol for diagnosis and treatment in Chapter 3 and Appendix 1.

Part 3: Sharing the knowledge widely

In 34 years of vitamin B12 experience and observations I amassed a great deal of knowledge which I have aimed to share in many different ways in conformity with the General Medical Council (GMC) guidelines on propagation of knowledge. Since 1981, I have engaged in debates, written to parliament, given presentations and educational workshops and spoken about B12 deficiency at many national and international conferences in Britain, India, Denmark and France, including the conferences of the Pernicious Anaemia Society (see list in Box i-2). My work and two of my patients were featured in the BBC documentary *Inside Out* broadcast on 31 October 2006.[5] In addition to collating two substantial patient surveys documenting the symptoms before and during treatment, and during a period of treatment withdrawal, I have also responded (and still respond) to enquiries from doctors, paramedics and patients all over the world about ways of diagnosing and treating B12 deficiency.

Other important work has included assembling evidence for submission to various regulatory authorities responsible for medical care guidelines. As described above, I conducted a retrospective study (1981-2006) on vitamin B12 deficiency in patients with neuropsychiatric symptoms and prepared a *Pathway of Care and Information for Patients* for the PCT (Chandy, 2006b). This study was also submitted to the British National Formulary (BNF) board. The BNF has since changed its guidelines, for example to remove any recommendation for use of cyanocobalamin (which it describes as "less suitable for prescribing"(BNF, 2017)), and to increase the recommended frequency of injections from three- to two-monthly for neurological conditions.

In early 2007, I wrote to the BNF editorial board, the House of Commons Health Select Committee and the editor of *The Times* to alert them to the risks associated with undiagnosed B12 deficiency in expectant mothers and the danger of homocysteinaemia and its consequences. If the mother has undiagnosed B12 deficiency, and is untreated or only given folic acid supplement, there is a risk that she could deliver the child with neuromuscular damage, SACD, congenital abnormalities, tumours (including brain damage) and spina bifida. This can be avoided with vitamin B12 replacement before and during pregnancy (Molloy et al., 2009).

BNF Guidance on treating newborns to eighteen-year-olds with vitamin B12 has since been published (BNFC, 2008). We believe that this came about as a result of our submission with a retrospective study.

I also wrote to the National Institute for Care and Excellence (NICE), in July and September 2014, concerning the lack of NICE Guidelines on vitamin B12 deficiency and hypoadrenalism. I requested a 'Patient-Safe Guideline' for vitamin B12 deficiency on the basis that a **pathway had been jointly prepared and approved by Easington PCT in July 2006,** eight years earlier, based on clinical evidence gathered over 25 years since 1981.

However, at the time of writing there is still no NICE Guideline available. This issue is addressed in Chapter 3.

The B12 Deficiency Support Group

I found that I was not alone. Concerned at the widespread ignorance and dismissal of this condition by the medical profession as a whole and its frequent misdiagnosis, a group of patients suffering from B12 deficiency at our Practice set up the B12 Deficiency Support Group which was later converted to a charity.[7] Its mission is to provide a voice for the sufferers and help them gain the support, guidance and treatment they require.

Cost savings to the NHS

NHS resources are under strain. Prevention is the key to a cost-effective health service which also delivers quality care for the population and improved economic output to the nation. Prevention requires planning, and the right mechanisms to be implemented in the first place. It has been

---

[7] Registered charity number 1146432. Further information is available from http://www.b12d.org.

calculated (figures from 2010) that failure to diagnose B12 deficiency is costing the NHS a minimum of £894 million per year in medical care required, quite independent of the additional social care, the loss in economic output for British commerce, and the damage to people's lives caused (Minney, 2010).

Our Patient-Safe Protocol

I am recommending tried and tested **Patient-Safe Protocols** that we have developed for diagnosing and treating B12 deficiency and hypoadrenalism. The respective Shinwell Medical Practice protocols for both conditions are in the appendices for your reference. Discussion and results of our treatments showing the long-lasting reversal of patient's conditions are found in the ensuing chapters. Other testimonies can be found on the B12 Deficiency Support Group's website.

We developed this Protocol following the recommendations in *Harrison's Principles of Internal Medicine* (Babior & Bunn, 2005; Hauser & Goodin, 2005, 2008; Hoffbrand, 2008) and United Kingdom National External Quality Assessment Scheme for Haematinic Assays (NEQAS) which advise that it must be a clinical decision to undertake a therapeutic trial in the suspicion of cases when a patient presents with classic signs and symptoms of B12 deficiency. See also up-to-date information in BMJ Best Practice (2018d).

The emphasis on the importance of the clinical picture is shown in the 20th edition of *Harrison's* which states (p. 701): "An important clinical problem is the non-anemic patient with neurologic or psychiatric abnormalities and a low or borderline serum cobalamin level. In such patients, it is necessary to try to establish whether there is significant cobalamin deficiency... A trial of cobalamin therapy for at least 3 months will usually also be needed to determine whether the symptoms improve" (Hoffbrand, 2018). NEQAS similarly states: "In the event of any discordance between clinical findings of B12 deficiency and a normal B12 laboratory result, then treatment should not be delayed. Clinical findings might include possible pernicious anaemia or neuropathy including subacute combined degeneration of the cord. We recommend storing serum for further analysis including MMA, or holotranscobalamin and intrinsic factor antibody analysis, and treating the patient immediately with parenteral B12 treatment" (NEQAS, 2014).

Similarly, the British Society for Haematology states: "The clinical picture is the most important factor in assessing the significance of test results assessing cobalamin (B12) status since there is no gold standard test to define deficiency". The Society reiterates that "Definitive cut-off points to define clinical and subclinical deficiency states are not possible" (Devalia et al., 2014).

Along with these protocols I advocate a holistic all-person (mind, body and spirit) approach to good medical care in place of the modern tick-box clinically unsafe methods.

Importance of holistic care: Mother Teresa's influence

The importance of caring for the whole person was brought home to me in my early days as a young medical student when I worked with the Mother Teresa mission among poor fishermen's families in the slums of Kerala, and later through my experience with one particular patient, Mr Norman Imms.

I had joined the mission after developing vitiligo which had a devastating psychological effect on me and led me to search for answers in prayer and charitable work. Working with poor families taught me to respect the poor, the sick and their suffering. To my surprise, after a few months my own health improved. This experience proved to be very valuable some years later when I was practising as a GP in County Durham and encountered a patient with particularly challenging problems. Mr Imms had been diagnosed as a paranoid schizophrenic manic depressive, also suffering psychosis and psychopathy. He had been removed from many other GPs' lists but over 17 years he was a daily visitor to my surgery, also demanding night-time consultations. I endured these visits because I felt that someone needed to help this poor man. Eventually, in 1990, I told him that I could not continue his care and that the only way to obtain help was for him to "spiritualise" his illness.

Figure i-1 Dr Chandy meets Mother Teresa

Photo © Norman Imms

He came with me to visit Mother Teresa and then wrote to her and was accepted as a co-worker. He met Mother Teresa 10 times in all. Each time his condition improved. On the last occasion, in 1997 not long before her death, she told him he was cured. This had a dramatic effect on him. When I next saw him he was truly a changed man: his hallucinations and delusions were completely gone. This taught me that a "true physician …must not only heal the body, but also touch the mind, and that the inner spirit of a human being is the most important part" (Independent, 1999).

This miracle prompted me to write to the Vatican to support the case for Mother Teresa to be made a saint. Mr Imms and I also participated in a BBC "Big Question" debate entitled "Does Mother Teresa deserve sainthood?" in October 2009. Mother Teresa was declared a saint in 2016.

What B12 therapy means to our patients

Each of my patients is saying "Doctor, you gave me my life back!" Every single patient has his/her own story to tell about how ill they were when their B12 level was low, and how well they are now with their B12 level normal. I would like to emphasise that it is not me, it is the result of a caring and logical approach to medical treatment in keeping with the Hippocratic Oath, the promise by all clinicians: *"May I always act so as to preserve the finest traditions of my calling and may I long experience the joy of healing those who seek my help"*.

There is perhaps no clearer way of communicating the difference this approach can make than by ending this Introduction with these heartfelt words from an appreciative patient:

> *"Hello Dr Chandy*
>
> *Not many people have a day in their life that is quite as inspiring, uplifting and as full of love and care as yesterday, but that is what it was for Elise and me.*
>
> *We wearily wended our way back to Northallerton, and then I drove home back to Sedgefield with more hope in our hearts than we have had for over four years. Thank you does not seem adequate for the huge amount of time you spent with us, and I will never forget the hug you gave me as we departed – a wonderful memory that will stay with me forever.*
>
> *Today I start getting us well, by getting the various tests put in place, ordering sharps, B12 etc and if you don't mind I will keep you updated with results etc.*
>
> *With the greatest respect and thank you to a very special man."*
>
> *Pauline Tweddell, 3 November 2016.*

Box i-1 Dr Joseph Chandy: Timeline	
1941, 16 January	Born Kerala, India
1965	Qualified MBBS, Trivandrum Medical College, Kerala University (India).
1966, June-August	Tutor, anatomy, Medical College Hospital, Allapy, South India.
1966, 26/27 August	Arrival in the UK and employment by the NHS. Prophetic message from the late Professor Jacob Chandy (1910-2007), world-famous professor of neurology at Christian Medical College, Vellore, India.
1966-69	Worked in paediatrics and general medicine in UK hospitals.
1969	Awarded Diploma in Child Health, Glasgow University.
1970	Appointed General Practitioner and senior partner to Shinwell Medical Practice, Horden, County Durham, UK.
1981	Encountered first case of vitamin B12 deficiency without macrocytosis or anti-IF antibodies.
1981-2002	Successfully treated many vitamin B12-deficient patients.
1988	Purpose-built a modern GP medical practice/nursing home complex in the heart of an ex-mining community, providing 50 new jobs. This won the Royal Town Planning Institute's Design Award for incorporating innovative adaptations so that the sick and disabled patients can help themselves.
1997	Meeting with Mother Teresa in Denmark.
1998-2005	Primary Care Group Board Member – elected to represent local GPs.
2002, March	Easington Primary Care Trust (PCT) delivered a blanket ban on my diagnoses of vitamin B12 deficiency in any patient whose B12 level was above the local laboratory threshold of 180 ng/L. The embargo remained in force until 2003.
2004, January	First draft of a *Pathway of Care and Information for Patients* regarding vitamin B12 treatment.
2004, 12 February	Easington PCT imposed an embargo on vitamin B12 treatment for new patients. The embargo remained in force, with some modifications, from 12 February 2004 to 3 July 2006.
2004, 2 September	Letter from Chief Executive of Easington PCT and referral to National Clinical Assessment Authority (NCAA).
2004, 26 October	Meeting with NCAA.
2006, 3 July	Joint work with the PCT on updated version of *Pathway of Care and Information for Patients* regarding vitamin B12 treatment overseen by Dr Jonathan Wallis

	(Consultant Haematologist, the Freeman Hospital, Newcastle-upon-Tyne). The Pathway was accepted by Easington PCT on 3 July 2006.
2007, 14 March	My *Pathway of Care and Information for Patients* was unilaterally rescinded by the new County Durham and Darlington PCT. This second embargo remained in force from 14 March 2007-10 February 2011. The PCT appointed Professor Mike Pringle to conduct an independent academic review of my work.
2007, 31 August	Professor Mike Pringle's report entitled *Vitamin B12 prescribing in the Shinwell Practice, Horden, County Durham*, dated 31 August 2007, highlighting my findings, recommended that the PCT provide ring-fenced funding to set up special dedicated clinics to continue to provide this "effective treatment". The report asked the PCT to assist the Practice with audits and support the Practice in sharing data and in sharing patients with independent researchers.
2009, 1 August	My *Pathway of Care and Information for Patients* was partially accepted by County Durham and Darlington PCT which allowed treatment to recommence for some categories of B12-deficient patients.
2010, 25 September	Received Glory of India Award for a lifetime of service in primary care and work on vitamin B12 deficiency.
2011, August	Shinwell Medical Practice develops its own *Protocol for excluding B12 deficiency (Megaloblastic anaemia/Pernicious anaemia)* from adult and child presentation based on the former *Pathway of Care and Information for Patients*. **The Protocol is given in full in Appendix 1 of this book.**
2015	Retirement from the NHS.

Box i-2 Presentations to raise awareness of B12 deficiency

1. Postgraduate meeting – Durham.
2. Research Interest Group – Sedgefield.
3. Paper on 'B12 deficiency with neuropsychiatric signs and symptoms with or without anaemia or macrocytosis' given at Northern Primary Care Research Network organised by Royal College of General Practitioners North of England Faculty Annual Research Presentation Day, Collingwood College, Durham, 16 November 2006.
4. Presentation to PCT board and Executive Committee – Durham.
5. Presentation to Professor Mike Pringle CBE (former President of the Royal College of Practitioners) at the Shinwell Medical Practice, County Durham.
6. Major International Research Conference organised by Pernicious Anaemia Society of UK - Bristol.
7. Annual Presentations at the Pernicious Anaemia Society, UK – Bristol.
8. Postgraduate Education Meeting – Sunderland.
9. Postgraduate Education Meetings – Peterlee and Easington District.
10. Postgraduate Education Meeting – Hartlepool General Hospital.

11. Presentation at a large conference - Denmark

12. Presentation – Delhi; India which was widely covered by the media both locally and nationally

13. Presentation – Kerala, India; again, widely published by the media

14. Postgraduate workshop – Kerala, India.

15. Poster Presentation B12d - BMJ: Future of Health Conference, London.

16. Poster Presentation on hypoadrenalism at *the Biannual International Forum on Quality and Safety in Healthcare*, Paris.

17. Participation in BBC documentary *Inside Out* broadcast on 31 October 2006.

18. Paper entitled 'Doctor, you have given me my life back' given at first international conference on B12 deficiency (*Congress B12 Integral "Cobalamin4All"*) held in Driebergen, the Netherlands, 28 May 2010.

19. Debate on Vitamin Supplementation; was one of four guest speakers – Westminster, London.

20. Paper entitled 'A Protocol for B12 Diagnosis and Treatment by Primary Care Clinicians' given at the Pernicious Anaemia Society symposium and study day in Porthcawl, Wales, June 2011.

21. Lecture tour of India, 2014.

22. Poster Presentation on B12d - 'Vitamin B12 deficiency, a common but forgotten illness'. *International Forum on Quality and Safety in Healthcare.* Paris, France, 2014.

23. Paper on "B12 deficiency and APS with a causal link to hypothyroidism, adrenal insufficiency." In *Thyroid Patient Advocacy Conference.* Crown Hotel, Harrogate, North Yorkshire, UK, 2015.

Chapter 1   Vitamin B12: a profile

"the word of the Lord was addressed to me, saying,
'before I formed you in the womb I knew you;
before you came to birth I consecrated you;
I have appointed you as a prophet to the nations.
So now brace yourself for action.
Stand up and tell them
all I command you.
Do not be dismayed at their presence,
or in their presence I will make you dismayed.
I, for my part, today will make you
into a fortified city,
a pillar of iron,
and a wall of bronze
to confront this land:
the kings of Judah, its princes,
its priests and the country people.
They will fight against you,
it shall not overcome you,
for I am with you to deliver you –
it is the Lord who speaks.'"

Jeremiah 1:4–5, 17–19

Figure 1-1 The role of vitamin B12 in the human body systems

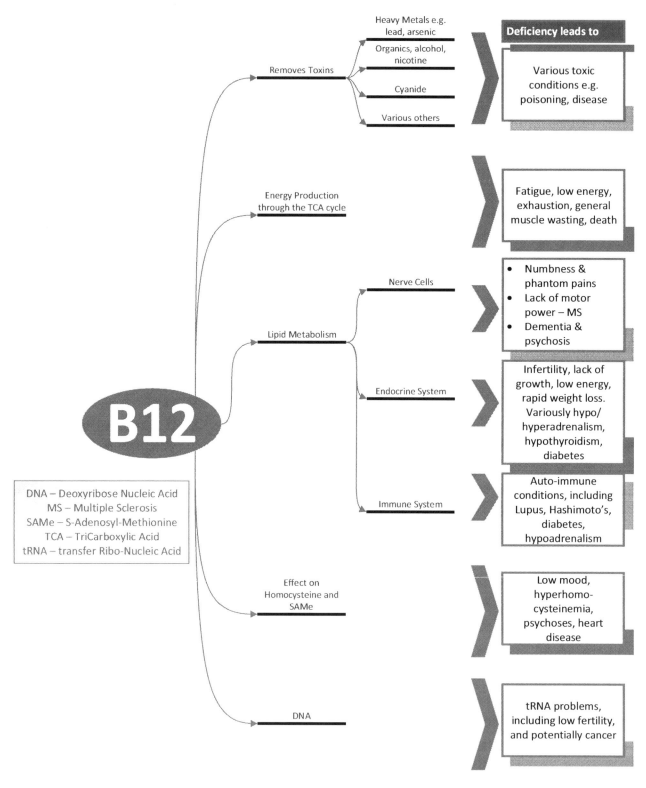

Based on clinical experience and Banerjee and Ragsdale (2003); Dowling et al. (2016); Green (2017); Koury and Ponka (2004); Stubbe (1994)

1.1 Vitamin B12 characteristics

Vitamin B12 is the generic name for a group of compounds based on the cobalamin molecule which has the trace mineral cobalt at its centre. Cobalamin is a highly active complex organometallic molecule. It is the largest and most chemically complex of all the 13 known vitamins (with an intricate chemical formula $C_{62}H_{88}CoN_{13}O_{14}P^+$) and is generally characterised as red in colour. Cobalamin, like the other B vitamins and vitamin C, is a water-soluble vitamin, a characteristic which influences how it is absorbed, excreted and stored by the human body. The other vitamins (A, D, E and K) are fat-soluble.

It is classed as a vitamin because it is an essential nutrient for humans which must be obtained regularly from food. Like other vitamins its role is to catalyse or regulate metabolic reactions in the human body. It plays a crucial role in many body processes. As described by the US PubChem Compound Database: "It is needed for hematopoiesis (the production of all types of blood cells), neural metabolism, DNA and RNA production, and carbohydrate, fat, and protein metabolism. It improves iron functions in the metabolic cycle and assists folic acid in choline synthesis."[8]

Vitamin B12 can only be made by microorganisms, such as bacteria and algae, providing the cobalt mineral is available to them from soil or water. The principal source of vitamin B12 for humans is animal products: the vitamin is made by microbes in the digestive tract of animals from where it is absorbed and deposited in their tissues. The main dietary sources for humans are therefore meat, fish, milk, eggs and cheese. There are virtually no plant sources of this vitamin, although some species of seaweed have been found to contain it (Watanabe et al., 2014). Vitamin B12 can also now be obtained from synthetic sources.

The absorption mechanism from the human gastrointestinal tract to circulation for crucial utilisation by the body's entire 100 trillion cells is a multi-step, delicate and complex process (Nielsen et al., 2012). This sensitivity means that absorption can be easily disrupted, for example by surgery, abnormal bacterial growth in the small intestine, intestinal disease or some medications that inhibit absorption. Prime causes are atrophic gastritis and lack of Intrinsic Factor (IF), a glycoprotein produced by the stomach that is necessary for absorption of vitamin B12. In addition to poor dietary intake, lack of vitamin B12 can arise from genetic conditions affecting the absorption pathway, or from many acquired conditions such as:

- Atrophic gastritis
- Pernicious anaemia (automimune destruction of the gastric parietal cells)
- Crohn's disease
- Intestinal infections
- Gastrointestinal surgery (especially if affecting the terminal ileum)
- Coeliac disease
- Treatment with antacids (acid is required to release vitamin B12 from food)
- Treatment with proton-pump inhibitors
- Use of some other medications and nitrous oxide (from anaesthetic or recreational use)

---

[8] Source: "Cobalamin", The NCI Thesaurus (NCIt), reproduced in the US National Center for Biotechnology Information (NCBI), (PubChem Compound Database) Compound ID 56840966 https://pubchem.ncbi.nlm.nih.gov/compound/56840966 (accessed 7 January 2019).

- Cyanide poisoning (for example, from smoke inhalation)

In the US National Library of Medicine's (NLM's) Medical Subject Headings (MeSH) vitamin B12 is described as "a cobalt-containing coordination compound produced by intestinal micro-organisms and found also in soil and water. Higher plants do not concentrate vitamin B12 from the soil and so are a poor source of the substance as compared with animal tissues. Intrinsic Factor is important for the assimilation of vitamin B12."[9]

Insufficient intake (from a diet lacking vitamin B12) or disrupted absorption of vitamin B12 results in a deficiency in all humans, including a pregnant woman, foetus and neonate, causing DNA damage.

1.1.1 Basic chemistry: B12 structure

Vitamin B12 is the largest vitamin with a molecular weight of 1355.388 grams per mole (g/mol), compared with: Vitamin A – 286.459 g/mol; Vitamin B3 – 123.111 g/mol; Vitamin B6 – 205.638 g/mol; Vitamin B9 (folate) – 441.404 g/mol; Vitamin C – 176.124 g/mol; Vitamin D – 384.648 g/mol; Vitamin E – 430.717 g/mol; Vitamin K – 450.707 g/mol.[10]

Figure 1-2 Cobalamin molecule

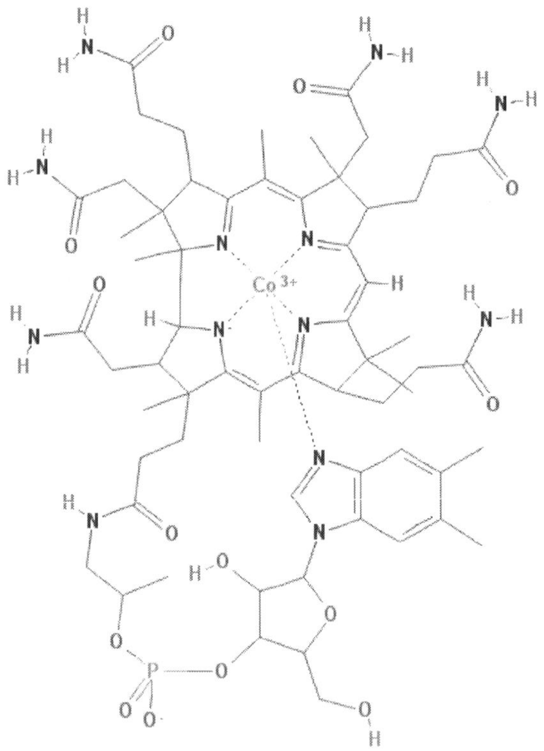

---

[9] Source: Medical Subject Headings (MeSH), US National Library of Medicine, Record Name: Vitamin B12, URL: https://www.ncbi.nlm.nih.gov/mesh/68014805 (MeSH).

[10] All figures from National Centre for Biotechnology Information, PubChem Compound Database, US. Accessed 29 January 2018. See also Kim et al. (2016).

Ions (charged molecules) are very important in biochemistry. They make a substance soluble or not soluble in water or fat, and help it to be selective in what it binds to.

The cobalamin molecule has a cobalt ion in the centre surrounded by a corrin ring structure with the four pyrrole[11] nitrogens coordinated to the cobalt (Shane, 2008). This combination means that B12 has a highly attractive centre, and then a protective layer around it. This gives vitamin B12 its main properties:

- as a binding site for toxins such as heavy metals and strongly radical ions such as cyanide and oxygen radicals (which bind to the centre and are then protected from releasing the heavy metal whilst the body takes the combined molecule to the kidney to get rid of it);
- as a carrier for highly reactive ions such as H+ which would otherwise react with the nearest molecule, both damaging the molecule and losing the energy stored within the highly reactive ion. This is why vitamin B12 is so important in the energy production cycles such as the TriCarboxylic Acid Cycle (TCA);
- as a catalytic site where normally stable molecules are brought together and reconfigure in a highly energetic state, protected by the amine rings from reacting with other nearby (but random) molecules and losing their energetic state (for a series of catalytic reactions, including lipid metabolism and conversion of homocysteine to methionine which is then converted to S-adenosyl-methionione (SAMe));
- as a donor for methyl groups which can bind to and release from vitamin B12 under specific conditions – for example, vitamin B12 takes a methyl group from 5-methylene tetrahydrofolate, thereby reducing it to tetrahydrofolate – a form of folate needed for further metabolic reactions which eventually lead to products required for DNA synthesis.

Figure 1-3 Detail of cobalamin molecule

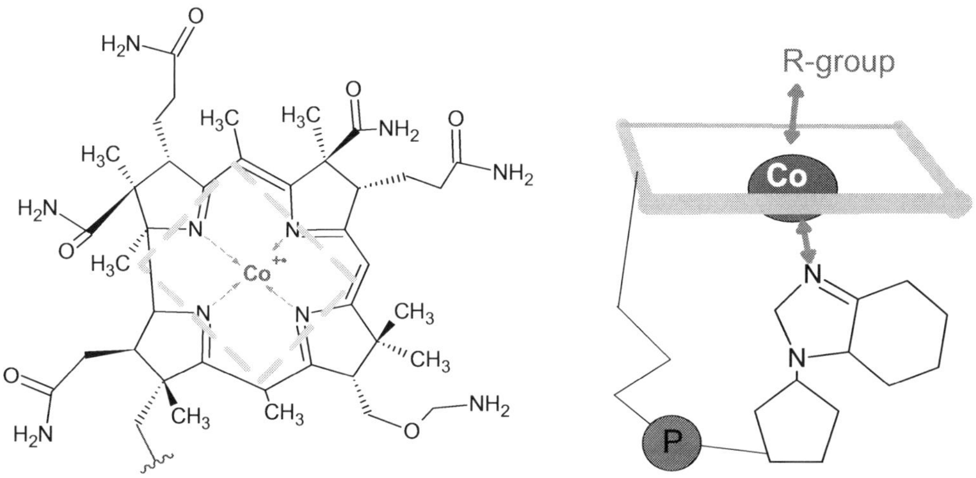

Graphics by Hugo Minney. The diagram on the left shows the cobalt atom positioned in the centre of a corrin ring by bonds of nitrogen from four pyrrole rings, illustrated as a square (tail foreshortened in blue, bottom

---

[11] A pyrrole ring is an organic compound characterised by a ring structure composed of four carbon atoms and one nitrogen atom.

left).The diagram on the right, a "side view", shows the molecular tail which allows the cobalt molecule to move relative to the pyrrole rings (up and down) so cobalt can bind to different-sized and different-strength R-groups, for example cyanyl, methyl, hydroxyl, adenosyl and heavy metals.

1.1.2   The B vitamins

Vitamin B12 is arbitrarily included amongst the B vitamins. We say "arbitrarily" because it has little in common with the chemical structure of other B vitamins. These vitamins are grouped together because they are water-soluble and have inter-related, cellular coenzyme functions (Kennedy, 2016). They act together in many human biochemical processes, for example the metabolism of homocysteine (Kennedy, 2016). Vitamin B12 has a particularly important interrelationship with folic acid (vitamin B9) in the folate cycle which leads to the synthesis of DNA and concurrently affects the methionine cycle as described in Chapters 4 and 9.

The eight B vitamins are listed in Table 1-1. Deficiencies in most of these are now rare, due to nutritional improvements (which begs the question: why does the same not apply to B12? – Maybe because of modern changes in agricultural methods which deplete cobalt in the soil?).

Table 1-1 Physiologic roles and deficiency signs of B-complex vitamins

Vitamin	Physiologic roles	Deficiency effects
Thiamine (B_1)	Co-enzyme functions in metabolism of carbohydrates and branched-chain amino acids	Beri-beri, polyneuritis, and Wernicke-Korsakoff syndrome, weight loss, confusion, anorexia, muscle weakness, cardiovascular symptoms.
Riboflavin (B_2)	Co-enzyme functions in numerous oxidation and reduction reactions	Growth, cheilosis (swollen, cracked lips), angular stomatitis (lesions at the corner of the mouth), and dermatitis, edema of the mouth and throat, hyperemia, hair loss, sore throat, reproductive problems, itchy or red eyes, degeneration of the liver and nervous system.
Niacin (nicotinic acid and nicotinamide)	Co-substrate/co-enzyme for hydrogen transfer with numerous dehydrogenases	Pellagra with diarrhoea, dermatitis, neurological symptoms such as apathy, headache, fatigue, loss of memory, and dementia.
Vitamin B_6 (pyridoxine, pyridoxamine, and pyridoxal)	Co-enzyme functions in metabolism of amino acids, glycogen, and sphingoid bases	Microcytic anaemia, electroencephalographic abnormalities, Naso-lateral seborrhoea (red itchy rash), glossitis, dermatitis with cheilosis, depression and confusion, weakened immune function, and peripheral neuropathy (epileptiform convulsions in infants).
Pantothenic acid	Constituent of co-enzyme A and phosphopantetheine involved in fatty acid metabolism	Deficiency is rare but symptoms include fatigue, sleep disturbances, impaired coordination, and gastrointestinal disturbances with anorexia.

Vitamin	Physiologic roles	Deficiency effects
Biotin	Co-enzyme functions in bicarbonate-dependent carboxylations	Thinning hair, red rash, conjunctivitis, ketolactic acidosis, aciduria, seizures, skin infection, brittle nails, fatigue, depression, nausea, hallucinations and paraesthesias of the extremities.
Folate/folic acid (Vitamin B_9)	A precursor needed to make, repair, and methylate DNA; a cofactor in various reactions; especially important in aiding rapid cell division and growth, such as in infancy and pregnancy.	Megaloblastic anaemia, atrophic glossitis, depression, raised homocysteine, Neural Tube Defects (NTDs) as described in this book.
Vitamin B_{12} Various cobalamins; commonly cyanocobalamin or methylcobalaminin vitamin supplements	A co-enzyme involved in the metabolism of every cell of the human body, especially affecting DNA synthesis and regulation, but also fatty acid metabolism and amino acid metabolism.	Neurological and neuropsychiatric impairment, megaloblastic anaemia, gastrointestinal disorders, autoimmune polyendocrine syndrome, as described in this book.

Compiled from: *Report of a joint FAO/WHO expert consultation* Table 5, page 27 (FAO & WHO, 2001) and National Institutes of Health Office of Dietary Supplements: *Thiamine, Riboflavin, Niacin, Pantothenic Acid, Biotin, Folate, Vitamin B12 Fact Sheets for Health Professionals* (NIH ODS, 2018a). Vitamin B12 information partly from our clinical experience.

1.1.3 Forms of vitamin B12

Cobalamin is the chemically pure form but it is normally bound to other atoms, resulting in several types of B12 (see Table 1.2).

Table 1-2 The most commonly used forms of B12 attached to different ions

Form of Vitamin B12	Molecular weight	Biochemistry in humans and animals
Methylcobalamin	Cobalamin (MW 1329) with a methyl group (MW 15) = Total MW 1344 g/mol or 0.744 mol per kg	Methyl donor to DNA. Co-enzyme in the folate cycle leading to DNA synthesis, and in the interlinked homocysteine-methionine cycle. By extension, affects DNA methylation and supply of S-adenosyl methionine (SAM), impacting on nerve Schwann cell insulation, hormone management, allergy and immune system management.

Form of Vitamin B12	Molecular weight	Biochemistry in humans and animals
		Can be manufactured, and can be injected or be given in oral tablet form. All forms of vitamin B12 are water soluble.
Adenosylcobalamin	Cobalamin (MW 1329) with an adenosyl group (MW 267) = Total MW 1596 g/mol or 0.627 mol per kg	Used in Krebs cycle to generate energy, in the mitochondria. Appears to be the active form of B12 in "active B12" (holotranscobalamin) in blood serum. Can be manufactured, and can be injected or given in oral tablet form.
Hydroxocobalamin	Cobalamin (MW 1329) with a hydroxyl group (MW 17) = Total MW 1346 g/mol or 0.743 mol per kg	Stable form of commercially manufactured cobalamin which converts relatively easily in the human body into methylcobalamin and adenosylcobalamin. Can be injected.
Cyanocobalamin	Cobalamin (MW 1329) with a cyanide group (MW 26) = Total MW 1355 g/mol or 0.738 mol per kg	Highly stable form of commercially manufactured cobalamin. Whilst the majority of humans can convert cyanocobalamin into an active form of B12 (methylcobalamin or adenosylcobalamin – the level of cyanide released from this conversion is fairly small and should not cause symptoms), a proportion are not able to make use of cyanocobalamin because the molecule is too stable, and the molecule is removed rapidly from the body by the kidneys because it is a recognised "B12 + toxin" molecule.

Source: All figures from National Centre for Biotechnology Information PubChem Compound Database, US. Compound ID numbers: 10898559, 70678541, 5460373, 5311498. Accessed 29 January 2018 (NIH, 2017).

See also 3.3 on page 70

Note Figure 1-3 on page 27 illustrates how the Cobalt atom can move to expose the bond and make the molecule more able to be used in the body (for less highly charged R-groups eg -CH3 and -adenosyl), or to hide the bond making it less able to be used (for highly charged and dense R-groups eg -CN)

1.1.4   Cobalamin isomers/analogues

In the same way that carbon monoxide is so similar to oxygen at a molecular level that it binds to haemoglobin, there are a number of molecules that look sufficiently like vitamin B12 that the body can be deceived. Perhaps the most obvious of these are the phytocobalamins: plant-manufactured molecules with a cobalt ion in the middle that are very similar, but are of no use in animal biochemistry.

In some ways, this is what IF in the stomach is for: to identify the real vitamin B12 and exclude phytocobalamins in the diet from entering the bloodstream in any more than trace amounts.

1.2   Vitamin B12 - history of discovery

Medical journals first began to report symptoms that we can now compare with the symptoms of vitamin B12 deficiency nearly 200 years ago. We have identified three distinct periods over the last two centuries:

1.2.1   Period I: 1824 to 1926

In the nineteenth century James S. Combe (1796-1883) of Edinburgh described a "deadly wasting disease" (Combe, 1824). The condition may have been known earlier as he refers to earlier works (Lieutaud, 1816; Parr, 1819). This description sparked a spate of medical papers reporting similar wasting diseases among people not obviously suffering from starvation or nutritional deficiency (Addison, 1849; Barclay, 1851; Fenwick, 1870; Flint, 1860). Thomas Addison (1793-1860) made an association with neuropsychiatric disorder (Addison, 1849; Vaidya et al., 2009). In 1872, Anton Biermer of Switzerland (1827-1892) gave the illness the name "pernicious anaemia" because it was almost always fatal (Biermer, 1872; Huser, 1966). Symptoms identified included megaloblastic red blood cells, and plaques in the spinal column (post-mortem of course) (Biermer, 1872; Charcot, 1868; Ehrlich, 1880). In 1900, Russell gave the first clinical description of the condition of Subacute Combined Degeneration (SACD) of the spinal cord (Russell et al., 1900).

In 1910, the American physician Richard C. Cabot (1868-1939) presented a natural history of the disease for 1,200 patients. Only six were in remission. The remainder usually survived only between one and three years after developing the symptoms (Cabot, 1910).

By the 1920s, government sources reported 10,000 unexplained deaths each year in the US alone, with similar symptoms. However, the haematologists began to consider this to be a haematological condition, and progress to identify the cause and develop a treatment was held back. The depletion of red blood cells was considered the most important aspect of the illness until more modern methods of investigation led to a broader view of its manifestations.

1.2.2   Period II: 1926 to 1979

Until the accidental discovery of the liver diet by George R. Minot and William P. Murphy in 1926 the strong connection with diet had not been made. These researchers were developing a more "integrative multidimensional view" of disease (Wailoo, 1997, p. 97). Almost by accident, they discovered that the liver diet could cure this deadly disease. It appears that George H. Whipple, Minot and Murphy were studying a cure for anaemia in dogs, and had already found that a liver diet helped bleeding dogs (dogs deliberately bled to give an artificial anaemia effect) recover more quickly. They tried the liver diet with adults who presented with pernicious anaemia, and found a similar recovery (Minot & Murphy, 1926). The disease, and death from the disease, must have been widespread at this time, because they were awarded the Nobel Prize for Physiology & Medicine in 1934 "for their discoveries concerning liver therapy in cases of anaemia".[12]

Even though the actual factor that cured the disease was not known, liver was readily accessible, and many people benefited. At one point, people would have an extremely painful injection of half a litre of liquefied liver monthly.

In 1929, the haematologist William Bosworth Castle (1897-1990) discovered that a gastric component, which he called "intrinsic factor" (IF), was missing in pernicious anaemia (Elrod & Karnad, 2003).

By the 1940s, vitamin B12 had been identified as the active factor in curing pernicious anaemia (Cohn & Surgenor, 1949; Smith, 1948). Then in 1948 the "extrinsic factor", that is, vitamin B12, was isolated in crystalline form as cyanocobalamin from liver by two independent scientific teams: Edward L. Rickes, Norman G. Brink, Frank R. Koniuszy, Thomas R. Wood and Karl Folkers at Merck laboratories in the US (Rickes et al., 1948b) and E. Lester Smith and F. Parker at Glaxo laboratories in the UK (Smith, 1948). Further work on the crystal structure analysis was done by the British chemist Dorothy Crowfoot Hodgkin (Scott & Molloy, 2012). In 1956 she described the structure of this large molecule in work which won her the Nobel Prize for Chemistry in 1964 (Hodgkin, 1958; Hodgkin et al., 1956; Hodgkin et al., 1955; Kamper & Hodgkin, 1955).[13]

We see this period as the "golden age" of understanding of vitamin B12. B12 deficiency was associated with neurological problems, including multiple sclerosis-like presentations (Simson et al., 1950; Sobotka et al., 1958; Welch, 1957), and problems with absorption had been connected with the failure of the stomach to produce acid (Colombo et al., 1955; Haq et al., 1952; Ott et al., 1948; Rickes et al., 1948a). There are even hints that in these early days people understood the way that B12 in the blood is activated (Lorber & Shay, 1950, 1952).

1.2.3 Period III: 1979 to date

More recently, there seems to be widespread refusal to accept that vitamin B12 deficiency exists. Chanarin laments in his book *The Megaloblastic Anaemias* (Chanarin, 1979):

> *"Nevertheless the investigation of these problems is increasingly a lost art. The pressures accompanying the management of patients with leukaemia has led to decreasing interest in other blood disorders. The simple elucidation of the cause of megaloblastic anaemia is poorly done, criteria on which diagnoses are made are often inadequate, and conclusions reached are often incorrect."*

There could be many reasons for this refusal. Conspiracy theorists might argue that pharmaceutical companies have nothing to gain from people getting well, and a lot to gain by keeping them away

---

[12] Nobelprize.Org. (2016) *The Nobel Prize in Physiology or Medicine 1934* [Online]. Available from: https://www.nobelprize.org/nobel_prizes/medicine/laureates/1934/ [Accessed 12 November 2016]. (NobelPrize.org, 2016).

[13] The Nobel Prize in Chemistry 1964 was awarded to Dorothy Crowfoot Hodgkin *"for her determinations by X-ray techniques of the structures of important biochemical substances"*. "The Nobel Prize in Chemistry 1964". *Nobelprize.org*. Nobel Media AB 2014. Web. 31 Jan 2018. http://www.nobelprize.org/nobel_prizes/chemistry/laureates/1964/

from simple and low-cost (and effective) solutions such as vitamin supplements. Nationalists might argue that developed countries like the UK or US could not possibly have nutritional deficiency in their populations. Eminent scientists might argue that the cause of the symptoms is far more complex. The result is that patients fail the test for B12 deficiency in spite of presenting with obvious symptoms; physicians set criteria for diagnosis that guarantee that only the most extreme cases will be diagnosed; and they promote expensive solutions and restrict access to a simple, cheap, and effective supplement. This means misery for a great many people.

In 1981, we identified our first B12-deficient patient, diagnosed with neuropsychiatric symptoms, in keeping with GMC guidelines. As it happens, hospital laboratory haematologists had refused to measure the B12 level for the above patient on three occasions, because there was "no macrocytosis".

In 1996, the above patient's daughter presented, aged 26, with symptoms similar to those of her mother in 1981. After careful investigation to exclude other possible causes, we diagnosed vitamin B12 deficiency and started B12-replacement therapy. We (and the patient) observed massive improvement. This sparked the realisation that:

1) **Vitamin B12 deficiency may be far more widespread in the Caucasian population in north-east England than commonly thought. We estimate that as much as 18% of the population (see below) may both be genetically sensitive to low vitamin B12, and at the same time have limited B12 intake from the diet. The same ratio may apply everywhere else where there is a Caucasian population.**

2) **Vitamin B12 deficiency is not always accompanied by megaloblastic (immature, volume greater than 97 fL) red blood cells (also known as macrocytosis). Neurological and neuropsychiatric symptoms may be far more common as early presenting symptoms.**

3) **The disease may be passed from parent to child, i.e. it may be a genetic sensitivity to low B12 in the diet, rather than something infectious or occurring randomly.**

1.3   Deficiency prevalence and manifestation

1.3.1   Prevalence of B12 deficiency in the modern population

The 1926 figure of 10,000 deaths per year in the US suggests that B12 deficiency was a serious problem. It means that in a population of 117 million[14] at least 0.5% would ultimately be given B12 deficiency as the cause of death. However, the vast majority of people with problems of B12 deficiency do not develop the fatal symptoms of rapid muscle wastage and death within two months that would lead to a post-mortem diagnosis. Most die from other causes. Many deaths likely to be related to B12 deficiency would be attributed to other causes (e.g. falling asleep whilst working with machinery, autoimmune disease, starvation due to inability to work, anaemia, other neurological conditions).

The true present-day prevalence of vitamin B12 deficiency is not known. This is because most studies so far undertaken have been localised and focused on specific groups (such as vegetarians)

---

[14] According to the US Census Bureau, the population of the United States was 117.4 million at 1 July 1926 (US Population by Year [online] http://www.multpl.com/united-states-population/table.)

rather than the general population. A recent World Health Organisation (WHO) technical consultation on folate and vitamin B12 deficiencies noted that vitamin B12 deficiency had the potential to be a worldwide public health problem, affecting millions of people, but that more research was needed to establish its prevalence. It recommended that population-based studies designed specifically to assess folate and vitamin B12 status in the whole population should be encouraged (McLean et al., 2008).

In addition, most studies use the serum B12 level as a marker of vitamin B12 deficiency but this is problematic for the following reasons:

- The serum B12 blood test itself has serious limitations (see Chapter 2 of this book);
- There is no consensus on deficiency cut-off points. In their report for the WHO, the authors noted that: "There is a need for international reference materials and more interaction and communication among laboratories regarding these analyses so that population prevalences of deficiency can be correctly determined and compared" (de Benoist, 2008).
- The threshold levels for deficiency are in any case questionable (Wong, 2015). For instance, people may have blood levels of B12 which appear "normal" but be suffering from functional B12 deficiency, due for example to failure of intracellular transport of B12 by transcobalamin II (Turner & Talbot, 2009).

It is our experience that vitamin B12 deficiency is very much under-recognised. At my medical practice in Horden, County Durham, in 2015, in a population of 5,760 patients, there were 1,036 patients (18%) diagnosed with vitamin B12 deficiency. This was confirmed by whether their symptoms were relieved by giving supplements of B12 by injection (Chandy, 2006a).

A major research project for the US Department of Agriculture in the Framingham (Massachusetts) Offspring Study led by nutritional epidemiologist Katherine L.Tucker found an even higher prevalence - 39% of those studied had low plasma B12 levels, suggesting that "Nearly two-fifths of the U.S. population may be flirting with marginal vitamin B12 status…" (McBride, 2000).

In the UK, the nutritional status of the population is assessed through the National Diet and Nutrition Survey (NDNS) rolling programme, begun in 2008, which is funded by Public Health England (PHE) and the UK Food Standards Agency (FSA). This relies, however, on a representative sample of just 1,000 people and what we would consider a very low cut-off point for serum B12 of 150 pmol/L (Public Health England and Food Standards Agency, 2018). A deficiency rate of 6% of the population aged under 60 in the UK is commonly quoted (Hunt et al., 2014).

According to National Health and Nutrition Examination Surveys in the US from 1999 to 2002, "the prevalence of deficiency (serum vitamin B-12 < 148 pmol/L) varied by age group and affected ≤3% of those aged 20–39 y, ≈4% of those aged 40–59 y, and ≈6% of persons aged ≥70 y. .. Marginal depletion (serum vitamin B-12: 148–221 pmol/L) was more common and occurred in ≈14–16% of those aged 20–59 y and >20% of those >60 y" (Allen, 2009).

In Latin America, Africa and Asia, vitamin B12 deficiency rates are even higher because of vegetarian diets or poor nutrition (Allen, 2009).

Vitamin B12 deficiency can occur at any age but is particularly prevalent in the elderly due mainly to malabsorption problems. Estimates of the prevalence of vitamin B12 deficiency among older people range between 5% and 40% depending on the definition of vitamin B12 deficiency used (Andrès et al., 2004; Wong, 2015). A population-based cross-sectional analysis of 3,511 people in the UK aged 65 or over found that 1 in 20 aged 65-74 years and 1 in 10 aged over 75 years had significantly low B12 blood levels (Clarke et al., 2004). These are the ratios also quoted by the NHS (NHS, 2016c).

1.3.2 Categories of B12 deficiency

The absorption route of vitamin B12 in the body is complex and delicate (see Chapter 2.1.6 *Causes of B12 deficiency*). Disruption of the process at any stage can lead to deficiency. This partly explains why we have found deficiency to be so widespread. Genetic factors also appear to play an important part (see Chapter 5.10 *Inheriting the genes for vitamin B12 deficiency*).

The main categories of vitamin B12 deficiency that we encountered at the Shinwell Medical Practice are listed in Section 2.3.1.

1.3.3 Body systems where vitamin B12 is important

Vitamin B12 plays a key role in many body systems and organs and the list of these is increasing (Volkov, 2008). It is needed for energy production through the Krebs cycle, for the synthesis of DNA via the folate cycle which affects every one of the trillions of cells in the body, and for the expression (activity) of genes through epigenetic processes.[15] It affects the proper functioning of the peripheral and nervous systems, cognitive function and mood, formation of blood in the bone marrow, skin and mucous membranes, bones (Clemens, 2014), the glandular system, the digestive system, the immune system, fertility, pregnancy and development of the embryo and neonate.

Vitamin B12 deficiency consequently manifests as a huge range of different symptoms, some of which appear to be unrelated to each other and have been misdiagnosed (as other conditions) because of this. Many examples of misdiagnosis are given in this book; others are described in the classic work by Sally Pacholok and Jeffrey Stuart *Could it be B12 An Epidemic of Misdiagnoses?* (2011). Vitamin B12 is so fundamental to animal life and metabolism that the symptoms are also widespread. However, all of the observed symptoms of deficiency relate to one or more of the **six fundamental functions of B12 in the human body**, which are:

1. Manufacture and normal functioning of blood cells. It therefore affects all rapidly dividing cells, epithelial cells (skin and mucous membrane) and bone marrow cells.
2. Energy production through the Krebs Cycle (also known as TriCarboxylic Acid Cycle or Citric Acid Cycle);
3. Lipid metabolism, affecting:
    a. Metabolism of fats, carbohydrates and the synthesis of proteins, with deficiency leading to general dysfunction in many systems;
    b. Nerve cell conduction (integrity of the myelin sheath) and neurotransmitters, including effects on the brain;
    c. Endocrine (glandular) systems;
    d. Immune systems;
4. Conversion of homocysteine to methionine, then to SAMe and amino acids, with effects on many metabolic processes.

---

[15] Epigenetics is the study of the effect of chemical compounds added to single genes (for example, through diet, including intake of vitamin B12) which regulate the activity of genes.

5. Correct synthesis and transcription of DNA (through interaction with folate), the genetic material of every cell.
6. Removing toxins, e.g. pollutants and poisons such as cyanide from cigarette smoke, lead and arsenic.

1.3.4   Vitamin B12 metabolism

The metabolism of vitamin B12 in the human body is complex and not fully understood (Shane, 2008). It is beyond the scope of this book to describe its extensive biochemistry but in what follows we provide an overview of the metabolic action of vitamin B12 as so far known. This biochemistry has far-reaching effects on DNA synthesis and DNA methylation (an epigenetic modulation of DNA through the transfer of methyl groups – consisting of carbon with 3 hydrogen atoms, CH_3 - between molecules), and on synthesis of myelin (the protective sheath surrounding nerves).

It is generally understood that vitamin B12 participates in three metabolic pathways via two coenzyme forms activated in different parts of the human cell:

- In the cytosol of cells, vitamin B12, in the form of methylcobalamin, is a cofactor in the methionine synthase enzyme necessary for a chemical reaction that converts the amino acid homocysteine to another amino acid methionine. Methionine is then further metabolised to S-adenosylmethionine (SAMe) which is a "methyl donor in many reactions, including the methylation of DNA, histones and other proteins, neurotransmitters, and phospholipids, and the synthesis of creatine. These methylation reactions play important roles in development, gene expression, and genomic stability" (Shane, 2008). SAMe is particularly important for maintaining cell membranes (Bottiglieri, 2002).

- The above reaction catalysed by methionine synthase is interlinked with the folate (vitamin B9) cycle: methionine synthase takes a methyl group from the folate compound N5-methyltetrahydrofolate (5-methyl-THF) and donates it to homocysteine, a reaction which generates tetrahydrofolate and methionine. If vitamin B12 is deficient, this reaction cannot take place and cellular folate accumulates as 5-methylTHF which cannot be used for further reactions. This is called the "methyl-folate" trap hypothesis. It leads to impaired DNA synthesis because folate is needed to synthesise thymidylate, a nucleotide required in formation of DNA and RNA. The methyl-folate trap and its consequences in megaloblastic anaemia and the occurrence of birth defects is described in more detail in Chapters 4 and 5.

- In the mitochondria of cells, vitamin B12 (in the form of adenosylcobalamin) is a cofactor for methylmalonyl coA mutase, an enzyme which catalyses the conversion of methylmalonyl CoA to succinyl CoA which then enters the Krebs cycle and heme biosynthesis (Shane, 2008).

Much of the damage caused by vitamin B12 deficiency is attributed to reduced action of the methionine synthase enzyme (Scott, 1999 quoted in Smulders) which causes homocysteine to accumulate and impairment of the methylation cycle. Some researchers hypothesise that the neuropathy typical of vitamin B12 deficiency is most likely to result from hypomethylation of myelin basic protein through this route (Smulders et al., 2006).

In the other enzymatic reaction, vitamin B12 deficiency causes methylmalonic acid (MMA) to accumulate in the mitochondria which in turn leads to the accumulation of unusual fatty acids in myelin (nerve sheaths), resulting in altered myelin with reduced components of phospholipids, sphingomyelin and ethanolamine, which has been suggested as another way in which vitamin B12 may affect myelin (Gröber et al., 2013; Shane, 2008; Smith & Coman, 2014).

1.3.5 How vitamin B12 deficiency manifests

Vitamin B12 deficiency is more common in females – significantly, 80% of sufferers (four out of five) are female. We think this is because the female body has considerably more metabolic challenges than the male, with monthly hormone cycles and the associated build-up and breaking down of the uterus, and the changes in the body due to pregnancy and lactation.

In order to understand more about the symptoms, it is useful to consider how vitamin B12 is used in the body, and therefore what might stop working in the event of deficiency. Vitamin B12 is:

- Essential for the transport and storage of folate in cells and for conversion of folate to its active form;
- Essential for DNA synthesis and transcription and the growth and maturation of cells;
- Essential for the metabolism of fats, carbohydrates (carboxylic acid or Krebs cycle) and the synthesis of proteins (amino acid metabolism).

This means that all rapidly dividing cells, including epithelial cells and bone marrow cells, will have the greatest need for vitamin B12. These cells are particularly sensitive to nutritional deficiency and may malfunction, resulting in slower wound healing, disturbances in growth and development, and so on.

An example which is used as a diagnostic marker is the maturation of red blood cells (RBCs - erythrocytes). RBCs should mature into doughnut-shaped cells without a nucleus, with a high surface area-to-volume ratio for efficient oxygen and carbon dioxide transport. In B12 deficiency, the cells do not mature as far as they should; some still contain their nucleus and others have not progressed to the doughnut shape from spherical. This leads to the higher MCV (Mean Cell Volume) – not a larger diameter but a much lower surface area-to-volume ratio.

This would also indicate that vitamin B12 may be involved in the prevention (repair) of cancer. This is discussed in Chapter 9.

Vitamin B12 is also:

- Essential for lipid metabolism and the proper development of cell membranes.

In the brain and nervous system every neurone requires the myelin sheath (a fatty layer that insulates nerves) for the neurone to function. Vitamin B12 is essential for the integrity of the myelin sheath and also for the formation of neurotransmitters.[16] Some of the most obvious symptoms of B12 deficiency are neurological disorders, whether malfunction of the sensory nerves (pins and

---

[16] Neurotransmitter chemicals include serotonin, dopamine, acetylcholine and nor-epinephrine.

needles, numbness e.g. "gloves and socks", phantom pains), or of the motor nerves (paralysis such as Subacute Combined Degeneration (SACD), tremors such as Bell's Palsy, and eyesight disorders).

Lack of a properly formed myelin sheath, and potentially slow replenishment of neurotransmitter chemicals, may also contribute to poor memory, "the fogs" (feeling cut-off from the activity going on around), dementia, and psychoses and migraines. All of these have been observed in patients with diagnosed B12 deficiency, and all of these symptoms have reversed with appropriate vitamin B12 supplementation.

Another role of vitamin 12 is in the:

- Production of a mood-affecting substance, S-Adenosyl Methionine (SAMe), which is metabolised from methionine.

Vitamin B12 is required in the metabolism of homocysteine to methionine which is then converted to SAMe (elevated levels of homocysteine are a diagnostic marker for B12 deficiency). Homocysteine is a low-mood chemical, associated with depression. It is also associated with heart disease, vascular disease, and death from these diseases. In contrast, SAMe is a mood-raising chemical as well as being a precursor for some essential amino acids. Medical scientists have noted that "deficiencies of folate and vitamin B12, necessary co-factors in the synthesis of SAMe, may account for decreased SAMe levels, especially in patients with depression and dementia" (Sharma et al., 2017).

1.4   Illness groups and conditions linked to B12 deficiency

1.4.1   Neuropsychiatric disorders

Neuropsychiatric symptoms are some of the earliest presenting signs of vitamin B12 deficiency. These include irritability, mood swings, confusion, forgetfulness, fogginess, tension headaches, depression, anxiety/panic attacks, psychosis, hallucinations and delusion. We have found that these conditions are often missed as symptoms of vitamin B12 deficiency or misdiagnosed as other conditions. There is also evidence that vitamin B12 deficiency may contribute to the onset of dementia through its effect on homocysteine (see below). The neuropsychiatric symptoms of vitamin B12 are reviewed in Chapter 8.

1.4.2   Neurological disorders

As we show in Chapter 6, neurological disorders occur frequently in vitamin B12 deficiency and without any haematological signs such as macrocytosis and IF antibody. Some of these disorders are known under other names, such as Bell's Palsy, Chronic Fatigue Syndrome (CFS), Myalgic Encephalomyelitis (ME) and MS-like presentation, but as they respond well to vitamin B12 therapy – to the extent of complete remission of symptoms in many cases - we conclude that they are predominantly manifestations of B12 deficiency. The most severe of these is Subacute Combined Degeneration of the spinal cord (SACD) which we and others have found to be frequently misdiagnosed.

1.4.3   Illnesses associated with DNA disorders: birth defects and cancer

Vitamin B12 contributes to DNA synthesis through its interaction with folate (see Chapter 4). It is now well known that folate deficiency leads to severe neural tube defects (NTDs) – a fact which led to the fortification of food products with folic acid (the synthetic form of folate) in many countries.

What is less well known is that folate levels in the body appear to be closely related to vitamin B12 levels (see data in Chart 5-1) so that it may be just as important to screen pregnant mothers for B12 deficiency as for folate deficiency (see discussion of vitamin B12 and NTDs in Molloy (2018)). The importance of vitamin B12 in pregnancy is considered in Chapter 5.

Vitamin B12 also contributes to DNA methylation, an epigenetic mechanism which affects gene expression. The roles of vitamin B12 in both DNA synthesis and DNA methylation imply that adequate levels of this vitamin may help to prevent cancer (which is a disorder of DNA). Some researchers have gone farther and suggest that vitamin B12 could be used as an anti-cancer therapy. The role of vitamin B12 in relation to cancer is explored in Chapter 9.

1.4.4   Illnesses associated with high levels of homocysteine
Vitamin B12 deficiency disrupts the methionine cycle, leading to an accumulation of homocysteine. Elevated levels of homocysteine have been linked to cardiovascular disease (Harvard Health Publishing & Harvard Medical School, 2014; Rotter, 2005), the onset of dementia (Smith et al., 2018) and also with early pregnancy loss and neural tube defects in babies (Li et al., 2017).

1.4.5   Autoimmune disorders
Autoimmune disorders take many forms: they include overactive immune system disorders when the body's immune system attacks and destroys its own tissue and underactive system disorders when the body's defence against disease is reduced. Such disorders are frequent in vitamin B12-deficient patients. The list below from the AARDA (2018) shows some fairly common autoimmune disorders which many with B12 deficiency will immediately recognise:

- Addison's disease
- Amyloidosis
- Ankylosing spondylitis
- Coeliac disease - sprue (gluten-sensitive enteropathy)
- Crohn's disease
- Dermatomyositis
- Graves' disease
- Guillain-Barre Syndrome
- Hashimoto's thyroiditis
- Multiple sclerosis [MS-like presentation/SACD (Subacute Combined Degeneration)]
- Myasthenia gravis
- Pernicious anaemia/B12 deficiency
- Reactive arthritis
- Restless legs syndrome (RLS)
- Rheumatoid arthritis
- Sjögren's syndrome
- Systemic lupus erythematosus (SLE)
- Type I diabetes
- Ulcerative colitis

Note: text in square brackets added by the authors.

Many of these conditions have overlapping symptoms, for example fatigue, general ill-feeling, joint pain and rash. It is our experience that many of these conditions cease to exhibit their symptoms once vitamin B12 balance is restored in the body.

Several important findings have emerged in relation to autoimmune glandular disorders. The first is that over several decades of administering B12 therapy we noticed that autoimmune glandular disorders were particularly prevalent among B12-deficient patients. Some patients also suffered simultaneously from more than one of these disorders, particularly hypoadrenalism and hypothyroidism. It seemed to us that this was not a coincidence and that B12 deficiency was somehow disrupting the immune system pathway in the glandular system. We found that by administering vitamin B12 and the relative hormone-replacement medication, the patients' symptoms subsided without the need for elaborate drugs.

Secondly, the co-occurrence of these conditions in the same patient implied that they were suffering from Autoimmune Polyglandular Syndrome (APS) Type II or III, a condition which is normally considered rare but according to our findings is relatively common. The relationship of vitamin B12 to APS is described in Chapter 7.

Thirdly, our observation of the gastrointestinal symptoms characteristic of early-stage vitamin B12 deficiency suggested that pernicious anaemia (PA) was a progression of these symptoms: in other words, that it is preventable if the B12 deficiency is identified soon enough. PA – the illness through which vitamin B12 deficiency was originally discovered - is itself an autoimmune condition in which the body attacks the parietal cells of the stomach, leading to loss of the glycoprotein IF which is necessary for absorption of vitamin B12. In our view it is an illness which arises *from* vitamin B12 deficiency and then accentuates the deficiency through its effect on IF. We were led to this conclusion partly by the fact that we did not have any cases of PA in our Practice among patients being treated for vitamin B12 deficiency. This issue is considered in Chapter 4.

1.5 Common diagnoses that respond well to B12 supplementation

It is our contention that vitamin B12 deficiency is already observed in the population, but that clusters of symptoms have been given other names than straightforward B12 deficiency, for a variety of reasons including national pride (a developed nation should not admit to a nutritional deficiency), commercial interests (painkillers and anti-psychotics are far more profitable than B12), and academic pride (once you have discovered a new symptom, you may be reluctant to admit that it is not new at all).

Some common diagnoses that respond well to vitamin B12 supplementation include:

1.5.1 ME (Myalgic Encephalomyelitis)/CFS (Chronic Fatigue Syndrome)/ FM (Fibromyalgia)/Anxiety and Depression

The above conditions are often treated with vitamin B12, with excellent results. The likely mechanisms include: poor nerve transmission (poor development of myelin sheath); accumulation of homocysteine; and failure of the Carboxylic Acid (energy-producing) cycle.

1.5.2 MS-like presentation

Multiple Sclerosis (MS) is a characteristic failure of the myelin sheath causing nerves to stop functioning, demonstrated by detecting plaques in areas of the spinal cord and brain where a large number of myelin sheaths are malformed or missing. These plaques and corresponding symptoms have been induced by restricting intake of vitamin B12, and repaired by B12 supplementation, in laboratory experiments (Scalabrino, 2005, 2009; Scalabrino et al., 2006; Scalabrino et al., 2007).

Not only is the mechanism clear and logically related to B12 deficiency, but the association has been demonstrated and appears to be causal.

1.5.3   Dementia

There is known to be an association between vitamin B12 deficiency and cognitive impairment as in dementia and other signs of brain atrophy because of the role of vitamin B12 in maintaining safe levels of homocysteine (Douaud et al., 2013; Nurk et al., 2010; Smith et al., 2015; Smith et al., 2016). It is known that the body's ability to absorb vitamin B12 reduces with age (Andrès et al., 2004) and that dietary supplementation is recommended. A population study supplementing elderly people with B12 in order to determine if dementia risk could be reduced showed that the group with B12/folate/B6 supplements did indeed have lower homocysteine, suffered less brain atrophy, and also retained their cognitive function better (Smith et al., 2010).

1.5.4   SACD (Subacute Combined Degeneration)/Single Limb Paralysis

Subacute Combined Degeneration (a known consequence of vitamin B12 deficiency) and Single Limb Paralysis are neurological disorders which, in the author's experience, have responded well to B12 supplementation – see Chapter 6 (Chandy, 2006a).

Chapter 2   How to diagnose vitamin B12 deficiency

You will not have to do anything but stay calm.
The Lord will do the fighting for you.

Exodus 14:14

Message from a patient to the world

Is Dr Joseph Chandy a miracle worker? YES, I believe he is – yet he alone cannot perform miracles. His work is in The Hands of God!

For no less than 25 years this man has more or less single-handedly conducted research into medical dilemmas. Dr J. Chandy is a warm-hearted family man who cares deeply for the population of today – now that his work is being recognised we must keep up the fight. As a long term B12 sufferer I say, "we must unite together to get the treatment we deserve". In my condition I'd do almost anything to have a full head of hair and full use of my hands. Maybe in my future this will come but until that time I'm relying on my B12 injections and I'll back Dr J. Chandy, his family and dedicated members of staff all the way in his quest for B12.

My greatest thanks to all involved.

Jannette Chapman, 2 November 2006

Figure 2-1 The range of categories of vitamin B12 deficiency signs and symptoms

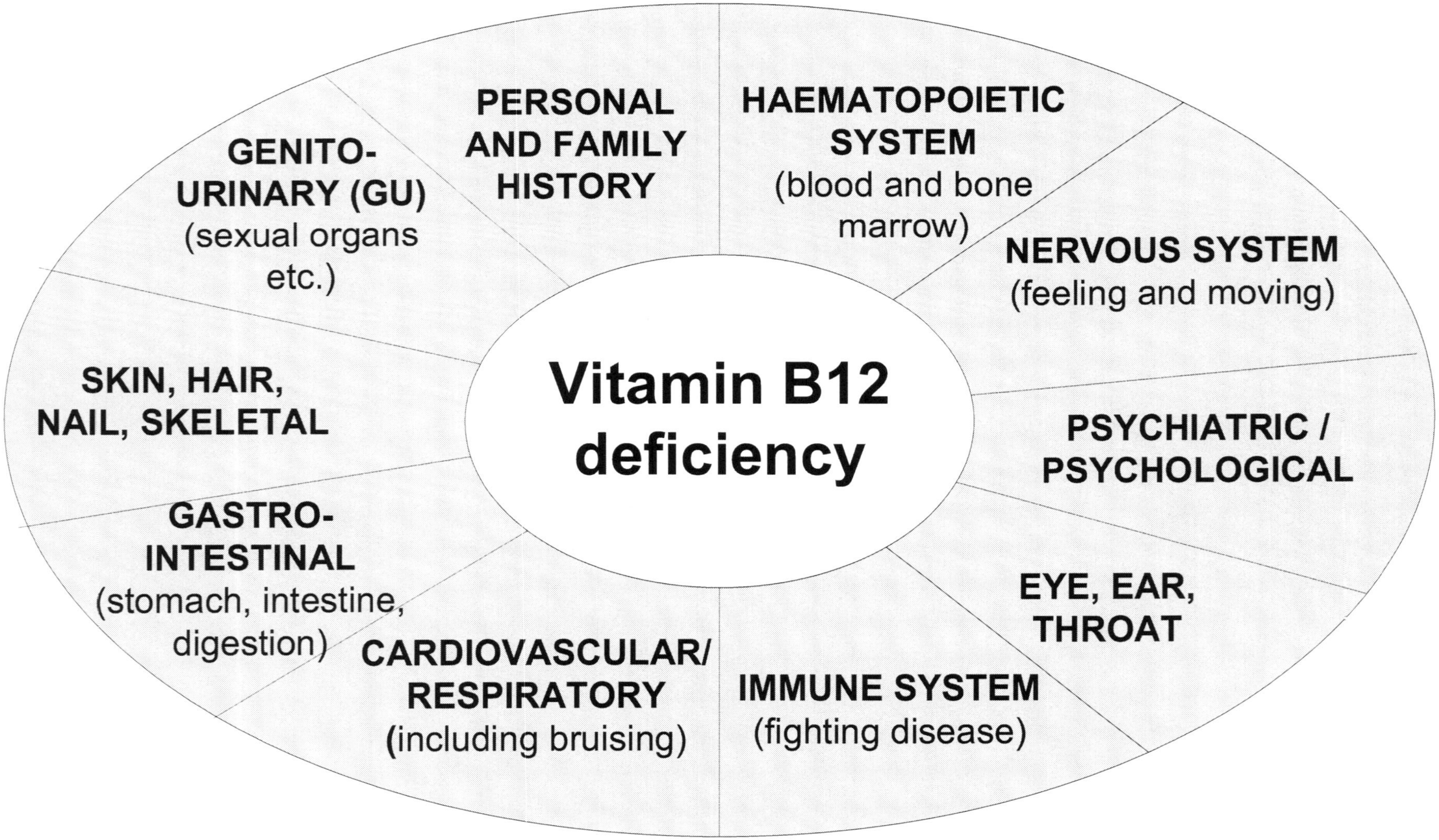

Vitamin B12 deficiency

NERVOUS SYSTEM (feeling and moving)

PSYCHIATRIC / PSYCHOLOGICAL

EYE, EAR, THROAT

IMMUNE SYSTEM (fighting disease)

HAEMATOPOIETIC SYSTEM (blood and bone marrow)

PERSONAL AND FAMILY HISTORY

GENITO-URINARY (GU) (sexual organs etc.)

SKIN, HAIR, NAIL, SKELETAL

GASTRO-INTESTINAL (stomach, intestine, digestion)

CARDIOVASCULAR/ RESPIRATORY (including bruising)

Chapter 2 How to diagnose vitamin B12 deficiency

2.1 Background to diagnosis of vitamin B12 deficiency

The traditional means of diagnosing vitamin B12 deficiency has been by a serum B12 blood test to determine the patient's B12 level, and the presence of the signs and symptoms of pernicious anaemia (PA) – the disease historically associated with causing lack of this vitamin. These signs are: macrocytosis (enlarged red blood cells), other changes in the blood and the presence of anti-Intrinsic Factor (IF) and anti-gastric parietal cell (GPC) antibodies.

In our experience, and in the views today of many experts and researchers of B12 referenced in this book, this is an outdated means of diagnosing B12 deficiency. It has a serious flaw in that it does not capture the many sufferers who do not have anaemia at all, or any other haematological signs. They may even have a serum B12 blood level which, according to the widely accepted cut-off point of 200 nanograms per litre (ng/L), would be considered to fall within the "normal" range. Instead, they have varying degrees of neuropsychiatric and neurological symptoms. Cases where the deficiency is "subtle" (i.e. not yet strongly manifested) are particularly at risk of being missed. As one expert says: "The proscription that cobalamin deficiency should not be diagnosed unless megaloblastic changes are found is akin to requiring jaundice to diagnose liver disease" (Carmel quoted in Smith & Refsum, 2011).

In this chapter we consider the limitations of the classical method of diagnosis and present our own diagnostic method, based mostly on signs and symptoms, and refined over three decades of clinical practice. This began as a formal "Pathway" in 2004 which we originally developed using our experience and following the recommendations in *Harrison's Principles of Internal Medicine*, the *BMJ Best Practice* guide and United Kingdom National Quality Assessment Scheme for Haematinic Assays (NEQAS) which advise that it must be a *clinical* decision to undertake a therapeutic trial in the suspicion of cases when a patient presents with classic signs and symptoms of B12 deficiency (see Introduction). The Pathway was further refined in the light of new knowledge and overseen by a senior haematologist from the Freeman Hospital, Newcastle-upon-Tyne. It was accepted as an official Pathway by Easington Primary Care Trust in 2006. This Pathway (since evolved into our Protocol) provides sufficient guidance for a clinician to diagnose vitamin B12 deficiency at an early stage and also enables patients to recognise their own symptoms through the **One Minute Health Check**. The Protocol is given in full in Appendix 1. To our knowledge, there is as yet no set of guidelines, other than our own, which specifically emphasises the neuropsychiatric and neurological signs and symptoms of B12 deficiency. The most helpful guidance we have otherwise encountered can be found in *BMJ Best Practice* [online] and in the *British Journal of Haematology* (Devalia et al., 2014). Our Protocol has been successfully used to diagnose and treat many B12-deficient patients.

2.1.1 Traditional link with anaemia

In Chapter 1 of this book we saw that vitamin B12 was first discovered in relation to PA, which was highly prevalent in the late eighteenth and early nineteenth centuries when nutrition was poor. To recap, two haematologists, George R. Minot and William P. Murphy, discovered by accident in 1926 that eating liver could cure, or at least alleviate, this disorder – which was at the time almost always fatal (hence its name "pernicious") – and concluded that liver contained a substance vital for human health. Two decades later, the vitamin B12 compound was isolated.

This particular historical trajectory had a number of consequences (Wailoo, 1997). Because vitamin B12 was discovered in relation to PA and by haematologists (who were subsequently awarded a Nobel Prize for their work), B12 deficiency came within the "scope and expertise" of haematologists

(Green, 2017). The diagnostic markers of B12 deficiency came to be, in the classical view, the haematological signs of PA. Collectively, these are: macrocytosis, other blood cell abnormalities, and the presence in the blood of signs of autoimmune attack. Although PA was known to be accompanied by neurological and neuropsychiatric signs and symptoms, these were not given foremost importance and were not viewed as indicators of B12 deficiency if present without macrocytosis and anti-GPC or anti-IF antibodies.

This was despite the fact that the early literature documenting this type of anaemia had described its neurological associations (Leichtenstern, 1884; Lichtheim, 1887; cited in Reynolds, 2006), and that these were recognised by James Samuel Risien Russell (1863-1939) in the early twentieth century when he described Subacute Combined Degeneration of the spinal cord – SACD (Russell et al., 1900). For discussion of SACD, see Chapter 6 of this book.

This connection with anaemia has persisted in traditional methods of diagnosis even though it has become clear that B12 deficiency has many other symptoms and that it may not be accompanied by anaemia at all.

The criteria for diagnosis of B12 deficiency which developed out of diagnosis of PA are still commonly found in traditional guidelines (see, for example, 'Anaemia – B12 and folate deficiency' in (NICE CKS, 2018a), 'Vitamin B12 or folate deficiency anaemia' in the (NHS, 2016c) online and 'Megaloblastic Anemias' (Babior & Bunn, 2005) in the medical textbook *Harrison's Principles of Internal Medicine*). They are known as the "Addisonian criteria", named after Thomas Addison (1793-1860) who is credited with the first description of PA in 1849, before it was given the name which identified it as fatal (Pearce, 2004). These criteria are summarised in Figure 4-1 at the beginning of Chapter 4. They have various drawbacks (described below) and are, we believe, a complicated diagnostic method which often leads to misdiagnosis of B12 deficiency or the diagnosis being entirely missed.

2.1.2   B12 deficiency *without* anaemia is common

Not only is the Addisonian system complicated, but its main drawback is that it makes no allowance for patients presenting with neurological and/or neuropsychiatric symptoms *without* anaemia. There is plenty of evidence in the medical literature that this type of presentation is far more common and even that there is often a "dissociation" between the two conditions: "Patients may present to haematologists and physicians with megaloblastic anaemia or to neurologists and psychiatrists with predominantly nervous-system symptoms". There is often no evidence of either anaemia or macrocytosis and researchers have even found "a significant inverse correlation between the degree of anaemia and the severity of neurological involvement…" However, if either set of symptoms is left untreated, the patients will generally develop the other strand (Reynolds, 2006).

Dr Ralph Green, an established authority on vitamin B12, says: "it became clear that the effects of B12 deficiency were not restricted to the hematopoietic system but were often overshadowed by neurological complications and were sometimes entirely absent. Just as folate deficiency is associated with effects beyond anemia, B12 deficiency also can be associated with nonhematological complications" (Green, 2017).

A reason for this may be that vitamin B12 is implicated in two distinct metabolic pathways in the human body: one leading to haematopoiesis (the formation of blood cells) and one to myelination (the formation of myelin sheaths around nerves) (Solomon, 2007).

Our long experience has shown that anaemia is rarely present in B12 deficiency, and that a patient may be deficient despite having what would commonly be described as a "normal" serum B12 level. In contrast, in the many cases we have encountered, neuropsychiatric and neurological signs and symptoms are far more prevalent and may be the only evidence of a deficiency state which is then confirmed through a therapeutic trial. Modern research is increasingly confirming this finding.

In the early 1980s we were a lone voice, but there is now plenty of evidence to support our view. For example, in a classic study in 1988 researchers found that 28% of 141 patients had no anaemia or macrocytosis and yet clearly had neuropsychiatric signs of B12 deficiency: "We conclude that neuropsychiatric disorders due to cobalamin deficiency occur commonly in the absence of anemia or an elevated mean cell volume and that measurements of serum methylmalonic acid and total homocysteine both before and after treatment are useful in the diagnosis of these patients" (Lindenbaum et al., 1988).

Individual case reports from all over the world confirm this view. Ralph Green writes: "Although considered an 'old' disease, new information is constantly accruing about B12 deficiency, the broad array of its effects, and methods for its diagnosis. B12 deficiency primarily affects the hematopoietic system, but its effects extend to other tissues and organs, most notably the nervous system. The spectrum of clinical presentations is broad so that diagnosis depends first on a high index of suspicion and then on the judicious application of appropriate testing" (Green, 2017).

This view is also reflected in the medical textbook *Harrison's Principles of Internal Medicine* which states:

> *"Cobalamin [the chemical name for vitamin B12] deficiency without hematologic abnormalities is surprisingly common, especially in the elderly. The risk of a non hematologic presentation for cobalamin deficiency is increased by the folate food fortification because folate can mask the hematologic effects of B12 deficiency. Between 10 and 30% of persons over age 70 years have metabolic evidence of cobalamin deficiency, either elevated homocysteine levels, low cobalamin – TCII levels or both.*
>
> *Only 10% of these patients have defective production of IF and the remainder often have atrophic gastritis and cannot release cobalamin from their food. Serum cobalamin levels may be normal or low, but serum levels of methylmalonic acid are almost invariably increased due to a deficiency of cobalamin at the tissue level. The neuropsychiatric abnormalities tend to improve and serum methymalonic acid levels generally return to normal after treatment with cobalamin. Neurologic defects do not always reverse with cobalamin supplementation."*
>
> (Babior & Bunn, 2005, p. 605)

Despite the increasing evidence emerging from medical research, still in recent years health authorities frequently "refuse prescriptions for vitamin B12 in patients with clinical signs of neuropathy because the patients have no haematological sign, and their plasma vitamin B12 levels are reported as 'normal'" (Smith & Refsum, 2011). This is especially worrying because, as *Harrison's Principles of Internal Medicine* points out: "An important clinical problem is the nonanaemic patient with neurologic or psychiatric abnormalities and a low or borderline serum cobalamin level. In such patients, it is necessary to try to establish whether there is significant cobalamin deficiency..." (Babior & Bunn, 2005)

2.1.3 Limitations of the blood tests

This brings us to discussion of other hurdles in the diagnosis of vitamin B12 deficiency. It is reasonable to assume that if the blood serum level of B12 is low, then a person has B12 deficiency. The corollary is that if the blood serum level of B12 is within a "normal" range, then a person cannot have B12 deficiency. There are two problems with this assumption: the first is the unreliability of the blood test.

In a letter defending my diagnostic method in 2012, Professor A. David Smith, [17] a recognised expert on the scientific aspects of vitamin B12, described the "uncertain reliability of commercially-available assays for blood levels of B12" (the full text of this letter is provided in Box 2-1 at the end of this chapter on page 62). There is currently only one commercial assay (procedure for assessing the quantity of a substance in a sample) in widespread use in laboratories worldwide for assessing the level of serum B12. This is the chemiluminescence-based assay (Combined Binding Luminescence Assay, CBLA). However, in 2012, a leading B12 researcher Professor Ralph Carmel cast doubt on the reliability of this method in a report showing that CBLA kits gave falsely high readings with blood from patients with pernicious anaemia, with failure rates ranging from 22% to 35% (Carmel & Agrawal, 2012). This was not the first time that such difficulties had been reported. In a letter to the Editor of Clinical Chemistry in 2000, Professor Carmel wrote: "We wish to report a serious problem in the ... chemiluminescence assay for cobalamin ...The problem is urgent for two reasons: (a) our findings suggest that many cobalamin-deficient patients are being missed; and (b) the assay is used by increasing numbers of laboratories..." (Carmel et al., 2000).

Examples of patients who were clearly clinically B12-deficient but whose blood tests showed results within the "normal range" can be found in Devalia (2006), and examples of contradictory results produced by different test methods are shown in Hamilton et al. (2006). In 2010, the American Society for Hematology also reported a case of false normal vitamin B12 levels caused by assay error (American Society of Hematology, 2011). Again, in 2016, another study reported only 19% sensitivity of the serum B12 test (Olson et al., 2016). In Japan, where other types of automated competitive protein binding (CPB) assays are used, inconsistency between results produced by three different tests has been reported (Ihara et al., 2008). Many experts now consider that the serum B12 blood test is of "limited diagnostic value as a stand-alone marker" (Hannibal et al., 2016).

The CBLA replaced older microbiologic and radioisotope-dilution assays during the past couple of decades, and may measure more than simply B12. The CBLA test gives reliable readings when measuring test solutions of pure B12 in saline (albeit that it has an upper limit of 2000 ng/L).

---

[17] Professor A. David Smith is Emeritus Professor of Pharmacology, Department of Pharmacology, Medical Sciences Division, University of Oxford.

However, when testing samples of human blood, it may give "normal" range readings for people who clearly have B12 deficiency symptoms, and who would get a low blood serum B12 under the previous radioisotope dilution assay to confirm their symptoms (Carmel & Agrawal, 2012). What CBLA is binding to instead of B12 is still not known, but we know that people are being told that they have a "normal" (above minimum threshold) level of B12 in their blood (and therefore a diagnosis of B12 deficiency should be excluded) when not only do they clearly have symptoms which indicate B12 deficiency, but B12-replacement therapy (loading dose of B12 by injection) often reverses those symptoms.

The second problem is that the standard B12 blood serum test (in common use) does not differentiate between the active (holotranscobalamin) and inactive forms of B12 so may give a false reading of the B12 actually available for use, described as "functional vitamin B12" (Turner & Talbot, 2009) (see Chapter 1). In the 1980s, a pioneering New York-based physician/scientist Victor Herbert (1927-2002), put forward the view (which is still held although some aspects are disputed – see Golding (2016)), that about 80% of B12 in the body is bound to haptocorrin, a storage protein, and is therefore inactive, while the remainder is bound to Transcobalamin II (this combination is called holo-transcobalamin [HoloTC]), the active fraction which enters the cells for metabolic reaction (Herbert, 1987)). If both are measured, total serum B12 may appear within the normal reference range, despite the important TC-bound fraction being lower (Green, 2017).

In addition to these risk factors, there is no international, or even national (in the UK) agreement about where the cut-off point lies for the B12 in blood below which a patient needs treatment. The cut-off point varies greatly between laboratories worldwide and there is no globally accepted reference range (Tsiminis et al., 2016). The *BMJ Best Practice* suggests the following: >200 picograms/mL[18] probable deficiency, 201-350 pg/mL possible deficiency, >350 pg/mL unlikely deficiency (BMJ Best Practice, 2018d). However, as Professor Smith points out in his letter, serious B12-deficiency symptoms can manifest in patients with B12 levels across the whole normal range.

Under these circumstances, arguments about what the threshold minimum level of B12 should be in the blood become academic. It is better to diagnose B12 deficiency using a combination of signs and symptoms, which should certainly include the blood serum B12 level, but focus mainly on symptoms and family history, and on confirming the diagnosis by a trial of B12-replacement therapy.

2.1.4 Other possible B12 deficiency biomarkers

There are several other methods that can be used to determine vitamin B12 deficiency:

- **Measurement of plasma total homocysteine (tHcy)**
  Levels of tHcy increase from the early stages of vitamin B12 deficiency. However, one drawback to using homocysteine levels as a biomarker of B12 deficiency is that high homocysteine levels can indicate other conditions, such as folate or vitamin B6 deficiency or other illnesses.

- **Measurement of plasma methylmalonic acid (MMA)**
  Levels of MMA increase with vitamin B12 deficiency. As with tHcy, raised MMA can also be caused by other illnesses but it is more specific to vitamin B12 deficiency than raised tHcy.

---

[18] See Table 2-1 for pg/mL and ng/L unit equivalences.

The main drawback of this test is its high cost. There is no routine national quality assessment scheme for plasma MMA assays in Britain.

- **Measurement of holotranscobalamin (holoTC)**
  As explained above, holoTC is the "active" fraction of plasma B12 and may be an earlier indicator of B12 deficiency than serum B12. A new measurement, The Abbott ARCHITECT Active-B12 assay, has been developed for detecting levels of serum holotranscobalamin which claims to be a more accurate marker of B12 deficiency (NICE, 2015). The appropriateness of this test is, however, disputed (Golding, 2016).

- **Bone marrow aspiration/biopsy** is rarely used.

- **The Schilling test**
  This test, introduced in 1953 to determine whether a patient was producing Intrinsic Factor, is now rarely used due to its cumbersome nature and use of a radioactive element (though this was harmless).

There are also arguments against the reliability of all these indicators (Carmel, 2011). It seems, therefore, that "Whatever screening criteria are used, a number of B12-deficient patients will be missed. Therefore, there may be a case for universal vitamin B12 screening [haematinic screening]" (Chui et al., 2001).

In summary, the British Society for Haematology recommends considering plasma tHcy and/or plasma MMA as supplementary tests (if available) and suggests use of holoTC as a more indicative routine test for vitamin B12 deficiency than serum B12 in the future (Devalia et al., 2014). Other experts also recommend a combination of tests (Green, 2017).

2.1.5 Scarcity of guidelines

While guidelines for diagnosing B12-deficiency-induced anaemia can be found in the publications of medical authorities, guidelines for diagnosing vitamin B12 deficiency in the *absence* of anaemia are distinctly lacking. The UK's National Institute for Care and Excellence (NICE) *Clinical Knowledge Summaries*, for example, a key online reference work for GPs, have no separate entry for vitamin B12 deficiency which is only mentioned in relation to anaemia (NICE CKS, 2018a). The same applies to *NHS* online (NHS, 2016c).

The key question then becomes: how do we diagnose vitamin B12 deficiency in the absence of guidelines which take into consideration the neurological and neuropsychiatric symptoms?

2.1.6 Causes of B12 deficiency

Vitamin B12 deficiency has many causes which can be grouped under the headings of poor dietary intake, increased requirements, malabsorption, other illnesses, and some medications. There are also inborn errors of cobalamin metabolism and gene mutations affecting the B12 absorption pathway (Hannibal et al., 2016). These causes need to be explored in a patient because type and frequency of treatment will depend partly on the cause.

Dietary intake may be the cause where patients follow a vegan or vegetarian diet, or where their diet is unbalanced as in eating disorders or a poor nutritional environment.

Increased requirements occur during pregnancy and while breastfeeding, at times of stress and as a result of other illnesses. Our advice from clinical evidence is that both mother and the developing foetus require optimum amount of vitamin B12 and folic acid to prevent neural tube defects (NTDs) and other related conditions in the newborn. It is good medical practice to screen all would-be mothers three months in advance with routine haematinic screening for vitamin B12 and folic acid and commence physiological supplementation of iron, vitamin B12 and folic acid.

Malabsorption is a prime cause of deficiency. The absorption route is complex and has several steps, damage to any one of which can disrupt the process. Vitamin B12 in food is bound to protein. This bond is broken by gastric acid and enzymes in the stomach which free the vitamin. The free vitamin B12 then binds to a protein called haptocorrin (a glycoprotein formerly known as Transcobalamin I or R-binder) which is made in human saliva and parietal cells in the stomach and which protects the vitamin B12 against stomach acid. As this complex passes into the more alkaline duodenum, pancreatic enzymes destroy the haptocorrin, again freeing the vitamin B12 which now binds to a molecule produced by the parietal cells called Intrinsic Factor (IF). In the ileum, the vitamin B12-IF complex is recognised by special receptors and absorbed into the blood. In the blood it is bound to two carrier-proteins. Some is stored in the liver and the remainder available for immediate use.

Disruption of this process can be caused by:

- chronic gastrointestinal disorders such as Crohn's disease;
- autoimmune reactions such as the production of anti-IF antibodies (as is the case in pernicious anaemia);
- atrophic gastritis (an inflammatory condition) and gastrointestinal surgery;
- lack of pancreatic proteases;
- long-term use of some medications such as antacids, proton-pump inhibitors, diabetic medications and oral contraceptives;
- tapeworm and other infections;
- alcohol abuse and heavy smoking.

(More detailed descriptions are found in Briani et al. (2013)).

Other illnesses Our advice is that the incidence of B12 deficiency is substantially increased in patients with other diseases thought to be immunological in origin, including Graves' Disease, myxoedema, thyroiditis, idiopathic adrenocortical insufficiency, vitiligo and hypoparathyroidism. Anti-IF antibody is usually absent from these patients.

Other causes are nitrous oxide anaesthesia (nitrous oxide inactivates B12 in the body, including brain cells) and smoke inhalation (cyanide poisoning).

2.1.7 Failure to activate B12 – failure of the entero-hepatic system

Deficiency can also arise from failure of the entero-hepatic system. As described above, the concepts of "active" and "inactive" B12 were first proposed by Herbert. However, it is not fully known how inactive B12 (thought to be stored in the liver, although this may simply be because there is a lot of blood in the liver) can be converted into active B12 and how this impacts on deficiency. One possible mechanism may be entero-hepatic circulation whereby materials carried in the blood are captured by the liver and passed into the small intestine via the bile duct. From here, they are activated with secreted intestine products (in the case of B12, IF secreted by parietal cells in the stomach) and then reabsorbed through the intestinal wall into the bloodstream already activated. In this mechanism, the IF "passes" the B12 to Transcobalamin II.

Entero-hepatic circulation appears to be widespread and may serve a number of different functions:

- bile salts are needed in the intestine to help with the digestion of fats/lipids, and are reabsorbed and recirculated after they have done their job;
- expired or degraded haemoglobin may be secreted as bilirubin to assist digestion of fats. A higher proportion of this is not absorbed.

Figure 2-2 Entero-hepatic circulation

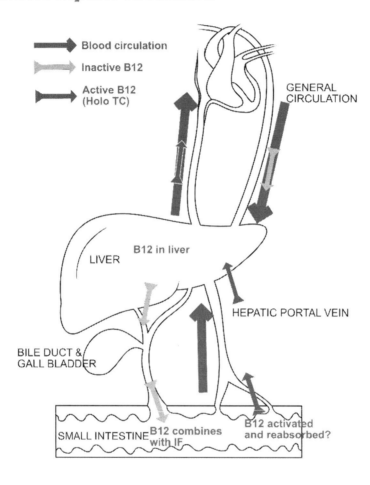

Graphic by Hugo Minney

Because the vitamin B12 circulates through this route frequently, if there is impaired absorption, this implies that large quantities could be lost through the gut (O'Leary & Samman, 2010). We suggest this could be one of the major causes of vitamin B12 deficiency, as the body stores are depleted.

2.2 Wide-ranging effects of B12 deficiency

2.2.1 Historical presentations

Before the Second World War, there were four principal presentations (medically recognised classifications) of B12 deficiency. The following classification is based partly on Chanarin's work (1990).

1) **Megaloblastic anaemia** (presence of megaloblastic bone marrow precursor cells). Requires bone marrow aspiration, presence of anti-intrinsic factor and anti-parietal cell antibodies, and typically, low serum B12/low serum folic acid/low Hb%

2) **Pernicious anaemia** (fatal) resulting in ineffective erythropoiesis. Anti-Intrinsic factor and/or anti-parietal cell antibodies present, low serum B12/ low folic acid and low Hb%

3) **Macrocytic anaemia** (macrocytic red cells MCV >100 fL appear in the peripheral blood)

4) **Vitamin B12 deficiency** (nutritional cause)

2.2.2 Postwar presentations

With improved nutrition in Britain and many countries after the war, a new set of five presentations were used to diagnose B12 deficiency:

1) **Microcytic anaemia** ((MCV <75) B12 deficiency caused by iron deficiency)

2) **Macrocytic vitamin B12 deficiency** (with or without anaemia or macrocytosis) subtle B12 deficiency

3) **Neuropsychiatric vitamin B12 deficiency** (with or without neuropsychiatric signs and symptoms)

4) **Vitamin B12 deficiency – APS** (autoimmune polyglandular syndrome – multisystem polyendocrine failure)

5) **Vitamin B12 deficiency – nutritional cause**

All of these categories may present with mild, moderate or severe signs and symptoms, and all appear to be associated with a strong family history (genetic preponderance).

In our experience at the Shinwell Medical Practice, pernicious anaemia (MCV> 97 fL; Intrinsic Factor/parietal cell antibody +ve; low B12; low folic acid) accounts for less than 10% of B12-deficiency presentations today. Note that UK laboratories are no longer routinely carrying out IF/parietal cell antibody tests.

Two more common presentations of anaemia also exist: microcytic (iron deficiency) anaemia and macrocytic (folic acid deficiency) anaemia. These two conditions are treated as follows:

2.2.2.1 *Microcytic anaemia: iron deficiency*

In most cases, iron deficiency (microcytic anaemia) can be easily diagnosed by low levels of blood iron or haemoglobin (Hb%), and easily corrected with oral iron (ferrous sulphate 200 mg TDS * 3/12; severe cases require regular iron IM injections). Because of the way the information on MCV is presented, a combination of low iron and low B12 may result in a normal "average" MCV even though the blood contains both macrocytic and microcytic red blood cells.

2.2.2.2 *Macrocytic anaemia: folic acid deficiency*

Routine haematinic screening identifies folate deficiency which is easily corrected by oral folic acid given daily for 3 to 4 months. However, due to folic acid food fortification in developed countries, folic acid deficiency is encountered much less frequently than previously. For effective DNA synthesis and maturation, both B12 and folic acid are crucial.

Folic acid supplementation can correct the megaloblastic cells in the bone marrow, but this may lead physicians to miss the neurological manifestations of the undiagnosed/untreated B12 deficiency. Hoffbrand and Provan advise that vitamin B12 deficiency should be "excluded in all patients starting folic acid treatment at these [specified] doses as such treatment may correct the anaemia in vitamin B12 deficiency but allow neurological disease to develop" (Hoffbrand & Provan, 1997).

2.2.3 Neuropsychiatric symptoms presentation

Our experience is that 90% of patients who are diagnosed with vitamin B12 deficiency present with neuropsychiatric symptoms (percentage derived from Shinwell Medical Practice patient survey). More information is given in Chapter 8.

Neuropsychiatric symptoms include: sensory nerve symptoms, such as tingling or numbness; motor nerve symptoms, such as tremors or paralysis; brain symptoms such as "brain fog", migraine headaches, psychoses. A huge range of presentations is possible as illustrated by the two cases below.

Case 2-1 Neuropsychiatric symptoms and alopecia

Paul Atchinson presented in March 2011 with neuropsychiatric symptoms and extensive alopecia. His B12 level was in the normal range (591 ng/L). Conventional treatment by a dermatologist had no impact. We started intensive B12 treatment. Four months later, in July 2011, his condition was much improved. By August most of his hair had grown back and by November 2011 he had completely recovered.

 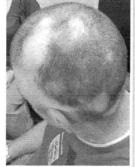 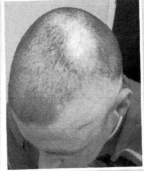 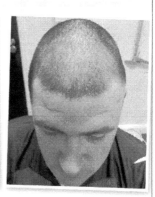

| March 2011 | 9th July 2011 | 20th August 2011 | 3rd Nov 2011 |

Case 2-2 Lupus, rheumatoid arthritis and Raynaud's disease

Susan Laidler (born 1964) suffered joint inflammation, skin lesions, lip and mouth ulcers and poor circulation (blue fingers). In 2008 her B12 level was 674 ng/L but had dropped to 266 ng/L by March 2011. She was taking two immunosuppressant medications for the rheumatoid arthritis. The ulcers, joint inflammation and all her symptoms disappear when she receives frequent (weekly) injections of vitamin B12, but reappear when she misses an injection or two. She no longer takes the immunosuppressant medicine (of her own volition).

 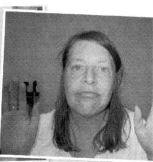 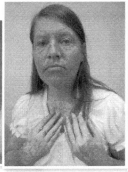 

| May 2011, after 4 wks treatment | June, after 2 more weeks' | 2 Aug | 8 Aug |

2.3 Our diagnostic method

2.3.1 Seven categories of deficiency

We consider that B12 deficiency can be categorised into seven categories, with four stages. It requires a clinical diagnosis by a clinician (as opposed to overreliance on a single number from a pathology laboratory), and diagnosis between these seven categories may include overlaps and multiple comorbidity.

Treatment may also be complex as absorption/transport/utilisation are complex, and regular reviews/monitoring with blood tests are essential. The proposed Protocol is enclosed as Appendix 1 to this book.

The seven categories that we have observed are:

I. Clinically significant B12 deficiency (with moderate to severe neuropsychiatric symptoms) B12 level <200 ng/l – with other related features (gastrointestinal, haematological symptoms)

II. Clinical B12 deficiency (with mild to moderate neuropsychiatric symptoms), a B12 level <200 ng/l with or without related features (such as gastrointestinal or haematological symptoms)

III. Subclinical cobalamin deficiency (blood serum B12 >200 ng/L) without signs or symptoms

IV. 'Subtle cobalamin deficiency', that is a subnormal/normal B12 level with some signs and symptoms

V. Functional cobalamin malabsorption (unable to absorb B12 from food but able to absorb oral B12)

VI. Transient cobalamin deficiency (condition remains reversed once corrected)

VII. Dietary B12 deficiency due to a vegetarian or vegan diet, or poor diet (takes 10-20 years to manifest)

2.3.2 Four stages of deficiency

I.	Serum B12 concentration low; no clinical or metabolic abnormalities. Low plasma level of holotranscobalamin II
II.	Increased level of HCY and MMA and low holotranscobalamin II – low B12 level. Damaged metabolism. Neuropsychiatric signs and symptoms with mild haematological changes without anaemia
III.	The plasma and cell stores of B12 become depleted. Serum B12 is low with metabolic abnormalities
IV.	Clinical signs become recognisable (Addisonian criteria) a. Macro Ovalocytosis b. Elevated MCV or Erythrocytosis c. Lowered haemoglobin d. Patients presenting with the classical features of pernicious anaemia (PA)/vitamin B12 deficiency would therefore be expected to have progressed through stages I, II and III over several years. Some vegans and patients with malabsorption of food cobalamin may also progress through these stages sometimes over many years, but others may not progress beyond stage I or II. These considerations imply that there are many more individuals in stages I, II, and III of vitamin B12 deficiency than in stage IV (PA).

Low nutritional intake of vitamin B12 may lead to negative balance and finally to functional deficiency when tissue stores of Vitamin B12 are depleted.

Early diagnosis (stages I and II) of vitamin B12 deficiency seems to be useful because irreversible neurological damage may be prevented by cobalamin supplementation at this early stage (Chandy, 2006a).

2.3.3 Our Protocol for diagnosis

Our Protocol (Appendix 1) is based on Signs (including family history and blood values for various components) and Symptoms, which enables a clinician to make a differential diagnosis with a high level of certainty. The method for using the Protocol is as follows:

2.3.3.1 Trigger symptoms

The clinician should be immediately alert if a patient presents with **tiredness, depression, hair loss, pins and needles, numbness in hands or feet, tremors and palsies, palpitations, recurrent headache or dizziness**, and B12 deficiency should be considered. The above symptoms may be marker symptoms for a wide variety of conditions, and differential diagnosis can identify the correct diagnosis.

2.3.3.2 One-minute Health Check

B12 deficiency often occurs alongside other deficiency conditions and degenerative diseases. It is important to perform blood tests in order to ensure a comprehensive diagnosis, so that treatment for co-occurring conditions can be given at the same time as B12-replacement therapy.

Order blood tests for: FBC; Serum vitamin B12; folic acid; TSH; U+Es; LFT; Serum ferritin; Glucose; 8-9am fasting cortisol; vitamin D. This will confirm or exclude the most common conditions found alongside vitamin B12 deficiency. Other appropriate diagnostic tests at this point include parathyroid, pituitary, adrenal and ovarian hormone tests.

Ask the patient to score using the **One Minute Health Check – B12 Deficiency Signs and Symptoms** (Table 2-1 One Minute Health Check on page 58). The patient circles their actual symptom(s) in each group and scores severity of the most severe from 1-10 (where 0=no symptom (leave blank), 5= symptom affects daily life to a moderate extent, all the way up to 10 where the symptom is present all the time and severe and debilitating).

Table 2-1 One Minute Health Check

A quick score will reveal if B12 deficiency, underactive thyroid or iron deficiency anaemia are possible diagnoses, and if the physician should order further tests and commence treatment.

	Signs and Symptoms	Score 1-10		Signs and Symptoms	Score 1-10
	Energy/ haemopoetic			**Cardiovascular/respiratory**	
	Weariness, lethargy, tiredness, fatigue, faints			Shortness of breath, wheeziness	
	Sleepy, tired in the afternoon			Palpitations, chest pain	
	Nervous system			Pallor, lemon yellow complexion	
	Tremor, foot drop			Bruising, vasculitis	
¥	Loss of balance (ataxia), seizures, falls			**Gastro-Intestinal (GI)**	
¥	Tingling or numbness in hands and/or feet, burning sensation			Sore tongue, bleeding gums	
	Restless leg syndrome			Red beefy tongue	
	Facial palsy			Cracking the angles of mouth	
	Spastic movements, crampy pain in limbs			Metallic taste, unusual taste, loss of appetite, loss of weight	
¥	Stiffness of limbs, muscle wasting			Gastric symptoms- acidity, heartburn	
¥	Weakness or loss of sensation in limbs, shooting pain in back/ limbs, paralysis			Intermittent diarrhoea, IBS	
	Migrainous headache			**Skin, hair, nail, skeletal**	
	Psychiatric			Premature greying	
	Irritable, snappy, disturbed sleep			Alopecia, unexplained hair loss	
	Confused, memory disturbance/ forgetful, fogginess			Joint inflammation, swelling, pain	
	Tension headaches			Dry skin, brittle nails	
*	Mental slowness, mood swings, anxiety/ panic attacks, depression			**Genito-Urinary (GU)**	
*	Psychosis, hallucinations, delusion			Heavy painful periods, irregular periods, infertility and frequent miscarriages	
	Eye, Ear, Throat			Polycystic ovarian disease	
	Blurred vision/ double vision/ drooping of eyelid (lid lag), orbital pain			Loss of libido	
	Dizziness, tinnitus			Shooting pain from groin to perineum	
	Difficulty swallowing, persistent cough			Incontinence	
	Immune System			**Personal and Family History**	
	Prone to recurrent URTI, UTI, Respiratory infections			Family history of B12 deficiency (Pernicious Anaemia), underactive thyroid, diabetes, vitiligo, depression	
	Other auto-immune conditions			Vegetarian, vegan, poor diet	
	Hypoadrenalism, myxodoema/ underactive thyroid			Alcoholism, smoking	

✳ PHQ9 Patient Health Questionnaire to be completed

¥ Neurological examination and appropriate referral if indicated

The physician should also order routine blood tests, including serum B12, in the following cases:

- ME, CFS, fibromyalgia, hypoadrenalism, MS-like presentation;
- Children born to B12-deficient mothers, presenting with behavioural problems, learning disability, dyspraxia, dyslexia and autistic spectrum disorders.

Before making a provisional diagnosis of B12 deficiency, exclude all other possible diagnoses, with appropriate blood tests as clinically indicated.

Refer to the Decision Tree below for diagnosis and treatment and await blood test results if appropriate. Note that for patients with severe signs and symptoms, treatment may need to be initiated *without waiting* for the results of blood tests.

Figure 2-3 Decision Tree

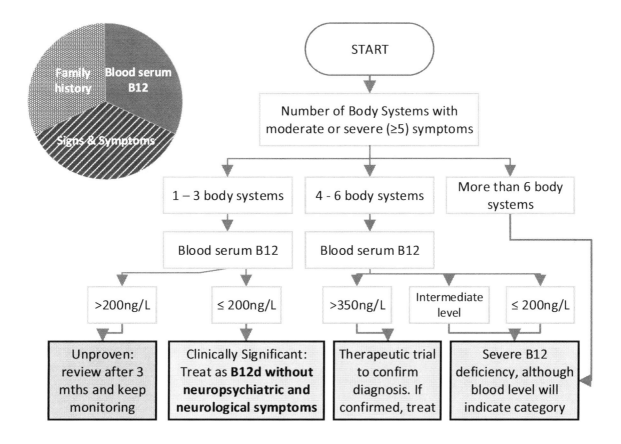

Blood tests are categorised as follows when combined with signs and symptoms indicative of B12 deficiency:

Table 2-1 Vitamin B12 deficiency by blood serum level

Blood serum B12 nanograms per litre (ng/L)	Blood serum B12 nanomole/millilitre (nmol/ml)	Classification
< 200 ng/L	< 148 nmol/ml	Clinically significant/ severe B12 deficiency
200-350 ng/L	148 – 259 nmol/ml	Moderate deficiency
>350 ng/L	> 259 nmol/mL	"Subtle" (subnormal/low normal blood serum B12 but with signs and symptoms)

Note: picograms per millilitre (pg/ml) are the same as nanograms per litre (ng/L) (100 picograms/millilitre = 0.1 nanograms/millilitre), so the numbers are the same for the same classifications of condition.

Results of other blood tests: many conditions are commonly found alongside vitamin B12 deficiency, and should be treated in the normal manner at the same time as administering B12-replacement therapy. See also the hypoadrenalism (Addison's disease or adrenal insufficiency) treatment protocol in Appendix 2.

2.3.4   Therapeutic trial

In addition to these classifications, patients can be assigned to a therapeutic trial (to confirm a suspected diagnosis) or prophylaxis (where the clinician has evidence to suggest this is needed to prevent symptoms developing or getting worse). For example, if the patient is diagnosed as having moderate or subtle deficiency (>180ng/L or >200ng/L with signs and symptoms, other autoimmune condition or family history) then they should be clinically reviewed every 4 weeks until the clinician reaches a clinical decision whether to commence treatment – even when the B12 level does not drop below 180-200ng/L. A deterioration of condition demonstrated by signs and symptoms is sufficient to commence a **therapeutic trial**.

2.3.5   Prophylaxis of vitamin B12 deficiency

In the following instances, B12-replacement therapy should be instituted as a prophylactic measure (to prevent further deterioration or even development of symptoms) regardless of blood serum B12 concentration: Prophylaxis is expected to continue for life.

1- **Specific medical history** renal imbalance, diabetes, >65 years old, or following GI surgery, Crohn's colitis, early onset dementia

2- **Moderate/subtle B12 deficiency with mild signs and symptoms**

3- **Moderate/subtle B12 deficiency with severe signs and symptoms:** patient presenting with strong family history, presence of other autoimmune conditions, major signs and symptoms which could become irreversible if treatment is not commenced urgently e.g. optic neuritis/neuropathy, sudden onset blindness, Subacute Combined Degeneration (SACD), ME, CFS, MS-like presentation, single limb paralysis, sudden loss of muscle mass (Motor Neurone Disease-like presentation), non-epileptic seizures, dysphagia, Bell's Palsy/Ramsey Hunt syndrome, Parkinson's like presentation, dementia, total alopecia, migrainous headache, temporal arteritis, recurrent miscarriages, dysfunctional uterine bleeding, or psychosis.

2.3.6   Other actions to take

- If clinical depression is suspected – complete PHQ9 and treat/refer as appropriate
- Neurological manifestation – neurological examination and refer to neurologist for further investigation

Provisional diagnosis of any other condition – refer to appropriate speciality.

Box 2-1 Document: Letter from Professor A. D. Smith

Comments on Allegations in Annex A (ES/C1-701040697) regarding
Dr J. Chandy

By Professor A. David Smith,
Emeritus Professor of Pharmacology, University of Oxford

29 November 2013

I have been asked to comment on Allegations 1, a to f, excluding d. I have done this after reading the relevant sections of Dr Tidy's report of 6 October 2013.

I note that Dr Chandy is a very experienced GP who over the years has developed a particular interest in pernicious anaemia and vitamin B12 deficiency. My comments will be confined to scientific aspects of these conditions since I am not able to comment upon the specific claims about particular patients as I am not medically qualified. One area of my research since 1995 has been in the field of B vitamins and in particular B12 (cobalamin) in human health. I have become a recognised expert in this field and, for example, have been invited to write editorials in medical journals on B12 and to serve on an expert panel of the National Institutes of Health in Washington. I therefore consider myself qualified to make the comments below.

The allegations concern the use of vitamin B12 replacement therapy in patients who were thought to be B12 deficient. It should be recognised that severe B12 deficiency, such as pernicious anaemia, is a fatal disease. It is first necessary to give some scientific background before I can comment on the allegations.

The scientific and clinical challenges in this field can be divided into four categories:
1. The uncertain reliability of commercially-available assays for blood levels of B12
2. The introduction of more specific assays for the functional status of B12
3. The uncertainty about where the cut-off value lies for these assays in order to initiate treatment with B12
4. The variable response of patients to B12 treatment

1. The uncertain reliability of commercially-available assays for blood levels of B12

Three main methods have been used to measure the concentrations of B12 in body fluids: the radio-isotope dilution assay (RIDA); the chemiluminescence-based assay (CBLA); and the microbiological assay. Only the first two methods have been used commercially but the microbiological method is widely considered to be the gold- standard and is used in research laboratories, including my own. There have been serious problems with both commercial assays. In the late 1970's it was found that the RIDA method sometimes gave falsely high values and so failed to identify B12 deficiency. The method has since dropped out of use, partly for this reason but mainly because of the need to use radioactive isotopes. The CBLA methods are used world-wide from kits supplied by several manufacturers. In the early 2000's occasional reports began to appear that the CBLA method was giving falsely high results and so missing B12 deficiency. This situation came to a dramatic conclusion in 2012 when one of the leading B12 researchers (Professor Ralph Cannel from New York) published a report in the New England Journal of Medicine showing that all 3 manufacturers' CBLA kits gave falsely high readings with blood from patients with pernicious anaemia, with failure rates ranging from 22 to 35%. The manufacturers have as yet not responded satisfactorily and this leaves the clinician with a major problem: how is he to assess the B12 status of his patients who he suspects are deficient?

2. The introduction of more specific assays for the functional status of B12

It has been known for more than 30 years that two blood markers exist that reflect the body's functional status of Bl 2: homocysteine and methylmalonic acid. Methods for measuring these markers are available, but only that for homocysteine is widely available. While the levels of these markers are raised in B12 deficiency, they are not widely used since homocysteine is not specific to B12 and methylmalonic acid assays are expensive and still only found in research laboratories. So, at present, these markers are mainly used in research settings and in the UK they are not available on the NHS. More recently, an assay method for so-called 'active-B12' has been introduced and is commercially available. Active-B12 is the form bound to a protein called transcobalamin and it is this complex which is taken up into cells of the body. Active-B12 only comprises about 20% of the total amount of B12 in the blood. In time, the Active-B12 method may become the method of choice for determining a patient's B12 status, but at present the expert advice is that more research is needed to establish its validity.

3. The uncertainty about where the cut-off value lies for these assays, in order to initiate treatment with B12

A clinician needs to know a value for the B12 level in blood below which he can say that a patient needs treatment with Bl 2. The original cut-off value and still the most widely used internationally, was 148 pmol/L, which is equivalent to 200 pg/mL (the conversion factor from pg/mL to pmol/L is 0.738). This cut-off value identifies most patients with pernicious anaemia and at this level the characteristic haematological signs are usually found, which has led to *the view that the haematological signs are a requirement for a diagnosis.* However, it is now well-documented that patients can have pernicious anaemia without the typical haematological signs, but will show neurological and/or psychiatric signs. In a classic paper in 1988, Lindenbaum at al. found that 28% of 141 patients had no anaemia or macrocytosis and yet clearly had neuropsychiatric signs of deficiency. Since then, there have been many reports that stated that haematological signs should not be a requirement for a diagnosis of B12 deficiency. Thus, the cut-off of 200 pg/mL, originally defined on haematological grounds, has to be reconsidered in case patients with higher blood levels will suffer neurological harm. In an authoritative review, Herrmann and Obeid (2012) found that a high proportion of patients defined as B12 deficient by functional criteria had serum B12 levels above 200pg/mL They concluded *"No single parameter can be used to diagnose cobalamin deficiency. Total serum cobalamin is neither sensitive nor is it specific for cobalamin deficiency. This might explain why many deficient subjects would be overlooked by utilizing total cobalamin as status marker."*
The BMJ Best Practice Guidelines for B12 deficiency (2013) propose the following cut-off values:
< 200 pg/mL probable deficiency 201-350 pg/mL possible deficiency
> 350 pg/mL unlikely deficiency
In a recent editorial in *Journal of Internal Medicine* I reviewed the evidence that people with B12 levels above 200 pg/mL and up to about 500 pg/mL were at risk of a variety of harmful outcomes. In particular, in a paper in *Neurology* in 2008 we showed that B12 levels across the whole normal range were associated with atrophy of the brain, the atrophy being the more rapid as the levels fell towards the traditional cut-off of 200 pg/mL.

4. The variable response of patients to B12 treatment

It is well known in clinical practice that patients with B12 deficiency show widely varied responses to the same treatment doses (see the web site of the Pernicious Anaemia Society). One of the early reports in the medical literature was by Tudhop et al. (1967) who stated: *"It is impossible to foretell, from clinical and haematological examination at the time of diagnosing pernicious anaemia, which patients will have a prolonged elevation of serum vitamin B12 of 1-2 years, and which will relapse quickly in 3-4 months following an injection of 500 pg. of hydroxocobalamin..*They concluded: *"Variation between patients makes it impossible to anticipate the duration of effect of a single injection of one of these drugs in any patient."*

Comments on the specific allegations

A. I cannot comment upon allegation '1f' since this is clearly a matter of how a child is defined in the NHS.

B. The other allegations, Ta,b,c and e', all relate to the prescribing of vitamin B12 to treat symptoms consistent with B12 deficiency.

C. Dr Tidy (page 335) considers that Dr Chandy should not have prescribed B12 to patients whose blood level was in the normal range, i.e. above 200 pg/mL. In my background material above I hope I have made it clear that there is no consensus in the field about what is an appropriate cut-off value for prescribing. Furthermore, the validity of the results of current methods for B12 is open to question and so a clinician has to use his/her judgement in making a decision about prescribing, according to the nature and severity of the symptoms and signs.

D. Dr Tidy (page 336) expresses the opinion that Dr Chandy should have referred three patients with neurological symptoms for further investigation by specialists before he started treating them. In my view, this would have risked harming the patients because some of the neurological consequences of B12 deficiency are irreversible and it is good practice to treat the patient as soon as possible. I found statements to support this view in the medical literature, including the following:

a. "Empirical treatment, to assess any clinical response and to prevent neurological damage, may be pragmatically justifiable as the dangers of treatment are not as devastating as those of not treating"(Devalia, BMJ 2006).

b. "A therapeutic trial of cobalamin will prevent delay in treatment and adverse clinical consequences." Hamilton & Blackmore BMJ, 2006)

c. "... our experience further supports the fact that when the diagnosis of B12 deficiency is suspected on the basis of clinical findings and additional tests, supplementation treatment should be administered even if the assayed level of the vitamin is not low..(Scarpa et al. Blood Transfusion 2012.)

d. "B12 assays may be vulnerable to interference resulting in normal values despite severe cobalamin deficiency. Where there is discordance between the clinical features of neuropathy - parasthesiae, loss of joint position sense, or megaloblastic anaemia and a "normal" B12 result, clinicians are advised to request storage of serum for further testing and are advised to treat the patient with B12 replacement therapy... .Treatment with B12 should not be delayed to avoid progression of neurological damage." (UK NEQUAS, 2013)

E. Dr Tidy (page 337) says that in his opinion a 'rigorous clinical trial would be indicated'. In my view, this would not at all have been in the interests of Dr Chandy's patients. The nature of their symptoms were such that to randomise them to a placebo tablet would have been unethical.

Furthermore, the great variability in the responses of patients with B12 deficiency to replacement therapy would have made such a trial scientifically in valid unless it was done on a very large scale, way outside the scope of a GP practice.

F. My overall conclusion with regard to the prescribing of vitamin B12 by Dr Chandy is that he has put the welfare of his patients first and has treated them as best he could with regard to timing and the dose used in the context of the considerable uncertainties about the scientific basis for treatment decisions.

Chapter 3   Treating B12 deficiency

You are the light of the world – like a city on a hilltop that cannot be hidden. No one lights a lamp and then puts it under a basket. Instead, a lamp is placed on a stand, where it gives light to everyone in the house. In the same way, let your good deeds shine out for all to see, so that everyone will praise your heavenly Father.

Matthew 5:14-16

Figure 3-1 Key points regarding treatment

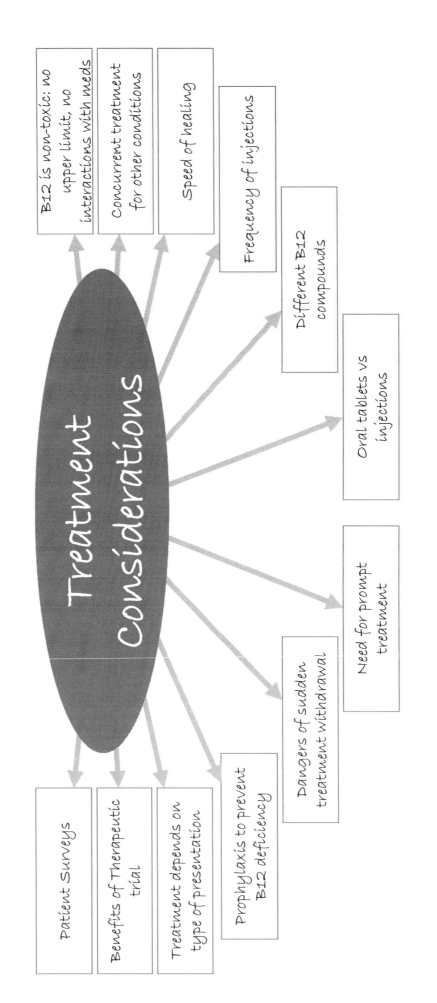

3.1   Vitamin B12-treatment regimes

Management of vitamin B12 deficiency poses a particular challenge because of the wide range of differing presentations and the fact that subtle cobalamin deficiency is non-specific. Correct diagnosis not only of the condition but also of the cause is key to correct treatment which will vary with the individual. Treatment regimes for the main categories of B12-deficient patient presentations are described on the third page of our Appendix 1: Protocol for excluding B12 deficiency (Megaloblastic anaemia/Pernicious anaemia) from adult and child patient presentation which starts on page 267) from adult and child patient presentation. The comments below provide additional and background information.

3.2   A note on safety

Experience has shown that vitamin B12 is completely safe, at any concentration in the diet and in the blood. In more than three decades of treating patients with high doses of vitamin B12 we never had any cases of adverse reactions. In contrast, the consequences of *not* treating a patient with vitamin B12 deficiency, or of treating them with suboptimal dosages, are devastating as described in the rest of this book.

The non-toxicity of vitamin B12 is confirmed by the US National Institute of Health Office of Dietary Supplements which states that the US Institute of Medicine (IoM) has not established any upper limit for vitamin B12 "because of its low potential for toxicity" (NIH ODS, 2018b). The IoM says: "no adverse effects have been associated with excess vitamin B12 intake from food and supplements in healthy individuals" (IoM, 1998c).

Whereas most vitamins have an optimal range (below which is deficiency, and above which would cause a different type of problem) (FAO & WHO, 2001, 2004), there appears to be no upper level of vitamin B12 intake where a problem might occur. Dr John Hathcock, the author of *Vitamin and Mineral Safety* published by the US Council of Responsible Nutrition (the leading trade association representing dietary supplement manufacturers and ingredient suppliers), states (Hathcock, 2014):

> *"No toxic effects of B12 have been encountered in humans or animals at any level of oral intake (IoM, 1998c; Miller & Hayes, 1982). The overall evidence indicates that vitamin B12 is virtually nontoxic. Doses of 1,000 µg per day were administered to a child by intravenous injection for a year without adverse effect (Merck & Co, 1958)."*

Similarly, the European Food Safety Authority (EFSA) states that the European Scientific Committee on Food (SCF) has concluded that "it is not possible to derive an Upper Intake Level, mainly because no clearly defined adverse effect could be identified" (EFSA, 2008). The Dutch charity Stichting Tekort further explains: "It is very clear this fear of overdosing is based on a misunderstanding. For over 60 years high dose vitamin B12 treatment has been used without any signs of the danger of an overdose" (Stichting Tekort, 2018).

Vitamin B12 is safe because:

- It is soluble in water. If there is too much in the blood then it will be excreted rapidly by the kidneys. Note that the fat-soluble vitamins A, D and K may pose a greater risk of toxicity than water-soluble vitamins because of this (JustVitamins, 2014);

- Vitamin B12 is a conveyor and catalyst. If it ceases to be the limiting factor, any extra B12 has no effect;
- From our experience with patients we have seen that the body can use increasing amounts of B12 well beyond the amount normally available to it, to good effect.

However, the same is not true of all the B vitamins. Folate, for example, has an optimal range above which it is thought to cause health problems (Smith et al., 2008), even though folate is often required alongside vitamin B12 in several biochemical processes. Some B vitamins, while needed in deficiency, should not be used at high doses. For example, niacin (vitamin B3) may cause flushing unless the dose is built up gradually, and at high levels of supplementation may cause liver or heart and other problems (NIH ODS, 2019). Similarly, vitamin B6 in high doses from supplements over a long time can cause nerve damage (NIH ODS, 2011a).

3.3   Different types of Vitamin B12

Vitamin B12, also called cobalamin, is the generic name for a family of compounds based on the cobalt atom. As described in Chapter 1, cobalamins consist of cobalt as the central ion in a corrin ring. The cobalt ion can attach to other compounds to create the following forms:

- With CN^- (cyanide): cyanocobalamin
- With OH^-: hydroxocobalamin
- With H_2O: aquocobalamin
- With NO: nitrocobalamin
- With CH_3^+: methylcobalamin
- With 5-Desoxyadenosyl: adenosylcobalamin

(Gröber et al., 2013)

Hydroxycobalamin and cyanocobalamin are synthetic forms (used for example, in vitamin supplements, pharmaceuticals, or food fortification) which are transformed to methylcobalamin and adenosylcobalamin in the human body. These latter two are the active forms used in metabolism.

3.3.1   Cyanocobalamin

Cyanocobalamin is the cheapest form of vitamin B12 on sale. It is a very stable form, produced through an industrial process by combining B12 with cyanide (a poison). The main disadvantage of this type of cobalamin is that it is lost from the body very quickly. Because it is linked to cyanide, which the body considers toxic, this form of B12 is one of the targets sought by the kidneys for excretion so body turnover of cyanocobalamin is rapid (IoM, 1998c, p. 307). Since most of the cyanocobalamin is therefore lost to the body shortly after injection, we believe that taking it may not be as effective as taking B12 in other forms.

In our experience, about one in 10 people receiving cyanocobalamin develop mild headaches. Some people also appear to be unable to make use of cyanocobalamin, which may be because the cyano bond is too strong to allow the cyano group to detach (which would free the cobalt ion to attach to another group and create a form more readily used by the body)(see Figure 1-2 Cobalamin molecule on page 26 and Table 1-2 The most commonly used forms of B12 attached to different ions on page 29 which illustrate that the cyano-group could be hidden by the Pyrrole ring from breaking the bond. These patients do derive benefit from other forms of vitamin B12, however.

We note that the BNF does not recommend use of cyanocobalamin in treatment: "Cyanocobalamin solution and Cytamen ® injection are not prescribable in NHS primary care" and "Hydroxocobalamin has completely replaced cyanocobalamin as the form of vitamin B12 of choice for therapy…" (BNF, 2017).

Figure 3-2 Cyanocobalamin – illustrating a possible structure which affects bioavailability

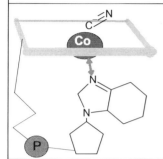

the CN- R-group (Cyano-) is small and highly charged, so the blue corrin square around the cobalt and cyanide make this bond less accessible to enzymes and co-factors, which means that this form of B12 is less bio-available in the body.

3.3.2   Hydroxocobalamin

Hydroxocobalamin is another artificial form of vitamin B12 (i.e. it is not found in living animals). However, it is rapidly converted to both of the biologically active forms. Hydroxocobalamin is the form of B12 used in injections in the UK and the most usual form of B12 recommended by the B12d.org charity to beneficiaries.

Hydroxocobalamin has a hydroxy- (OH⁻) group attached to the cobalt atom. The hydroxy- group is extremely soluble, and releases the B12 rapidly which frees B12 to interact with other biochemicals.

See the cross-references above.

Figure 3-3 Hydroxocobalamin – illustrating a possible structure which affects bioavailability

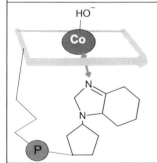

the Hydroxyl- group is charged but not as densely as Cyano-, the bond between this and the Cobalt ion is more available for replacement when B12 is used in reactions.

3.3.3   Methycobalamin

Methylcobalamin is a biologically active form which is used to transfer methyl groups from one molecule to another in cells and so assist with lipid metabolism and the regulation of DNA (gene switching on and off or epigenetics). The Methyl- (CH_3^+) group is exchanged in many biological reactions. For example, in the interaction between vitamin B12 and folate (vitamin B9), B12 takes a methyl group from folate, allowing the folate cycle to complete, leading to correct synthesis of DNA.

B12 then donates the methyl group to homocysteine to form methionine. The Methyl-group bond distance is the same as Adenosyl- so it is not illustrated.

Methylcobalamin is also used in treatment and is available in tablet (oral) form and injectable form. An injectable form is used in some countries, such as Japan (see, for example, Kira et al. (1994)). In India, it is available in injectable, oral and sublingual forms (Kamath & Pemminati, 2017).

Methylcobalamin appears to be the most important active form in the cell cytoplasm. However, in at least one organelle within the cell, mitochondria, the most important active form appears to be adenosylcobalamin. There are debates about the relative advantages of these two forms. Some suggest that adenosylcobalamin is responsible for myelin synthesis (with deficiency therefore leading to neurological disorders) and cannot be replaced by methylcobalamin. This assertion has been challenged with an alternative hypothesis that the block of the conversion of methionine to S-adenosylmethionine (which depends on methylcobalamin) is responsible for B12 deficiency neuropathy (Kamath & Pemminati, 2017).

We have not encountered any difficulties with hydroxocobalamin but a case where a patient with severe vitamin B12 deficiency responded to treatment with high dose oral methylcobalamin, but not to equally high dose oral hydroxocobalamin, has been reported (Rietsema, 2014).

3.3.4 Adenosylcobalamin – also known as dibencozide

The other biologically active form is adenosylcobalamin. In this case, adenosine in its active form, adenosyl-, is the active group attached to the reactive site of B12.

Figure 3-4 Adenosylcobalamin – illustrating a possible structure which affects bioavailability

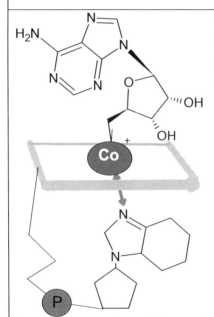

The Adenosyl- group is not charged, similar to the methyl-group, which means the Cobalt ion sits higher in the Corrin ring, permitting easier exchange of R-groups (OH, CH3, adenosyl, etc) during reactions which means that the B12 is at its most bio-available.

It is possible that this is the form of B12 that is active in the bloodstream when circulating. This appears to be the form that is used to create energy in mitochondria (the active organelles inside each cell).

Adenosylcobalamin needs particular conditions: a particular pH, and accompanying electrolytes, to become soluble. It is usual to take adenosylcobalamin in oral tablets rather than by injection. It is often sold as an athlete performance enhancer because it increases energy and enthusiasm.

3.4 When to start B12 therapy

The best advice when B12 deficiency is suspected is to start treatment straight after taking a sample of blood, even before receiving the results.

Some doctors delay until they have received the results of the blood analysis, to get a base level of serum B12, but the consequence of even such a brief delay is that symptoms could get worse – especially in cases of severe deficiency, whereas there is no risk from providing additional B12 if the body does not actually need it. The *BMJ Best Practice* states that patients with severe haematological or neurological symptoms require immediate treatment with an intensive regime of B12 therapy (BMJ Best Practice, 2018d).

Below (Case 3-1) is an example of the benefit to a patient of a therapeutic trial.

Case 3-1 Benefit of therapeutic trial in a case of Bell's Palsy

Karen Taylor, born 1981, presented with symptoms of Bell's Palsy (facial weakness, visible over her left eye in the photo and causing pain in the left ear). The standard treatment for this condition is large doses of oral steroids. We confirmed via a blood serum B12 test and signs and symptoms that she could be B12 deficient. Her B12 blood level came back as 345 ng/L on 2 August 2011 which is considered "low normal". As the treatment protocol agreed with the Primary Care Trust stated that therapeutic trials could be started at this level, and with that provisional diagnosis in mind, we commenced treatment with vitamin B12. Within three and a half weeks (by 26 August 2011) the Bell's Palsy resolved without the need for large doses of steroids (which have side-effects).

3.5 How much and how often?

Practices concerning both dose and method of administration of vitamin B12 vary considerably between countries. In most countries, vitamin B12 is given by intramuscular injection (IM) in the form of cyanocobalamin or hydroxocobalamin, although some countries (for example, Sweden) use predominantly oral tablets (Hvas & Nexo, 2006; Nilsson et al., 2005).

Everyone is different and the supplementation needed cannot easily be determined from the symptoms. We have found that in mild cases of B12 deficiency oral tablets may be given but that in moderate and severe cases injections are necessary.

Standard treatment is to give a loading dose of IM injections of 1 mg per 1 ml ampoule of hydroxocobalamin on alternate days for two weeks but in severe cases it may be necessary to give injections for up to eight weeks. This is a matter of clinical judgement. The BNF states that this dose should be continued until there is no further improvement (BNF, 2018) – in our experience some patients may need the loading dose for another month (see, for example, Case 3-2). The BNF recommendation is to follow this up with three-monthly injections. We have found, however, that the three-monthly frequency is not enough and that injections need to be given monthly. If patients have to wait for three months, the benefits of the loading dose may be eroded when there is no fresh B12 in the system. The frequency of injections has to be tailored to patient needs. Our experience based on clinical evidence is that the majority of patients (around 80%) need monthly injections. Also, many patients are ready for a further dose three weeks (rather than three months) after the loading dose has finished.

Hydroxocobalamin is the only form of vitamin B12 supplied for injection by the NHS (2016d). We have found that every patient can be managed on hydroxocobalamin because the body converts it to the usable forms.

Case 3-2 Example of patient needing unusually high number of loading doses

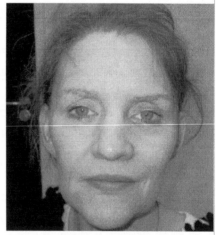

Jane Jermy, born 1965, used to run a creative media company. For ten years she had no strength in her writing hand (photo left) which limited her ability to work and look after her children. She had been diagnosed as suffering from ME, depression, fibromyalgia, joint pain and the psychological disorder Munchausen's by proxy. In February 2009 we found her blood serum B12 level to be 172 ng/L. Once treatment

was started she required 33 loading doses (1 mg B12 injections given two days apart), followed by injections every two months until an analysis of her symptoms led to a revision of the schedule to weekly injections. Her symptoms remitted; she became able to write and returned to work.

3.5.1 Oral supplements versus injections

Oral tablets containing vitamin B12 can be purchased from many health food shops and online. They are a convenient way of obtaining B12 supplements, and there are no obstacles to purchasing tablets. However, we do not recommend using tablets containing cyanocobalamin for the reasons given above.

B12 tablets are available which have a mixture of methylcobalamin and adenosylcobalamin, or vitamin B12 along with other associated vitamins and minerals (e.g. B12 and folate, B12 and folate and vitamin B6). These may work better for some.

As a rule of thumb, we have found that 1000 mcg (1mg) of methylcobalamin or hydroxocobalamin is a suitable amount for daily intake orally. This is a much higher dose than the 50-150 mcg indicated by the BNF which also suggests cyanocobalamin for oral intake which we normally would not recommend (BNF, 2017).

If B12 deficiency results from absorption problems in the digestive tract, tablets will be less effective because the B12 cannot be absorbed through this route. Some tablets circumvent this problem by being designed to be placed under the tongue. In this case, the vitamin B12 is absorbed directly into the bloodstream and is not dependent on secretions in the stomach or intestine.

In our own observations, oral supplements will generally stop symptoms getting worse, but for healing a course of injections is often required. Injected vitamin B12 reaches the bloodstream much more quickly than B12 absorbed through the stomach or intestine.

Case 3-3 Oral treatment inadequate: injections needed

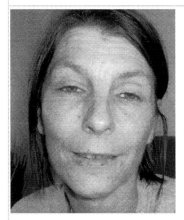

Sharon O'Brian presented in 2000, aged 37, with neuropsychiatric symptoms, suffering from falls, facial palsy, paralysis on her right side and a weight of only 5 stone. Because her B12 level was 268 ng/L, which was above the NHS cut-off point for B12 deficiency, we were at that time (due to a PCT embargo) not allowed to treat her with injections. Instead she started oral B12 treatment. Because in reality she was severely B12 deficient – see Chapter 2 for an explanation of the limitations of B12 blood levels as indicators of deficiency - this course of action proved ineffective and her B12 level fell to 237 ng/L in 2006 and 148 ng/L in 2009. At this point she was referred to a neurologist with an MS-like presentation. The neurologist gave no diagnosis and no treatment. As the embargo on injections was by then lifted, we instituted intensive B12-replacement therapy: her facial palsy and paralysis were totally reversed and she gained weight to 8 stone. We believe that had we been allowed to start treatment when she first presented in 2000 we would have been able to save her 10 years of suffering and the loss of her job. Both her son and daughter have been diagnosed with B12 deficiency and are receiving treatment.

3.5.1.1   Intramuscular injection (IM)

Vitamin B12 for injections is a nutritional supplement, not a medicine. With proper use of sterile technique, there is no reason why individuals should not self-inject. It is usual to inject into the muscle (intramuscular - IM). This is because B12 is water-soluble and flows into the fluids surrounding the cells of the muscle. It therefore easily transfers into the bloodstream from an intramuscular injection.

3.5.1.2   Subcutaneous injection (SC)

The other common form of self-injection is sub-cutaneous (SC), i.e. into the fatty layer just below the skin. This is ideal for fat-soluble vitamins such as A, D, E and K. Many people self-inject subcutaneously. However, in the case of vitamin B12, the vitamin may not pass into the bloodstream and reach the parts of the body that need it quickly. For example, some people observe a red bruising effect around the injection site, which, unlike a normal bruise, does not change and darken. This may be the B12 (which is red) trapped in the fatty layer, and therefore not circulating in the bloodstream.

3.5.2   Frequency of injections

Chart 3-1 shows the results of a review (part of our Patient Survey – see below) of how often our patients needed injections in order to function optimally which was presented at the IHI/BMJ International Forum *Quality and Safety in Healthcare* conference in Paris (Chandy & Minney, 2014). The vast majority (80%) needed injections monthly or more frequently. (See also the patient comments in Box 3.1 on the effects of prolongation of the time between injections which resulted from the PCT decision to require the Practice to prescribe injections according to guidelines rather than clinical need.) The BNF confirms that during the period that symptoms are improving, alternate-day injections should be continued. The Best Practice guidance from the BMJ website (BMJ Best Practice, 2018d) also confirms that the frequency of injections should be tailored to the severity of the patient's condition.

Chart 3-1 Frequency of B12 injections required

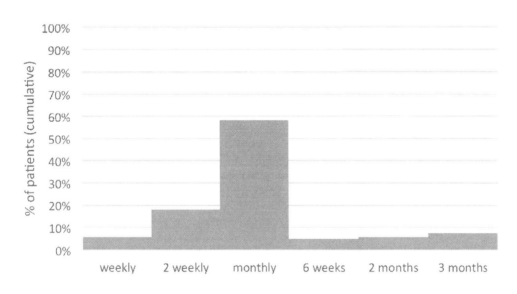

Source: Patient records and Shinwell Patient Survey 2008-9. Data extracted from 344 individual patient survey forms.

As explained in Chapter 2, the body is recycling vitamin B12 all the time. It is possible that if the body is very efficient at recycling, then improved intake of B12 in the diet or by injection every few months will be quite sufficient, because the body is only using a very small amount each time it cycles B12. However, if it is less efficient at recycling, B12 blood levels could go down quite quickly.

The following chart shows how often injections might be needed for different efficiencies.

Chart 3-2 Effect of vitamin B12 recycling efficiency on frequency of injections

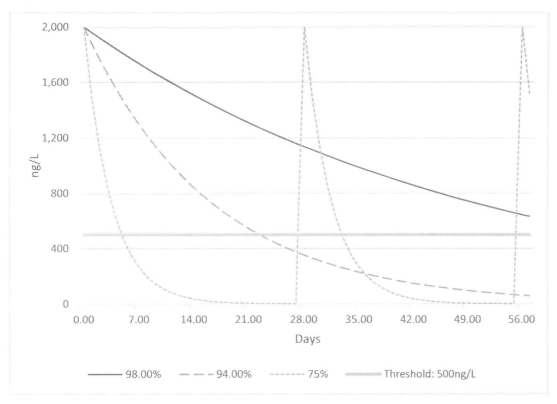

Chart 3-2 shows that, following an injection, the B12 level of a person whose vitamin B12 recycling efficiency is low (grey dotted line) will drop sharply below the 500 ng/L threshold within about 5 days. In contrast, the B12 level of a person whose recycling efficiency is 94% (dashed orange line) will remain above the threshold for about three weeks, and that of a person whose recycling efficiency is 98% (solid blue line) may remain above the threshold for up to three months. The numbers used for recycling efficiency are for illustrative purposes only. Chart prepared by Hugo Minney based on observation at the Shinwell Medical Practice.

The above chart shows the concentration of plasma B12 in the days following an injection. We suggest that where entero-hepatic circulation is reclaiming B12 highly efficiently (and there are no other causes for loss of B12 – such as presence of lead or nicotine toxins which deplete B12), then the level of B12 remains above threshold for longer. So injections every three months may be sufficient to maintain blood B12 above the threshold. However, if the blood serum B12 falls faster, then more frequent injections are needed. At high rates of loss, injections daily or on alternate days may be needed to maintain plasma B12 at a level sufficient for normal function.

This also illustrates why it is more important to inject frequently, than to inject a large dose at each injection.

3.6   Dangers of withdrawing treatment

During the two PCT embargos[19] on B12 treatment, B12 therapy was withdrawn from a number of our patients. We observed that a relapse (the symptoms returned) occurred much more quickly than the textbooks would suggest. Since most patients will have B12 deficiency caused by malabsorption – which is a permanent condition – they will in most cases need lifelong treatment. It is especially important to monitor these patients because symptoms can return rapidly if treatment ceases. The difficulties that cessation of treatment during embargos caused for patients are illustrated in their comments in the Patient Survey questionnaires – see extracts listed in Box 3-1 on page 84.

3.7   Body stores and daily losses

Patients with symptoms of vitamin B12 deficiency which has been caused by insufficient dietary intake (for example, vegetarians) often ask why, if diet is the cause, it has taken so long for their symptoms to manifest (Rizzo et al., 2016). The answer lies in the way the body stores and recycles vitamin B12.

Various studies have been undertaken since the 1950s on the amount of vitamin B12 stored in the body of a healthy adult (for example, Adams et al. (1970)). Such studies are difficult to conduct and use different methods (such as Whole Body Counting (WBC) or vitamin B12 excretion in bile), all of which involve many assumptions and estimates so are not easily comparable. It is generally recognised by medical scientists that more research is needed in this area.

However, a recent overview of the current state of knowledge concerning daily vitamin B12 losses and bioavailability of vitamin B12, which looked at more than 6,000 academic journal articles on vitamin B12, concluded that studies so far conducted had shown a total body store of vitamin B12 ranging on average from 1.06-3.9 milligrams (mg) (Doets et al., 2013 Table 3). For purposes of determining dietary requirements, most estimates of the total body store used by authorities are between 2 and 3 mg (IoM, 1998b). Most of this is held in the liver and appreciable amounts in muscle, bone marrow and the gut, although vitamin B12 is distributed throughout all cells in the body (Chanarin, 1990).

Much of the vitamin B12 held in the liver is recycled, via the bile to the intestines (the process known as entero-hepatic recycling), and reabsorbed into the bloodstream. Depending on the initial size of a person's store of B12, it may take a number of years for daily losses from the body to result in deficiency if their B12 stores are not being replenished.

The study by Doets et al. showed that a summary estimate of the rate of loss based on the WBC method was 0.13% per day. When calculated by measuring vitamin B12 excretion in bile, two studies produced results of 1.1% and 1.5% (Doets et al., 2013). However, much of the B12 excreted in bile is reabsorbed as described in section 2.1.7, although reabsorption may not occur in individuals who

---

[19] For two periods during the Shinwell Medical Group's treatment of patients with B12 deficiency (12 February 2004 to 3 July 2006 total embargo followed by partial embargo; 14 March 2007 – 1 August 2009 total embargo followed by partial embargo), the medical Practice was forbidden by the PCT to treat patients for B12 deficiency. In both periods, the patient group had to lobby the PCT to have treatment restored. As far as we know, no other doctor or medical practice has been restricted in diagnosing B12 deficiency, or treating with this very safe nutritional supplement.

lack IF which explains why sufferers of pernicious anaemia, for example, experience dramatic B12 losses (IoM, 1998b).

Reports vary on the percentage that is reabsorbed in a healthy individual, but range from 55% (IoM, 1998b) to 90% (EFSA, 2008). Authorities tend to assume a loss rate of 0.1-0.2% of total body vitamin B12 per day (EFSA, 2008; IoM, 1998a). Vitamin B12 is lost mostly through the faeces but also through urine, the skin and metabolic reactions. The losses include unabsorbed B12 from food or bile, shedded cells, gastric and intestinal secretions, and B12 synthesized by bacteria in the colon (IoM, 1998b).

If it is assumed that the smallest B12 body store consistent with health is 300 mcg (derived from Bozian et al. (1963)) with a 0.1 % daily loss rate, no absorption of B12 from food or supplements, and an intact entero-hepatic circulation, then stores of 1 mg would be expected to meet the body's needs for 3 years, 2 mg for about 5 years, and 3 mg for about 6 years. A 1.5 % loss would reduce these estimates to 2, 3.6, and 4 years (IoM, 1998b). This is why it may take several years for symptoms of deficiency to appear.

3.7.1   How much B12 (and in what form)?

Patients may ask why it is necessary to take oral supplements (or have injections): could their symptoms not be rectified by an improved diet containing more vitamin B12?

Many patients will have malabsorption problems that prevent vitamin B12 being absorbed from food in sufficient amounts to maintain health. Or they may have congenital defects that interfere with B12 metabolism. Large doses, whether through tablets or injection, are needed to overcome these barriers.

These amounts are not easily obtained from food. The amount of vitamin B12 in any meal is very small compared with injected doses or supplements. In Europe, the average daily intake of vitamin B12 from a normal diet has been found to be 2-6 mcg although individual intakes may be as high as 32 mcg (EFSA, 2008). A vegetarian diet, however, may provide only 0.5 mcg per day (Chanarin, 1990).

It has also been shown that there is a limit to the amount of vitamin B12 that can be absorbed from any meal, even in a healthy person, because of saturation of the IF-receptors (Doets et al., 2013). Also, not all vitamin B12 in a portion of food is absorbed – estimates show that absorption varies widely from different B12-containing foods (IoM, 1998b Table 9-1; Tucker et al., 2000).

However, some vitamin B12 (about 1-5% of a dose) is absorbed through passive diffusion, that is it bypasses the need for binding to IF (Andrès et al., 2004). This percentage is insignificant when amounts of vitamin B12 are small, as in a single meal, but may become more influential when a large dose is taken, for instance through a tablet. Tablets placed under the tongue, and injections which send vitamin B12 directly into the muscle or bloodstream, are likely to be more effective in most cases.

Carmel provides figures to show that the *percentage* of B12 absorbed from oral doses <u>decreases</u> as the dose <u>increases</u> in healthy people (although the actual amount does increase a little). For instance, from a dose of 1 mcg, 56% (0.56 mcg) would be absorbed, but from a dose of 1 mg, only about 1.3% (13 mcg) would be absorbed. In patients suffering from malabsorption illnesses, only

1.2% is absorbed – that is, the rate of passive diffusion. From injections, in both healthy and ill people, 97% (9.7 mcg) of a 10 mcg dose is absorbed but the rate decreases to 15% (150 mcg) of a 1 mg dose (Carmel, 2008). This still represents a substantial fraction of the total body store in a healthy person (using the figures given above).

We know from experience that some people seem to need higher levels of B12 circulating in the blood in order for their symptoms to be remitted. This implies that people short of B12 in their cells process B12 less efficiently than healthy people and need higher levels circulating in the blood (Smith & Refsum, 2011).

3.7.2   Recommended dietary intake

Opinions about the amount of vitamin B12 needed per day from a normal diet vary between countries, and researchers have questioned whether the Recommended Dietary Allowance (RDA) of 2.4 mcg for adults set by the US National Institutes of Health Office of Dietary Supplements, or 2.5 mcg set by the European Community, is high enough (Bor et al., 2010).[20] The UK uses a lower figure of 1.5 mcg (Doets et al., 2012; Public Health England, 2016 Table 4).

The US RDAs for different age groups are given below.

Table 3-1 Recommended daily amounts of vitamin B12

Life Stage	Recommended Amount, Micrograms (mcg)
Birth to 6 months	0.4 mcg
Infants 7-12 months	0.5 mcg
Children 1-3 years	0.9 mcg
Children 4-8 years	1.2 mcg
Children 9-13 years	1.8 mcg
Teens 14-18 years	2.4 mcg
Adults	2.4 mcg
Pregnant teens and women	2.6 mcg
Breastfeeding teens and women	2.8 mcg

Source: *Vitamin B12 Fact Sheet for Consumers* (NIH ODS, 2011b).

---

[20] Following a new European regulation effective from December 2014, nutritional information on packaging formerly known as the Recommended Daily Allowance (RDA) has been expressed as Nutrient Reference Values (NRV). The European Community NRV for vitamin B12 was set at 2.5 mcg (µg) in May 2016. NRVs are based on current scientific knowledge and state how much of a given nutrient needs to be taken per day to prevent deficiency in healthy people (JustVitamins, 2016).

3.8   How long will it take for symptoms to recover?

B12 is a vital vitamin, and plays a role in many different biochemical functions within the body. The rate of improvement is different in each patient and is unpredictable. We know from experience that there will be improvement but it is not possible to put a specific time limit on recovery.

In our experience, most people seem to notice improvements in their symptoms in the following order:

Table 3-2 How long does it take for symptoms to heal?

Timeframe	Symptoms affected (from observations at the Shinwell Medical Practice)
Within hours	Enjoyment of friends, sociability and mood improvements.
Within a day or so	Fatigue should lessen although patients may expect to feel a general tiredness for some weeks.
Within a week	The Brain Fog should lift and patients should start to want to be more sociable, and to be able to remember better. HOWEVER, note that all symptoms do not improve at once. Numbness and pins and needles should start to remit.
Within two weeks	Some strength may return to muscles and joints. However, progress will be gradual.
Within a month	Some of the longer nerves (e.g. those of the hands and feet) may take up to a month to show signs of recovery. Pains in hands and feet, strength and grip strength may take longer to remit/restore but some improvement should be detected. Cyclical hormones such as those of the fertility cycles and associated disorders should be normalising. Hormone-controlled energy levels, e.g. production of cortisol and thyroid hormones should be normalising. Note that the body may not be responding to them yet even though hormone levels in the blood should be much better.
Longer than a month	Recovery from some conditions takes longer. For example, in relapsing/remitting MS (Sub Acute Combined Degeneration (SACD)/MS- like presentation), muscles will need time to regain their tone even though the nerves may now be functioning correctly.

3.9   Reversing-out syndrome

About one in 10 people have observed that they experience similar symptoms to those experienced from deficiency, as they start a programme of B12-replacement therapy. We term this "Reversing-out syndrome".

The most obvious such symptoms are neurological. For example, where there was numbness, patients may start to feel pain as the nerves recover. They may experience twitches when the nerve axons that instruct the muscles to move start to work again and transmit random signals. Or they may experience shooting pains, when nerves in hands and feet start to transmit sensations and the brain initially interprets these signals as pain.

Another common symptom is a red rash on the skin, sometimes accompanied by itching. The skin is the largest organ in the human body and plays an important role in eliminating toxins. The human body is able to selectively push substances from the bloodstream outside the skin. The red rash may be caused by the body getting rid of homocysteine, by pushing it through the skin onto the surface. Many people apply skin cream but we are concerned that this may trap the homocysteine next to the skin. It is preferable to wash it away with a wet cloth instead.

Patients may also experience sudden tiredness, which may be caused by low potassium or low magnesium. When the body is performing below par, due to low B12, then low levels of magnesium and potassium may be quite sufficient. Once the B12 level is restored, low levels of other nutrients may make themselves felt.

Other symptoms may also manifest as B12 levels are restored. Unfortunately, some patients think this is a result of taking B12 and cease the therapy. We advise that patients persist with treatment in order to pass through Reversing-out syndrome.

3.10 Other considerations

3.10.1 Anaphylactic shock from injections

It is reassuring to confirm that during the past 37 years since commencing B12 injections in 1981, not a single one of our patients has experienced local or systemic anaphylactic shock. Anaphylactic shock affects the whole body and can cause a sudden feeling of weakness (from a drop in blood pressure), abdominal pain, nausea or vomiting, and collapse and unconsciousness. It is very serious; if a patient has an anaphylactic reaction, they may need an observation period in hospital.

Anaphylactic shock is a hypersensitive reaction to an allergen (something that the patient is allergic to). There is nothing in B12-injectable solutions that patients are allergic to. We must emphasise again that we have never observed such a reaction to B12 injections.

In contrast, reactions such as a stinging sensation from injection are common but this is harmless. It may be caused by temperature difference (e.g. injecting straight from the fridge), or because of injecting an unbuffered solution. We advise anyone who self-injects to keep the ampoule out of the fridge and to let it (or the syringe) reach as close to body temperature as possible before injecting (e.g. hold the syringe in the hand for a few minutes).

3.10.2 Mineral or vitamin deficiencies highlighted by B12 supplementation

Prolonged B12 deficiency can result in low levels of other minerals and vitamins, such as magnesium, potassium and vitamin D, or imbalances in many other vital substances the body needs to function well.

For example, magnesium is needed to maintain health. Adequate amounts can be obtained from a well-balanced diet or by taking multivitamin multi-mineral one-a-day supplements. Following prolonged B12 deficiency, however, a patient's body levels of magnesium may have dropped. A patient may not have noticed low levels of magnesium because they feel so tired and inactive.

Once the normal level of B12 has been restored it is possible that deficiencies of other nutrients may manifest. In our experience, once the B12 level is sufficient to maintain health, the fundamental metabolism of the body is restored to harmony. We have regularly checked the U+Es of our B12-deficient patients but never found it necessary to prescribe additional nutrients (except in the case of patients who had iron deficiency anaemia or folic acid deficiency).

However, taking a multivitamin multi-mineral one-a-day supplement before the first B12 injection to top all nutrients up will not cause harm.

3.11 Vitamin B12 as a prophylactic measure to avoid deficiency

In the following instances B12-replacement therapy should be instituted as a prophylactic measure (to prevent further deterioration or even development of symptoms) regardless of blood serum B12 concentration: prophylaxis is expected to continue for life.

1- **Specific medical history:** renal imbalance, diabetes, >65 years old, or following GI surgery, Crohn's colitis, early onset dementia.

2- **Moderate/subtle B12 deficiency with mild signs & symptoms**

3- **Moderate/subtle B12 deficiency with severe signs & symptoms:** patient presenting with strong family history of B12 deficiency, presence of other autoimmune conditions, major signs and symptoms which could become irreversible if treatment is not commenced urgently e.g. optic neuritis/neuropathy, sudden onset blindness, Subacute Combined Degeneration (SACD), ME, CFS, MS-like presentation, single limb paralysis, sudden loss of muscle mass (Motor Neurone Disease-like presentation), non-epileptic seizures, dysphagia, Bell's Palsy/Ramsey Hunt syndrome, Parkinson's like presentation, dementia, total alopecia, migrainous headache, temporal arteritis, recurrent miscarriages, dysfunctional uterine bleeding, or psychosis.

3.12 Shinwell Medical Practice Patient Surveys on vitamin B12 therapy

Complying with good medical practice, the Shinwell Medical Group conducted two Patient Surveys on the experience of patients undergoing B12 therapy. The surveys took the form of questionnaires issued to patients:

- Patient Survey 1 took place between December 2005 and January 2006, that is, during the ban on B12 treatments imposed by Easington PCT. There were 225 respondents to this survey.
- Patient Survey 2 was conducted from May 2008 to August 2009, after Professor Pringle's report had been published (see Introduction). There were 344 respondents to this survey.

Patient Survey 1 (2005-6): Seven questions were asked concerning the severity of symptoms on first diagnosis, how patients felt after treatment had started, when treatment was stopped (due to the withdrawal of treatment by Easington PCT), and again when treatment resumed (when the ban was partially lifted). Patients were also asked whether they felt any side-effects during treatment and how often they thought they should receive B12 injections when they were on treatment. The results confirmed the effectiveness of the B12 therapy: 87% of patients responded that they felt better after treatment started; 75% said their symptoms reappeared when treatment was withdrawn; more than half said their symptoms improved again after treatment was restored. Almost all the group (96% of respondents) said they experienced no side-effects during treatment. Another important finding was that patients' B12 blood serum levels, which were tested to accompany the survey, fell much more quickly than is predicted by the textbooks when treatment was withdrawn.

Patient Survey 2 (2008-9): This survey was carried out after County Durham PCT had ordered a change to the B12 treatment protocol from one based on clinical need to one based on guidelines only (which fails to address all aspects of patient presentation). This resulted in the frequency of injections being reduced (to three-monthly from two-monthly or one-monthly) for some patients and treatment being completely withdrawn for others. Patients were asked to complete a survey during their treatment review. They described their symptoms before diagnosis and after treatment had started on a scale of 0 to 5 where 5 was the most severe. They were also asked whether they consented to the new treatment regime imposed by the PCT. Patients were grouped into two categories: those whose minimum blood serum B12 was below the 200 ng/L guidelines' cut-off point, and those where the level was above 200 ng/L. A total of 344 surveys were collected.

The symptoms described covered the wide range of body systems affected by B12 deficiency. B12 levels were recorded at three points: at diagnosis, during treatment (the highest level reached) and the level reached during the withdrawal period if the patients had been affected by the previous Easington PCT ban. The blood serum levels of those with low levels at diagnosis (typically 160-167 ng/L) rose to a range of 1387-1692 ng/L during treatment but fell to a range of 271-574 ng/L when treatment was withdrawn. The levels of those with initially higher starting points (208-256 ng/L) rose to 1044-1391 ng/L but fell back to 140-479 ng/L during the withdrawal period. Over 71% of patients explicitly did not agree to the change to the PCT-imposed regime. A striking point to emerge from the data was the impact of B12 injections on blood serum B12 levels. It is commonly assumed that the "normal" B12 levels in the UK are 200-900 ng/L but patients receiving supplements have levels substantially above this. At the same time patients reported that their symptoms were mostly remitted. This indicates that the "normal" range for one individual may be different from the "normal" range for another. The "normal" range given by manufacturers of testing assays varies from one manufacturer to another, and there is more variation between one laboratory and another, calling into question whether there is any such thing as a "normal" range.

Box 3-1 Extracts from the Shinwell Medical Practice Patient Survey 2008-9
Patient descriptions (in their own words) of the effects of B12 treatment, cessation of treatment or prolongation of time between injections, and symptoms during treatment.
All clear, able to swallow. Dizziness improved; more energy; no cramp; no hair falling out.
Much improvement. When treatment stopped became worse; much improvement since treatment re-commenced.
A lot better when getting monthly injections; tingling still in hands.
Patient can taste food (without salt); hair stronger; a lot fitter; health in general very good; no symptoms reappearing.

A lot better; even got a job; could drive again; could walk in a straight line; whole life has improved; feel and look healthy; not depressed; occasionally feel memory loss when B12 is due.

Patient feels a totally different person; he is 76 in August: I feel much healthier and a happier person than when I was 72.

Feel much better; all of the symptoms have gone.

Big improvement on all symptoms while have regular treatment. But now the time [is greater] between treatments, symptoms have returned and feel much worse.

Though diagnosed with MS she has found that from the initial treatment her symptoms have been reduced in severity, and her condition only declined when on two occasions her treatment was stopped. The treatment improves [her condition] at every level as well as slowing the onset of MS.

On monthly injections symptoms cease. Since going on 2-monthly in January, she feels like she did before the injections started - all the symptoms return. 2-monthly injections - she only feels better for the first 2 weeks then she has another 6 weeks where she spends most of the time in bed with severe exhaustion.

Lack of energy; other symptoms start to reappear as time between injections passes.

Much better; no tiredness; twice tried - monthly + by 6th week dropping and bad tempered; most of the symptoms return; no interest in anything; could not tolerate oral medication.

Much better; mild symptoms at the end of the month when needing another injection.

Much better whilst on treatment. On stopping or reducing the interval to 2- or 3-monthly old symptoms return - mainly tiredness.

Much better after he gets the injection; in the 3rd week the symptoms come on and wife notices it.

Less tired; hasn't fainted; pins and needles gone; not confused.

Improves after treatment, but after 4 or 5 weeks symptoms come back.

She felt very well as she was on the B12 injections every 2 weeks in the beginning then monthly injections were stopped for about a year, and she completely fell apart again having her original symptoms. Injections were started again every month as then they had to be 2-monthly; 2-monthly are no good as she starts having symptoms again. She would like to go back to monthly injections as she feels this is more beneficial

Her health improved over a number of years; then injections stopped for 2 years and she deteriorated really bad to the point when the injections started again - by then her level was really low.

Monthly injection everything was 90% better; when changed to 2-monthly symptoms would reappear in-between injections - tiredness, headache, unable to concentrate at about 5 to 6 weeks, numb feeling in arm at some time, gradually symptoms start reappearing one at a time. She cannot manage on 2-monthly treatment, as cannot cope at work or at home; she needs monthly injections to feel like she can work and take care of her family.

Since changing to 2-monthly injections the patient feels very tired, always wanting to sleep, irritableness, tingling feet, ratty, feeling drawn, weepy, pressure on head. Feeling ok up to 2/3/weeks after injection, then after that goes back downhill. Feels better getting injection on a monthly basis as after the 3rd week she knows she is ready for it again. However, getting injection 2-monthly she feels terrible, miserable, weepy, and all the symptoms start again.

Tired, feeling down the same as before he started the injections. Felt much better with injections monthly, going into the second month he could feel himself going back to the way he felt before the injections started.

One-monthly injections no symptoms (2nd time injections have stopped); 2-monthly very tired, numbness in arms, twitching in face, aches all over, physically drained.

The patient was so well on monthly injections, then felt unwell on 2-monthly; lost weight - 4.5 stone in the last year; couldn't eat, tiredness, sleeping all the time, right forefinger partially paralysed.

When receiving monthly injections she felt very well in herself and had none of the symptoms. Then started 3-monthly and has gone back to suffering all symptoms. Having tried 3-monthly injections she feels she is unable to manage this; she feels that she needs the supplement at around the 4th/5th week.

When she was getting the injections every 2 weeks she felt better than she had done for a lot of years. But since they went to 2-monthly her symptoms come back just as bad after about 3 weeks. She states she needs the injection at least monthly to function properly and lead a normal life.

When she had monthly B12 injections she was fine, but since having the injections every 3 months she feels a lot worse. She now has blurred vision, constant tiredness, no energy, neuropathic pain and numbness down her right leg.

A lot better, not as tired, no other symptoms are there.

Left-sided headache, shooting pain from back to the head, left orbital pain, palpitations, panic attack, tiredness, going to bed at 8.30pm, pins and needles and numbness in hands, burning sensation in fingers, hair falling. Since 2-monthly injections many of the signs and symptoms returned but much worse, especially palpitation, shooting pain and headache on left side of head and left eye, tiredness.

Was initially on B12 injection (monthly), then it stopped and she was on oral OC Vit B12 tablet. She is a lot better, left side weak, left knee locks, using a walking stick. She was very well on B12 injections. However, she can manage reasonably well on oral OC B12 tablets 100mg.

Oral medication - did not respond; whilst having regular injections feel much better.

Feel well after injection but towards needing next dose she begins to feel tired, dizzy, feeling of choking, unable to swallow.

A lot better, feel well when getting monthly injections, and since 3-monthly injections tiredness, swaying, palpitations.

Felt much better with injections; all symptoms back since treatment stopped.

Since the treatment stopped she is back to square one. When she did have treatment she was so much better, she does not think she should have to be taken off the B12.

Yes, definitely, when stopped symptoms returned. She was really worried.

When she was getting 1 monthly injections she was so much better, able to go to work and lead a normal life at work and home. When stopping injections on 21/10/2008 she has started to have all the symptoms if not worse.

When she was getting regular injections she felt a lot better but when she stopped having injections in 2004 her symptoms came back again, also when in 2008 injections stopped severe symptoms came back.

Chapter 4 Megaloblastic anaemia – not the only way to diagnose B12 deficiency

---

Remember, dear brothers and sisters, that few of you were wise in the world's eyes or powerful or wealthy when God called you. Instead, God chose things the world considers foolish in order to shame those who think they are wise. And he chose things that are powerless to shame those who are powerful. God chose things despised by the world, things counted as nothing at all, and used them to bring to nothing what the world considers important. As a result, no one can ever boast in the presence of God.

---

1 Corinthians 1:26-29

Figure 4-1 The Addisonian Criteria for diagnosing megaloblastic anaemia

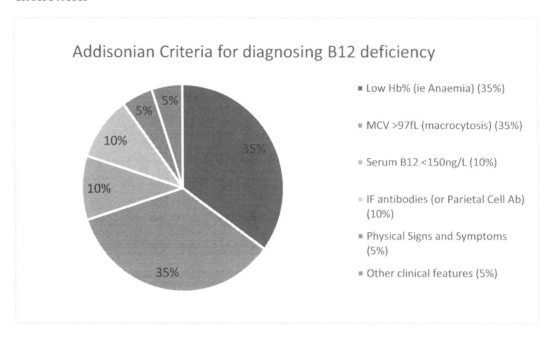

Optional additional tests

- Schilling test (radioactive materials used to determine whether B12 can be absorbed – not usually permitted because of radioactivity)
- uMMA (urinary Methyl-Malonic Acid)
- Plasma homocysteine
- Transcobalamin II estimate (sometimes called "active B12 test")
- Bone marrow examination

Figure 4-2 Chandy criteria for diagnosing vitamin B12 deficiency

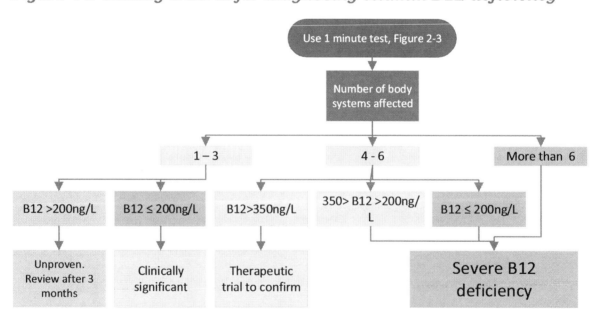

4.1   B12 deficiency and haematopoiesis (formation of blood cells)

As explained in Chapter 2, vitamin B12 is essential for multiple body systems which explains the many varied symptoms of deficiency. In this chapter we consider the effect of vitamin B12 deficiency on the blood where it manifests as megaloblastic anaemia. This is a blood cell maturation disorder which results from impaired DNA synthesis. In this condition, red blood cells (RBCs) are enlarged (macrocytic) and other blood cell changes occur. The impairment of RBC formation reduces the oxygen-carrying capacity of the blood and leads to the typical symptoms of anaemia, including fatigue, weakness and other acute disorders.

Megaloblastic anaemia can result from any cause of vitamin B12 deficiency. It can also result from folate deficiency or some other disorders, but B12 deficiency is the leading cause. Where it results from autoimmune attack on stomach cells (which leads to lack of secretion of Intrinsic Factor – IF – necessary for the absorption of vitamin B12) it is known as "pernicious anaemia" (PA). This illness has historically been the condition most associated with vitamin B12 deficiency, to the extent that the two conditions have been viewed as almost synonymous. This is so much so that in classical medicine, vitamin B12 deficiency is diagnosed through the symptoms of PA (see Chapter 2). What we wish to emphasise in this book, however, is that today vitamin B12 deficiency presents far more frequently with neurological or neuropsychiatric symptoms *without* anaemia and that PA is relatively rare.

In this chapter we go further and propose a new view of PA, suggesting that rather than being a cause of B12 deficiency, PA is an end-stage manifestation of this condition and can be prevented by early recognition of the neurological/neuropsychiatric symptoms. We investigate this issue and also draw attention to other aspects of the relationship of PA to B12 deficiency which are not usually well communicated to GPs.

4.2   What is megaloblastic anaemia?

There are many types of anaemia. In general, anaemia is defined as too few or abnormal RBCs (also known as erythrocytes), or too little haemoglobin (the pigment in red blood cells which carries oxygen). An analysis by Kassebaum et al. showed that in 2010 mild, moderate and severe anaemia had a worldwide prevalence of 32.9% which indicates that it is a serious health problem (Kassebaum et al., 2014). Anaemia results in insufficient oxygen delivery to the tissues, causing symptoms such as fatigue, frequent headaches, shortness of breath, pale skin, loss of appetite and mood changes. The symptoms vary according to the type of anaemia.

The BMJ Best Practice (BMJ Best Practice, 2018c), quoting World Health Organisation data, states that anaemia is defined as a haemoglobin (Hb) level <12 grams per decilitre (g/dL) in females and <14 g/dL in males, or as a Hb level <12.5 g/dL in adults. The BMJ also says that it is the most common haematologic disorder seen in general medical practice.

Anaemias can be classified in different ways. Under one classification system, the most common is iron-deficiency anaemia, with other important groups being vitamin-deficiency anaemia (including vitamin B12 and/or folic acid deficiency anaemia), aplastic anaemia, haemolytic anaemia, sickle cell anaemia and anaemia caused by other diseases (American Society of Hematology, 2018).

When organised by the functional defect in red cell production, there are three main classes of anaemia: marrow production defects (hypoproliferation); red cell maturation defects (ineffective erythropoeisis); and decreased red cell survival (blood loss/hemolysis). Megaloblastic anaemia comes in the second category in this list.

In megaloblastic anaemia, the deficiency of vitamin B12 or folate, which leads to a lack of the components required for DNA synthesis, means that RBCs do not form properly in the bone marrow (Green, 2017). They appear as malformed immature cells (known as megaloblasts) seen both in the bone marrow and in the blood. The malformations include the retention of a nucleus (healthy RBCs shed their nucleus as they mature) and an oval shape rather than a doughnut-shape which results in a cell size larger than normal (macrocytic = mean corpuscular volume (MCV) > 97fL). The nucleus in these cells is more immature than the cytoplasm, producing nuclear/cytoplasmic asynchrony (Aslinia et al., 2006). The cells may also have a shorter life than normal RBCs (120 days) which means there are fewer of them than in a healthy person because the cells are released before they have matured enough to divide. The incomplete DNA synthesis affects all cells but is most pronounced in the RBCs. Other changes in the blood include hypersegmented neutrophils (with up to six lobes) and a reduction in the number of granulocytes (white cells) and platelets (Hoffbrand & Provan, 1997).

Harrison's Principles of Internal Medicine (2008) explains:

> *"The megaloblastic anaemias are a group of disorders characterised by a macrocytic anaemia and distinctive morphological abnormalities of the developing haemopoietic cells in the bone marrow. In severe cases the anaemia may be associated with leucopenia and thrombocytopenia. Megaloblastic anaemia arises because of the inhibition of DNA synthesis in the bone marrow, usually due to deficiency of one or other of two water-soluble B vitamins, vitamin B12 (B12 cobalamin) or folate. B12 deficiency may also cause a severe neuropathy but whether this occurs with folate deficiency is controversial. In a minority of cases, megaloblastic anaemia arises because of a disturbance of DNA synthesis due to a drug or a congenital or acquired biochemical defect that causes a disturbance of B12 or folate metabolism or affects DNA synthesis independent of B12 or folate"* (Hoffbrand, 2008).

4.2.1 Effect of macrocytosis – enlarged Red Blood Cells

Macrocytic cells are defined as cells with a Mean Corpuscular Volume (MCV)[21] greater than 80-95 femtolitres (fl) in adults, which is detected in a blood count (Hoffbrand & Provan, 1997). They are found relatively frequently and do not always indicate illness, unless there are other signs and symptoms (Aslinia et al., 2006).

RBCs carry oxygen from the lungs to the rest of the body (wherever it is needed), and carbon dioxide back to the lungs. They do this through the haemoglobin molecule, which is what gives blood its red colour. RBCs need to be able to absorb and release oxygen and carbon dioxide at a fast rate in response to activity. A healthy RBC has a doughnut shape – thin in the middle and thick around the outside, which gives it a greater surface area-to-volume ratio than a sphere or ball shape. This means that the cytoplasm, containing the haemoglobin which transports oxygen, is as close as possible to the cell membrane at all times. In order to get this shape, the cell has lost its nucleus. In

---

[21] MCV (fl) = [Hematocrit (per cent) x 10]/[TBC count (10^6/μL)] (Aslinia et al., 2006)

humans, the healthy RBC has an average MCV around 90 femtolitres (fL). In megaloblastic anaemia, the diameter of the RBC is still 6 – 8 μm, but the MCV can be up to 150 fL.

If the RBCs are either too large or too small or differently shaped, neither oxygen nor carbon dioxide can be effectively transported. This leads to lack of energy and even muscle pains. How many B12-deficiency sufferers have experienced these?

4.2.2   Causes of megaloblastic anaemia

The vitamin B12 deficiency which leads to megaloblastic anaemia can have many causes. These include any condition which disrupts the B12-absorption pathway, such as intestinal diseases, atrophic gastritis (chronic inflammation of the stomach which increases with age and reduces the production of acid and enzymes needed for digestion as well as of intrinsic factor), gastric surgery, pancreatic insufficiency, bacterial overgrowth, medications which inhibit production of stomach acid (e.g. antacids and proton-pump inhibitors), or autoimmune attack on stomach cells (PA). Other factors leading to deficiency include low dietary intake and genetic predisposition to deficiency. PA has been assumed to be the most common cause in elderly patients, but researchers have shown that food malabsorption rather than PA may be the leading cause: "If an image of an elderly patient with pernicious anaemia is the first thing that comes to mind when you think of B12 deficiency, take note: That image could obfuscate a more common case of B12 deficiency—one caused by food-B12 malabsorption" (Andres et al., 2007).

Megaloblastic anaemia can also be caused by folate deficiency and some other disorders, but vitamin B12 deficiency is the most common cause (Rosenblatt & Fowler, 2006). Folate/folic acid deficiency can have a dietary cause or can be induced by vitamin B12 deficiency because of the interaction of the two vitamins (see Chart 5-1 on page 113, and Chart 5-2). Other possible causes of megaloblastic anaemia are drug damage, congenital defects and myelodysplasia (a type of cancer) (Babior & Bunn, 2005, pp. 604-605).

4.2.3   Pernicious anaemia

As stated above, when the cause is specifically autoimmune attack on stomach cells, or on cells which secrete Intrinsic Factor (IF – essential for B12 absorption), the illness is called "pernicious anaemia" (PA). An autoimmune condition is where the body's defence mechanism, intended to destroy foreign cells and so prevent infection or disease, turns on the body's own cells and destroys them. Note that atrophic gastritis can also be an autoimmune condition (Minalyan et al., 2017).

The autoimmune attack in PA is caused by several types of antibodies which affect production of gastric acid necessary for separating cobalamin from food, and production of IF, which is needed for cobalamin absorption. (For further information on the B12-absorption route in the human body, see Chapter 1.) In PA, the production of gastric juice is much reduced and contains no or little hydrochloric acid (a condition known as achlorhydria) (Chanarin, 2000).

Anti-gastric parietal cell (GPC) antibodies attack principally the gastric enzyme H^+/K^+ -ATPase proton pump which regulates hydrochloric acid secretion in the stomach. Two types of anti-IF antibodies are known. Type I IF[+] blocks the binding of vitamin B12 to IF (thus preventing the formation of the B12/IF complex) while Type II IF[+] binds to the B12/IF complex, preventing it being absorbed across the intestinal wall (Andrès & Serraj, 2012). Since both hydrochloric acid and IF are required for the proper digestion and absorption of B12, people with this condition are usually unable to absorb B12 in the quantities needed to maintain health.

The UK Pernicious Anaemia Society (PAS) explains: "Parietal cells are found in the lining of the stomach. As well as producing Intrinsic Factor, parietal cells also produce hydrochloric acid. Intrinsic Factor is essential for B12 absorption whilst hydrochloric acid allows B12 to be released from food. Parietal Cells may fail due to infection (from *Helicobacter pylori*, for example) or because the body produces antibodies that kill off the parietal cells – parietal cell antibodies" (PAS, 2018c).

It is thought of as a disease of the elderly: the average patient presentation is around 60 years old. However, it is seen in other ages, and even in children - typical PA symptoms can be seen in children under 10 years old (juvenile PA).

PA develops gradually as the body's stores of B12 are used up. Typical common symptoms include shortness of breath, extreme fatigue, lack of coordination, brain fogs, brittle nails and dry skin. Many other symptoms are also seen in increasing degrees of severity. The effects of this debilitating condition on patients have been described in detail by Martyn Hooper, Chairman of the Pernicious Anaemia Society, in his book *What you need to know about Pernicious Anaemia and Vitamin B12 Deficiency* (Hooper, 2015).

4.3   Delays in diagnosis via the "Addisonian criteria"

PA is traditionally diagnosed through the Addisonian criteria described in Chapter 2. Although well established, these criteria have a number of serious drawbacks and delays in diagnosis are common as demonstrated in a survey of PA patient experience of diagnosis and treatment in the UK conducted between 2010 and 2012 (Hooper et al., 2014). A total of 889 patients registered with the PAS completed an online survey or postal questionnaire. The results showed that: one-third of patients experienced symptoms for up to one year before diagnosis and 14% waited more than 10 years for a diagnosis! Neurological features – which should have triggered prompt diagnosis - were highly prevalent, the most common being memory loss and poor concentration. Other findings were (PAS, 2018a):

- 44% were initially wrongly diagnosed as having some other problem
- 22% had to wait 2 years for a correct diagnosis
- 19% for 5 years
- 4% for 10 years
- 14% waited 10 years or more.

In answer to the frequent question "Why did it take so long for me to be diagnosed" in its Patients' FAQ, the PAS says:

> "There are three main reasons. Firstly, doctors don't specifically look for B12 deficiency and all too often believe that the symptoms patients complain of are associated with other diseases. Where doctors actively look for B12 deficiency they diagnose many more cases of B12 deficiency than doctors who aren't actively looking for the deficiency.

Secondly there are problems associated with the current test used to measure the amount of B12 in the patient's blood. [See Chapter 2 and below.]

Thirdly, the test used to find out if the B12 deficiency is caused by Pernicious Anaemia also appears to be thoroughly flawed [See explanation below.]" (PAS, 2018b).

On the face of it, PA appears easy to diagnose and confirm. The small intestine requires Intrinsic IF to absorb B12, and this is produced by parietal cells (gastric cells) in the stomach wall. Where IF is not being produced, it is because the parietal cells are damaged and it should be easy to detect either IF antibodies (IF^{+ve}), or parietal cell antibodies (PC^{+ve}).

The challenge, as with so many tests, is the number of false negatives (when the result of the test indicates that there is no problem, or excludes a diagnosis). Unconfirmed reports indicate that perhaps only one-third of people with obvious symptoms of PA actually get a positive result for IF antibodies (IF^{+ve}), so we believe that many people fail to get a diagnosis because of a "false negative" (i.e. IF^{-ve}), and therefore do not get the treatment they need.

4.3.1 Drawbacks of the Addisonian Method

4.3.1.1 Macrocytosis – not a specific marker

The normal diagnostic tools are a Complete Blood Count (CBC) and a peripheral blood smear. The most common haematological signs of megaloblastic anaemia are the presence of macroovalocytes and hypersegmented neutrophils on peripheral blood smears (Andrès & Serraj, 2012). However, there are many other causes of macrocytosis which can occur without anaemia. So macrocytosis alone is far from being a sufficient indicator of B12 deficiency. Macrocytic anaemias are grouped into megaloblastic and non-megaloblastic types. If macrocytic cells are found, further tests are needed to determine the cause (Nagao & Hirokawa, 2017).

Other signs in the blood can help to confirm the diagnosis, such as neutropenia (abnormally low levels of neutrophils), thrombocytopenia (an abnormally low level of platelets), pancytopenia (low blood counts for both red and white cells and platelets), intramedullary haemolytic component (see, for example, Khalil et al. (2012)) and pseudothrombotic microangiopathy[22] (Andrès & Serraj, 2012). A case of pseudothrombotic microangiopathy due to severe vitamin B12 deficiency, for example, is described in Veit (2017).

4.3.1.2 Serum B12 blood test not reliable as a stand-alone marker

As described in Chapter 2, the method for measuring serum B12 in common use is not completely reliable although it can be a used as an indicator in conjunction with other markers. Another drawback of the test is that it measures all B12 in the blood, rather than just the bioactive B12 which is the significant portion. In addition, there is no agreed national or international standard reference range for B12 levels. Finally, it is our experience that many patients whose B12 blood level is "normal" nevertheless manifest clinical symptoms of deficiency, suggesting that requirement differs

---

[22] Pseudothrombotic angiopathy is anemia, thrombocytopenia (abnormally low platelet level), and schistocytosis (circulating red blood cell fragments) caused by vitamin B12 deficiency.

by person (see, for example, case showing that "normal cobalamin serum levels do not rule out a cobalamin deficiency" in Roessler and Wolff (2017)).

4.3.1.3   IF⁺ and GPC⁺ antibodies – tests not totally reliable

Antibodies present in the blood usually indicate the presence of a pathogen (a disease-causing organism that should not be there). The body creates antibodies to attack the pathogen, and antibodies are very specific – they only attack exactly what they are designed to attack. Because the antibodies are so specific, if they can be detected, they are considered a reliable indication of whether the pathogen is present, or has been present recently.

The presence of antibodies (Ab⁺) to either parietal cells or IF (Parietal Cell Ab+ (PC⁺) or IF Ab+ (IF⁺)) shows that vitamin B12 deficiency is probably due to absorption issues. This is a useful diagnostic criterion to confirm vitamin B12 deficiency.

However, the results for tests for antibodies are not totally reliable. For IF⁺, a negative result (lack of the presence of antibodies) is true for everyone who does not have the condition (it is *specific*), but *sensitivity* (the percentage of people who are actually suffering from the condition but reported falsely as "negative") is reported to be only about 37-50% (Andrès & Serraj, 2012) or 40-60% (Devalia et al., 2014) so a "negative IFAB assay does not therefore rule out pernicious anaemia [vitamin B12 deficiency]" (Devalia et al., 2014). The equivalent figures for anti-GPC antibodies are higher, at 81.5% and 90.3% (Andrès & Serraj, 2012) but this test is less useful because it also shows 10% positivity in healthy individuals. Therefore, "a positive GPC antibody test is not definitive for pernicious anaemia" (Khan et al. (2009) cited in Devalia et al. (2014))".

A common reason why doctors do not diagnose B12 deficiency is because B12 deficiency is progressing down a different route, e.g. neurological pathology. It is also possible that a diagnosis may be refused even though anti-GPC antibodies are present, because the doctor was looking for anti-IF antibodies.

We note that the British Society for Haematology (BSH) **Guidelines for the diagnosis and treatment of cobalamin and folate disorders** begin by saying that the clinical picture should be "the most important factor in assessing the significance of test results assessing cobalamin status because there is no 'gold standard' test to define deficiency" (Devalia et al., 2014). The Guidelines advise (quoting Carmel et al. (1996)): "Identification of hypersegmented neutrophils, defined as >5% of neutrophils with five or more lobes and the presence of oval macrocytes, may suggest either cobalamin or folate deficiency, but they are not sensitive in early cobalamin deficiency". They also state: "Oval macrocytes, hypersegmented neutrophils and circulating megaloblasts in the blood film and megaloblastic change in the bone marrow is not a specific indicator of cobalamin deficiency (Galloway & Hamilton, 2007) and the possibility of underlying myelodysplastic syndrome has to be considered (having excluded alcohol excess, drugs and other causes of an elevated MCV)."

4.3.2   Landmark case did not show macrocytosis or IF-antibody

The patient whose condition initially started me on my voyage of discovery of the widespread effects of vitamin B12 deficiency (Glenise Mason, Case 5-7, also described in the Introduction) is an illustration of the above points. Her blood test did not show either macrocytosis or anti-IF antibody; in fact, it showed *micro*cytosis (RBCs smaller than normal - indicative of iron-deficiency anaemia). It was her pallor, neuropsychiatric and other symptoms that alerted me to the possibility of B12 deficiency. Because there were no classical signs of B12 deficiency, the laboratory was reluctant to do a B12 blood test. After some considerable persuasion, they finally agreed to do the test which showed her B12 level to be very low at only 185ng/L. I therefore diagnosed B12 deficiency and instituted B12-replacement therapy by injection. Her B12 level rose, the *micro*cytosis resolved and her haemoglobin level normalised.

From that time (the early 1980s), realising the inadequacy of the classical guidelines, I began to develop other means of diagnosing vitamin B12 deficiency. With experience, I became able to diagnose B12 deficiency at an early stage of its development, through neurological and neuropsychiatric signs and symptoms. These were subsequently confirmed either by a serum B12 blood test alone, or (where the serum B12 level was above the level considered by the NHS as "normal") by a therapeutic trial.

As a result of this approach, from then onwards I encountered no cases of PA. I continued to order full blood count tests for patients whom I suspected had vitamin B12 deficiency but these regularly did not show macrocytosis. Nevertheless, their B12 level on presentation had been low as demonstrated subsequently either by a serum B12 test or by their favourable response to a therapeutic trial. For a while, I also ordered anti-IF antibody tests because these were required at the time but as these *always* proved negative (because I was identifying cases of B12 deficiency before the autoimmune reaction had developed), I eventually abandoned them as unnecessary. (The anti-IF antibody test is expensive so this also resulted in some saving to the NHS.)

As there are generally no effective guidelines for diagnosing vitamin B12 deficiency without anaemia, we developed our own which are given in the **Protocol for excluding B12 deficiency (Megaloblastic anaemia/pernicious anaemia) from adult and child patient presentation** (provided in full in Appendix 1).

Our method for diagnosing vitamin B12 deficiency, including megaloblastic anaemia, shown in Figure 4-2 at the head of this chapter, is straightforward and accords much more attention to family and dietary history and signs and symptoms than the Addisonian method. Of course, we also consider blood test results but, because of their unreliability described above, we do not depend solely on these.

In our method, the presenting signs and symptoms are first assessed using the **One-minute health check** (part of our Protocol in Appendix 1, see page 56 and page 271). If B12 deficiency is suspected, blood tests are ordered for the full blood count, serum vitamin B12 and folic acid, TSH, U+Es, LFT, serum ferritin, glucose, early morning cortisol and vitamin D to confirm or exclude the most common conditions found alongside vitamin B12 deficiency. Figure 4-2 summarises how decisions on treatment are made using our system. The decisions are fully described in our Protocol. The two main categories of presentation that we observed at the start were: (1) a small number of people with the typical haematological signs of B12 deficiency anaemia but no neurological effects; and (2) patients with neurological signs and symptoms but no macrocytosis.

It is useful to determine the cause of B12 deficiency if found, and to establish whether this is a problem of genetics, low dietary intake or malabsorption (including PA). The presence of GPC antibodies and/or IF antibodies will help in this, with the provisos stated above.

4.3.3   Pernicious anaemia – is it preventable?

Ever since the cure for PA was discovered in the 1920s it has, to our knowledge, tended to be assumed that PA is the cause of vitamin B12 deficiency, in other words that PA develops first (from origins which are not well understood). Careful observation in clinical practice has suggested to us, that far from being the beginning of the cycle, PA may be the *end-stage* of a process of gradually increasing vitamin B12 deficiency.

It is well known that atrophic gastritis, for example, which is prevalent in the elderly, can lead to vitamin B12 deficiency because of reduced release of cobalamin from food (Andrès et al., 2004). The ensuing B12 deficiency produces further gastrointestinal disorders, such as IBS/diverticulosis, unexplained diarrhoea, Crohn's colitis, mouth ulcers, bleeding gums (see, for example, Case 4-1 and Case 4-2). These may weaken the digestive system to the point at which the autoimmune condition of PA develops.

Case 4-1 Gastrointestinal symptoms and speech difficulties

This patient, John Derek Marlow, aged 74, presented with difficulty swallowing, incoherent speech and colitis. Tests indicated a B12 level of 155 ng/L. After six months of B12 treatment (loading dose, followed by monthly injections) he was transformed. He reported that his throat felt clear; he no longer choked on fish nor had swallowing difficulties. His speech was lucid. His hair was also growing back! At that stage, however, his colitis had not improved – in many patients colitis is one of the first gastrointestinal symptoms to improve.

We also observed the frequent co-occurrence of autoimmune conditions in our B12-deficient patients. We would therefore like to suggest that B12 deficiency itself is in some way contributing to the onset of autoimmune illness (see Chapter 7). It is documented elsewhere that PA/vitamin B12 deficiency often occurs in patients with Autoimmune Polyglandular Syndrome (APS) (Zulfiqar & Andrès, 2017). Vitamin B12 deficiency usually develops over a number of years; damage to the digestive system as it progresses may exacerbate the deficiency by preventing further absorption of B12. In our view, there is a possibility that these cumulative disorders may be contributing to the development of PA and APS.

The link between B12 deficiency and the immune system is also demonstrated by a case in my Practice where a patient sadly died of pneumonia during the period of the PCT embargo when her B12 injections were stopped and her immune system was thereby compromised. Her twin sister had the same condition but survived because she was resumed on B12 treatment sooner.

This makes us consider that PA/vitamin B12 deficiency appears to be preventable. In other words, there is strong clinical evidence that PA, which is an autoimmune illness, is a *result* as well as an *accentuating cause*, of vitamin B12 deficiency. I was led to this conclusion by the fact that from the moment I developed an effective system for diagnosing vitamin B12 early deficiency, I had no more cases of PA/end-stage vitamin B12 deficiency *whatsoever* in my Practice for the three ensuing decades that I worked there as a GP. This is, in my view, overwhelming evidence that, if diagnosed and treated soon enough, B12 deficiency will not progress to the PA stage. What I am suggesting is that the autoimmune attack on parietal cells of the stomach and IF-secreting cells in PA is a **result** of the deterioration in body systems resulting from B12 deficiency.

I therefore propose that B12 deficiency is progressive, and easily treated in the early stages, preventing progression.

Case 4-2 Difficulty swallowing, weight loss, fatigue and depression

Beverley Winfield, born 1968, suffered from difficulty swallowing (glossopharyngiditis). Her blood

serum B12 level was recorded as 224 ng/L. If she had been treated from the start, the demyelination of the glossopharyngeal nerve could have been prevented. She was referred back and forth to various specialties to find the cause of her swallowing difficulties, loss of weight, fatigue and depression. One hospital had suggested that she might have throat cancer. She accidentally came to see me in

November 2006. I diagnosed B12 deficiency although her B12 blood level recorded as 446 ng/L. I commenced her on an intensive course of vitamin B12-replacement therapy and soon she was able to swallow without difficulty and to join her husband and children for tea. The transformation in her appearance can be seen by comparing the two photographs.

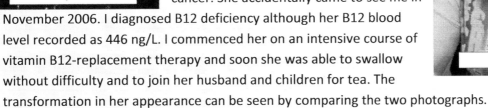

4.4 The importance of early diagnosis

4.4.1 Early: simple B12 deficiency

In my view, the difference between 'simple', or immediately treatable, B12 deficiency and End-Stage/Potentially Fatal Pernicious Anaemia is substantial and identification of B12 deficiency early is of crucial importance. We can prevent fatal/pernicious anaemia (the common pre-war period presentation – see Chapter 2) if we treat proactively and methodically when a patient first presents with vitamin B12 deficiency. The following example illustrates:

Example

- For example, a person (male/female/child), possibly non-meat-eater/vegetarian/vegan, presents to their GP with classic neuropsychiatric signs and symptoms and/or an autoimmune disorder.

- A blood test confirms vitamin B12 deficiency (blood serum B12 less than 200 ng/L (pg/ml) or between 201-350 ng/L (pg/ml) (classed as 'subtle B12 deficiency' (Babior & Bunn, 2005) and (BMJ Best Practice, 2018d)).

- Prompt vitamin B12-replacement therapy prevents progression to lifelong PA, or to any other end-stage presentation, such as Multiple Sclerosis-like presentations.

4.4.2   B12 deficiency end-stage presentation

PA/fatal anaemia results when vitamin B12-replacement therapy is delayed or totally missed. If a patient is not diagnosed promptly, perhaps due to a "mixed bag" of symptoms, or has not sought medical advice from the outset, then the body will deteriorate further. Without sufficient vitamin B12 the body is not able to sustain itself as optimally as it could. As explained earlier (see Chapter 1 or Chapter 2) this is because B12 is vital for all bodily functions and cell processes to work effectively and efficiently. In layman's terms, the body weakens overall; the person becomes excessively fatigued and unable to cope with standard daily tasks and sometimes generally to deal with life. In addition to an increase in classic neuropsychiatric signs and symptoms, the delay may result in a multi-system polyendocrine syndrome (APS) where the body attacks its own cells (see Chapter 7). This is an extremely serious condition. There could be demyelination of the nerves which progresses from the simple inflammation which mostly only occurs in Stage One.

The following will occur:

- IF antibody will be positive.

- Parietal cell antibody may be positive. (The parietal cell secretes IF but if the parietal cell is damaged then the IF will not be secreted to carry the B12 throughout the body.)

- Gastric cells will atrophy.

- With poor stomach acid production, food will not be digested by the stomach and B12 will not be released from food.

The solution is to commence vitamin B12-replacement therapy urgently and to screen for accompanying autoimmune polyglandular disorders. If such disorders are found, appropriate hormone-replacement treatment, for example with physiological doses of hydrocortisone or levothyroxine will be needed. The B12/cortisol combination reverses the autoimmune tendency and speeds up remyelination of the nerves. (Note that standard treatment for MS-like presentations in hospital is to give intravenous B12 with physiological doses of cortisol (a steroid hormone), but patients are then sent home and there is no follow-up. So after about a month their symptoms return.)

To conclude: *pernicious anaemia/fatal anaemia* will still exist if a person's vitamin B12, folic acid, haemoglobin or ferritin levels are extremely low. In these cases, the patients may need a blood transfusion. But it ***should not still exist if we treat proactively with haematinic screening and replace as per the deficiency.***

4.5   Vitamin B12 interactions with folate

4.5.1   The "methyl-folate trap"

As stated above, megaloblastic anaemia can be caused by either folate[23] deficiency or vitamin B12 deficiency. The effects on blood cells are the same so from the point of view of haematological signs,

---

[23] "Folate" is the term used to describe natural sources of this vitamin. "Folic acid" describes the synthetic form. They are both also known as vitamin B9.

the two conditions are identical. The reasons for this as so far understood are a result of the interaction of the two vitamins. The folate cycle (a series of chemical reactions involving folate in the body) is responsible for producing thymidine, a constituent of DNA and needed for the healthy formation of RBCs. It follows that if there is insufficient supply of folate/folic acid, then RBC formation will be impaired. A deficiency of folate/folic acid can be caused by poor diet (such as diets lacking in green leafy vegetables or cow's milk), or by alcoholism, some gastrointestinal diseases, increased requirements as in pregnancy, severe blood loss and use of some medications (Nagao & Hirokawa, 2017). Most importantly, folate deficiency can also be, and often is, caused by vitamin B12 deficiency: B12 deficiency leads to megaloblastic anaemia because it impairs the folate cycle. Direct folic acid deficiency is less common in developed countries today because of food fortification with folic acid which was introduced to prevent the severe birth defects discovered to be caused by folate deficiency in pregnancy. (However, some consider folate supplementation without B12 supplementation to have drawbacks (Smith et al., 2008)).

The biochemistry of folate has been investigated by many researchers since the isolation of folic acid from spinach in 1941. In the 1950s and 1960s the role of folate compounds in single-carbon unit transfer in amino acid conversions, including homocysteine to methionine and in purine and pyrimidine synthesis was elucidated (Hoffbrand & Weir, 2001). One chemical reaction has been shown to be especially important in DNA synthesis: thymidylate synthesis in which deoxyuridine monophosphate (dUMP) is methylated by the folate compound 5, 10 methylene tetrahydrofolate (THF) to thymidine monophosphate (dTMP).

That a lack of B12 could lead to folic acid deficiency was first proposed in the early 1960s when it was noticed that most patients suffering from megaloblastic anaemia had deficiencies of either vitamin B12 or folic acid or both (Herbert & Zalusky, 1962). This provoked investigation of the interaction between the two vitamins and led to formulation of the hypothesis that vitamin B12 deficiency leads to folate being trapped in cells in an unusable form.

The biochemistry of the interaction between B12 and folic acid is complex and beyond the scope of this book to describe in detail but explanations are provided in, for example, Shane (2008) and Green (2017), among others. What follows is a simplification to provide some general understanding of the processes involved.

A vital step in the folate cycle is the conversion of the folate compound 5 methyl-tetrahydrofolate (MTHF) to 5, 10 methylene THF. In vitamin B12 deficiency, this conversion does not occur, or occurs at a lower rate. The folate gets "trapped" in the MTHF compound and is not available for other reactions, including thymidine synthesis. It is trapped because the conversion cannot take place without a cobalamin (vitamin B12)-dependent enzyme, methionine synthetase (MS). In the normal folate cycle, this enzyme takes a methyl group (consisting of carbon with 3 hydrogen atoms, CH_3) from MTHF, thereby converting it to THF from which it can be recycled to 5, 10 methylene THF.

This is known as the "methyl-folate trap" hypothesis. The trap occurs at the point where the folate cycle intersects with the methionine cycle. When the cycles function normally, the cobalamin molecule takes the methyl group and forms methylcobalamin. It then donates the methyl group to homocysteine which is thereby converted to methionine. This frees the THF which becomes available for other reactions. In summary: "Impairment of methionine synthetase activity in vitamin

B_{12} deficiency results in the accumulation of methyltetrahydrofolate which can neither be utilized for other reactions nor demethylated to provide free tetrahydrofolate" (Bender, 2003).

Until relatively recently, the hypothesis had never been tested in human beings but the presentation of a rare case (Smulders et al., 2006) provided an opportunity to demonstrate most features of the methyl-folate trap and thereby provide evidence for it.

4.5.2 Masking of B12 deficiency

Conversely, there is concern that high doses of synthetic folic acid can temporarily correct megaloblastic anaemia and mask vitamin B12 deficiency, leading to an undiagnosed progression of neurological damage to an irreversible stage. This concern first arose in the 1950s when it was seen that patients treated with the newly-discovered folic acid, on the assumption that it would cure pernicious anaemia, developed a rapid worsening of their neurological symptoms after an initial improvement (Reynolds, 2006).

The fact that large doses of folic acid can correct megaloblastic anaemia implies that the methyl-folate trap can be overriden. One possible mechanism for this is that high-dose folic acid overcomes the block "through dihydrofolate reductase (DHFR) reduction to tetrahydrofolate" (Green, 2017 Figure 3). Varela-Moreiras et al. (2009) explain:

> "Since folic acid (pteroylglutamic acid, the synthetic form of folate) is reduced directly to tetrahydrofolate, it escapes the metabolic block caused by insufficient cobalamin. Thus, folic acid treatment corrects the megaloblastic anemia caused by cobalamin deficiency. As a result, the hematological marker of the deficiency (anemia) is corrected, and the clinical sign of the deficiency is masked. The resulting delay in diagnosis of the deficiency can lead to irreversible neurological damage."

It is not clear whether the same effect would occur in a vitamin B12-deficient patient with a high natural folate intake (such as in a vegetarian diet). The issue seems mainly to relate to administration of folic acid, which can be given in much higher doses than a normal diet would provide and which is more readily bioavailable than dietary folate.

The potential masking of B12 deficiency can in our view be easily avoided through meticulous family history-taking and observance of signs and symptoms as described above which would obviate a misdiagnosis.

4.5.3 Hyperhomocysteinaemia

The trapping of folate because of cobalamin deficiency has another important consequence: it means that another vital biochemical reaction, the methionine cycle, cannot complete. In a healthy person, following conversion of homocysteine to methionine, the latter is converted in further steps to S-adenosyl methionine (SAMe) which is important for the production of neurotransmitters and for DNA methylation. In this reaction, SAMe gives off its methyl group and thus becomes homocysteine, starting the whole cycle again.

If this cycle is impaired, levels of homocysteine in the blood rise, creating the condition known as hyperhomocysteinaemia. "Homocysteine, otherwise a normal amino acid, is both vasculotoxic [poisons or damages the heart and vascular/circulatory system] and neurotoxic [poisons or damages the nerve system] when elevated to 17 or more µmol/l [in the blood serum]" (Herbert, 2002). At vasculotoxic levels, there is a high risk of heart attacks, thrombotic strokes and peripheral venous occlusion. High levels of homocysteine also have adverse effects on pregnancy (see Chapter 5 of this book and Refsum (2001)). Herbert further explains:

> "Three publications have suggested folic acid deficiency is the cause of hyperhomocysteinaemia in the elderly. However, if analysed appropriately, all subjects – folic-acid deficient patients with hyperhomocysteinaemia – also have B12 deficiency. I [Victor Herbert] strongly suggest that it is the B12 deficiency, rather than the folate deficiency, that is causing the hyperhomocysteinaemia. The B12 deficiency may also be causing the folic acid deficiency in these patients. In summary, the low serum folates are secondary to malabsorption due to gut B12 deficiency, and the low red cell folates are secondary to malabsorption because B12 is necessary both to get folate into red cells and to keep it there (by polyglutamating it)." (Victor Herbert, answer to discussion on Carrazana (2002) in Herbert ed. **Vitamin B12 deficiency**, (p.26)).

Researchers have found that the majority of cases of hyperhomocysteinaemia result from low levels of vitamin B12 and/or folic acid. Some have suggested that hyperhomocysteinaemia may be a direct result of severe gastric damage as in atrophic gastritis (Santarelli et al., 2004). Others have also found a link between atrophic gastritis and coronary heart disease via hyperhomocysteinaemia (Senmaru et al., 2012).

4.5.4   Vitamin B12-replacement therapy for hyperhomocysteinaemia

When vitamin B12 supplement (B12 replacement) is given to a patient who is deficient in B12 and in folate, tests show that the folate levels in the blood increase to non-deficient (normal) levels (Chandy, 2006a) even without folate supplementation. Vitamin B12 enables the utilisation of folate which is in many foods (vegetarian and non-vegetarian), raising the levels in blood serum and other body tissues. Even the erythropoietic process (development and maturation of RBCs) is enhanced. The risks of hyperhomocysteinaemia are therefore reduced.

4.6   Risk of other conditions and associated autoimmune disease

In addition to the neurological and neuropsychiatric conditions that are described elsewhere in this book, patients with vitamin B12-deficiency anaemia may develop other complications. Investigations should include endoscopy to determine whether the patient suffers from atrophic gastritis or other conditions such as gastric carcinoma or gastric polyps which are more common in this type of anaemia than in healthy people (Hoffbrand & Provan, 1997). Patients with vitamin B12 deficiency anaemia may also develop iron deficiency anaemia if the cause of their condition is chronic atrophic gastritis (Devalia et al., 2014).

Multiple autoimmune conditions are also found in patients with pernicious anaemia. The most common such conditions are (Hoffbrand & Provan, 1997):

- Graves' disease

- Myxoedema

- Thyroiditis (hypo- or hyper- thyroidism)

- Idiopathic adrenocortical insufficiency (hypoadrenalism, low cortisol)

- Vitiligo

- Hypoparathyroidism

To shame what is strong, God has chosen what the world counts as weakness. He has chosen things low and contemptible, near nothings, to overthrow the existing order.

1 Corinthians 1:27b to 30

Figure 5-1 Preventive programme summary

4 to 6 months before pregnancy:

Routine blood test for: FBC + B12 + folic acid, serum ferritin, fasting blood sugar, TSH - T3 - T4, LFT + U+E, Lipid/Vitamin D/AM Cortisol (if indicated).

Follow up one- to three-monthly as required.

Newborn:

Routine B12 and folic acid screening test in the newborn, along with current practice of Guthrie and phenylketonuria.

Commence without delay optimum replacement therapy for any of the above deficiencies diagnosed.

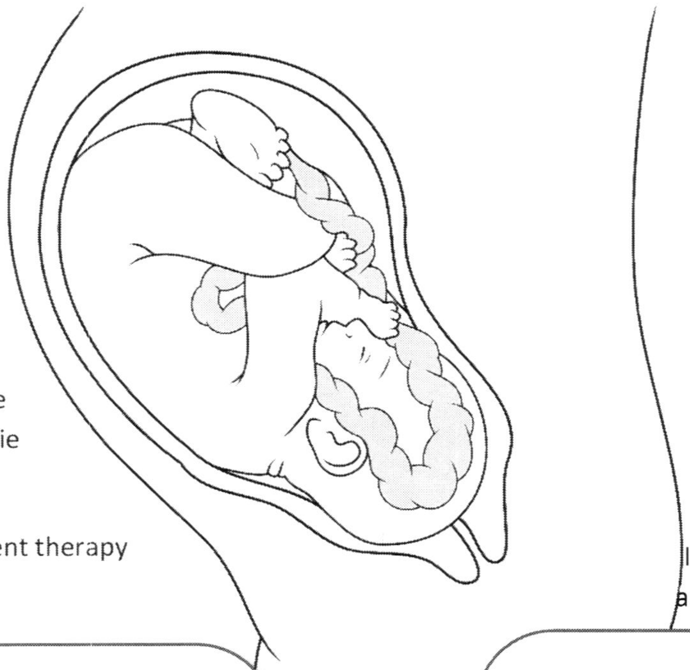

Mother and Father should:

Stop smoking (CO + CN poisoning).

Reduce alcohol consumption.

Follow a healthy balanced diet.

Withdraw and stop any harmful or unneeded prescription medication.

Avoid stress and have adequate rest and leisure activities.

Identify vegetarian and vegan would-be mothers, advise appropriately and follow them up monthly.

Avoid these potential problems:

Hypotonia (floppy baby syndrome); cleft lip; cleft palate; Down Syndrome; Neural tube defects (NTDs); Spina Bifida; Attention Deficit Hyperactivity Disorder (ADHD); foetal alcohol spectrum disorder (FASD); Meningocele. Mother avoids miscarriages, haemorrhage, postnatal depression, hair loss, fainting, eclampsia and morning sickness during pregnancy.

Achieve these beneficial results:

Baby advanced neurologically and physically (milestones);

Avoids many neurological and psychiatric diseases in later life: impact on dementia and cancer;

Mother enjoys pregnancy and breast-feeding without fatigue or depression;

Baby continues to receive B12 and folic acid via breast milk – and maternal bonding achieved.

5.1 Advance preparation for a healthy pregnancy

In this chapter we explain that women contemplating pregnancy should be tested for vitamin B12 deficiency and supplemented if necessary just as they are currently for folate (folic acid). Vitamin B12 is completely safe for adults, for pregnant women, for foetuses and babies, for small children, for any age in fact. Lack of vitamin B12 presents a serious risk for the health of both mother and child.

It is vital to provide an optimum vitamin and nutritional status in the mother to achieve gene expression correctly in the neonate. Couples preparing to conceive should consider all factors illustrated in the Preventive Programme Summary (Figure 5-1). Vitamin B12 is needed for folate metabolism in the body which leads in various steps to compounds necessary for the synthesis of DNA (which contains the instructions for all life processes) and the correct functioning of every cell in the human body (see Figure 9-1). It is also needed to convert homocysteine to methionine, which in turn leads to production of S-adenosyl methionine (SAMe) used in building thousands of compounds and proteins needed for healthy cells, tissues and organs. Vitamin B12 has wide-ranging effects on fertility, the health of the mother during pregnancy, the health of the child as embryo, neonate, infant and into later life. Low vitamin B12 levels in pregnant women have been linked to increased risk of early and recurrent miscarriage, premature births and low birth weight (Obeid et al., 2017). They have also been linked to increased risk of having a child with congenital heart defects and hyperhomocysteinaemia in the mother, leading to risk of cardiovascular problems in both mother and child in later life (Verkleij-Hagoort et al., 2006). Most importantly, vitamin B12 deficiency can lead to functional folic acid deficiency (because of the interaction between the two vitamins) which is well known to cause neural tube defects (NTDs).

The following summarises some key points regarding vitamin B12 in pregnancy:

1. "Both folate and cobalamin [B12] deficiency have been implicated in recurrent fetal loss and fetal neural tube defects" at birth (Hoffbrand, 2018, pp. 701-702). Folate deficiency is now rare due to dietary supplementation, but B12 deficiency is largely ignored.

2. Vitamin B12 and folic acid (together) lower homocysteine in both mother and baby, and prevent future cardiovascular disease risk.

3. "Long-term nutritional cobalamin deficiency in infancy leads to poor brain development and impaired intellectual development. In infancy there may be feeding difficulties, lethargy, and coma" (Hoffbrand, 2018, p. 701). Continued vitamin B12 deficiency, if left untreated, may predispose a person to dementia in later life.

4. The nutritional status in mother, foetus and neonate has a substantial impact on all aspects of development at this critical time. Vitamin B12 is a methyl donor for DNA and gene expression. Providing a methyl donor in the diet, before and during pregnancy, alters the state of methylation of the offspring's DNA. This means that genes either express correctly or incorrectly.

5. Mononuclear DNA damage is increased in children and their mothers as a result of vitamin B12 deficiency (Minnet et al., 2011). As well as the importance of vitamin B12 in enabling genes to turn on and off (vital for correct development of the child), the donated methyl groups appear to be important in preventing damage to DNA. (The importance of nutrition in epigenetic alterations in the embryo is discussed in Wu et al. (2004)).

6. Vitamin B12 is needed for folate metabolism, and interaction of the two vitamins is essential for the conversion of homocysteine to methionine, for the synthesis of purines and pyrimidine, for methylation reactions, and for the maintenance of cellular levels of folate. One consequence of vitamin B12 deficiency is raised homocysteine which may lead to pregnancy complications. Research has suggested that maintaining optimal vitamin B12 status may be crucial to lowering homocysteine levels in the mother (Molloy et al., 2002).

5.2 Birth defect preventive programme: vitamin B12 supplementation

A couple planning to conceive should consider healthy lifestyle choices and have blood test checks for deficiencies and then appropriate supplementation. It is well understood that pregnant mothers usually need nutritional supplements, because of the high nutritional demands of pregnancy. We recommend that mothers-to-be should have vitamin B12 supplementation to ensure optimal health of the foetus and baby.

There are many different causes of B12 deficiency (see Chapter 2) but the most common are limited dietary intake and problems with absorption (Hoffbrand, 2012). If the mother is not getting enough vitamin B12, then the foetus will not get enough vitamin B12 through the placenta and umbilical cord.

Case 5-1 Teenage female: delayed periods

In an unusual case, the mother of a fifteen-year-old girl requested a home visit. Her concern was that although her daughter had the normal breast development of a teenager, so far there had been no sign of her starting a monthly period. The hospital performed a vaginal examination and identified that she had only a rudimentary vagina. There was no visible or palpable cervix or uterus. An ultrasound scan confirmed the above abnormality.

This mother and several members of her family had been diagnosed with vitamin B12 deficiency in previous years. Sadly, compliance to regular B12-replacement therapy had been very poor. We suggest that non-compliance with both folic acid oral supplements and B12 injections by the mother during pregnancy resulted in this birth defect (mononuclear DNA damage) which would have been totally preventable, since the treatment was preventive rather than reactive medicine.

5.3 Vitamin B12 and fertility

It is well known that severe vitamin B12 deficiency (as in pernicious anaemia, for example) leads to temporary infertility (NHS, 2016a). Research has shown that prolonged B12 deficiency results in infertility by causing changes in ovulation or development of the ovum or changes leading to defective implantation (Bennett, 2001). Vitamin B12 is necessary for the proper functioning of the endocrine system, which is necessary both for preparing a woman's body for pregnancy, and for maintaining the pregnancy. A significant number of women diagnosed with vitamin B12 deficiency in our Practice also suffered from hormonal disturbances (see, for example, Cases 7-5 and 7-6 in Chapter 7).

Case 5-2 Cardiomyopathy and mitral-aortic defect in pregnant mother

Hayley Matthews (born 1979) presented in February 2011 with cardiomyopathy/mitral-aortic regurgitation and closure of the ventricular tunnel. She was concerned about getting pregnant because of her own frailty and likely heart defects in the baby. Her blood serum level was found to be 283 ng/L (normal range 350-900 ng/L) and replacement therapy commenced. She rapidly gained strength, and when she wanted a baby folic acid supplements were added. Hospital cardiology clinics were surprised that she had a healthy pregnancy and no post-natal problems. Her baby was born in July 2013 healthy and with no heart defect.

Case 5-3 Vital role of vitamin B12 and folic acid in fertility

Donna Dyson already had an 11-year-old daughter. For the previous three years or so she had been trying for a baby but unfortunately had been having irregular periods, or no periods for months. She suspected some early miscarriages, and experienced extreme fatigue, headaches, mood swings and depression, and fainting attacks. She was losing hope of becoming pregnant again.

A routine blood test confirmed vitamin B12 deficiency, and we commenced her on B12-replacement therapy. Following the initial loading doses, she was given weekly (and subsequently monthly) injections as part of ongoing treatment programmes.

Her regular periods returned; her fatigue symptoms diminished, and she became energetic. Folic acid was commenced and given alongside vitamin B12 as she was very keen to have another child. She became pregnant and had a healthy child.

An interview with Donna Dyson is available on the B12d.org website: www.b12d.org/testimonials

Hormones, particularly cyclical hormones, are controlled by the pituitary (which is itself controlled by the hypothalamus from the brain). The pituitary protrudes out into the bloodstream and samples the blood, determining levels of hormones going around the body and comparing these levels to the levels that the pituitary expects. If blood levels are lower than expected, then the pituitary sends a signal to the hormone-producing gland (endocrine gland) to increase production, and if the levels are higher than expected then the pituitary either stops stimulating the endocrine gland, or may in a few cases send a suppressing signal.

The female sex hormones (oestrogen and progesterone) are no exception. The levels and relative proportions of these two vary over a lunar month cycle (28 days) when a woman is not pregnant, and the endocrine glands (the ovaries and uterus) that produce them, need to be finely tuned to secrete them in the correct proportions. This cycles the thickening of the uterus wall, release of an ovum, and subsequent refreshing and expulsion of the ovum.

During pregnancy, a number of hormones need to act together to ensure that the usual cycle of uterus wall breakdown and subsequent release of another ovum does not happen. The uterus needs to support the growing child, including formation of placenta, and the stretching and repositioning of muscles and bones of the mother to accommodate the size of the child.

5.4 Considerations during pregnancy: the myth of haemodilution

> *"I also have another query. I am a midwife and so interested to know the normal B12 levels in pregnancy during each trimester. A client with symptoms was tested and it was 63 in her first trimester. Her GP prescribed 1 injection and her consultant obstetrician has said that 63 is normal in pregnancy and she should not be treated. Her only symptom is excessive tiredness which does keep her in bed. She did get improvement from the injection. She is now nearing the end of her pregnancy. I'd be interested to know your opinion on B12 in pregnancy. Thank-you."*
>
> Erika Thompson – Beautiful Births, *Wessex Independent Midwives (Thompson, 2017)*

The level of vitamin B12 in the blood has been found to decrease during pregnancy. This was noted by Chanarin (1990, p. 141). A more recent longitudinal study on the effect of pregnancy on maternal and foetal cobalamin status showed that the mother's vitamin B12 levels (measured both as cobalamin and as holoTranscobalamin) dropped from the 8th to 32nd weeks of pregnancy compared with the levels at preconception (which were in the "normal" range), but were higher in umbilical cord blood. In this study, levels were measured in 92 women, showing an average of 293 pmol/L at preconception to 198 pmol/L at the 32nd week, but the average level in the cord was 325 pmol/L. The researchers' interpretation of these figures was that "there is a strain on cobalamin status during pregnancy" (Murphy et al., 2007).

We would interpret these findings as indicating that the mother's body stores of vitamin B12 are being used up. This natural drop makes it all the more important to monitor vitamin B12 levels in pregnant women because any unusually low serum vitamin B12 (which a GP might mistakenly attribute to haemodilution during pregnancy as in the example quoted above) could lead to severe consequences. Haemodilution of any of the important markers should be an immediate flag to a doctor that something is deficient.

We suggest that pregnant women mobilise their body stores of B12 to increase the blood serum B12 level to meet the needs of the growing embryo and foetus. Vitamin B12 is a key component for healthy cell growth and division, so this makes sense. Researchers have shown that during pregnancy the placenta "actively concentrates cobalamin [vitamin B12] in the foetus, resulting in foetal serum levels twice those of maternal serum" (Smith & Coman, 2014). If the mother's levels are healthy, this gives the newborn enough stores of vitamin B12 to last for 6-12 months.

However, for a vitamin B12-deficient mother, the drop in maternal vitamin B12 levels has important consequences: her vitamin B12 status will worsen during pregnancy and, depending on her degree of deficiency, the foetus may also become deficient. It has also been shown that mothers with low vitamin B12 levels have raised homocysteine (HcT)and methylmalone (MMA) levels and, predictably, low cobalamin and high Hct/MMA levels in their newborns (Li et al., 2017; Smith & Coman, 2014).

5.5   Identifying the non-anaemic B12-deficient mother

An important clinical problem which is often overlooked is the non-anaemic mother-to-be who does not typically present with obvious vitamin B12 deficiency. She (the patient) may have neurological and psychiatric abnormalities and, if tested, typically have a low or borderline serum vitamin B12 level. Psychiatric disturbance is common in both folate and vitamin B12 deficiency.

In such people, it would be useful to confirm a diagnosis by a trial of vitamin B12-replacement therapy for at least three months (therapeutic trial). Vitamin B12 is completely safe and beneficial for adults, children and people preparing to be parents, and is inexpensive. A trial will assess whether the symptoms improve.

If the mother is under-diagnosed, untreated or only given folic acid supplement, there is a higher likelihood that she would deliver a child with neuromuscular damage, Subacute Combined Degeneration of the spinal cord (SACD), congenital abnormalities, tumours (including brain damage) and NTDs. It is a straightforward matter to ensure that the mother is not vitamin B12 deficient by giving vitamin B12-replacement therapy before and during pregnancy, at the time that the mother is often already prescribed mandatory folic acid supplementation (see Table 5-3).

5.6   Vegetarian/vegan mothers and vitamin B12 deficiency

Because of the high demands on the body during pregnancy, vegetarian/vegan mothers may well have subclinical vitamin B12 deficiency. Infants born to vitamin B12-deficient mothers, including those with subclinical deficiency, may be predisposed to develop disease or disabilities, particularly so when they are exclusively breast-fed. Some may develop haematological diseases such as anaemia and pancytopenia. Breast-fed infants born to vegetarian/vegan mothers have been observed to experience substantial neurological damage manifested by developmental delay, irritability, tremor and convulsions. Furthermore, these conditions may persist as long-term cognitive and developmental delay, despite adequate therapy.

> *Case 5-4 Vegetarian mother from London*
>
> A young couple moved up from London to manage a shop they bought in the north-east. The lady was in her twenties, 10 weeks' pregnant with her first child and had been receiving antenatal care from the GP and the midwifery team in London. She was already receiving mandatory folic acid 400 µg daily. She transferred her care to our surgery and complained of fatigue and other symptoms which she associated with the pregnancy. On enquiry, she said she had been a lifelong vegetarian. Blood serum B12 and folic acid levels had not been done in London.

A blood test we carried out reported an extremely low serum B12 level of 28 ng/L. We commenced her immediately on an intensive B12-replacement programme while continuing her on folic acid. She enjoyed her pregnancy from this point on, and remained exceptionally well. She gave birth to a healthy baby who was breast-fed during the ensuing months. Although she remained a vegetarian, she continued monthly vitamin B12 injections and as a result the baby continued to receive sufficient B12 from the breast milk.

5.7   Neural tube defects: the roles of folic acid and vitamin B12

In the 1970s researchers discovered a connection between the occurrence of neural tube defects (NTDs) and folate (vitamin B9) status in pregnant women. Because the roles of vitamin B12 and folate are interlinked, lack of vitamin B12 similarly puts the growing foetus at significant risk of NTDs (see Case 5-5). These are among the most common birth defects reported worldwide. NTDs are extremely serious and include spina bifida, anencephaly, and encephalocele. They result from failure of closure of the neural tube after the third or fourth week of gestation – that is, very early in the pregnancy (Thompson et al., 2009).

5.7.1   Food fortification with folic acid

As a result of the discovery of the importance of folate, in the 1990s several countries, including the US, introduced mandatory folic acid fortification of food. Since then, the incidence of NTDs in these countries has dropped but not been eliminated entirely so ways of minimising the risk further are being sought (O'Leary & Samman, 2010). At the same time, questions have been raised about the desirability of food fortification with folic acid since high levels of folic acid in the blood have been linked to various unsatisfactory outcomes, such as insulin-resistance and obesity in children born to pregnant women with this status. High folic acid levels have also been linked to reduced response to antifolate drugs used against malaria, rheumatoid arthritis, psoriasis, and cancer (Smith et al., 2008). A further concern is that supplementation with folic acid to ensure all mothers receive enough folate during pregnancy may mask vitamin B12 deficiency because high levels of folic acid can correct some of the effects of B12 deficiency, such as macrocytosis, but not others – so neurological damage could progress undetected.

5.7.2   Vitamin B12 and folate/folic acid interlinked metabolisms

As described in Chapters 1 and 4, adequate vitamin B12 is vital for the proper functioning of the folate cycle. Therefore, lack of vitamin B12 can lead to a functional lack of folate even if there is sufficient folate in the diet. The action of vitamin B12 on the folate cycle is through the coenzyme methionine synthase (MS) which is needed to convert a folate compound, 5-methyltetrahydrofolate, to tetrahydrofolate which can then be used in a series of biochemical reactions leading to the production of nucleotides for DNA synthesis (that is, for cell replication). If vitamin B12 is deficient, the role of methionine synthase is reduced and, according to the "methyl-folate trap" hypothesis, methyl folate accumulates in cells and cannot be further metabolised. This compromises folate-dependent DNA synthesis (Molloy, 2018).

At the same time, this coenzyme plays a key role in converting homocysteine to methionine in the methionine cycle, leading to another chain of reactions necessary for DNA methylation. "The continuous recycling of homocysteine to methionine through this enzyme is an essential cellular reaction wherein folate-derived methyl groups are transferred to a multitude of products, including methyl-DNA and methylated proteins that contribute to gene expression and gene silencing mechanisms (i.e., epigenetic control of cellular functions). One current hypothesis for the role of folate in neural tube formation relates to the importance of such epigenetic processes in orchestrating the flow of molecular processes that must be achieved during neural tube closure" (Molloy, 2018).

It is not known whether impairment of one of these cycles alone is responsible for NTDs or whether they result from a combination of these effects. High-dose synthetic folic acid supplementation can override the effects of lack of methionine synthase on the folate cycle, but they cannot substitute for the homocysteine-methionine reaction. So a vitamin B12-deficient mother would, at the very least, suffer from impaired DNA methylation.

A great deal of research has been done into the effects of folate/folic acid deficiency on NTD occurrence but considerably less into the role of vitamin B12 deficiency in these defects. As a result, vitamin B12 supplementation is rarely considered (Obeid et al., 2017). This general lack of awareness of the impact of vitamin B12 deficiency on pregnancy has been attributed to the assumption that vitamin B12-deficient women could not conceive because pernicious anaemia – previously considered the main cause of vitamin B12 deficiency - was known to lead to infertility (Molloy et al., 2008). However, it is now known that there are many other causes, and stages, of vitamin B12 deficiency which do not rule out pregnancy.

It is interesting to note, for example, in the clinical guidance listed in Table 5-1, the recommendations for folic acid/folate supplements, considering that folic acid deficiency is rarely encountered due to food fortification, and that folic acid is available in a far wider range of foodstuffs (both vegetarian and non-vegetarian) than vitamin B12. Supplementation with vitamin B12 is much less emphasised although deficiency may be far more common.

Additionally, absorption and utilisation of folic acid may be much reduced if vitamin B12 levels are lower. In contrast, folic acid absorption and utilisation are guaranteed if the vitamin B12 level in the circulation and amniotic fluid are maintained normal before, during and after pregnancy, especially if the mother is breast-feeding. We conclude that careful consideration needs to be given to vitamin B12 supplementation alongside folate supplementation during pregnancy.

5.7.3   Impact of vitamin B12 deficiency on occurrence of Neural Tube Defects

Nevertheless, some studies on the impact of vitamin B12 status on the occurrence of NTDs have been undertaken. A survey of such research in different population groups showed that studies consistently reported a two-to-fourfold increased risk of NTDs in mothers with low vitamin B12 status (O'Leary & Samman, 2010). Research in Canada, for example, on the impact of food fortification with folic acid, found a threefold increase in the risk of NTDs in mothers who had low vitamin B12 levels (Thompson et al., 2009). The researchers concluded that vitamin B-12 fortification of foods might reduce NTDs more than fortification with folic acid alone.

Several studies have reported that births with NTDs correspond with low B vitamins in the amniotic fluid. In one study, low vitamin B12 occurred more frequently than low folate in amniotic fluid associated with NTD pregnancies at between 15 and 20 weeks' gestation (Dawson et al., 1998). Folate supplementation reduces the risk of recurrent NTDs, but the research shows that both folate and vitamin B12 deficiencies may be independent risk factors. An overview of current research has called for a wider observational study of the impact of vitamin B12 status on NTDs (Ray & Blom, 2003).

Case 5-5 Neural tube defect in severe vitamin B12 deficiency

A few years ago, one late evening I received a phone call from a very distressed lady, requesting an urgent home visit to her 30-year-old daughter. The daughter was discharged from hospital following her first confinement. Her mother was weeping; the father stood silent but handed over the hospital discharge letter to me: "full-term baby born with NTD/anencephaly (absence of cerebral cortex and skull vault); heartbeat and breathing stopped 20 minutes from the time of birth". I remained speechless for a while and departed saying that I would revisit in a few days' time which I did.

Three generations of this family, including this mother, had been diagnosed with severe vitamin B12 deficiency and had been receiving regular parenteral B12 replacement. Unfortunately, she had stopped the one-monthly repeat injections. She was aware of the importance of continuing the injections before and during the pregnancy. She therefore only received mandatory folic acid during the pregnancy.

I reassured her she would have a healthy baby if she recommenced vitamin B12 injections and that, when pregnant, she should continue with B12 injections and daily folic acid. She followed my advice and became pregnant again and was blessed with two healthy and alert babies, a boy and a girl, both without any birth defects whatsoever. The whole family is thankful for this miracle.

In a recent discussion of whether foods should be fortified with vitamin B12 as well as folic acid, one researcher (Molloy, 2018) makes the following observations:

1. Folate/folic acid status does not appear to be the sole determinant of NTD susceptibility;
2. NTDs have been found still to occur particularly in women with low vitamin B12 levels;
3. The neural tube closes in the first 20-28 days of pregnancy, so the pre-pregnancy folate/vitamin B12 status of the mother is crucial;
4. Factors influencing the folate/vitamin B12 status of the mother may include a combination of genetic variants affecting vitamin B12 metabolism and poor dietary intake of these vitamins.

5.7.4   Our finding: serum folate levels mirror vitamin B12 levels

We would like to add to this debate observations from our own clinical experience. As described in the Introduction, we first came across a case of vitamin B12 deficiency without macrocytosis in the 1980s (Case 5-7). At that time, the importance of folic acid was not well known so although we instituted vitamin B12 replacement, we did not think of supplementing the patient with folic acid. She received vitamin B12 injections between 1992 and 2001, and again between 2003 and early 2007, but continued to eat broadly the same diet. In reviewing the effects of the B12 therapy in subsequent blood tests, we were surprised to note that, despite non-supplementation with folic acid and no change in the patient's diet, her serum folate levels had risen and continued to mirror closely those of vitamin B12. The same pattern was observed in a second patient (see Charts 5-1 and 5-2).

We monitored our first patient over a long time and were thus able to observe that this pattern persisted. This is to us clear evidence that adequate vitamin B12 can restore and maintain folic acid levels; in other words it appears to optimise folic acid absorption. We suggest, therefore, that maintaining adequate vitamin B12 status may be just as important as maintaining adequate folic acid status in preventing NTDs. It might also reduce the need for very high-dose folic acid, so avoiding the known detrimental effects of such high doses.

Chart 5-1 Glenise Mason, blood vitamin B12 and folate levels (note B12 supplementation only, folate follows B12 even without folate supplements)

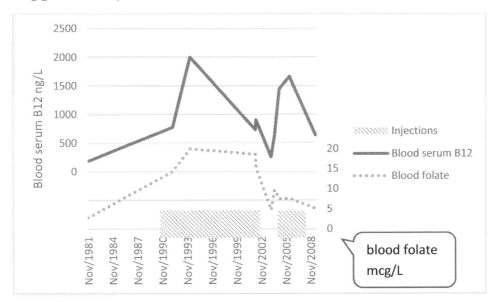

Source: Patient records

Note how blood folate levels (the dotted lower line, units 0 – 20 mg/L) follow blood serum B12 (upper solid line, units 100 – 2000 ng/L). The grey boxes at the bottom show periods when vitamin B12-replacement injections were being administered; the white areas indicate when no vitamin B12 was being administered. The same effect was observed in another patient:

Chart 5-2 Patient A, blood vitamin B12 and folate levels (note B12 supplementation only, folate level follows B12 level)

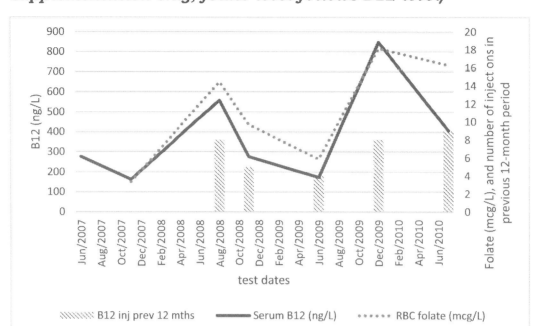

Source: Patient records

See also table Table i-2 on page 7.

UK guidance (see Table 5-1) recommends supplementing the mother's diet with folate or folic acid to ensure the child's proper neurological development. We suggest that a pregnant or pre-pregnant woman diagnosed as folate deficient on the basis of blood serum folate levels may benefit more from vitamin B12 supplements raising her blood serum folate and available folate by mobilising body stores, than from dietary or mandatory folate supplements. It is also important to consider whether the diet of both vegetarians and non-vegetarians contains adequate amounts of folic acid.

5.8 Embryo and neonate B12-deficiency manifestation

Vitamin B12 deficiency has been described in infants born to severely B12-deficient mothers. These infants develop megaloblastic anaemia at about three to six months of age, presumably because they are born with low stores of vitamin B12 and because they are fed breast milk with low B12 content. The vitamin B12 content of breast milk is largely determined by the mother's recent vitamin B12 intake. Supplementation with vitamin B12 during pregnancy and breast-feeding can prevent depletion of the mother's stores and deficiency in infants (Obeid et al., 2017).

Babies born to vitamin B12-deficient mothers have also shown growth retardation, impaired psychomotor development, and other neurological sequelae.

We are surprised that newborns are not already screened for vitamin B12 deficiency during a Guthrie test[24] which already screens to identify the much less common (but easily treated) condition of phenylketonuria.

Paediatricians in Australia have reported:

> "On average, the cobalamin concentration in breast milk is 0.42 mcg/L (Allen, 2002). Breast milk B12 concentrations have been found to be lower in women consuming a strict vegetarian diet compared to omnivorous women (0.23 ± 0.09 mcg/L vs. 0.38 ± 0.08 mcg/L). Infants fed breast milk containing less than 0.36 mcg/L had elevated methylmalonate levels. Additionally the milk B12 concentration was inversely proportional to the length of time the vegetarian diet was consumed (Specker et al., 1990). Exclusively breast fed infants of deficient mothers are most at risk as most commercially available infant formulas are fortified with cobalamin" (Smith & Coman, 2014).

A recent study of maternal supplementation (with 50 µg of daily oral vitamin B12) during pregnancy and early lactation in a resource-poor area of India showed that this measure significantly improved maternal plasma and breast milk measures of vitamin B12 status, as well as multiple measures of infant vitamin B12 status. The researchers noted that this was the first such study of the effects of supplementation and the results could be of global interest because of the potential benefits of such a programme to poor communities worldwide (Duggan et al., 2014).

5.9   Clinical symptoms of vitamin B12 deficiency in infants and children

Vitamin B12 deficiency in infancy may manifest in many different ways, making it difficult to diagnose. In 2007 I wrote to the British National Formulary (BNF) Editorial Board to say that there should be a guidance on vitamin B12 deficiency for babies and young children. At the same time, I wrote to the parliamentary Health Select Committee and to the editor of *The Times*. Thankfully, we now have patient-safe BNF Guidelines on vitamin B12 deficiency for children (BNFC, 2008) which appeared shortly after my letter.

We recommend that a child born to a mother with known vitamin B12 deficiency, a child who presents with delayed development, hyperactivity, dyspraxia, behavioural problems, learning disabilities, autistic spectrum disorder-like symptoms, should initially be screened by a blood test. This is to exclude a number of common conditions, including vitamin B12 deficiency, underactive thyroid and inborn errors of metabolism. Treatment should then follow the BNF guidelines. Regardless of the cause, babies and toddlers found to be anaemic due to low ferritin (hypoferritinaemia), should have iron supplementation instituted.

The Australian team referred to above also noted the urgency of being alert to possible vitamin B12 deficiency in infants. They state: "Vitamin B12 deficiency is an important and possibly under recognised cause of neurological morbidity in infants. The causes of infantile vitamin B12 deficiency are heterogeneous, ranging from dietary deficiency in a breast feeding mother to specific inborn errors of metabolism". They noted that the infant brain appears to be "particularly susceptible to the myelination based mechanisms of B12 deficiency as myelination occurs mostly in the first 2 years of

---

[24] For description of the Guthrie test, see NHS: 'Your pregnancy and baby guide: Newborn blood spot test' at https://www.nhs.uk/conditions/pregnancy-and-baby/newborn-blood-spot-test/

life, but is at its peak in the first 6 months of life". Neurological symptoms are common: infants might show "Hypotonia [low muscle tone], developmental delay, developmental regression, eye movement abnormalities, irritability, chorea, tremor and seizures" but at the same time have no unusual haematological signs (Smith & Coman, 2014).

They observe that in older children the symptoms commonly include: paraesthesia, ataxia, abnormal movements, glossitis and personality change. Abnormal pigmentation of the dorsum of the fingers, toes and in the axillae, arms and medial thighs; hypotonia, hyperreflexia and choreoathetoid movements are also found.

Evidence from other research confirms this severe impact of vitamin B12 deficiency on infants. For example, Casella et al. (2005) report a case of a 6-month-old infant (born to a strict vegetarian mother) who showed insidious developmental regression and brain atrophy but who recovered after vitamin B12 therapy. Another case report (Glaser et al., 2015) describes an infant (born to a mother suffering from undiagnosed pernicious anaemia and exclusively breast-fed) whose MRI scan showed cerebral atrophy and delayed myelination: the infant was treated with vitamin B12 and on follow-up at 8 years' old was symptom-free. A study of 40 breast-fed infants (aged around 4.5 months) suffering from vitamin B12 deficiency showed a range of consequences. These included failure to thrive (48% of children), hypotonia (40%), developmental delay (38%) and microcephaly (23%). Two-thirds of children had anaemia (megaloblastic in 28% of all children). The majority had methylmalonic aciduria, hyperhomocysteinemia and increased aminotransferases (Honzik et al., 2010). A study of neurological symptoms in infants with vitamin B12 deficiency aged about one year in Turkey showed principally hypotonia (100%), anorexia (92.8%), neurodevelopmental (85.7%), and social retardation symptoms (80.9%)(Taşkesen et al., 2011).

If untreated, the vitamin B12 deficiency will persist into later life. The condition Juvenile Pernicious Anaemia/B12 deficiency resembles PA/B12 deficiency in adults. Children with this condition suffer from the expected associated glandular disorders, particularly those most relevant to their stage of life, such as autoimmune thyroiditis, Addison's disease, or hypoparathyroidism. Some have mucocutaneous candidiasis (Hoffbrand, 2018, p. 704):

Case 5-6 Child treated and mother diagnosed

The child in the photo (born 2006) was lacking energy, becoming withdrawn and not going out to play; on testing he had low levels of serum B12 (133 ng/L compared with the normal range 350-900 ng/L), folic acid 4.9 mg/L (normal range 5-20 mg/L) and ferritin 18 mg/L (normal 25-280 mg/l). Treatment for deficiency of all three resulted in the happy child who can be observed in the photo.

A genetic link was suspected so the mother (Sallyann Phillips) was tested. Her vitamin B12 level was found to be very low at 112 ng/L, with folic acid 3.7 mg/L and ferritin 25 mg/L. She is much better now she is receiving treatment. She had previously thought tiredness was due to having her young son.

5.10 Inheriting the genes for vitamin B12 deficiency

One of the known causes of vitamin B12 deficiency is inherited genetic conditions which impair vitamin B12 metabolism. Genetic variants (polymorphisms) can influence the amount of vitamin B12 in tissues by affecting the proteins involved in vitamin B12 absorption, cellular uptake and intracellular metabolism (Surendran et al., 2018). A number of such genes have been identified. Interestingly and encouragingly, researchers also found that high doses of vitamin B12 could override these disorders: "The remarkable feature of vitamin B12 utilisation disorders has been their potential for treatment. The discovery that high-dose vitamin B12 can overcome pathway deficits in some patients has given new life to individuals with an otherwise potentially severe or fatal disease" (Froese & Gravel, 2010). These researchers have recommended screening of newborns for homocysteine and methylmalonate (markers of vitamin B12 deficiency) so that any disorders can be identified and treated before serious stages of deficiency develop.

In a study of twins by Swedish researchers, the heritability of vitamin B12 levels was found to be 59%, indicating that the genetic influence on vitamin B12 levels is high (Nilsson et al., 2009). These genetic effects are not properly understood but researchers suggest that they result from a combination of factors, including environmental influences (which include diet).

This means that if a person has these genes in their genome (DNA), then in conditions where their metabolism is stressed (for example by lack of vitamin B12 in the diet), they are more likely than others to exhibit the symptoms of, and suffer from, vitamin B12 deficiency.

Folate metabolism is known to be affected by polymorphisms of six genes in Caucasians (MTHFR, MTRR, FOLH1, CβS, RFC1, SHMT) (McKay et al., 2012). Some of the same genes (MTHFR) and others (TCbIR, BHMT, TCN2, CUBN, AMN, FUT2) affect vitamin B12 metabolism (Beech et al., 2011; Mills et al., 2012; Tanaka et al., 2009; Zittan et al., 2007). The polymorphisms may be different, or certainly have different prevalences, in Asians (Sukla & Raman, 2012).

In our Practice we encountered a number of instances in which vitamin B12 deficiency was inherited, as illustrated in the cases described below.

In our Practice, we observed that vitamin B12 deficiency seems to run in families. Our landmark case – the one that started us on our journey of discovery of the widespread effects of vitamin

B12 deficiency – is an example. Both the mother, Glenise Mason, and her daughter, Nicola Lonsdale, presented with similar symptoms.

Glenise Mason presented with recurrent anaemia and neuropsychiatric symptoms which did not respond to iron supplement. However, she had no macrocytosis or anti-IF antibodies so initially I did not think of vitamin B12 deficiency. As described in the Introduction, in 1981, after ten years of treating her, it suddenly struck me that her symptoms resembled those of the Brahmin women I had treated in India many years previously. I persuaded the laboratory to run a serum B12 test which gave a result of 185 ng/L. I then diagnosed vitamin B12 deficiency and instituted vitamin B12-replacement therapy by injection. She recovered and her anaemia cleared up.

In 1996, her daughter attended with similar symptoms and a blood B12 level of 137 ng/L. She was also treated with vitamin B12-replacement therapy and recovered.

This example illustrated **three ground-breaking discoveries**:

(1) B12 deficiency can occur without macrocytosis (previously considered a necessary symptom) but with neuropsychiatric signs and symptoms.

(2) Genetic inheritance of vitamin B12 deficiency - the transcription defect is passed down from one generation to the next: mother's B12 deficiency – 185 ng/L (low with significant signs and symptoms); daughter's B12 deficiency – 137 ng/L (low with significant signs and symptoms).

(3) Folic acid availability to the body is very dependent on the vitamin B12 status. Both mother and daughter had dietary folate intake which was considered adequate, but the folate was not available to the body without sufficient vitamin B12 (see Chart 5-1).

Case 5-8 Mother champions the case for her daughters

This is another example of predisposition to vitamin B12 deficiency being inherited. Hilda Wiffen (born 1931) came to the surgery with neuropathy in December 2005. Her vitamin B12 level at the time was 211 ng/L, and she was commenced on oral B12 tablets.

She asked the surgery to check for vitamin B12 deficiency in each of her daughters. One daughter, Brenda, was diagnosed with Multiple Sclerosis (MS) by a neurologist, and since June 2006 she was treated with immuno-suppressants. However, she did not improve, and her general condition and left-sided weakness worsened.

In the light of our knowledge of the effects of vitamin B12 deficiency and treatment (that treatment does not interfere with other medications and there is no risk in taking B12 supplements), Brenda was offered vitamin B12-replacement therapy. Her condition has since improved. This prompted her sisters to consider whether they might have vitamin B12 deficiency. They were subsequently treated and are also improving.

Subsequently, Hilda's granddaughter presented, aged 15, suspecting that she might have inherited B12 deficiency. Our provisional diagnosis, on the basis of signs and symptoms, was in fact B12 deficiency, which was later confirmed by a blood test.

Case 5-9 Inherited vitamin B12 deficiency in the Storey family

The data below show the vitamin B12 levels of several generations of the same family (ages are given after the names). The first figure shows the vitamin B12 level at diagnosis. The much higher figure is blood serum B12 during treatment. Treatment should not be stopped when the blood level is higher: this shows the treatment is working.

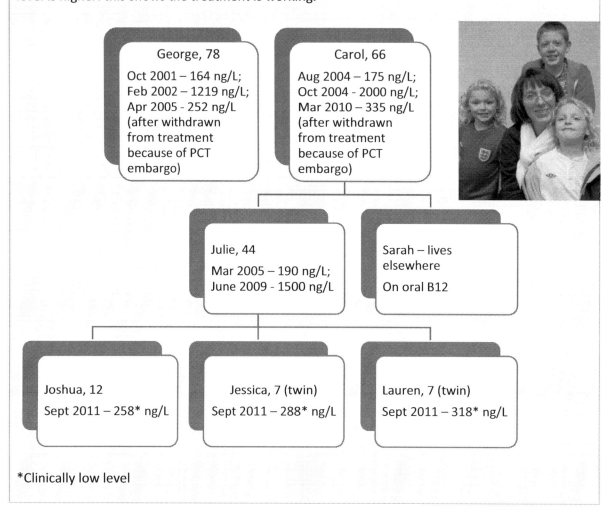

George, 78

Oct 2001 – 164 ng/L;
Feb 2002 – 1219 ng/L;
Apr 2005 - 252 ng/L
(after withdrawn
from treatment
because of PCT
embargo)

Carol, 66

Aug 2004 – 175 ng/L;
Oct 2004 - 2000 ng/L;
Mar 2010 – 335 ng/L
(after withdrawn
from treatment
because of PCT
embargo)

Julie, 44

Mar 2005 – 190 ng/L;
June 2009 - 1500 ng/L

Sarah – lives elsewhere

On oral B12

Joshua, 12

Sept 2011 – 258* ng/L

Jessica, 7 (twin)

Sept 2011 – 288* ng/L

Lauren, 7 (twin)

Sept 2011 – 318* ng/L

*Clinically low level

The figure below shows the vitamin B12 level (ng/L) of members of one family across four generations. The first number is the B12 level at diagnosis with date. The second number (following →) is the level after treatment (>200ng/L = not permitted to inject due to clinical guidelines at the time).

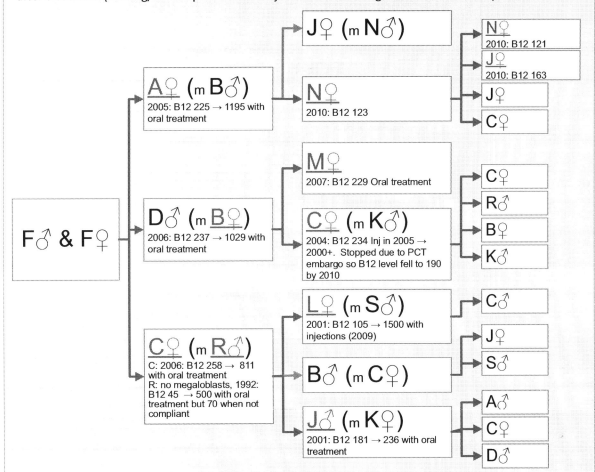

Initial <u>underlined and highlighted in red</u> indicates known B12 deficiency. All others have not been tested.

Oral = oral administration of B12; inj = administration of B12 by injection

Many young children (right-hand side) have not been tested

Upper case letters are initials of first name

Table 5-1 Supplementation with vitamin B12: current UK guidance

Doctors in the UK rely on a number of sources for guidance and for keeping their clinical practice up to date. Official sources are the National Institute for Health and Care Excellence (NICE) and NHS [online]. The British National Formulary (BNF) and BMJ "Best Practice" are important professional guides. Aside from this last (the BMJ), at January 2019 there is little information about vitamin B12 supplementation from these official sources.

VITAMIN	NICE UK	BNF	NHS	Good Medical Practice[1]
B12	NICE acknowledges that there is a significant gap, with no NICE guideline made available for vitamin B12 deficiency, but has not at the time of writing addressed it. Dr Chandy wrote to NICE (4/9/14) about the "Urgent need for a patient-safe Vitamin B12 deficiency NICE Guideline".	2006 – BNF for Children recommended vitamin B12 injections for pregnant women and toddlers with B12 deficiency. Some variation in the length of time between injections has been noted in the different official sources. However, the BNF (2019) states: "There is no justification for prescribing multiple ingredient vitamin	Yes, if mother is vegetarian then they may have some trouble with their iron and B12 levels and will need to talk to their midwife or GP. The website states, with reference to vegetarian and vegan eating well: "Vegetarian and vegan mums-to-be need to make sure they get enough iron and vitamin B12, which are mainly found in meat and fish, and vitamin D" (NHS, 2018).	If vitamin B12 deficiency is suspected (whether by signs and symptoms, or blood serum level), then begin replacement therapy. The blood serum test for B12 is known to give false negatives (say that someone is replete when they are actually deficient). For people planning pregnancy and parenthood, blood tests should direct supplementation from 3 months before pregnancy onwards. Ranges (based on our experience): Normal B12 level: 550 ng/L and above Subnormal with Signs and Symptoms < 500 ng/L < 400 ng/L < 300 ng/L < 200 ng/L

[1] BMJ Best Practice [online] is used by many healthcare professionals to update their Continuous Professional Development (CPD). We sent a detailed academic paper highlighting our recommendations, and shortly afterwards they produced a "Good Medical Practice" section on Vitamin B12 which closely agrees with our recommendations.

VITAMIN	NICE UK	BNF	NHS	Good Medical Practice[1]
		preparations containing B12 or Folic Acid."		Low - below 200 ng/L Normal Folic Acid 6-20 ng/ml Normal Ferritin >50-200 µg/L
Folic Acid	400 mcg daily from planning the pregnancy until 12 weeks' pregnant, and postnatal, if deficient.	Yes, for prevention of the occurrence of neural tube defects (NTDs). Up to 5 mg daily for women who are in the high-risk group who want to conceive.	400 mcg daily from planning the pregnancy until 12th week of pregnancy.	Screening and treatment as described.
Vitamin D	No official guidance.	No; see above statement regarding vitamin preparations.	Healthy Start Vitamins* (containing vitamins C, D and folic acid) are available free of charge to women on the Healthy Start Scheme during pregnancy and until the baby is one-year old.	Screening and treatment as described.

* "Healthy Start" drops: if the neonate needs help with vitamin supplements then they need: vitamin A 223 mcg; vitamin C 20 mg; vitamin D 7.5 mcg. We would also suggest, for a child, methyl B12 500 mcg (sublingual lozenges) daily for four weeks.

Table 5-2 Characteristics of vitamin B12 and folate (vitamin B9) deficiency

CHARACTERISTICS	VITAMIN B12 (COBALAMIN)	VITAMIN B9 (FOLATE/FOLIC ACID)
Symptoms of deficiency (basic biochemistry)	Failure to remove toxins/radicals from cell and body fluids. Impaired energy production (failure to produce NADPH – an energy carrier in metabolic pathways - and Adenosine Triphosphate (ATP), an organic chemical involved in energy transfer). Impaired DNA synthesis and lipid metabolism leading to: • Neuropathy • Autoimmune complications • Imbalance of endocrine system • Digestive impairments and related conditions • Impaired DNA transcription and replication • Megaloblastic or immature red blood cells • Failure to switch genes off or on at appropriate points in cell development	DNA transcription: the folate cycle leads to production of thymidine necessary for DNA synthesis. Folate is also needed in the conversion of homocysteine to methionine. The folate cycle can be disrupted by lack of vitamin B12. Deficiency of folate can lead to impaired cell and foetal development.
Dietary source of vitamin	Meat, fish, milk and milk products, poultry. Not available from vegetables.	Both plant and animal foods, including fruit and vegetables.
Daily requirement	For non-deficient humans: recommended dietary intake for adults is set at 2.4 mcg per day in the US; 2.5 mcg per day in the European Union; 1.5 mcg per day in the UK. Impairment of entero-hepatic recycling mechanism can lead to much greater requirements.	Adults and children over 11 years old in the UK = 200 mcg per day; 400 mcg per day in pregnancy.

CHARACTERISTICS	VITAMIN B12 (COBALAMIN)	VITAMIN B9 (FOLATE/FOLIC ACID)
Enhanced metabolic demand during pregnancy	Yes – for all body functions.	Yes – typically for neural tube development (both folate and vitamin B12 needed).
Deficiency symptoms before and during pregnancy	MOTHER: fatigue, depression, dizziness, eclampsia, bleeding, frequent miscarriages, morning sickness; could be a major cause of postnatal depression; may be associated with hair loss. FOETUS/NEWBORN: retarded development of all vital parts or vital parts missing in the newborn, e.g. kidney, ureter, vagina, uterus. Prone to NTD; encephaly; cleft lip/palate; Down syndrome; autistic spectrum disorder. Newborn with moderate to severe CNS/PNS and mild-to-moderate neuromuscular damage of the growing child.	Due to folate food fortification, moderate to severe folic acid deficiency is not often seen. Also, mandatory supplementation before pregnancy and up to 12 weeks of pregnancy minimises the possibility of folic acid deficiency causing similar damage to the mother, foetus and newborn child to the same extent as vitamin B12 deficiency.
Making it available: • Absorption • Transportation • Utilisation by the cell receptors	The absorption process of vitamin B12 is complex and delicate. Disruption at any point (whether through autoimmune attack on gastric parietal cells or other cause) results in deficiency and multisystem disease manifestations, such as neurological, neuropsychiatric, haematopoetic or polyglandular conditions (often irreversible if not treated promptly). Normally, about 2 mg cobalamin is stored in the liver and another 2 mg is stored elsewhere in the body. The steps of the absorption route are:	Folate is easily absorbed through the proximal jejunum and transported to the cell by a carrier. Normal individuals have 5-25 mg of folic acid in various body stores, half in the liver. Deficiency will occur in months if the dietary intake is curtailed. Our clinical evidence/finding is that: if there is not an adequate amount of vitamin B12 in the circulation, folic acid will not be absorbed or utilised to provide the crucial methyl donor for perfect DNA transcription.

CHARACTERISTICS	VITAMIN B12 (COBALAMIN)	VITAMIN B9 (FOLATE/FOLIC ACID)
	Saliva – transcobalamin I combines with vitamin B12 to aid subsequent absorption. Stomach – stomach acids and proteases digest whey protein around vitamin B12. True B12 (i.e. not pseudo-vitamins) bind with R-binder. Intrinsic factor (IF) is released in the stomach by the crypt cells. Duodenum – IF combines with usable vitamin B12 to aid absorption. Terminal ileum – vitamin B12 binds to receptors in the intestinal wall and is absorbed and transferred into the blood. This happens preferentially to B12 combined with IF. Blood – "active B12" (approximately 20% of total blood serum B12) is a combination of transcobalamin II (TCII) and vitamin B12. The form of the rest of vitamin B12 in blood is not understood, although cells cannot absorb non-active B12.	
Active form	There are two active forms of vitamin B12 in the cell: **Methylcobalamin:** is the cofactor in the enzyme methionine synthase (MS) which participates in the homocysteine-methionine cycle in the cytosol of cells. This cycle is crucial for the regeneration of S-adenosyl methionine (SAMe) required for lipid metabolism and methylation of DNA. MS also plays a	Folate is the name for a group of related compounds. Folic acid is the synthetic form. The active form is Tetrahydrofolate.

CHARACTERISTICS	VITAMIN B12 (COBALAMIN)	VITAMIN B9 (FOLATE/FOLIC ACID)
	key role in the metabolism of folate/folic acid which leads through a series of steps to products needed in DNA synthesis.

Adenosylcobalamin: is the cofactor in the enzyme MethylMalonylCoA mutase which works in the mitochondria of cells. It is used in the Krebs cycle for energy production.

In blood, free (not bound to TCII) vitamin B12 can combine with a number of radicals to protect the body, e.g. heavy metals, organic toxins, free radicals.

Other forms of vitamin B12, including cyanocobalamin and hydroxocobalamin, are inactive biologically and need to have the radical group changed to one of the active forms to become useful.

Cobalamin analogues (e.g. phytocobalamins) are typically inactive and cannot be converted to an active form. | |
| Biological role | Vitamin B12 is required for biochemical pathways in both the cytosol and mitochondria of cells.

The B12-dependent enzyme methionine synthase catalyses the conversion of homocysteine to methionine. At the same time, in an interlinked reaction, it converts the folate compound 5-methyl-tetrahydrofolate to tetrahydrofolate, a form needed for other reactions, leading to DNA synthesis. | Folate performs several crucial metabolic roles in the body. It is vital for cell division and DNA synthesis, regeneration of methionine from homocysteine and for accepting and donating one-carbon units for normal metabolism and regulation.

The first step in its metabolism is conversion of Tetrahydrofolate (THF) to 5,10-methylene-THF. Some of the 5,10-methylene-THF is then reduced to 5-methyl THF by the enzyme methylene tetrahydrofolate reductase |

CHARACTERISTICS	VITAMIN B12 (COBALAMIN)	VITAMIN B9 (FOLATE/FOLIC ACID)
	When this reaction is impaired, the folate cycle is deranged, leading to lack of products for DNA synthesis which affects the formation of red blood cells (causing megaloblastic haematopoiesis). Large doses of folic acid can overcome this block and produce a partial haematological remission in patients with vitamin B12 deficiency which may therefore "mask" the vitamin B12 deficiency. As a result, vitamin B12 deficiency may advance to a severe stage before it is recognised.	(MTHFR). The N5 group of 5-methyl-THF is used to donate a one-carbon group to homocysteine, thereby converting it to methionine, via the action of the B12-dependent enzyme methionine synthase. If vitamin B12 is deficient, this reaction cannot take place, even when folate levels are high. This is the "methyl-folate trap" hypothesis.

Tissue folate deficiency therefore develops which results in megaloblastic haematopoiesis. |
| | Tissue folate stores in vitamin B12 deficiency are substantially reduced despite normal or supernormal serum folate levels.

Vitamin B12 in the form of adenosylcobalamin is required for the enzyme MethylMalonylCoA mutase which is involved in catabolism of some fats and amino acids (Molloy, 2018). Deficiency of vitamin B12 impairs this reaction and may be another route leading to the neurological complications of vitamin B12 deficiency. | The methionine synthase reaction also regenerates THF required for the formation of 5,10-methylene-THF and 10-formyl-THF used directly in synthesis of thymidylate and purines, precursors of DNA.

Methionine is required for protein synthesis and, through its conversion to S-adenosyl methionine (SAMe), is a key methyl donor involved in more than 100 methyltransferase reactions with a wide variety of acceptor molecules, including methylation of DNA, RNA, proteins, and phospholipids. Methylation of DNA affects gene expression and specialisation. |
| The homocysteine connection | One chemical (and blood) characteristic of vitamin B12 deficiency is the build-up of **homocysteine because this amino acid cannot be converted to** methionine in the absence of vitamin B12. High levels of homocysteine are a risk factor for venous and arterial thrombosis. | Homocysteine elevated risk factor for arterial and venous thrombosis.

Due to folate food fortification, combined deficiencies of B12 and folic acid are not common. |

CHARACTERISTICS	VITAMIN B12 (COBALAMIN)	VITAMIN B9 (FOLATE/FOLIC ACID)
	Impairment of conversion of homocysteine to methionine may also contribute to neurological complications of vitamin B12 deficiency because it leads to reduced production of S-adenosyl methionine (SAMe) which has consequences for fatty acid synthesis and the integrity of the myelin nerve sheath.	Deficiency of vitamin B12 can lead to functional folic acid deficiency.

Table 5·3 Suggested specific vitamin B12 replacement for the pregnant mother

Vitamin B12 status of the mother	During pregnancy	Recommended treatment for the mother	Recommended treatment for the child
Non-vegetarian woman with normal blood serum B12 level.	Anticipate that blood serum vitamin B12 levels may fall, indicating that the mother is using her stores of vitamin B12 to supply the growing baby. If vitamin B12 levels decrease during pregnancy, then the mother has exhausted her stores of vitamin B12.	If vitamin B12 levels fall sharply during pregnancy, the mother should receive B12-replacement therapy during pregnancy and especially during the first three months. If vitamin B12 levels in the blood rise or remain normal during pregnancy, then this is a normal physiological state and no replacement is required (usual pregnancy supplement containing B12 is fine).	If the mother's B12 levels rise or remain normal during pregnancy, whether naturally or through vitamin B12 supplementation, then the child should be born normal and have no requirement for vitamin B12 supplementation. Providing a methyl donor[1] (B12) before and during pregnancy may permanently alter the state of methylation of the offspring's DNA, restoring normal gene expression, and development throughout life.
B12-deficient woman on normal diet who may not be diagnosed as B12 deficient.	Vitamin B12 deficiency will worsen due to high demand from the growing baby. The mother's signs and symptoms will worsen, including fatigue and low mood (tearful and depressed). We now know that this is NOT	**Symptoms** • Post-natal depression ("baby blues") • Hair loss • Extreme lethargy	Risk that the baby will be born vitamin B12 deficient – "floppy" and with neuromuscular damage. This requires urgent treatment with vitamin B12 injections – 1000µg hydroxocobalamin daily for 10 days. Review clinically and continue replacement therapy accordingly.

---

[1] A methyl donor is any substance that can transfer a methyl group (a molecular group composed of one carbon atom bonded to three hydrogen atoms — CH_3) to another substance. Methylation is important for gene expression. Vitamin B12 is an important methyl donor in the complex chain of reactions which lead to DNA methylation. The importance of B12 in proper function of DNA is discussed in Chapter 9.

Vitamin B12 status of the mother	During pregnancy	Recommended treatment for the mother	Recommended treatment for the child
	"just being pregnant", and the mother can have a happier pregnancy.	• Dizziness/fainting Vitamin B12-replacement therapy should alleviate this.	In severe cases the infant may require hospital admission for vitamin B12-replacement therapy.
Vegetarian/vegan woman with B12 deficiency; diagnosed B12-deficient woman with Signs and Symptoms. Always requires treatment, which should commence three months prior to pregnancy.	Continue the already established replacement therapy as both mother and baby require vitamin B12 (the baby for its neuromuscular development).	Continue vitamin B12-replacement therapy for the woman during nursing and afterwards.	With sufficient vitamin B12-replacement therapy for the mother, the baby is expected to be born normal and require no vitamin B12-replacement therapy. Vitamin B12-replacement therapy for the mother should ensure sufficient vitamin B12 in the mother's breast milk. If vegetarian milk (soya milk) is used as an alternative then vitamin B12 supplementation for the child will be needed.

Chapter 6 Neurological disorders – SACD/MS-like presentation

Though the mountains may fall, and the hills turn to dust,
yet the love of the Lord will stand as a shelter
for all who will call on his name.
Sing the praise and glory of God.

Could the Lord ever leave you?
Could the Lord forget his love?
Though the Mother forsake her child,
he will not abandon you.

Should you turn and forsake him,
he will gently call your name.
Should you wander away from him,
he will always take you back.

Go to him when you're weary;
he will give you eagle's wings.
You will run, never tire,
for your God will be your strength.

As he swore to your Fathers,
when the flood destroyed the land.
He will never forsake you;
he will swear you again.

Daniel L. Schutte, Society of Jesus

Figure 6-1 Key points regarding B12 deficiency and neurological disorders

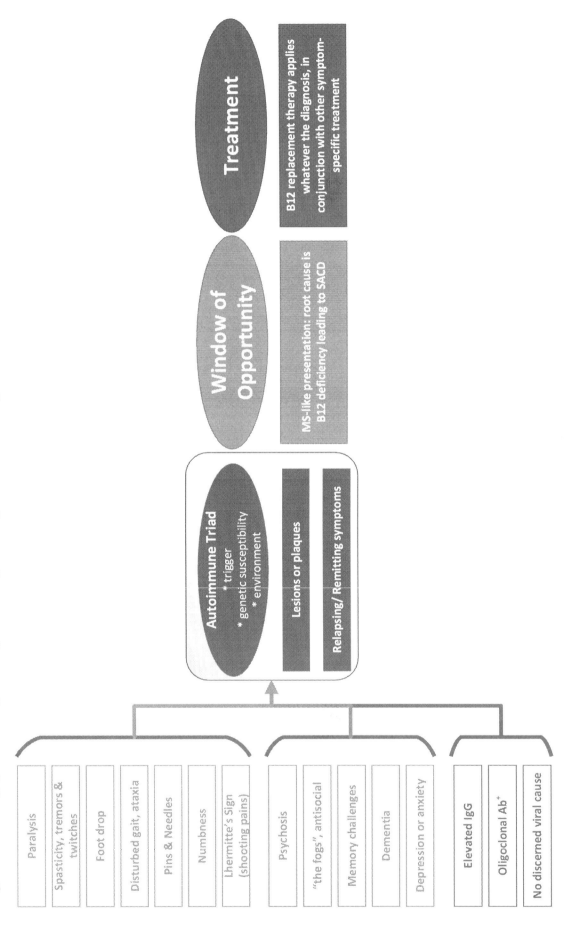

6.1   Vitamin B12 deficiency and neurological disorders

Vitamin B12 is essential for the proper functioning of the nervous system through several routes. Through the action of the B12-dependent enzyme methylmalonyl CoA mutase, it contributes to synthesis of fatty acids which are required for the integrity of the myelin[27] sheath (Scalabrino, 2001). Vitamin B12 affects every single cell, including the Schwann cell,[28] which is vital for neurological function (Nishimoto et al., 2015). Another B12-dependent enzyme, methionine synthase, is crucial for the proper functioning of the methionine cycle which leads to supply of S-adenosylmethionine (SAMe). B12 deficiency affects levels of SAMe, leading to impaired methylation reactions needed for the synthesis of proteins and neurotransmitters[29] in the Central Nervous System (CNS) (Varela-Rey et al., 2014). It has also been suggested that vitamin B12 may have other effects on the nervous system, for instance as a regulator of cytokines[30] (Scalabrino, 2001).

In our experience, neurological and neuropsychiatric signs and symptoms are the most frequently encountered presentations of vitamin B12 deficiency today. Research has shown that neurological symptoms manifest in up to 75% of B12-deficient patients (Carrazana, 2002). If untreated these symptoms may lead rapidly to the severe vitamin B12-deficiency condition known as Sub Acute Combined Degeneration of the spinal cord (SACD). This can be a devastating condition causing irreversible nerve damage and eventually death. Symptoms include debility, abnormal sensations such as tingling and numbness, mobility difficulties, mental disorders, and problems with vision, all of which gradually worsen if undiagnosed and untreated. The term "combined" is used because the condition affects the brain and the peripheral (body) nerves as well as the spinal cord.

6.2   SACD: a "forgotten" illness

SACD has been known for more than a century (see below) but today it is scarcely mentioned in medical textbooks and clinical guidelines. To our knowledge there are no guidelines – other than our own – which deal specifically with its clinical symptoms. For instance, SACD did not feature in the 16th edition of the medical textbook *Harrison's Principles of Internal Medicine* and is mentioned only in a short paragraph in the 20th edition (Hauser, 2018). Similarly, at the time of writing, there is no mention of SACD in the National Institute for Care and Excellence (NICE) Clinical Knowledge Summaries [online], one of the foremost reference authorities for clinicians. It is for this reason that we have termed vitamin B12 deficiency a "forgotten illness".

A few decades ago, SACD was a more generally recognised diagnosis than it is today. The condition is also known as Putnam-Dana Syndrome or Lichtheim's disease after early interpreters of the condition. James Jackson Putnam (1846–1918), Charles Loomis Dana (1852-1935) and Ludwig Lichtheim linked anaemia with spinal cord degeneration in the late 1880s and early 1890s (Pearce, 2008).The first complete clinical description of the condition, however, was given by the eminent neurologist James Samuel Risien Russell (1863-1939) in a paper published in *Brain* (Russell et al., 1900). At that time, much of the diagnosis had to be made from post-mortem dissection. He described plaques in the diseased brain and spinal cord, which have now become diagnostic

---

[27] Myelin is an insulating sheath around nerves which is made of protein and fatty acids. It allows electrical impulses to transmit effectively along nerve cells.

[28] Schwann cells play a crucial role in maintaining the peripheral nervous system (PNS).

[29] Neurotransmitters are chemicals used by the nervous system to transmit messages between neurons or from neurons to muscles.

[30] Cytokines are proteins released by cells that aid cell communication in immune responses.

characteristics of Multiple Sclerosis (MS) (viewed on MRI scans today). Many other early clinical studies also identified a link between vitamin B12 deficiency and severe neuropathy (Scott & Molloy, 2012). For example, in a chapter on "Vitamin B12 Neuropathy" published in 1969, Chanarin gave a detailed description of the condition (Chanarin, 1969).

6.3 SACD: difficulty of diagnosis by traditional means

Carrazana (2002) describes the effects of SACD thus: "[It...] is the classic nervous system manifestation of vitamin B12 deficiency. It affects the dorsal columns with resulting deficits of position and vibration sense, broad-based ataxic gait and, occasionally, Lhermitte's sign. Involvement of the corticospinal tracts leads to weakness, spasticity, hyperreflexia, clonus, Babinski sign and urinary/faecal incontinence".

From our own experience, and as tabulated in Table 6-2, we have encountered the following neurological symptoms in vitamin B12-deficient patients (note that this list is not exhaustive): weakness of limbs; fatigue; disturbance of gait; loss of tendon reflex; spasticity; paresthesia (unusual sensations); hypoesthesia (reduced sensation); painful spasms; sensory impairment; eyesight disorders; depression; memory loss; impaired attention; paroxysmal symptoms; slow information processing; facial weakness. In other words, neurological symptoms predominate in these patients and may, or may not, be accompanied by haematological evidence in the form of macrocytosis, anti-IF antibodies and low serum B12 levels.

Partly because of the lack of prominent guidelines, SACD is often missed as a diagnosis and its symptoms attributed mistakenly to other illnesses or even viewed as being "all in the patient's mind". In our experience it has been misdiagnosed as a variety of other conditions, such as Chronic Fatigue Syndrome (CFS), Myalgic Encephalomyelitis (ME) and particularly MS. Neurologists often fail to consider SACD as a differential diagnosis for MS whose symptoms it mimics. The similarities between the two conditions (mapped in Table 6-2) are very close but the diagnosis of SACD is frequently overlooked, we believe, because of lack of knowledge of the condition and/or over-reliance on serum B12 levels and whether macrocytosis and anti-IF antibodies are present – the classic signs of vitamin B12 deficiency (whose drawbacks as diagnostic criteria are discussed in Chapter 2). For example, in the brief mention of SACD in *Harrison's Principles of Internal Medicine*, we read: "The diagnosis is confirmed by the finding of macrocytic red blood cells, a low serum B12 concentration, and elevated serum levels of homocysteine and methylmalonic acid" (Hauser, 2018, p. 3181).

As emphasised throughout this book, we advocate a holistic approach to patient care which has proved indispensable in vitamin B12-deficiency diagnosis. It is through applying such an approach (via our Patient-Safe Protocol) that we have been able to diagnose and treat many missed cases of SACD – some of long standing – with successful results. The five cases presented here are evidence of this success.

6.4 Examples of misdiagnosis of SACD

In their case report on rapid healing of a patient with dramatic SACD, researchers Roessler and Wolff (Roessler & Wolff, 2017), noting the lack of consensus or guidelines for the diagnosis of vitamin B12 deficiency, state: "Frequently, the diagnosis of cobalamin deficiency is difficult, because anaemia or macrocytosis are frequently absent, cobalamin concentrations are mostly borderline (Lindenbaum et al., 1988), and solely psychiatric syndromes are present which are sometimes variable, unspecific, subtle, and uneven in rate (Reynolds, 2006; Wong, 2015)". Roessler and Wolff's study is of a 57-year-old man suffering from myelosis of the cervical posterior columns whose symptoms were initially thought to stem from a traumatic injury. He demonstrated neurological symptoms but no others, particularly no provable gastrointestinal, haematological or psychiatric disorders. His cobalamin (vitamin B12) serum level was normal. The diagnosis of SACD was confirmed by an elevated methylmalonic acid, and hyperhomocysteinaemia, together with the neurological evidence. The authors conclude, as we and others have also found, that "normal cobalamin serum levels do not rule out a cobalamin deficiency".

Another example of how misleading blood serum levels of vitamin B12 can be in diagnosing this condition is provided by a case report from the Department of Neurology, University Hospital Zürich (Ulrich et al., 2015). The patient was suspected to be suffering from SACD but initial tests showed nearly normal holotranscobalamin, suggesting no vitamin B12 deficiency. Further testing showed high methylmalonic acid (MMA) and plasma total homocysteine levels, indicating impaired vitamin B12-dependent metabolism. The cause of the mismatch between the blood serum vitamin B12 level and the underlying condition of vitamin B12 deficiency was found to be oral supplementation of vitamin B12 that the patient had taken for three days prior to hospital admission. His blood serum B12 level was by then almost "normal" but this would not have been enough to reverse the neurological damage.

The number of misdiagnosed or undiagnosed cases of SACD that we have encountered in our Practice leaves us in no doubt that a broader approach to diagnosis is needed as well as clear and prominent guidelines. As described in the case notes below, if a holistic approach is followed that takes into account family and dietary history, signs and symptoms, as well as blood test results, SACD can be effectively diagnosed and treated before it becomes an irreversible condition.

In saying this, we realise that we are challenging accepted medical wisdom, but as Dr Jonathan Wallis (Consultant Haematologist, the Freeman Hospital, Newcastle-upon-Tyne) said in the BBC programme *Inside Out* in answer to a question from the interviewer:

> *"I think we should all question the perceived wisdom and the norm, and a lot of medical progress has been made by people who have taken on the medical profession. So I think it is credible what Dr Chandy is doing, but you have to be careful to get it right" (Jackson, 2006).*

6.5   Misdiagnosis as MS (Multiple Sclerosis)

One of the most frequent misdiagnoses of SACD that we have encountered is its diagnosis as MS because SACD gives an MS-like presentation. As shown in Table 6-2 the parallels are so close that the two conditions are almost indistinguishable. MS, however, is given much greater publicity in medical textbooks and guidelines (a whole chapter, for example, is dedicated to it in various editions of *Harrison's Principles of Internal Medicine* (Cree & Hauser, 2018; Hauser & Goodin, 2005, 2008, 2012)) whereas SACD appears to have almost disappeared from view.

As stated above, some of our patients had been diagnosed by neurologists as suffering from MS. After we had treated one of these patients with vitamin B12 and their condition had improved, one neurologist wrote to us: "This is to confirm that the above patient was investigated several years ago in the neurology clinic for episodes of possible recurrent optic neuritis. A diagnosis of possible MS was considered but her investigations including several MR brain scans and spinal fluid analysis failed to confirm the diagnosis. Her clinical course has remained uneventful and the previous possible diagnosis of MS now seems unlikely."

In other cases the diagnosis was inconclusive, but all responded well to vitamin B12 therapy, demonstrating that SACD was the true diagnosis. Ours is not an isolated finding; Polish researchers reported two cases where SACD had been misdiagnosed as MS, explaining that: "Because of heterogeneous manifestations of MS, an incorrect diagnosis is not uncommon" (Kurkowska-Jastrzębska et al., 2006).

Others have commented on the similarities between the two conditions and a possible "significant" or "causal" relationship between them: "Multiple Sclerosis (MS) and vitamin B12 deficiency share common inflammatory and neurodegenerative pathophysiological characteristics. Due to similarities in the clinical presentations and MRI findings, the differential diagnosis between vitamin B12 deficiency and MS may be difficult. Additionally, low or decreased levels of vitamin B12 have been demonstrated in MS patients. Moreover, recent studies suggest that vitamin B12, in addition to its known role as a co-factor in myelin formation, has important immunomodulatory and neurotrophic effects. These observations raise the questions of possible causal relationship between the two disorders, and suggest further studies of the need to close monitoring of vitamin B12 levels as well as the potential requirement for supplementation of vitamin B12 alone or in combination with the immunotherapies for MS patients" (Kocer et al., 2009; Miller et al., 2005). The possibility of a causal link between B12 deficiency and MS is also discussed by Pacholok and Stuart (2011, pp. 53-80).

One researcher has suggested that the two conditions are indeed both caused by vitamin B12 deficiency but by different routes. After being diagnosed with MS, he researched the illness and experimented on himself over 10 years by injection of 4 mg (or more) of B12 in the form of adenosylcobalamin (AdoCbl). Following this research, he put forward the 'MS-AdoCbl hypothesis', which is that MS results from autoimmune attack induced by bacteria from particular agricultural crops (legumes with rhizobia class bacteria) which could enter the bloodstream through, for example, a cut. The attack targets an enzyme called adeno-syltransferase (ATR) that is needed to convert cobalamins to the bioactive form adenosylcobalamin AdoCbl. "When the concentration of ATR is reduced, production of AdoCbl is limited resulting in metabolic changes" that damage the nervous system. He found that almost all his CNS symptoms were eliminated and the improvement continued for about two days, but the MS symptoms returned if the injections were stopped. He recommends that further research be conducted on treatment of MS with AdoCbl (Boucher, 2017).

It is well known that MS is particularly difficult to diagnose. In their chapter on MS in *Harrison's Principles of Internal Medicine 20th edition*, 2018, pp. 3191-3192, Cree and Hauser write:

> **Diagnosis:** "There is no single diagnostic test for MS."

> **Differential Diagnosis:** "The possibility of an alternative diagnosis should always be considered…"

Similarly, the UK's *NHS* web site states (February 2016) in relation to MS: "Diagnosing MS is complicated because no single test can positively diagnose it. Other possible causes of your symptoms may need to be ruled out first" (NHS, 2016b).

The advice given by NICE UK is that a patient showing signs and symptoms suggestive of MS should be referred promptly to a consultant neurologist, and that "Only a consultant neurologist should make the diagnosis of MS" (NICE CKS, 2018b). NICE does recommend arranging blood tests, which includes screening for vitamin B12 deficiency but, as reported above, serum B12 levels are often misleading.

In classic treatments, there is "no cure" for MS. Symptom-relieving treatments only are given.[31] In the long term, patients are admitted to nursing homes and eventually require PEG feeding (costly nutritional drinks). If treatment is offered, it mainly consists of symptom-modifying drugs such as beta interferons (typical cost £7,000 per year) and Fincolimod (typical cost £17,640 per year) which treat the symptoms and not the cause, in combination with other drugs to treat the side-effects. The above drugs are contra-indicated in patients with immunodeficiency because of the risk of opportunistic infection, and in those with severe liver impairment.

Since there is a real possibility that the condition may in fact be SACD, at the very least doctors might try a therapeutic trial of three months of vitamin B12 injections. There is no known toxicity of vitamin B12 whereas the consequences of SACD being left untreated are devastating. Researchers into this condition in 1998 concluded that the clinical, electrophysiological, and MRI findings associated with SACD in vitamin B12 deficiency are so diverse that "vitamin B12 deficiency should be considered in the differential diagnosis of all spinal cord, peripheral nerve, and neuropsychiatric disorders" (Hemmer et al., 1998). Japanese researchers have also concluded that use of massive dose vitamin B12 as an additional therapy is warranted in MS because of the potential toxicity of the immunosuppressant drugs currently used. They treated patients with 60 mg a day of methylcobalamin for six months (Kira et al., 1994).

6.6 Comparison of symptoms: SACD and MS

By definition, MS involves scleroses in the spinal column. It takes at least two forms: relapsing/remitting or coming and going; and progressive or steadily deteriorating.

Typical presenting signs are:

- Unilateral optic neuritis, cerebellar signs, Lhermitte's sign (shooting electric shock-like pain) in arms/legs/back on flexing neck (e.g. turning head), facial palsy, epilepsy, aphasia, euphoria, dementia, depression, often accompanied by fatigue (Hauser & Goodin, 2005);

- Remissions and relapses with later progressive accumulation of disability.

A diagnosis of vitamin B12 deficiency accounts for all of the symptoms of MS just as it does for SACD. Whereas there is no treatment that improves MS (although some treatments may modify the

---

[31] New stem cell treatment has brought hope that disability can be slowed or even reversed. The treatment, called "Autologous Haematopoietic Stem Cell Transplantation (AHSTC)", is being developed at Sheffield Teaching Hospitals. Sufferers are given high-dose chemotherapy to destroy the faulty immune system. However, the MS Society warned that the treatment may not help every sufferer and it does come with chemotherapy side effects (Radowitz, 2016). Perhaps B12-replacement therapy is a better solution? Further information is available from http://www.sth.nhs.uk/news/news?action=view&newsID=787

symptoms), treatment with vitamin B12-replacement therapy appears to remit many of its symptoms (symptoms are no longer present or minimal so the patient has a normal life).

We are confident in saying this because all the patients diagnosed by us as suffering from SACD responded to vitamin B12-replacement therapy, which confirmed our original diagnosis.

In diagnosing MS, the tests required are cerebrospinal fluid (CSF) and an MRI scan. What is not considered as part of the differential diagnosis is the patient's family history in relation to vitamin B12 deficiency, their dietary history and haematinic screening e.g. FBC, vitamin B12 or folic acid level. The Protocol we have developed for diagnosing vitamin B12 deficiency (see Appendix 1) takes all these factors into account. It is on the basis of this holistic Protocol that we have been able to diagnose the patients described in the case notes here as vitamin B12 deficient and treat them accordingly.

Table 6-1 Some possible inadvertent misdiagnoses of SACD

Acute Disseminated Encephalomyelitis (ADEM)
Balo's Concentric Sclerosis
Behçet's disease
Chronic Fatigue Syndrome (CFS)
Chronic inflammatory demyelinating polyneuropathy (CIDP)
Fibromyalgia
Leukodystrophies
Lyme Disease
Myasthenia Gravis
Myalgic Encephalopathy (ME)
Neuromyelitis optica spectrum disorder (NMOSD)
Sarcoidosis
Sjögren's Syndrome
Systemic Lupus Erythematosus (SLE)

Compiled from (Godman, 2017), (Jewells et al., 2015) and (Singhal & Berger, 2012).

More than 100 disorders can mimic MS (Singhal & Berger, 2012). Given the frequency with which SACD is mistaken for MS, this implies that SACD could equally be confused with many other disorders. Above (Table 6-1) is a list of other illnesses which we believe could be caused by vitamin B12 deficiency and cured or relieved by vitamin B12 therapy. In this regard, Swedish researchers have reported favourable response to vitamin B12 injections with oral folic acid in ME and Fibromyalgia (Regland et al., 2015). *Harrison's Principles of Internal Medicine* notes that "vitamin B12 injections are used in a wide variety of diseases, often neurologic, despite normal serum B12 and folate levels and a normal blood count and in the absence of randomized, double-blind, controlled trials. These conditions include multiple sclerosis and chronic fatigue syndrome/myalgic encephomyelitis (ME)..." Unfortunately for patients, *Harrison's* attributes any benefit from these injections to "the placebo effect of a usually painless, pink injection" and states that oral vitamin B12 administration in ME has "not been beneficial, supporting the view of the effect of the injections being placebo only" (Hoffbrand, 2018, p. 707).

6.7 "Window of opportunity" for treatment

We understand a great deal about the risks of withdrawing vitamin B12-replacement therapy in relation to neuropathic symptoms because of the enforced cessation of our treatment of our patients on two separate occasions. This cessation of treatment by a Primary Care Trust (PCT), and later its successor, affected hundreds of our patients and resulted in re-emergence of the patients' previous symptoms. This was particularly noticeable for major disabilities such as those implicated in SACD. For some, their disabilities became irreversible in spite of later recommencing the former vitamin B12-replacement regime, leading us to think there may be a "window of opportunity" during which a patient's health can be restored (see cases in this chapter which demonstrate this), and after which the symptoms become irreversible. However, the timeframe for this window appears to be unique to each person and unpredictable. We cannot stress enough the importance of quick action on first diagnosis. For example, when Brenda Berry (Case 6-3) presented in June 2006 we offered vitamin B12 therapy but she asked for a referral. She was treated by a neurologist for MS for four years. Her condition nevertheless deteriorated and her blood serum B12 level dropped to 157 ng/L in July 2010. It was only then that, at her mother's recommendation, she came to us for vitamin B12 therapy. Her serum B12 rose to 544 ng/L in May 2011 after injections and she has steadily improved.

6.8 Patterns emerging from our cases

The following patterns are seen in the cases in this chapter:

- A clear sign of the likelihood of vitamin B12 deficiency is where patients have a family history of the condition. For example, in the family of Brenda Berry (Case 6-3) vitamin B12 deficiency had been diagnosed in other family members. We were able to detect deficiency in seven generations (Figure 6-2), five of which we diagnosed ourselves over several decades. We also suspected B12 deficiency in the two earlier generations because Brenda's mother recalled that her grandfather had been diagnosed with pernicious anaemia and been treated with liver extract (not something that a grandchild would likely forget!).

- Patients may have "normal" blood serum B12 levels but nevertheless be severely deficient. For example, Linda Skilton (Case 6-6) had a vitamin B12 blood level of 707 ng/L on presentation in November 2006, considered well into the normal range, but which we read as "false normal" because of her other symptoms. Questioning revealed that oral supplementation she was taking had falsified the results.

- Patients presented with multiple symptoms, which would not be consistent with a single diagnosis such as MS. These could include tiredness and sickness. Patients from the same family (Case 6-4) had different symptoms.

- Characteristic neurological symptoms include a non-symmetrical weakness, Lhermitte's Sign (shooting pain in weaker side limbs and back, often triggered by stretching the neck), sometimes symptoms manifesting on the head (outside the skull), such as nystagmus, blurred vision, depression. Two of the patients were misdiagnosed with MS (Cases 6-1, 6-5).

- The hospital will often run CT and MRI scans, and on failure to find plaques, may suggest a hysterical or mental cause of the condition and recommend no treatment.

- All patients recovered well, and some experienced dramatic improvement, on receiving vitamin B12 therapy.

6.9   Genetic link in MS

In this chapter we have shown that vitamin B12 deficiency is often mistaken for MS; and in Chapter 5 we showed that there is often family inheritance of vitamin B12 deficiency – that is, in some people it may have a genetic cause. It is therefore interesting to note that in the 1990s researchers Rothwell and Charlton interpreted the unusually high incidence of MS in Scotland (12.2 per 100,000 in the Lothian Region and 10.1 per 100,000 in the Border Region) as being of genetic origin, rather than resulting from an environmental risk factor (Rothwell & Charlton, 1998). Could it be that at least some of these cases are of inherited vitamin B12 deficiency?

Case 6-1 SACD - not stroke or MS (Chelsea Chicken)

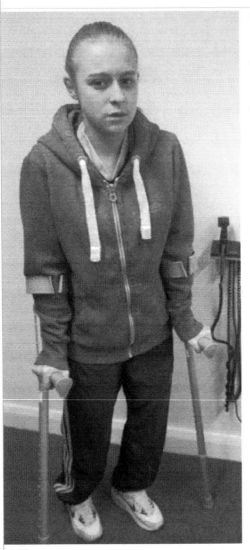

Chelsea presented aged 17 (in 2014) having attended an Urgent Care Centre (three times), a GP surgery, and Acute Hospital A&E due to falls and shooting pains, constipation and aches and pains all over her body.

The initial diagnosis by a neurologist had been stroke because the patient was wheelchair/crutches' dependent, and the scans and tests did not give the signs of MS. In consequence, the neurologist advised that the patient must have been attention-seeking, and the condition must have been all in her mind.

I knew the family well. I was shocked to see this young lady walking along the corridor with the aid of two crutches, accompanied by a relative. It was evident that she was struggling to walk, even with the crutches, and in considerable pain. We had previously diagnosed and treated her mother and other members of the family for vitamin B12 deficiency with successful outcomes.

Following detailed history-taking and thorough neurological examination, I explained our findings and the provisional clinical diagnosis I had arrived at:

1) The patient must have been suffering from undiagnosed B12 deficiency for a few years (most females in her family, including her mother, were suffering from vitamin B12 deficiency).

2) The shooting pain travelling down her left side and left leg was Lhermitte's Sign.

3) The weakness, pain, absence of reflexes etc. was more pronounced in the left side than the right (non-symmetrical). This is commonly called **single limb paralysis.**

4) If left untreated, the patient could be expected to develop Subacute Combined Degeneration (MS-like presentation).

Further blood tests were ordered to exclude other conditions and confirm this diagnosis. Loading doses of vitamin B12 were commenced immediately.

One month later, the patient had already gained weight and was able to walk without crutches part of the time. The pain was diminishing.

Case 6-2 Left oculomotor nerve paralysis

Julia Johnson presented with double vision, ptosis in the left eye, and an orbital headache (symptoms of nerve damage, either optic nerve or oculomotor nerve) in May 2009, and when tested, her plasma B12 level was 252 ng/L. We referred her to a specialist eye hospital where she spent 9 days, but was subsequently discharged with no diagnosis and no treatment (she was given an eye patch and sent home – the photo right shows the blanked-off glasses lens).

Because of her low B12 level and obvious neuropathy, we started her on injections of vitamin B12 every 2 months. This did not prove adequate, but when we increased the frequency of the injections to monthly, her sight was fully restored. She now works in SpecSavers.

Case 6-3 "Incurable with various symptoms" – Brenda Berry

This patient, Brenda Berry, aged 34 (when she presented in 2014), had a long history of anaemia and fainting, collapse and tiredness, and more recently of spastic contractions. Her family medical history (sisters, grandparents and cousins) included diagnoses of vitamin B12 deficiency and under-active thyroid.

Brenda Berry: vitamin B12 blood serum levels				
Date of Test	June 2006	July 2010	May 2011	May 2013
Blood serum B12 (ng/L)	268	157	544	375

The local acute hospital had attempted a number of diagnostic and treatment interventions, including lumbar puncture attempts (1997), and had recorded progressive loss of sensation/loss of tone and muscle weakness, although these symptoms were accompanied by non-specific pains and weakness which could have indicated an alternative diagnosis.

Although her serum B12 level, 268 ng/L in June 2006, had fallen to 210 ng/L and then 157 ng/L four years later, the neurologist did not diagnose vitamin B12 deficiency, but rather treated her with immunosuppressants because he considered her condition to be MS. Her general condition, and weakness of the left side, worsened.

We diagnosed vitamin B12 deficiency as the most likely underlying cause and commenced treatment. However, this safe replacement therapy had to be stopped on two occasions because of the PCT restrictions on administration of treatment (see the Introduction).

To us, the diagnosis had been clear as her blood serum B12 levels had dropped and symptoms not normally used to diagnose MS were reported in hospital letters making this diagnosis. However, we had a restriction on our ability to make a diagnosis of vitamin B12 deficiency.

Due to the intervention of her mother, who was aware of the family history of vitamin B12 deficiency, the diagnosis of MS was overturned. We confirmed the true diagnosis of Subacute Combined Degeneration (SACD) due to demyelination of the spinal column. Now she is on regular vitamin B12 injections and is steadily improving, and less dependent on crutches and a wheelchair.

Her mother, Mrs Hilda Wiffen, had been diagnosed as B12 deficient in December 2005 (her vitamin B12 level was 211 ng/L) and she received OC (oral) B12-replacement therapy.

See also Figure 6-2 Family history of vitamin B12 deficiency identified in seven generations, where Brenda Berry is identified in the fourth generation.

Figure 6-2 Family history of vitamin B12 deficiency identified in seven generations

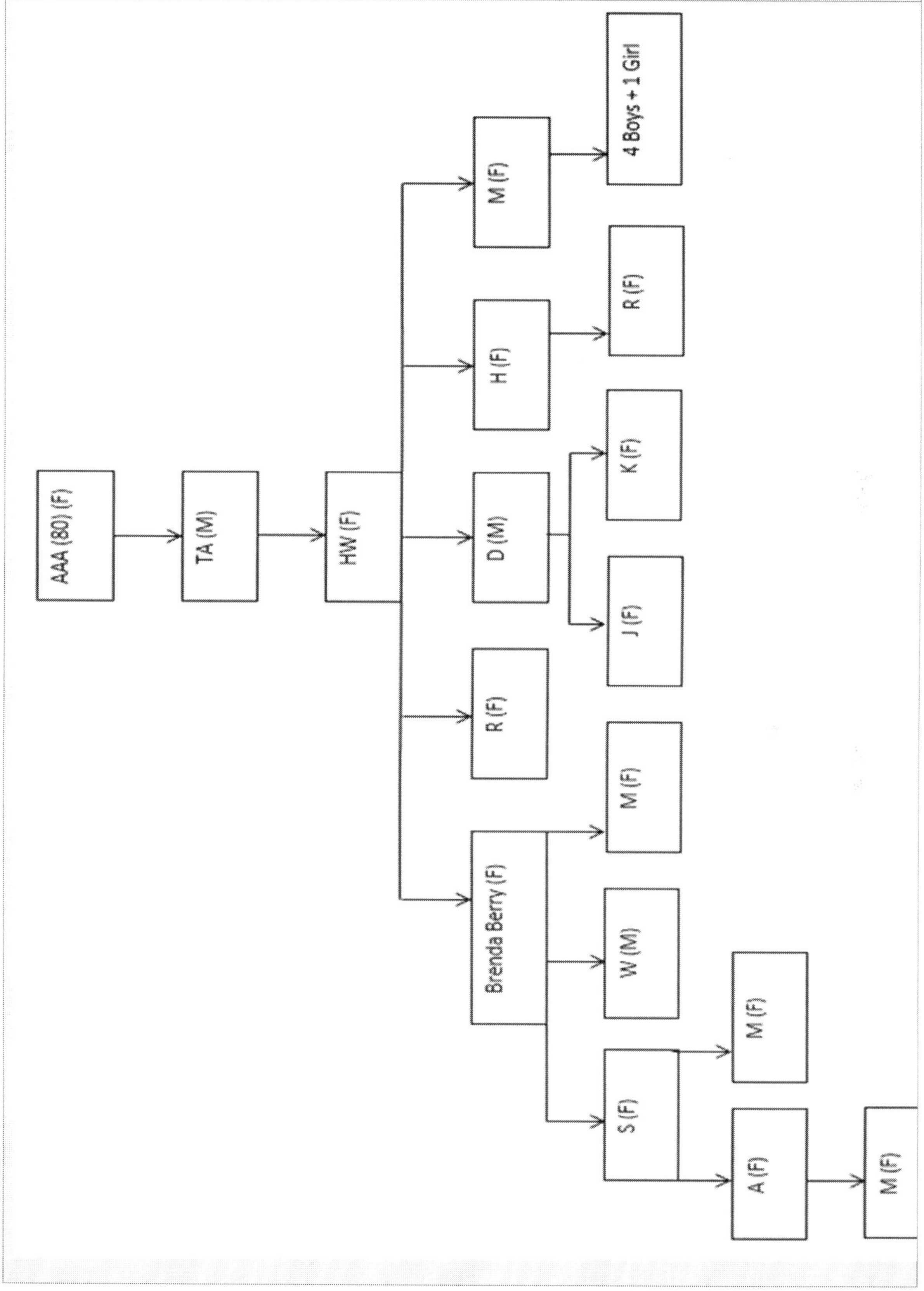

This case group concerns three members of the same family (maternal uncle, mother and daughter) who all presented with MS/SACD but with different symptoms.

Male born 1940

This patient's vitamin B12 level in May 2006 was 120 ng/L. He opted for OC ("Over the Counter") vitamin B12 tablets, which maintained the patient with minimal signs and symptoms.

In January 2011 he presented with worsening symptoms, classified as "moderate". They did not include SACD or severe neurological symptoms although his serum B12 level at that time was very low at 90 ng/L. At the patient's request, vitamin B12 injections commenced. This reduced the symptoms.

Female born 1952

This patient was diagnosed with myxoedema in 1995. In July 2004, she presented with moderate-to-severe neuropsychiatric symptoms. Her vitamin B12 level was 363 ng/L.

Because of the Easington PCT embargo on diagnosis and treatment, I refrained from treating her on this occasion.

During the five-year period (2004-9) her lower limbs became weak and she had to rely on a wheelchair. In September 2009, a diagnosis of SACD was made. She was referred to hospital. The neurologist report stated: "I note her family history of B12 deficiency although her levels have been 'normal'. On 1 May 2009 she developed sudden onset neuropathy and paralysis of her entire left leg [single limb paralysis], suspecting worsening B12 deficiency". Her vitamin B12 level was checked. **The level had dropped to 258 ng/L.** At this level, treatment was not allowed by County Durham PCT which had taken over from Easington PCT. However, I felt clinically obliged to treat her (as per GMC guidelines on Good Medical Practice).

Following the commencement of treatment, she began to improve steadily. She recovered fully from her left upper limb paralysis and was able to discard the wheelchair. At the time of writing she uses two crutches when required and most of the time does not use aids.

Female born 1987

In January 2004 at the age of 16, this patient presented with fainting attacks three to four times a month, passing out without warning for one to two minutes at a time (no fits), and shaking of head when reaching out with her hand. She had a pale yellow complexion, dizziness, pins and needles in her fingers, hair loss, depression, paralysis of her left leg below the knee and loss of sensation. She was walking with two crutches (her vitamin B12 level was 247 ng/L).

During February 2004, I clinically diagnosed her with severe vitamin B12 deficiency with neuropsychiatric signs and symptoms. Unfortunately, at that time the embargo by Easington PCT (from February 2004 to March 2005) prevented me from diagnosing or treating any new patient for vitamin B12 deficiency. However, I knew that if I missed this "window of opportunity" she

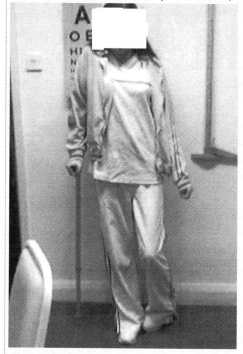

would develop SACD/lower limb paralysis and would be wheelchair-bound for the rest of her life. Therefore, in contravention of the embargo, I gave a loading dose of six injections over two weeks, followed by weekly injections. (This was recorded clearly on the patient record, along with the decision for the diagnosis and a record that we were aware of the embargo. This was supported by reference to the BNF (BNF, 2009), which gives clear instructions for loading doses followed by regular frequent injections "until no further improvement".)

The patient was able to report symptom improvement, starting with her dizziness abating and no further fainting, by 30 March 2004. In July 2004 the patient reported that power had returned to her left leg. In September 2004 she reported regaining sensation below the knee. From December 2004 to January 2005 she was able to discard first one crutch then the other.

The patient was assessed week by week. On a few occasions her regular treatment was interrupted (for example, she decided that she was well and needed no further injections; holidays; etc.) and the weakness in her left leg as well as other signs and symptoms reappeared. She again had to rely on crutches until she made the connection between vitamin B12 injections and symptoms returning, and returned to the surgery for injections.

It is widely known that if we miss the "window of opportunity" to provide treatment the first time we suspect a neurological condition, and fail to treat decisively and rigorously, the patient will end up with irreversible conditions (this is also emphasised in BMJ Best Practice (2018d)). In the case of failure to treat vitamin B12 deficiency, the condition may result in paralysis (SACD-like presentation), depression, psychosis etc. The decision to treat despite the embargo was commended by a letter from the neurologist on 25 August 2004 which read, "Coming to our mutual patient, I hope that the Vitamin B12 replacement helps her. On several discussions with her I could never detect any pressures or other reasons why this functional behaviour should have come about, but in my experience this is the case in the majority of patients. I think it is great that you have the enthusiasm to look at this in your patients."

Case 6-5 MS-like presentation - Wendy Imms

Wendy Imms, born 1972, had a family history of vitamin B12 deficiency. Her mother was diagnosed with B12 deficiency and her maternal aunt was diagnosed with both vitamin B12 deficiency and MS.

In 1995, Wendy suffered from depression and was under the care of a Community Psychiatric Nurse (CPN). In 1996 she developed menorrhagia and dysmenorrhoea.

In 1997 (aged 25) she presented with pins and needles in her hands and feet, unsteadiness, dizziness, depression, fatigue and sleepiness, heavy periods and pain. She was referred to a neurologist who reported: - "mildly disarthria, angle clonus, bilateral finger nose and heel shin ataxia, impaired sensation to pain below Rt knee ... ?demyelinating. MRI – brain plaques of demyelination. Cervical cord signal abnormality is consistent with demyelination. CSF - oligoclonal bands in CSF and not in serum."

Her vitamin B12 level was 189 ng/L. In April 1997, I commenced treatment. Five months later, in September, the neurologist reported: "She has improved considerably since I last saw her in May. There is mild limb ataxia".

In early 2002 the **PCT embargo required me to discontinue the vitamin B12 treatment.**

In late 2002 she again presented with depression and anxiety, using a wheelchair more, registered blind with optic atrophy and incontinence. Her blood serum B12 level was 340 ng/L, dropping to 158 ng/L in August 2003.

Treatment was restarted in that month. By 2006, both patient and husband were delighted with the improvement in both her mental and physical states. She was managing to get through most household chores and no longer wheelchair dependent. Her blood serum B12 had risen to 819 ng/L.

Case 6-6 When it's hard to go on - Linda Skilton

On 16 November 2006, having worked in the south of England all week, Mr Skilton returned home to spend the weekend with his wife; to his shock he found Linda in a terrible state (in the same pose as pictured in the photograph, taken at Christmas 2006). She was sitting with a cat in her lap and a note for her husband stating that she did not wish to live in this dreadful state any longer. Mr Skilton was aware that his wife had seen a number of specialists in south England. Since moving north to Easington she had seen numerous local practitioners and specialists. Until then she had not been my patient.

That evening I received a call from Mr Skilton. Although it was nearing surgery closing I agreed to see Linda straightaway. Within 30 minutes Mr Skilton brought Linda to the surgery in a

wheelchair. I could sense that Linda had almost given up on ever getting out of the wheelchair. I listened to them both intently until they finished conveying the whole story to me. I spent some time going through Linda's background history. I made the decision not to trouble her getting in and out of her wheelchair to do a physical or neurological examination. After a short pause, I said to Linda and her husband: "I know what is the matter with Linda, the true diagnosis, and I will treat her; I will get her out of that wheelchair and enable her to drive the car by herself in three months". There was a total silence for five minutes then Linda declared: "I will call you the Jesus of Peterlee".

Linda Skilton: Blood test results						
	23/11/05	27/03/06	31/08/06	16/11/06	18/01/07	25/05/07
B12 blood serum (ng/L)	524	418		707	520	2000
Folate blood serum (µg/L)	7.4	7.2		14.3	10.9	15.6
Thyroid Stimulating Hormone	4.4	6.78	2.32		4.13	1.77
Haemoglobin	13.9	13.7	13	13.9	13.7	13.6
Mean Corpuscular Volume (fL)	90.9	89.5	89.2	87.1	88.7	90.5

History of illness:

15/07/1975 Hospital A: Polymyositis/adenopathy and sarcoid myopathy affecting lungs with enlarged liver and abnormal liver function tests (LFTs). Has a poor prognosis of ultimate functional recovery.

21/11/1986 Hospital B: Total abdominal hysterectomy.

Oct 1992 Hospital C: Past history of nephrectomy.

16/09/1994 Road traffic accident: limited neck movement.

02/11/1999 Hepatitis. Raised LFTs. No cause found.

13/01/2001 Hospital B: Phlebitis right calf.

22/10/2001 Patient of another practice: excessive twitching getting worse at night and depressed.

04/02/2002 Complaining of excessive twitching all over the body and now affecting the left eye. Referred to consultant neurologist.

04/02/2002 Private referral to neurologist. Shaking getting worse: could not even hold a cup of tea; "can't live on this way". Medication prescribed by neurologist: Clonazepam 0.5 mg two tablets at night and Temazepam 10 mg one tablet at night.

13/05/2002 Previous history of sarcoidosis.

13/05/2002 Consultant neurologist private appointment: "EMG arranged. She has a neurological syndrome with invisible ocular twitching and restlessness as well as more overt myoclonic movements. Please note that three years ago she had hepatitis."

25/09/2002 History of myoclonic seizure so is taking Clonazepam.

31/02/2003 Complaining of headache, blurred vision, heartburn and pins and needles in right arm for seven weeks.

11/04/2003 Deep Vein Thrombosis. Warfarin commenced.

12/06/2003 "Please find enclosed the report on this lady's EMG which would be in keeping with sensory neuropathy."

31/12/2003 Headache, blurred vision, heart murmur and pins and needles in right arm for seven weeks. Blood pressure (BP): 180/100.

02/01/2004 TSH 4.17 (0.2 – 4.0), Free T4 13 Pmol/L (11-30).

13/02/2004 Well. All bloods normal.

26/11/2004 Shinwell Medical Practice: Letter from neurologist dated 24/11/2004: "Periodic movements during sleep and myoclonic jerks. Controlled 90% of the time on Clonazepam. She does have some slurred speech which I suspect is a side-effect of the medications. I do not think any of these symptoms represent any significant recurrence of Polymyositis".

27/03/2006-16/11/2006 Due to general deterioration in condition, patient taking vitamin B12 supplements (OC - "over the counter" or purchased by self).

16/11/2006 When requested appointment at Shinwell Medical Practice by husband: extreme fatigue, sleepy all day, experiencing dizziness, falls, blurred vision, low mood, suicidal feelings, depression, weepy, agitation, tingling in hands and feet, unexplained hair loss, headache, loss of libido, neuropathic pain (painful hips), spasm of lower limb.

Though her serum B12 level was recorded as 520 ng/L clinically I came to the conclusion from signs and symptoms that this was a false normal B12 level. (This has since been shown to be common (Carmel & Agrawal, 2012).) I diagnosed that she was suffering from subtle vitamin B12 deficiency (Babior & Bunn, 2005), and to confirm this I treated her with daily vitamin B12 injections.

Medical orthodoxy would have maintained that because of her serum B12 level she was not B12 deficient, but a holistic approach, including 45 minutes of history-taking, convinced me that she was severely B12 deficient.

On each of her visits to the surgery I noticed massive improvement in all systems of the body, especially the neuropsychiatric area. As I had promised Linda and her family, she was out of the wheelchair and able to drive to the surgery herself within 3 months of commencing treatment and her B12 level rose to 2000 ng/L without any adverse reactions. Unfortunately, this was the time (March 2007 to February 2011) when the local PCT enforced a further embargo on vitamin B12 injections to all the Practice patients. This caused untold mental and physical damage to all my patients, including Linda, who began to suffer when her B12 level dropped to 380 ng/L within 2 months of the embargo being imposed and her previous symptoms (for instance, Restless Leg Syndrome) began to re-emerge. Fortunately, the Practice has since managed to have the embargo reversed once and for all.

The photo above is from June 2007: Linda at her niece's wedding.

Clinical record for her recovery period shows:

16/11/2006 Injections commenced/three-month therapeutic trial.

16/01/2007 Feeling much better.

14/06/2007 Dramatic improvement in all areas. Says she feels like a new person; walking stick discarded; no longer uses commode.

Gemma Bates, born 1982, presented with MS-like symptoms and muscle spasm due to Lhermitte's Sign which caused her to lean to the right. She was also unable to sleep because of the pain. In July 2013 her vitamin B12 level was 194 ng/L.

Injections of vitamin B12 were commenced and within two months there was significant improvement. She was so delighted with the improvement that she asked to be photographed posing in her previous twisted posture to show the change.

Case 6-8 Glossopharyngeal nerve pathology causing persistent cough

Mr Billyards had been a delivery driver but was unable to sleep because of a cough, so he could not stay awake at the wheel. He also had difficulty swallowing. His vitamin B12 level in March 2010 was 164 ng/L. He is now receiving 1 mg vitamin B12 each month by injection which has restored his nerve function. He no longer has either the cough or swallowing difficulty. By March 2011 he was back to his previous job.

The next chapter will explore the possibility that vitamin B12 deficiency is also responsible for autoimmune conditions. In this regard we note the comment by John Snowden of Sheffield Royal Hallamshire Hospital:

> *"It is unclear what causes MS but some doctors believe it is the immune system itself that attacks the brain and spinal cord"* (Priestley & Cummings, 2016).

Table 6-2 Comparison of Multiple Sclerosis and vitamin B12 deficiency symptoms

This detailed comparison illustrates that Multiple Sclerosis (MS) is an indefinite diagnosis, whereas vitamin B12 deficiency accounts for all of the symptoms and offers a specific treatment with a strong possibility of recovery.

Clinical features	Multiple Sclerosis	Vitamin B12 deficiency causing SACD	Observations and comments
	Vitamin B12 deficiency-like signs and symptoms in MS	Subacute Combined Degeneration of the posterior and lateral spinal column: vitamin B12 deficiency paralysis	
General			
Demyelinating disorder.	Yes.	Yes.	These disorders may be caused by impaired DNA synthesis in rapidly dividing cells (red blood cells, gastrointestinal (GI), genito-urinary (GU), RS, CNS, skin) which all require vitamin B12 for maturation and are in a constant state of breakdown/repair. Vitamin B12 deficiency leads to incomplete maturation of these cells, which in red blood cells results in megaloblastosis.
Characterised by inflammation.	Yes.	Yes.	
Selective destruction of Central Nervous System (CNS).	Yes.	CNS is involved (but not necessarily).	True disease process in MS has not been proved clinically or scientifically.
Peripheral Nervous System (PNS).	Is spared in some cases.	PNS is involved.	Many, if not all, cases of MS record that the patient also suffers other systemic illnesses, particularly autoimmune conditions.
Evidence of associated systemic illness.	No. Textbook claims this is not found in clinical practice (but see Observations and comments column).	Yes – multi-system polyglandular/endocrine disease.	
Pathogenesis Physiology			
Characterised by triads of inflammation, demyelination, Gliosis (scarring).	Yes.	Yes.	

Table 6-2 Comparison of Multiple Sclerosis and vitamin B12 deficiency symptoms

Course of illness relapsing-remitting or progressive	Yes.	Insidious onset and progressing steadily. Irreversible end stage if no vitamin B12 replacement given.
Lesions or plaques visible on MRI scan of brain or spinal column: Size from 1-2 mm.	Yes.	
Myelin specific autoimmune antibodies cause demyelination and stimulate macrophages and microglia cells.	Vitamin B12 deficiency disrupts lipid metabolism which is essential for the formation of myelin sheath.	In vitamin B12 deficiency the cause of demyelination is clearly identified.
Fundamentally different pathologies in different patients. Cause/pathology unknown so far.	Vitamin B12 deficiency the main cause.	In MS is possibly due to different pathologies. However, no definite causative factor identified so far.
Total or partial axonal destruction.	Yes.	Vitamin B12 deficiency is the cause of axonal destruction.
Axonal loss is a major cause of irreversible neurologic disability.	Yes, but this is preventable by vitamin B12 therapy to ensure correct myelination of the adult and correct expression of DNA in offspring.	Reversed and restored by vitamin B12 replacement.
Conduction block occurs in the demyelination.	Yes.	Also early diagnosis/treatment of vitamin B12/folic acid deficiency prevents demyelination/conduction block.

Table 6-2 Comparison of Multiple Sclerosis and vitamin B12 deficiency symptoms

Epidemiology			
Incidence Male : Female	M : F 35% : 65%	M : F 20% : 80%	See prevalence below.
Age of onset.	20 to 40 years. Rarely under 2 years of age.	Usual onset is in adults. However, the condition can occur in children.	This is a genetic condition and we have come across children as young as five who are diagnosed with vitamin B12 deficiency.
Highest prevalence.	205 per 100,000 in the Orkney Islands, north Scotland (Rothwell & Charlton, 1998).	200 per 100,000 (0.2%) suffering from pernicious anaemia (PA) in Scotland.	Prevalence in Shinwell Medical Practice, in 2015, out of a Practice population of 5,760, approximately 1,060 patients observed to have vitamin B12 deficiency with neuropsychiatric symptoms. This equals 18% of the Shinwell Medical Practice population.
Higher prevalence.	North European Caucasian population, northern US and Canada.	High prevalence in these same areas amongst similar population. Some prevalence in India due to vegetarian diet.	
Low prevalence.	Japan, Asia, Equatorial Africa and Middle East. Japan: 2 per 100,000; fish diet may be preventative.	Similar low prevalence within these same areas.	
Immunology			
Autoimmune cause.	Yes.	Yes.	
Cerebrospinal fluid (CSF).	Elevated CSF immunoglobulins (IgG), oligoclonal antibody present.	Raised protein (IgG) immunoglobulins.	Oligoclonal immunoglobulins (IgG) are also detected in other inflammatory conditions, including infections, and thus not specific to MS or vitamin B12 deficiency. Oligoclonal bands seen on spectrometry.
Subclinical disease			
MRI has demonstrated bursts of disease activity 7 to 10 times more frequently than is clinically apparent.	There is a large reservoir of subclinical disease activity in MS, especially during the early stages of the disease.	There is clear evidence of a large number of patients in subclinical state of vitamin B12 deficiency (due to insidious onset). Also, a group of patients whose serum B12 level is 300-500 ng/L but whose tissue level of B12 is low.	The triggers causing these bursts are unknown in MS. Vitamin B12 deficiency also causes myelin destruction of CNS.

Table 6-2 Comparison of Multiple Sclerosis and vitamin B12 deficiency symptoms

		Both these groups respond to empirical treatment with vitamin B12 supplementation.	Demyelination of both CNS and PNS.
Viral-induced demyelinating disease.	No clear proof to implicate viral infection.	Demyelination solely due to vitamin B12 deficiency.	
Microbiology			
			Similar onset and progression of the disease.
Clinical manifestations			
Onset.	Abrupt or insidious.	Abrupt or insidious.	
Severity of symptoms.	May be severe, or seem so trivial that the patient may not seek medical attention for months or years.	Similar.	
Asymptomatic cases.	Yes.	Yes.	
Symptoms extremely varied.	Yes.	Yes.	
Signs and symptoms			
Weakness of limbs.	Weakness of limbs, fatigue, disturbance of gait.	Yes.	As a result of posterior and lateral column involvement of the spinal cord due to Subacute Combined Degeneration of the spinal cord (SACD), which develops as a result of vitamin B12 deficiency.
	Upper motor neurone type, weakness of limbs, spasticity, hyper-reflexa, Babinski reflex positive.	Yes.	
	Tendon reflex lost (simulating lower motor neuron lesion – spinal cord involvement).	Yes.	
Spasticity.	30% of MS patients have moderate to severe spasticity, especially in the legs. Painful spasms.	Yes.	Eventually progresses to Subacute Combined Degeneration presentation (SACD).

Table 6-2 Comparison of Multiple Sclerosis and vitamin B12 deficiency symptoms

Symptom	Description		Similarity
Optic neuritis and monocular pallor of the optic disc.	Diminished visual acuity. Decreased colour perception. Progress towards severe visual loss, usually mono-ocular.	Yes.	
Peri-orbital pain.	Peri-orbital pain often precedes or accompanies the visual loss.	Yes.	
Visual Blurring. Diploplia. Nystagmus.	This may result from internuclear opthalmoplegia (INO) or palsy, via the oculomotor cranial nerve (CNIII) or optic nerve (CNII).	Yes.	
Sensory symptoms			
Paresthesias.	Tingling, prickling, pins and needles, painful, burning.	Yes.	Strong similarity.
Hypoesthesia.	Reduced sensation, numbness or a dead feeling.	Yes.	
Unpleasant sensation.	Feeling that body parts are swollen, wet, raw or tightly wrapped.	Yes.	Similar onset and progression of the disease.
Sensory impairment of the trunk and legs below horizontal line.	Indicator - spinal cord is the origin of the sensory disturbance. Often accompanied by a band-like sensation of tightness around torso.	Yes.	
Pain.	Pain is a common symptom of MS experienced by >50% of patients. Pain can occur anywhere in the body.	Yes.	

Table 6-2 Comparison of Multiple Sclerosis and vitamin B12 deficiency symptoms

Ataxia.	Manifests as ataxia. May involve head, trunk and cerebellar dysarthria (scanning speech).	Yes.	Eventually progresses to Subacute Combined Degeneration (SACD) presentation due to B12 deficiency.
Bladder and bowel dysfunction.	90% of MS patients suffer from bladder dysfunction.	Yes.	
Constipation.	Occurs in >30% of patients. Bowel continence 15%.	Yes.	
Cognitive dysfunction.	Memory loss; impaired attention; difficulties in problem solving. Slowed information processing; euphoria (elevated mood).	Yes.	
Depression.	Experienced by 50-60% of patients. Can be reactive or endogenous. Can contribute to fatigue.	Yes.	SACD/MS-like presentation due to vitamin B12 deficiency.
Fatigue.	Experienced by 90% of patients. Moderate to severe. Generalised motor weakness; limited ability to concentrate; extreme loss of energy; an overwhelming sense of exhaustion that requires patient to rest or fall asleep. Fatigue maximum during mid-afternoon. Exacerbated by elevated temperatures, by depression and by effort to accomplish basic tasks.	Yes.	

Table 6-2 Comparison of Multiple Sclerosis and vitamin B12 deficiency symptoms

	Is common in MS.	
Sexual dysfunction/loss of libido.	Yes.	
Facial weakness.	Due to a lesion in the intraparenchymal pathway of the seventh cranial nerve, may resemble idiopathic Bell's Palsy.	Yes.
Vertigo.	Appears suddenly and resembles acute labyrinthitis.	Yes.
Heat sensitivity symptom.	Hot shower may cause transient blurring.	Yes.
Paroxysmal symptoms.	Electric shock-like sensation includes: Lhermitte's Sign; tonic contractions of a limb, face or trunk (tonic seizures); paroxysmal dysarthria; ataxia; paroxysmal sensory disturbance.	Yes.
Trigeminal neuralgia (hemifacial spasm; glossopharyngeal neuralgia).	Occurs when demyelinating lesions involve root entry or exit zone of 5th, 7th and 9th cranial nerves (CN V, VII and IX).	Yes.
Facial myokymia.	Persistent rapid flickering contractions of the facial musculature (orbicularis oculi).	Yes.

Table 6-2 Comparison of Multiple Sclerosis and vitamin B12 deficiency symptoms

		Diagnosis	
Five diagnostic criteria to be fulfilled for definite MS (see *Harrison's Principles of Internal Medicine*, 16th, 17th and 18th edns): 1.Relapsing/remitting MS 2. Secondary progressive 3.Primary progressive 4. Progressive/relapsing 5. The patient's neurological condition could not be better attributed to another disease.	There are no definitive tests, symptoms or signs. MRI, spectrometry. No single clinical sign or test is diagnostic of MS. Possibility of an alternative diagnosis should always be considered, especially when clinical course is progressive from the outset. Uncommon or rare symptoms in MS (aphasia, Parkinsonism, chorea, isolated dementia, severe muscular atrophy, peripheral neuropathy, episodic loss of consciousness, fever, headache, seizures, coma) should increase concern about alternative diagnosis.	A definite diagnosis of vitamin B12 deficiency can be reached using our Protocol – see Appendix 1. Vitamin B12 deficiency with neuropsychiatric symptoms is diagnosed and where patient shows positive response to empirical treatment with vitamin B12, the diagnosis of vitamin B12 deficiency is confirmed. Improvement following three-month therapeutic trial reconfirms original diagnosis of SACD/vitamin B12 deficiency. Vitamin B12 deficiency (most common demyelinating condition in which we see these uncommon signs and symptoms).	Signs and symptoms severe; low/subnormal B12 level; strong family history of vitamin B12 deficiency or symptoms associated with vitamin B12 deficiency. SACD diagnosis due to vitamin B12 deficiency. MS-like presentation, not MS. *Harrison's Principles of Internal Medicine* (18th edition (Hauser & Goodin, 2012)) states that another condition must be considered first before a diagnosis of MS can be made. Page 3402 lists 'Disorders that can mimic MS' which include vitamin B12 deficiency.
		Prognosis	
Prognosis	Most patients with MS experience progressive neurologic disability.	Neurological disability can be totally reversed if vitamin B12 deficiency is diagnosed early and treated promptly and the correct diagnosis of SACD not missed.	**Withholding or delaying treatment can result in irreversible neurological symptoms.**

Table 6-2 Comparison of Multiple Sclerosis and vitamin B12 deficiency symptoms

	Disease Process	
	MS disease process may have two separate phases: Inflammatory (demyelination resulting in attacks); Neurodegeneration (gradual loss of axons underlines progressive MS).	Similar process in vitamin B12 deficiency: demyelination followed by axonal deaths.	Totally preventable by early diagnosis and vitamin B12-replacement therapy. SACD presentation due to vitamin B12 deficiency.
Treatment		
Treatment	No satisfactory treatment available for MS. Treatment that promotes remyelination or neural repair does not currently exist. Symptom-modifying treatments include: Fingolimod 0.5mg daily: cost = £1,470 for 28 days = £17,640 a year. B-interferon injection: cost = £7,000 for a year. Copaxone injection: cost = £18.36 per injection.	Satisfactory vitamin B12-replacement therapy with no side-effects is available which provides full and total recovery. Prompt initiation of vitamin B12-replacement therapy leads to remyelination and neural repair and prevents irreversible damage. Plaque formation (characteristic of MS) is also reversed. Vitamin B12-replacement therapy costs £1.10 per injection, loading dose 6 injections alternate days, followed by one injection every 28 days = £20.90 a year.	Vitamin B12 deficiency may occur with autoimmune polyendocrine syndrome (APS) Type II or III. Therefore, exclude all other possible co-existing conditions: primary/secondary adrenal insufficiency; underactive thyroid; vitamin D deficiency; low ferritin. also exclude gout. WHAT ARE WE WAITING FOR?

Source: Multiple Sclerosis symptoms from Hauser and Goodin (2012). SACD symptoms as observed in our patients at the Shinwell Medical Practice.

Chapter 7   Autoimmune glandular disorders, with special reference to APS and hypoadrenalism (Addison's disease)

I watch the sunrise
lighting the sky
casting its shadows near.
And on this morning
bright though it be
I feel those shadows near me.

But you are always close to me
following all my ways.
May I be always close to you
following all your ways, Lord.

I watch the sunlight
shine through the clouds,
warming the earth below.
And at the mid-day, life seems to say:
'I feel your brightness near me.'

For you are always...

I watch the sunset
fading away,
lighting the clouds with sleep.
And as the evening closes its eyes
I feel your presence near me.

For you are always...

I watch the moonlight
guarding the night,
waiting till morning comes.
the air is silent, earth is at rest
only your peace is near me.

John Glynn

Figure 7-1 Visual Reference Diagram: Vitamin B12 and the endocrine glands

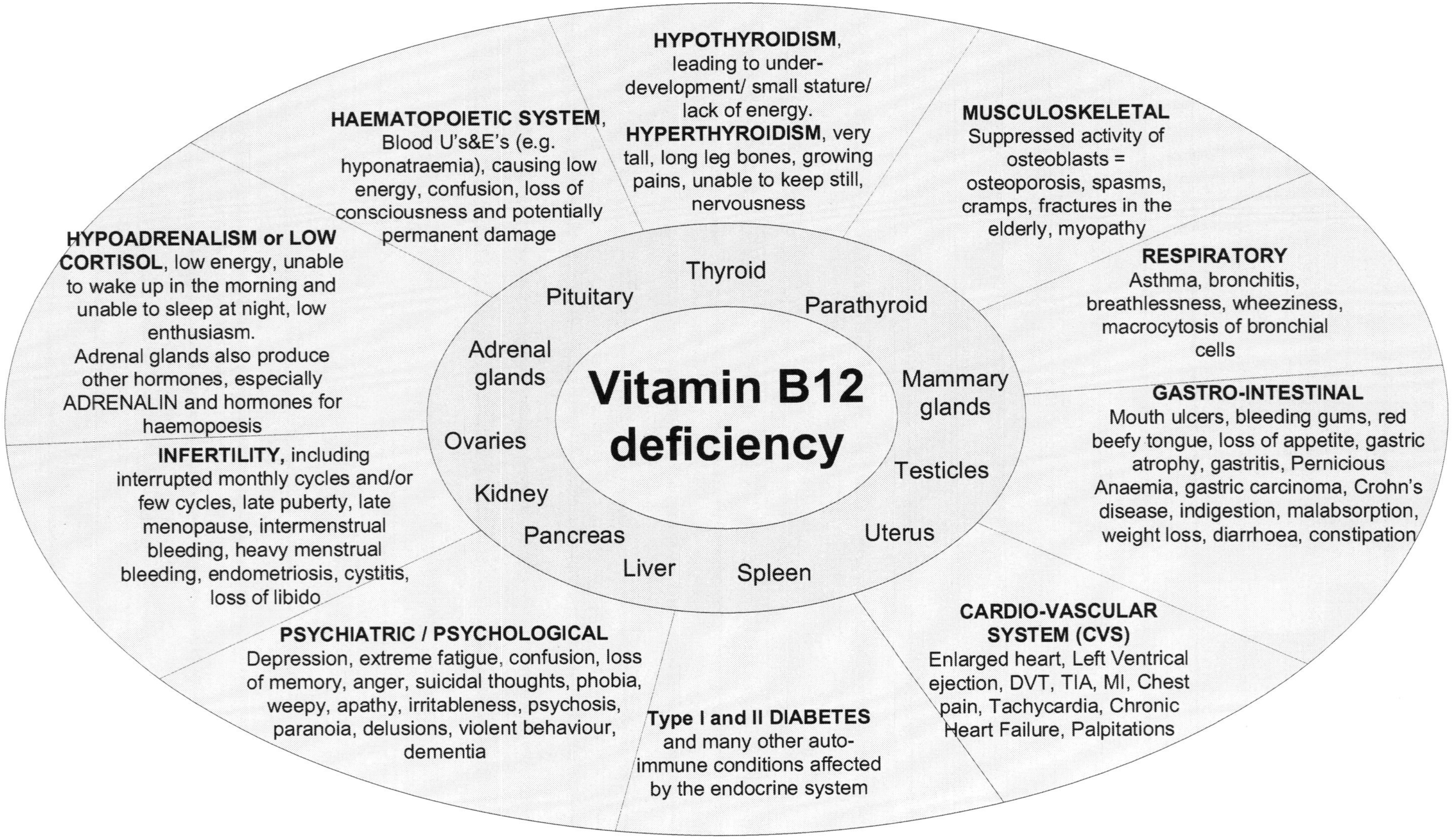

Vitamin B12 deficiency

Inner ring glands: Pituitary, Thyroid, Parathyroid, Mammary glands, Testicles, Uterus, Spleen, Liver, Pancreas, Kidney, Ovaries, Adrenal glands

MUSCULOSKELETAL
Suppressed activity of osteoblasts = osteoporosis, spasms, cramps, fractures in the elderly, myopathy

RESPIRATORY
Asthma, bronchitis, breathlessness, wheeziness, macrocytosis of bronchial cells

GASTRO-INTESTINAL
Mouth ulcers, bleeding gums, red beefy tongue, loss of appetite, gastric atrophy, gastritis, Pernicious Anaemia, gastric carcinoma, Crohn's disease, indigestion, malabsorption, weight loss, diarrhoea, constipation

CARDIO-VASCULAR SYSTEM (CVS)
Enlarged heart, Left Ventrical ejection, DVT, TIA, MI, Chest pain, Tachycardia, Chronic Heart Failure, Palpitations

Type I and II DIABETES and many other auto-immune conditions affected by the endocrine system

PSYCHIATRIC / PSYCHOLOGICAL
Depression, extreme fatigue, confusion, loss of memory, anger, suicidal thoughts, phobia, weepy, apathy, irritableness, psychosis, paranoia, delusions, violent behaviour, dementia

INFERTILITY, including interrupted monthly cycles and/or few cycles, late puberty, late menopause, intermenstrual bleeding, heavy menstrual bleeding, endometriosis, cystitis, loss of libido

HYPOADRENALISM or LOW CORTISOL, low energy, unable to wake up in the morning and unable to sleep at night, low enthusiasm.
Adrenal glands also produce other hormones, especially ADRENALIN and hormones for haemopoesis

HAEMATOPOIETIC SYSTEM, Blood U's&E's (e.g. hyponatraemia), causing low energy, confusion, loss of consciousness and potentially permanent damage

HYPOTHYROIDISM, leading to under-development/ small stature/ lack of energy.
HYPERTHYROIDISM, very tall, long leg bones, growing pains, unable to keep still, nervousness

Chapter 7 Autoimmune glandular disorders, with special reference to APS and hypoadrenalism (Addison's disease)

SECTION 1 Autoimmune glandular disorders and vitamin B12 deficiency

In treating vitamin B12-deficient patients over many years we noticed that a significant number of them also suffered from autoimmune glandular disorders. Prominent among these illnesses were the life-threatening condition of hypoadrenalism[32] (under-active adrenal glands) and hypothyroidism (under-active thyroid gland). These patients also had other autoimmune glandular conditions such as diabetes, vitiligo, premature ovarian failure, hyper/hypo parathyroidism and others.

For instance, in 2015, in a total of 1,036 vitamin B12-deficient patients in our Practice, 366 had hypothyroidism (Chandy, 2015). We also had 15 patients with hypoadrenalism (Table 7-1), out of a total Practice population of 5,760 (a much higher incidence of hypoadrenalism than the figure given in *Harrison's Principles of Internal Medicine* of 5 patients in 10,000 in the general population (Arlt, 2012; 2018, p. 2733)). Fourteen of these also had vitamin B12 deficiency and nine had severe hypothyroidism.

Table 7-1 Prevalence of vitamin B12 deficiency and myxoedema among patients with hypoadrenalism, 1981-2015				
Name (some names withheld to preserve anonymity)	**Sex**	**Hypoadrenalism**	**Myxoedema (severe hypothyroidism)**	**B12 deficient**
Angela Abraham	Female	Yes	No	Yes
Patient A	Female	Yes	Yes	Yes
Patient B	Female	Yes	No	Yes
Leanne Walker (née Chandy)	Female	Yes	No	Yes
Lisa Henderson	Female	Yes	Yes	Yes
Joan Richardson	Female	Yes	Yes	Yes
Patient C	Female	Yes	Yes	Yes
Patient D	Male	Yes	No	Yes
Donna Lawton	Female	Yes	Yes	Yes
Patient E	Male	Yes	No	Yes
Donna Kennedy	Female	Yes	Yes	Yes
Patient F	Male	Yes	Yes	Yes
Patient G	Male	Yes	Yes	No
Patient H	Female	Yes	Yes	Yes
Patient I	Female	Yes	No	Yes
Total ratio		**15/15**	**9/15**	**14/15**

Note: Shinwell Medical Practice Population (SMP) = 5,760 patients

Total number of patients on levothyroxine (for underactive thyroid): 366 (Male: 82; female: 284). Prevalence of hypoadrenalism in the SMP – 15 patients out of 5,760 (much higher incidence than the figure given in *Harrison's Principles of Internal Medicine* of 5 patients in 10,000 in the general population (Arlt, 2018).

Of those with hypoadrenalism, 9/15 also have severe hypothyroidism ($\chi^2=1500$, df=1, p=0.00) and 14/15 also have diagnosed B12 deficiency ($\chi^2=58$, df=1, p=0.00), showing a strong correlation.

---

[32] Hypoadrenalism is also known as adrenal insufficiency or Addison's disease (after Thomas Addison who gave the first clinical description of the condition in 1855).

Glands produce hormones which are essential for regulation of all body activities. Groups of glandular disorders occurring together can produce devastating effects and a host of diverse symptoms which vary from patient to patient.

7.1   Vitamin B12 deficiency – an underlying cause?

We observed that, if untreated, these conditions became progressive (moved from one gland to another) which suggested to us that there was an underlying cause which was likely to be vitamin B12 deficiency. To our knowledge we are the first to suggest this, although many researchers have noted the frequent occurrence of autoimmune glandular disorders, and other autoimmune conditions, in B12-deficient patients. For instance, autoimmune hypothyroidism has been found to be prevalent in patients with vitamin B12 deficiency (Issac et al., 2015; Morel et al., 2009; Ness-Abramof et al., 2006).

Our hypothesis that vitamin B12 deficiency was implicated in these glandular disorders was vindicated because our patients recovered well when treated with vitamin B12 alongside the relevant hormone replacement *without the need for an elaborate complex of drugs*. The results were dramatic and patients' symptoms improved much more sharply than with hormone-replacement therapy alone. Although our patients would mostly need to remain on this combined treatment for life, the vitamin B12 appeared to effect some glandular repair; the disease progression was stopped and the patients' quality of life greatly improved.

7.2   Need to screen for autoimmune glandular conditions in B12-deficient patients

In view of the above, this chapter aims (in Section 1) to alert clinicians to the importance of screening for autoimmune glandular disorders in vitamin B12-deficient patients. Its second aim, in Section 2, is to share expertise in the diagnosis and treatment of hypoadrenalism in particular. This is a serious illness which frequently co-occurs with vitamin B12 deficiency but is easy for the clinician to miss as its symptoms, such as dizziness, leg pain, blurred vision and breathlessness, may be unspecific. Many patients with hypoadrenalism are still today not diagnosed until an emergency arises (Leelarathna et al., 2009). Because of the co-occurrence of hypoadrenalism with vitamin B12 deficiency, we developed some expertise in its diagnosis. Unfortunately, we found the current clinical guidelines inadequate for diagnosing and treating this condition, so we developed our own (given in full in Appendix 2 at the end of this book). We hope that by sharing this knowledge we will contribute to ensuring prompt diagnosis of patients with this condition.

The last part of the chapter, Section 3, gives a brief overview of the relationship of vitamin B12 deficiency to other autoimmune glandular disorders.

7.3   Autoimmune Polyglandular Syndrome

The condition described above in which a person suffers from multiple autoimmune glandular disorders at the same time is called Autoimmune Polyglandular Syndrome (APS).[33] It was classified in the 1980s into Types I, II, III and IV according to the pattern of glands involved (see Box 7-1) (Neufeld & Blizzard, 1980; Neufeld et al., 1980; Tincani et al., 2008). Since then, further discoveries have widened the classification.

---

[33] APS is also known as Polyglandular Autoimmune Syndromes or Polyendocrine Autoimmune Syndromes: not to be confused with anti-phospholid syndrome which has the same acronym.

Box 7-1 Types of APS

APS TYPE I is very rare. It is an inherited disorder (involving mutation of the AIRE gene) with prevalence ranging between 1 in 9,000 in susceptible communities to 1 in 80,000 (Betterle et al., 2002). It has three main component diseases: chronic candidiasis (affecting the skin, nails, tongue, mucous membranes); chronic hypoparathyroidism (affecting calcium and phosphorus levels – leading to muscle cramps, spasms and seizures), and **autoimmune Addison's disease (described in detail below).**

APS TYPE II (also known as Schmidt's Syndrome) combines autoimmune Addison's disease with autoimmune thyroid disease (Hashimoto's thyroiditis). It can also include a range of other autoimmune disorders, such as Type I diabetes mellitus, hypoparathyroidism, vitiligo, PA/vitamin B12 deficiency and gonadal failure.

APS TYPE III groups thyroid autoimmune diseases and other autoimmune diseases (but excludes autoimmune Addison's disease, hypoparathyroidism and chronic candidiasis). It can be associated with diabetes mellitus, PA/vitamin B12 deficiency, vitiligo, alopecia, hypogonadism, myasthenia gravis and rheumatoid arthritis, among others.

APS TYPE IV covers other associations of autoimmune conditions, such as Addison's disease with hypogonadism, PA/vitamin B12 deficiency, vitiligo, alopecia, hypophysitis, but excludes chronic candidiasis, hypoparathyroidism, thyroid autoimmune diseases and type 1 diabetes mellitus.

Often, at least three glands are affected but researchers have counted up to 150 different autoimmune illnesses in patients suffering from this condition (Betterle et al., 2002, p. 338). These include, as mentioned above, hypoadrenalism and hypothyroidism but also diabetes mellitus, myasthenia gravis (weakness and muscular fatigue), coeliac disease (inflammation of the small intestine), hypo/hypergonadism (disorder of sex hormones), alopecia, pernicious anaemia, vitiligo (absence of skin pigment), autoimmune chronic active hepatitis, lymphocytic hypophysitis (autoimmune disease of the pituitary gland) and many others.

APS is considered to be a rare condition, but our experience suggests that APS Types II and III are more common than generally thought. This may be because autoimmune glandular disorders are often treated by the medical profession as isolated conditions, independent of one another, so APS is not being diagnosed and therefore an underlying cause (such as vitamin B12 deficiency) is not being sought. In a Practice population of 5,760 patients we had nine patients suffering from autoimmune hypoadrenalism with autoimmune thyroid disease (Table 7-1), therefore fulfilling the criteria for APS Type II. Eight of these were also vitamin B12 deficient. We also had patients suffering from APS Type III, with combinations of disorders including, for example, underactive thyroid and alopecia. Several cases in this chapter (Cases 7-1, 7-3, 7-5, 7-6, 7-7) are examples of patients suffering from a combination of autoimmune conditions with vitamin B12 deficiency.

Figure 7-2 Autoimmune progressive damage

```
  ┌─────────────────┐                        ┌──────────────────┐
  │Gastric parietal cell│                     │  IF Ab+ve or Ab-ve │
  │   Ab+ve or Ab-ve  │                       └──────────────────┘
  └─────────────────┘
                          ╱──────────────╲
                          │      APS       │
                          ╲──────────────╱
```

Pancreas	Thalamus/ Hypothalamus/ Parathyroid/ Thyroid	Pituitary / Adrenal glands	Ovary
Type I or Type II diabetes	Hyper/hypo thyroidism	Hypoadrenalism / Addisons	PCOS or Primary Ovarian Failure

Graphic by Hugo Minney

7.4 Treatment of APS and importance of early detection

The standard approach to treating glandular disorders is to treat each disorder separately. In our experience, misdiagnosis is common. Patients may be inadvertently misdiagnosed as suffering from Myalgic Encephalopathy (ME), Chronic Fatigue Syndrome (CFS), fibromyalgia (FM), depression or even Multiple Sclerosis (MS) (which cannot be treated: the medications only alleviate symptoms), when the correct diagnosis should be vitamin B12 deficiency/APS (hypoadrenalism), which can be treated and cured.

Case 7-1 Vitamin B12 deficiency with two autoimmune conditions

Tracey Baldam (born 1969) initially presented with many of the signs and symptoms of vitamin B12 deficiency 15 years earlier – the blood test showed that she had both vitamin B12 deficiency and underactive thyroid. A few years ago she stopped treatments for both conditions herself. Shortly afterwards she presented with classic rheumatoid arthritis symptoms: swollen painful joints. She did not make the connection between stopping the treatment and the pain. Diagnosis of rheumatoid arthritis was made by hospital consultants who commenced her on methotrexate.

As she was still in a lot of pain with swollen joints, she presented to our surgery. We suggested she should go back on vitamin B12 injections and thyroxine. Within three months (by August

2011) she had totally recovered and herself stopped the methotrexate (an immune-system suppressant).

Many patients with depressed (or hypo-) function in one gland have evidence of other endocrine gland dysfunction; therefore it is important for the clinician to be alert to the possibility of combinations of conditions. Where the doctor does recognise a progression of autoimmune glandular disorders, classical medicine concludes that the progression cannot be stopped and fails to see that simple treatment can resolve or alleviate these conditions. Alongside the standard treatments, we would recommend vitamin B12 therapy which, in our experience, appears to help to correct dysfunction of the HPA Axis (see Figure 7-3 below). As with many conditions, early detection and prompt effective action can prevent irreversible end-stage crisis presentation.

7.5   Vitamin B12 – the link with autoimmunity

Autoimmune disorders result from the body's immune system mistakenly attacking its own cells instead of invading pathogens. The incidence of autoimmune disease worldwide is increasing, especially in developed countries, and is estimated to affect 3% or more of the world population (Bolon, 2012). Autoimmunity can occur in any body system or tissue and dozens of different conditions have been identified.

How may vitamin B12 deficiency be linked to autoimmunity? There is evidence that vitamin B12 may play a general role in preventing autoimmune attack. Researchers have shown that vitamin B12 strengthens the body's immune systems. A Japanese team, for example, found that vitamin B12 injections increased the number of CD8[+] T cells that fight infection: "We conclude that vitamin B12 acts as an immunomodulatory for cellular immunity" (Tamura et al., 1999). In this connection it can be noted that CD8+ T-cell deficiency is a feature of many chronic autoimmune diseases (Pender, 2012). Others have found that vitamin B12 "has important immunomodulatory effects on cellular immunity, and abnormalities in the immune system in pernicious anaemia are restored by B12 replacement therapy" (Erkurt et al., 2008). An example from our own Practice of a patient suffering from these effects is given in Case 7-2.

Case 7-2 Common immunodeficiency

Douglas Stephenson presented in 2007 (aged 37) with recurrent infections and bronchiectasis. On referral, the hospital diagnosed immunodeficiency and commenced immunoglobulin treatment.

In May 2013, we identified low blood serum B12 of 140 ng/L, and commenced treatment. By July 2013 he reported to the immunology clinic that he was very well, suffered no more infections and no diarrhoea. Blood tests confirmed no proteinuria, although vitamin D supplementation is still required.

7.6   Overview: glands, hormonal cycles and the HPA axis

This sub-section is included for the benefit of the general reader to explain how the glandular system is interlinked and therefore how cumulative and progressive effects may occur.

The human body secretes and circulates about 50 different hormones (chemicals) from nine specialised glands (the pituitary, the thyroid, the four parathyroids, the two adrenals and the thymus) and several organs which can produce hormones (including the pancreas, heart, kidneys, ovaries, testicles and intestines). For example: the pancreas secretes insulin which regulates glucose metabolism; the thyroid gland secretes thyroxine (T4) and triiodothyrone (T3) which regulate metabolism and growth; and the adrenal cortex secretes glucocorticoids (cortisol), mineralocorticoids (aldosterone) and androgens. Cortisol stimulates glucose synthesis and anti-stress and anti-inflammatory processes. Aldosterone affects the sodium/potassium balance (Society for Endocrinology, 2018).

Hormones are released by the glands or organs directly into the intercellular fluid and carried through the bloodstream to target organs. They carry messages which control many body processes such as metabolism (energy levels), homeostasis (internal balance of body systems, such as temperature), reproduction, response to stress, and contraction of muscles.

The entire network is controlled by the hypothalamus (part of the brain) and the pituitary gland (at the base of the brain and which has two parts: the anterior and the posterior). The hypothalamus is the link between the hormonal and nervous systems. It receives messages through the nerves (such as the presence of daylight or heat and cold) and produces hormones in response to these stimuli. Some of these hormones stimulate other glands. The hypothalamus is important for regulating heart rate, blood pressure, body temperature, fluid and electrolyte balance, appetite and weight, glandular secretions of the stomach and intestines, sleep cycles and stimulation of the pituitary gland (Sargis, 2015). The pituitary also in turn secretes several hormones which act on other endocrine glands.

To function properly, all hormone-producing glands must release the correct amount of hormones at the right time. Many hormones are cyclical, with the cycle (circadian rhythm) ranging from a whole lifetime to a single day. For example, in a healthy human the level of cortisol begins to rise just before waking up, peaks at midday and reduces at night when the body needs rest (Chart 7-1). When a gland or the HPA axis malfunctions, hormonal disturbances occur.

Different amounts of hormone are needed at different times. In general terms, and for most of the cyclical hormones (those responsible for growth, fertility, circadian activity, etc.) the pattern is (see Figure 7-2):

- the brain informs the **hypothalamus** how much hormone should be present for a particular purpose (e.g. wakefulness, fight or flight, etc.);
- the **hypothalamus** informs the **pituitary** which checks this against current levels;
- if more hormone is needed, then the **pituitary** stimulates the appropriate hormone-producing gland (endocrine organ). The pituitary is too delicate and complex to produce the quantities of hormone needed, but can produce small quantities of the **stimulating hormones**.

Chart 7-1 Cortisol daily cycle (circadian rhythm) in a healthy human

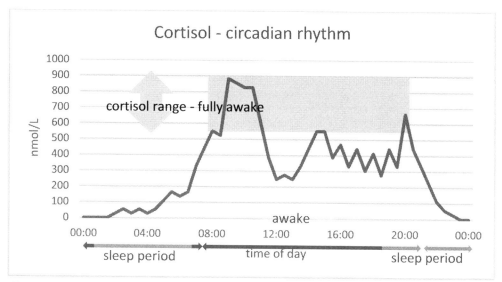

illustration by Hugo Minney

So, to break this into stages (using the example of cortisol):

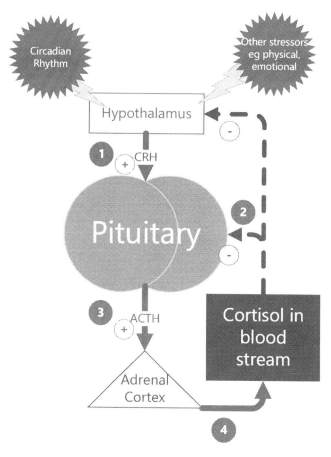

Figure 7-3 The hypothalamic-pituitary-adrenal (HPA) axis

(1). The brain sends a signal via a nerve impulse to the hypothalamus (the brain can see whether it is daylight, whether there is danger, whether food is required and so on). The hypothalamus converts it to a chemical signal (that is, it produces a Corticotropic Releasing Hormone or CRH) to send to the pituitary to convey the information.

(2) and (3). The pituitary checks the current hormone level and if more is required, sends an AdrenoCorticoTropic Hormone (ACTH), that is a stimulating hormone, to the adrenal glands.

(4) The endocrine gland that produces cortisol is the adrenal cortex (the outer layer of the adrenal gland, also known as the suprarenal gland).

Graphics by Hugo Minney

SECTION 2: APS component illnesses: Hypoadrenalism

Hypoadrenalism, a disorder in which the adrenal glands do not produce enough steroid hormones, is also called "Addison's disease" after Thomas Addison (1793-1860), who gave the first clinical description of the condition. An interesting point here is that even at this early date Addison noticed that the adrenal glands were damaged in all the 11 cases of pernicious anaemia (PA) on which autopsies were performed at that time (Graner, 1985; Pearce, 2004). In other words, he had spotted a connection between vitamin B12 deficiency (manifested in the form of PA) and glandular damage. Addison at first thought that hypoadrenalism was a cause of PA but later abandoned this idea (Addison, 1855). As we now know, PA induces vitamin B12 deficiency and may in fact itself be an end-stage presentation of B12 deficiency – see Chapter 4 of this book, so we believe it may have been the other way round: that is that vitamin B12 deficiency in PA had led to hypoadrenalism in Addison's patients.

Case 7-3 Importance of timely intervention in hypoadrenalism

Donna Kennedy, a hospital nurse, was diagnosed with vitamin B12 deficiency (with a B12 blood level of 248 ng/L in 2012) but initially did not follow any treatment. She attended the surgery in August 2013 with a red rash as shown in the photo. An allergic reaction was initially suspected but her cortisol level was 130 nmol/L (normal range 500-700 in the morning) and B12 level 243 ng/L (normal range 350-900 ng/L), which, in conjunction with extreme fatigue and breathlessness, confirmed vasculitis rather than urticaria. Emergency treatment was given before the cortisol results were known which proved to be the correct treatment. Donna was given B12-replacement therapy (injections on alternate days), along with oral hydrocortisone short-term to treat the transient hypoadrenalism and skin rash. Through this treatment her normal adrenal function was restored, indicating that this timely intervention had prevented long-term damage to the adrenal glands. She recovered completely and returned to her nursing duties.

Hypoadrenalism leads to multiple health problems resulting from under-production of the three types of hormone secreted by the adrenal cortex. These include (from the Society for Endocrinology (2018)):

- **Glucocorticoids**: Mainly cortisol, which is important for the body's response to stress, (including illness), for regulating metabolism, for stimulating glucose production and in anti-inflammatory processes.
- **Mineralocorticoids:** Mainly aldosterone, which is important for maintaining salt and water levels which regulate blood pressure.
- **Adrenal androgens**: Sex hormones (small amounts of oestrogen, testosterone, progesterone and dehydroepiandrosterone (DHEA)). DHEA is important for energy levels.

7.7   Forms of hypoadrenalism

There are three forms of the disease (primary, secondary and tertiary) depending on the cause of the disorder. Treatment depends on the form diagnosed. Unfortunately, hypoadrenalism is often undiagnosed until the crisis point is reached, where the adrenal glands are almost totally destroyed. Known as "Addisonian crisis", this condition can be fatal (see Figure 7-4 and Case 7-4).

This illness can occur as part of APS or on its own (as an isolated condition) (Arlt & Allolio, 2003). By definition, it is included in APS Types I and II and may also feature in Type IV. Through our work with B12-deficient patients in whom extreme fatigue was prevalent, we discovered that low cortisol – a result of under-active adrenal glands - was also contributing to their symptoms. In the absence of satisfactory diagnostic guidelines, this led us to develop our own diagnostic Protocol (Appendix 2) for capturing this condition in the early stages.

Figure 7-4 Newspaper report: Death from undiagnosed Addison's disease

19

News

Boy died after GPs 'ignored symptoms of rare disease'

Danielle Sheridan

Two doctors who ignored numerous signs that a 12-year-old boy was dying from a rare disease caused his death through negligence, a court heard yesterday.

Joanne Rudling, 45, and Lindsey Thomas, 42, are accused of manslaughter by negligence after Ryan Morse died at his home in Abertillery, south Wales, one week before his 13th birthday in 2012.

A court heard that Ryan, who was usually "fit and healthy", had had a series of appointments at Abernant surgery, the family's local GP practice, in the three months before his death.

Both doctors deny manslaughter. Dr Rudling also denies trying to pervert the course of public justice.

John Price, QC, for the prosecution, said that one GP carried out a telephone consultation with Ryan's mother, Carol, 54, who has four other children, 24 hours before her son died.

"The doctors should have visited Ryan at his home to personally examine him," Mr Price said. "They would have seen a very sick child in need of immediate attention. Ryan was, in fact, dying. They could have

Ryan Morse's skin went yellow and he had lost weight

called an ambulance. If they had done as they should, his life would have been saved."

Ryan was displaying symptoms of Addison's disease, which include progressive anaemia, low blood pressure, weakness and discolouration of the skin. Mrs Morse was concerned that her child's skin was "yellowing" and feared that he may have glandular fever.

Mr Price added: "Ryan's skin became so discoloured that his school friends had nicknamed him 'Teabag'.

"The cause of his death was what is called an Addison's disease crisis. Addison's disease is a rare but treatable disease."

A welfare officer at Ryan's school who was asked to look into his regular absences in the months leading up to his death noted

Lindsey Thomas left, and Joanne Rudling

that he looked "thin, grey and gaunt". A teacher said: "I noticed that his skin was dark. He looked Indian or Pakistani in race. There wasn't much of him."

Three days before his death his mother picked him up from school early because he was shaking, had vomited twice and complained of feeling ill.

At home his temperature changed from "very cold" to "burning", and his mother was so concerned that she slept with him in his bed. By the next day Ryan was delirious and "talking rubbish".

Mrs Morse called the surgery and was told by Dr Thomas to "fetch him up" to see her, despite the fact he was "not able to carry his own weight". Later that day she made another phone call and spoke to Dr Rudling, who "also ignored" signs that Ryan was dying.

Dr Thomas later told an investigator from the Aneurin Bevan health board: "At no point did the mother ever ask me to visit him. But she said if he needed to be seen then she wouldn't be able to bring him in because he felt too ill."

Cardiff crown court heard that Dr Rudling later made false entries into Ryan's records two days after the boy's death. She allegedly made the notes look like they had been entered on the day his mother rang in for a consultation.

She is also accused of incorrectly noting that his genitals had "changed colour" when his mother had specifically said they were "black" in colour.

The trial continues.

D. Sheridan, *The Times*, 5 May 2016.

7.7.1 Primary hypoadrenalism

In primary hypoadrenalism, the adrenal glands themselves are damaged or destroyed. The main cause used to be tuberculosis which remains a problem in developing countries, but in developed countries it is autoimmune adrenalitis, in other words autoimmune attack on the adrenal glands (Nicolaides et al., 2017). It can also occur when antibodies block the binding of ACTH to its receptors, preventing a response to ACTH to release cortisol. Infectious fungal diseases, viral infections, tumours, adrenal haemorrhage and genetic defects are other causes.

In this condition, production of all three hormone groups listed above is affected.

Autoimmune Addison's disease is chronic (i.e. long standing) and antibodies to the adrenal cortex may or may not be detected in a person's blood many years before damage to the adrenal cortex is apparent through low levels of cortisol. Chronic primary hypoadrenalism is held to be extremely rare, with a prevalence of 93-140 per million in the developed world (Arlt & Allolio, 2003). However, autoimmune adrenalitis appears to be increasing, implying that the prevalence of hypoadrenalism may also be rising (Laureti et al., 1999). In our Practice we encountered 15 cases of chronic hypoadrenalism (see, for example, Cases 7-3 and 7-5) as well as the case of a GP colleague who was the patient of another Practice (Case 7-4).

In general, at least 80% of both adrenal glands have to be damaged in order for deficiencies to become clinically evident. Signs and symptoms become critical when 90% of the adrenal cortex is destroyed. This is a problem for diagnosis as discussed below.

7.7.2 Secondary hypoadrenalism

Hypoadrenalism can also result from any disruption of the action of the pituitary gland which affects

Figure 7-5 Causes of hypoadrenalism: factors affecting HPA Axis

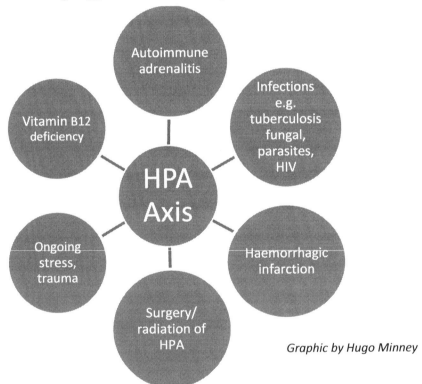

Graphic by Hugo Minney

secretion of the stimulating hormone ACTH as described in Figure 7-3. The most frequent causes of this condition are a pituitary tumour, surgery, or treatment with irradiation. In this case, the adrenal glands may still be intact. They are simply not receiving enough stimulation because the HPA axis is disrupted. Production of glucocorticoids will be affected but mineralocorticoid levels may be normal because mineralocorticoids are not controlled by the HPA axis. (They are under the control of the renin-angiotensin system – RAA.)

Secondary hypoadrenalism is more common than the primary form with an estimated prevalence of 150-280 per million (Arlt & Allolio, 2003). A frequent cause of secondary hypoadrenalism is therapeutic use of steroids for other conditions because this leads to atrophy of the pituitary corticotrophic cells. The dose given may be higher than the level the body normally produces, so if the patient takes corticosteroids for a long time, the adrenal glands produce less and may be slow to resume normal production when the prescription dose is stopped – which can cause adrenal insufficiency. For this reason, prescription doses should be reduced gradually. Conditions arising from this cause are usually reversible. In other cases, the cause may be autoimmune disorder (Kasperlik-Zaluska et al., 1998).

7.7.3   Tertiary hypoadrenalism

A third cause is any process that interferes with the hypothalamus and CRH production. As in secondary hypoadrenalism, the HPA axis is disrupted but the cause is different (Charmandari et al., 2014). The effect on hormone production will be the same as in secondary hypoadrenalism.

Among APS Type II patients, hypoadrenalism occurs with hypothyroidism in about 69% of patients, and with Type 1 diabetes in about 52% of cases (Sherman & Gagel, 2005). In established diabetes, a significant drop in the amount of insulin required to achieve the same glucose control may be a warning sign of developing hypoadrenalism.

Although the diagnosis is more common in people older than 30 years, children as young as five may also have symptoms which indicate Addison's disease.

7.7.4   Addisonian (adrenal) crisis

Untreated Addison's disease can be fatal and the deterioration can be rapid (see Plate 7.1). Adrenal crisis is likely to occur 6 - 8 times per 100 patient years, so a person with Addison's disease can expect four crises during their lifetime (Bancos et al., 2014).

Hypovolaemic shock, cardiac arrest, stroke, cerebral oedema or other circulatory complications can occur as a result of adrenal crisis. Complications may leave a patient with permanent disabilities, including permanent brain damage. Because of hyponatremia (low sodium, which affects the fluid balance in every part of the body), the doctor should recognise the condition and treat it correctly.

An acute exacerbation (adrenal crisis = patient collapse) should be considered an emergency and treated with IV hydrocortisone and a hospital admission. It can be brought on by a serious infection, acute stress, bilateral adrenal infarction or haemorrhage (Charmandari et al., 2014). In such cases, none or delayed treatment is more dangerous than treatment.

The symptoms of an Addisonian crisis include:

- Dehydration and/or severe vomiting and diarrhoea
- Stabbing pain in the abdomen, low back, or legs
- Low blood pressure (shock)
- Low blood sugar
- Loss of consciousness

Treatment includes:

- Rehydration by saline infusion at initial rates of 1 litre per hour (L/h), with continuous cardiac monitoring.
- Glucocorticoid replacement by bolus injections of 100 mg hydrocortisone followed by the administration of 100-200 mg hydrocortisone over 24 hours.
- Mineralocorticoid can be initiated once the daily hydrocortisone dose has been reduced to <50 mg, because at higher doses hydrocortisone provides sufficient stimulation of mineral corticoid receptors.

Life-saving treatment with steroids can only be given if the emergency medical team knows that the patient has hypoadrenalism. Addisonian crisis can affect a patient's thinking and even cause loss of consciousness, so all patients with adrenal insufficiency are advised to wear a medical alert bracelet or necklace that clearly states their diagnosis (Toft & Spinasanta, 2016). Patients should keep extra supplies of tablets at home or when on holiday as well as vials of hydrocortisone that they can inject.

Case 7-4 End-stage Addisonian Crisis presentation

In January 2013, Dr Jane Leigh joined the Shinwell Medical Practice GP Team of 4 GPs.

The Senior Partner (Dr Chandy) was concerned as she appeared quite ill and struggled to cope, asking for 20 minutes for each consultation and using a nebuliser (containing steroids) between consultations.

The Senior Partner decided to discuss her health issues with her. She told him that she had been ill for 17 years and had a diagnosis of ME/CFS, and that the immunology clinic at the teaching hospital had been searching for a viral cause (Epstein-Barr virus) for at least 10 years, without finding anything.

Her symptoms were classic symptoms of Addison's disease (extreme fatigue, weight loss, breathlessness, dizziness, syncopal attacks, feeling extremely ill and no energy to get out of bed etc.). It appeared that her early morning cortisol level had not been tested. On prompting, the immunology clinic carried out a straightforward blood test to determine her early morning cortisol level.

The result was:	
Baseline cortisol (0 m)	0 nmol/L

She was immediately referred to the endocrinologist. A diagnosis of primary hypoadrenalism was confirmed, and the endocrinologist commenced her on hydrocortisone: 10 mg (am) + 10 mg (midday) + 5 mg (5 pm).

Dr Chandy suggested that the initial dose was not high enough and in fact, two weeks later, she developed gastritis and vomiting. She then collapsed at home in the early hours of the morning. A 999 crew arrived, but they were unable to administer the Efcortisol injection (a form of hydrocortisone) without a protocol. Eventually, the patient was admitted as an emergency and received IV Efcortisol, fluids and electrolytes. She now takes a hydrocortisone dose tailored better to her physiological need. Following this treatment, her health improved dramatically.

The "window of opportunity" to diagnose promptly and initiate appropriate replacement was 17 years previously. During this critical 17-year period she and her family undoubtedly suffered intense physical and psychological trauma from the ups and downs of her condition. The current guidelines are preventing Doctors (GPs and Consultants) from early diagnosis and treatment of this deadly condition; better guidelines would save many precious lives (Wass, 2012, p. 5063) – see also newspaper report above (Figure 7-4 and Sands (2017); Wass (2012)).

7.7.5   Diagnosing Addison's disease

The progression of Addison's disease is often gradual and may not be detected until an illness or other stress precipitates an adrenal crisis. It can progress undetected to the critical or emergency stage which requires immediate hospital admission. Long-term hypoadrenalism, if left uncorrected, could be fatal.

The main presenting symptoms of all forms of hypoadrenalism (fatigue, anorexia, weight loss) are non-specific and could be the result of any number of different causes; thus, there is a risk that diagnosis may be delayed. The principal symptom is overwhelming exhaustion, which is a result of low cortisol. When three or more of the following symptoms are present in the same patient, hypoadrenalism should be considered as part of the differential diagnosis:

- Feels faint, dizzy, headache
- Weakness, fatigue
- Anorexia, weight loss
- Abdominal pain, salt craving
- Loss of muscle mass
- Breathlessness

Note: Many of the signs overlap with those of Type 1 diabetes (also an autoimmune condition); however, in Addison's disease you would expect blood glucose to be normal or even low. Fatigue, sleepiness, thirst, and unexplained weight loss occur in both conditions.

As a person with hypoadrenalism does not have enough cortisol circulating during waking hours, they feel very tired throughout the day and particularly immediately after waking.

Other symptoms are hypotension, electrolyte imbalances such as hyponatremia (low sodium), hyperkalemia (high potassium), or metabolic acidosis, hyperpigmentation (dark skin patches – in primary adrenalism only), autoimmune manifestations (vitiligo – white skin patches), decreased axillary and pubic hair, and loss of libido and amenorrhea in women. However, in secondary hypoadrenalism there is no hyperpigmentation of the skin, because the secretion of ACTH is not increased. Also, since the production of mineralocorticoids is mostly intact, dehydration and hyperkalemia are not present, and hypotension is less prominent (Charmandari et al., 2014).

Besides tiredness and the symptoms listed above, there are many other symptoms to help a physician diagnose hypoadrenalism:

- Joint and muscle pain/weakness;

- Increased pigmentation of the skin – due to raised ACTH level (only present in primary hypoadrenalism – not present in secondary/tertiary hypoadrenalism);
- Depression;
- Decrease in axillary and pubic hair – common in women;
- Neuropathy, myopathy;
- Unsteadiness/falls;
- Postural hypotension (low blood pressure on standing up – mainly present in primary hypoadrenalism);
- Impotence and amenorrhoea;
- Hypoglycaemia – reduced opposition to insulin action.

*Note: Blood pressure control is abnormal in severe cortisol deficiency (prone to postural hypotension). Very low blood pressure is a sign that the patient is in immediate danger of collapse. Patients with a severe deficiency of cortisol and the **related hormone aldosterone** often have a low sodium level and increased potassium level.*

7.7.6 Current diagnostic guidelines inadequate

From our patient experience, we believe that the current guidelines to diagnose hypoadrenalism are unsafe and damaging to the patient: they result in either a delayed diagnosis, or an end-stage diagnosis when it is too late to treat (Wass, 2012). Others have also found that delay in diagnosing is a "frequent cause of adrenal crisis" (Papierska & Rabijewski, 2013). We recommend following the Protocol for diagnosing hypoadrenalism included at the end of this book.

There are a number of diagnostic tests but none are completely reliable for reasons explained below. For example, the commonly used high dose Synachten Stimulation Test (SST), in which 250 mcg of ACTH is injected to test for adrenal response, is only reliable when 95% to 100% of both adrenal glands are destroyed. This is because such a high dose is likely to produce a reaction from the adrenal glands even if they are severely impaired. Mild secondary adrenal insufficiency can pass the test showing an intact HPA axis, and conversely healthy individuals might fail any single test by a small margin. "Thus, clinical judgment remains important. Persisting symptoms such as fatigue, myalgia, or reduced vitality should lead to reassessment" (Arlt & Allolio, 2003, p. 1887), p. 1887). There are cases of suboptimal responses to high dose SST being reported as normal and therefore no replacement therapy considered. There are also cases where replacement therapy is withdrawn from hypoadrenal patients with suboptimal responses to high dose SST who have been clinically and physiologically benefiting from the therapy.

Levels of cortisol and ACTH in healthy individuals and patients suffering from hypoadrenalism are given in Table 7-4.

7.7.7 Some questions for the clinician to ask

- Take blood pressure sitting and standing. If the blood pressure drop is greater than 20 points, diagnose postural hypotension.
- Ask the patient if they frequently drop keys, struggle to climb stairs or to get up from a sitting or squatting position.

- Check oral mucosa pigmentation and skin where clothes rub; for hyperpigmentation: this may be a soft muddy colour or darker, depending on patient's natural skin colour. If present, this can indicate high ACTH.
- Measure electrolytes (low sodium (Na), high potassium (K)), blood glucose, 9am cortisol (diagnosis highly likely if cortisol <100 nmol/L, and although unlikely if cortisol >400 nmol/L it should not be excluded if the patient is acutely unwell).

7.7.8 Quick patient questionnaire – hypoadrenalism

This questionnaire [which is part of our **Protocol for Hypoadrenalism** – see Appendix 2] should be completed by the patient. It is sometimes helpful if they circle the actual symptom experienced. Few patients report the full complement; some may also report psychoses.

Box 7-2 Hypoadrenalism questionnaire

Instruction to the patient: *Please grade these symptoms 1-10 and circle most relevant symptoms. 1 indicates that this symptom is mild and infrequent. 10 indicates the patient has it all the time and it is severe and debilitating. A score of 5 indicates that the patient has the symptom and it affects their daily life to a moderate extent.*

Symptom	score
Joint and muscle pain/weakness	
Increased pigmentation of the skin – due to raised ACTH level (not in all cases); pigmentation may be accompanied by vitiligo. Occasionally (in children) the opposite – alabaster-like pallor	
Intermittent abdominal pain and salt craving	
Vague stomach ache or other gut symptoms, diarrhoea and nausea	
Experiences weakness, fatigue, anorexia and weight loss	
Feels faint, dizzy and has headache	
Signs & Symptoms usually subtle	
Depression/anger/difficulty concentrating	
Decrease in axillary and pubic hair – common in women; alopecia	
Loss of muscle mass	
Neuropathy, myopathy	
Dizziness, unsteadiness, falls, syncope	
Breathlessness, difficulty with speech, chest pain	
Postural hypotension, hyponatremia (low sodium)	
Impotence and amenorrhoea	
Hypoglycaemia	

Table 7-2 Blood levels of cortisol and ACTH

	ACTH	CBG Cortisol (Corticosteroid-binding Globulin [attached] cortisol)	Serum Free Cortisol (SFC)*
Healthy subject, fasting levels 8am-9am	30-60 ng/L	550-800 nmol/L	20% of CBG-C
Healthy subject, midnight levels	<10 ng/L	<100 nmol/L	20% of CBG-C
Primary adrenal insufficiency, fasting 8am-9am	>30 ng/L	<275 nmol/L, signs and symptoms present	Variable
Secondary adrenal insufficiency, fasting 8am-9am	<20 ng/L	<275 nmol/L, signs and symptoms present	Variable

Note: for cortisol levels some sources use µg/dL. The conversion factor is 27.6 (i.e. 10 µg/dL = 276 nmol/L). SFC refers to cortisol available to be used by cells

Compiled with reference to: Schlaghecke et al. (1992), Debono et al. (2009), Erturk et al. (1998), Oster et al. (2017), BMJ Best Practice 'Adrenal Suppression Investigations' (2018b) and 'Addison's disease: Investigations' (2018a). Healthy ACTH levels from Oster et al. (2017).

7.7.9 Confirming the diagnosis

Typically, three or more symptoms would indicate that hypoadrenalism should be considered. Before making a provisional diagnosis of hypoadrenalism, exclude all other possible diagnoses with appropriate blood test and investigations as clinically indicated.

When patients present with mild to moderate symptoms, the GP should order tests for: early morning fasting cortisol levels (8am – 9am) along with Full Blood Count (FBC), vitamin B12, folic acid, ferritin, thyroid-stimulating hormone (TSH), triiodothyronine (T3), thyroxine (T4), parathyroid hormone, vitamin D, urea and electrolytes (U&Es), liver function, blood glucose etc. in order to differentially or concurrently diagnose ME, CFS, FM, MS-like presentation, depression, psychosis, vitamin B12 deficiency, myxoedema and so on.

The following table may be useful in making a diagnosis.

Table 7-3 Hypoadrenalism: Stages of disease progression

	Stage 1 Preclinical	Stage 2 Preclinical	Stage 3 Subtle	Stage 4 Clinically significant	Stage 5 Clinically critical	Stage 6 Clinical emergency
Signs and Symptoms	Mild	Mild to Moderate	Moderate	Significant	Critical	Emergency (adrenal crisis)
Early morning (fasting) cortisol	400-500 nmol/L	300-400 nmol/L	150-300 nmol/L	50-150 nmol/L	25-50 nmol/L	0-25 nmol/L

7.7.10 Tests to determine hypoadrenalism

7.7.10.1 Short Synacthen Test (SST)

The term "Synacthen" is an abbreviation of Synthetic ACTH Enhancement. In this test, a burst of artificial ACTH (cosyntropin) is given. Then blood samples of cortisol are taken at intervals (usually 0 mins, 30 mins, 60 mins after the ACTH administration) to test the response of the adrenal cortex and its ability to produce cortisol on stimulation. Where adrenal insufficiency is suspected, this test will distinguish between primary adrenal insufficiency (adrenal gland unable to produce cortisol in spite of stimulation), versus secondary adrenal insufficiency (adrenal gland functions as normal, but there is no ACTH to stimulate it until the SST is given).

We believe there are some problems with this test as routinely administered. The first derives from the size of the dose. SST provides a burst of 250 mcg of artificial ACTH (for a 65 kg person, with approximately 5 litres of blood, this is 50 mcg/L, or 50,000 ng/L). This is about 1,000 times as much as the expected concentration of natural ACTH at its peak (ACTH varies between 50 ng/L and 5 ng/L over the circadian rhythm, although it is delivered in a series of bursts (Oster et al., 2017)). This huge dose is likely to stimulate the adrenal cortex to produce some cortisol even if only 5% of the adrenal cortex remains (i.e. 95% is damaged and unable to function) which can lead to "falsely reassuring results" ("false negatives") (Abdu et al., 1999; Ferrante et al., 2012), whereas physiological doses of ACTH would not produce sufficient cortisol from such a small amount of remaining adrenal cortex.

However, ACTH does not affect only the adrenal cortex. It is contraindicated in some circumstances: a 250 mcg dose of cosyntropin can cause collapse in patients with allergies (Datapharm, 2017; Juno Pharmaceuticals, 2015), which is a risk because of the high dose being used for the standard SST.

7.7.10.2 Low-dose SST to detect partial hypoadrenalism

This test has the advantage that it can detect partial adrenal insufficiency that may be missed by the standard high-dose test. It is also preferred in patients with secondary or tertiary adrenal insufficiency, and is safer, for the reasons described above.

A low dose (500 nanograms – 1,000 ng (= 0.5-1 mcg) of ACTH – only slightly more than the 0.16-0.726 mcg that the pituitary naturally produces) is administered as an intravenous bolus. We believe that this test provides a more sensitive index of adreno-cortical responsiveness, because it results in physiological (appropriate to healthy or normal functioning) plasma ACTH concentration, i.e. the amount that the pituitary would normally produce when stimulated The low dose SST can be carried out in a primary care or community setting since it does not cause shock. The test should be carried out at 14.00 h, when natural ACTH production is low. A value of 500 nmol/L or more at any time during the test indicates normal adrenal function (Arlt & Allolio, 2003).

Note that these tests measure standard serum cortisol levels (not serum free cortisol). Since more than 80-90% of cortisol is bound to liver protein (Cortisol Bound Globulin (CBG)), serum free cortisol (SFC) is technically difficult to measure. So far there are no "gold standard" tests to measure unbound free/active cortisol.

The amounts of ACTH and cortisol in the blood naturally vary so a single random sample is not enough. Three or more weekly low or subnormal morning cortisol levels are clinically significant and should be clinically assessed and appropriate action taken.

7.7.10.3 Insulin tolerance test

This test, in which insulin is injected into a patient's vein, is an alternative for determining secondary hypoadrenalism. It helps to assess how well the HPA axis is functioning. This test can be dangerous. It is a powerful stressor and for this reason is contraindicated in patients over 60 years old, suffering from conditions such as ischaemic heart disease, seizures or cardiovascular disease, panhypopituitarism and severe hypoadrenalism. <u>If the patient is taking hydrocortisone this should be discontinued for 24 hours before the test.</u> It should also not be performed on children outside a specialist clinic.

7.7.10.4 MetyraponeTest

This test is used to detect secondary adrenal insufficiency. Metyrapone, which inhibits the conversion of 11-deosycortisol to cortisol, is administered overnight. In a healthy person, serum 11-deoxycortisol will increase as the HPA axis responds to the lack of cortisol. If the HPA axis is impaired, serum 11-deoxycortisol will not be more than 230 nmol/L at 8am (Arlt & Allolio, 2003, p. 1887).

7.7.11 Assessing cortisol levels

In a healthy person, cortisol is highest (550-750 nmol/L) in the morning within 30 minutes of waking up. Through the day, the level of cortisol is carefully regulated by the HPA axis: at midday it is around half the morning level, and by evening it will be 100-200 nmol/L to prepare the person for sleep.

An 8-9am cortisol level of less than <200 nmol/L is highly abnormal and strongly suggests a diagnosis of adrenal insufficiency. A cortisol level below <300 nmol/L (8-9 am fasting) should be cause for concern and anything below 400 nmol/L should be followed up. During acute illness, a cortisol level of less than < 500 nmol/L may be consistent with hypoadrenalism since the body would normally respond to such stress by producing more cortisol. Levels of 550 nmol/L or above exclude the diagnosis.

In primary hypoadrenalism, a patient's ACTH level is usually greater than 80 ng/L. But if the patient is suffering from pituitary disease or steroid suppression of the action of the hypothalamus, the ACTH level is undetectable (less than 10 ng/L). When early morning cortisol is <270 nmol/L or cortisol, ACTH and DHEAS levels are subnormal, hydrocortisone therapy is continued.

If three or more 8-9am weekly total cortisol CBG (cortisol binding globulin) levels are consistently reported as <270 /<300 nmols/L and the patient is presenting with moderate-to-severe classic signs and symptoms of hypoadrenalism and other autoimmune conditions, a three-month therapeutic trial of physiological replacement doses of hydrocortisone (total dosing of 15-25 mg/day) is commenced. This is followed by monthly clinical review and adjustment of the hydrocortisone dosing in accordance with a *Hydrocortisone Day Curve (HCDC)* carried out in the Primary Care setting (see the **Protocol for diagnosing hypoadrenalism (Appendix 2)**).

Prompt clinical diagnosis and physiological replacement can reverse the progression of the condition at early stages i.e. 2, 3 & 4 (Table 7-3) of presentation. Thus, possible regeneration of the adrenal glands can be achieved by this early intervention.

7.7.12 Limitations of the tests: high CBG levels

As with all laboratory tests, there are limitations. One of these is that the SST tests do not take into consideration a patient's level of CBG which affects their cortisol levels. Researchers have shown that: "CBG varies significantly within and between individuals. This is accompanied by changes in serum total cortisol large enough to affect the outcome of an SST and, by implication, other tests of the HPA axis" (Dhillo et al., 2002). Misleading results from the SST (and also the Insulin Tolerance Test) have life-threatening consequences so it is extremely important to interpret the results with reference to the individual's CBG levels.

Considerable work has been done on this subject by Dr Mike Welch who has shown that in a small proportion of patients who clinically manifest the signs and symptoms of adrenal insufficiency, the SST as currently performed fails to support the diagnosis of Addison's disease. Instead it may show either an unexpected normal result, or a sub-optimal response to ACTH from, often, a normal baseline. Furthermore, results may vary on subsequent repeated SSTs from previous investigations.

A modification to the SST whereby free cortisol in plasma is the required measurement, together with an assay of CBG, may be required to enable the clinician to establish a diagnosis of atypical, or high CBG, Addison's disease.

Current methodology for the assay of free cortisol in plasma is not yet established as an accredited technique. This requires urgent attention (Welch, 2006).

7.7.13 Sound and safe approach

The above simple but sound and safe approach to diagnosis that we have developed enables the physician to arrive at a clinically robust diagnosis of hypoadrenalism. A safe and side-effect free, medium-to-long-term treatment can then be instituted. The advantages are:

- Optimum physiological dosing prevents any further destruction of the remaining functioning cortical cells;
- Regular monitoring with an HCDC reassures the patient and enables the clinician to fine-tune the cortisol dosing accordingly;
- Normal cortisol circadian adrenal function is restored which allows the person to live a normal life;
- If the "window of opportunity" has not been missed, partial or total regeneration of the adrenal gland can take place once the adrenal cortex is given a rest;
- If and when the adrenal cortex regenerates, then replacement treatment is reduced, or even, in rare cases, withdrawn;
- Even when a hypoadrenal patient requires lifelong replacement of oral steroids, because the dose is physiological, there will not be any adverse effects, as one might expect when long-term pharmacological doses of steroids are administered in various other clinical situations.

7.7.14 Effect of hypoadrenalism on fertility and the female sexual cycle

Women with adrenal insufficiency often suffer from androgen deficiency which can contribute to low energy levels and cause loss of libido. Dehydroepiandrosterone (DHEA) supplementation of 25-50 mg (total daily dose) may be needed. Female fertility is broadly controlled by a number of hormones, including oestrogen and progesterone, which maintain the monthly cycle.

The hypothalamus and pituitary are closely involved in this monthly cycle, and the hypothalamus releases a hormone to make a follicle release an egg, when oestrogen levels in the blood are highest.

This cycle is particularly sensitive to vitamin B12 deficiency, not only because of the large number of hormones involved but also because of the sensitivity of the hypothalamus to oestrogen, before an egg can be released.

In our experience, a great many women who have had heavy menstrual bleeding (HMB or menorrhagia) have been completely cured, and their ability to conceive and have children has been restored, through vitamin B12-replacement therapy (see Chapter 5).

Case 7-5 Classic case of APS: Angela Abraham

From age 14 onwards, Angela suffered from dizziness, fainting, feeling cold all the time, nausea, muscle cramps, hair loss, IBS and stomach pain, palpitations, thirst, panic attacks and loss of concentration. She has a family history of autoimmune problems and vitamin B12 deficiency.

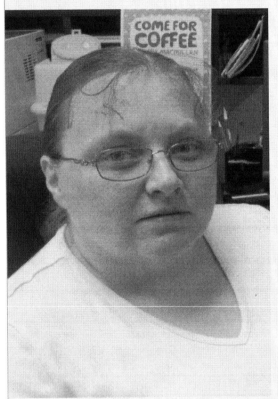

She had many previous diagnoses, including the glandular disorder Polycystic Ovary Syndrome (PCOS), vitamin D deficiency, depression, comfort eating, obesity, ME/CFS-, FM-like presentations.

In September 2000, we diagnosed her with vitamin B12 deficiency and began replacement therapy. Some of her symptoms improved. In 2006 she suffered from menorrhaghia with chronic pelvic pain and underwent an abdominal hysterectomy.

At this time, due to the PCT embargo (see Introduction) we were not able to administer B12 therapy and her symptoms re-emerged. Her morning cortisol level was found to be low at 212 nmol/L so we referred her to an endocrinologist who arranged a high-dose SST. This showed a sub-optimal response but a further test two months later showed slightly higher levels; the first test results were therefore attributed to long-term use of steroid inhalers and she was discharged by the endocrinologist in May 2012.

We were able to resume vitamin B12 therapy after February 2011 when the PCT embargo was lifted but by then the "window of opportunity" to prevent further deterioration had been missed. Her health symptoms worsened and in 2013 we again referred her to an endocrinologist with comprehensive clinical supporting evidence to suggest hypoadrenalism and possible APS. A further SST confirmed extremely low levels of cortisol and a low level of ACTH, giving a diagnosis of secondary hypoadrenalism. Once the diagnosis was confirmed, Angela was given the correct cortisol supplementation and her condition improved. With accompanying vitamin B12 injections

---

her overall condition improved dramatically. Follow-up management included routinely conducting HCDCs in the primary care setting.

Despite being given multiple high-dose SSTs, Angela was not diagnosed as suffering from Addison's disease until she was almost at crisis point. This illustrates that the adrenal cortex can continue to produce cortisol when stimulated by 250 mcg Synacthen, until it is completely burnt out (see 26/07/2013 line in the chart below).

Chart 7-2 Results of multiple SSTs on a single patient

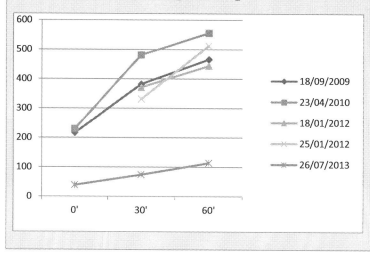

Table 7-4 Angela Abraham – timeline summary

Other conditions	B12 deficiency, PCOS, vitamin D deficiency, depression, comfort eating (sweet craving), obesity, ME, CFS, FM-like presentation											
Signs & Symptoms	Age 14 onwards – Dizziness, fainting, tiredness, weakness, feeling cold all the time, nauseous, muscle cramps, hair loss, IBS, stomach pain, palpitations, thirsty, headache, depression, panic attacks, loss of concentration, Mind switches off. (signs & symptoms) +++++											
Date / Hospital / GP	10/06/09 GP	06/08/09 GP	18/09/09 Hospital 1	23/04/10 Hospital 1	15/12/11 GP	18/01/12 Hospital 2	25/01/12 Hospital 2	24/08/12 GP	10/12/12 GP	11/02/13 GP	04/06/13 Hospital 3	26/07/13 Hospital 3
8-9am Cortisol	212 nmol/L fasting	146 nmol/L fasting	SST 250 mcg ACTH test 0' 216 30' 382 60' 466	SST 0' 230 30' 481 60' 556	209 nmol/L fasting	SST 0'* 30' 371 60' 444	SST 0'* 30' 331 60' 512	139 nmol/L fasting	263 nmol/L fasting	303 nmol/L fasting	**73** nmol/L fasting	**0' 39** 30' 74 60' 114
Signs & Symptoms severity marked by * (1-5)	S&S ***** ; Referred to Hospital 1 by Dr Chandy	S&S ***** ; Awaiting Hospital 1 appointment	S&S ***** ; ??ACTH level (not reported)	S&S ***** ; ??ACTH level (not carried out)	S&S ***** ; 28/12/11 Referred to Hospital 2	S&S ***** ; Baseline cortisol missing, ACTH 37 ng/L	S&S ***** ; Baseline cortisol & ACTH not reported		S&S *****	S&S ***** ; 24/04/13 – Referred to Hospital 3 by Dr Chandy	S&S ***** ; Clear Adrenal Insufficiency although not diagnosed by hospital	S&S ***** ; Adrenal Insufficiency confirmed
Treatment or time-specific medication	No steroids	No steroids	No steroids	No steroids	No steroids	No steroids	No steroids		Steroid inhalers	Steroid inhalers	Hydrocortisone 10mg – AM 10mg – 12 Mid-Day SPR – Hospital 3	Hydro-cortisone stopped for 2 days.
Comments/observations	GP suspects Hypo-adrenalism having treated/excluded other conditions. B12 248 ng/L	GP continues to be concerned	RVI '?Early Addison's disease, Impaired response will take this further'	RVI 'Could still be early Addison's. Long Synacthen Test Proposed' No appt received by patient, nor a discharge letter to GP		HGH Confirmed	HGH confirmed 'SST Normal, No follow up necessary, Discharged'		Fatigue, breathlessness. S+S worsening. On steroid inhalers.	Fatigue, breathlessness.	SPR from Hospital 3 telephoned Dr Chandy. **Urgent, Commence Hydrocortisone** **14.06.13** Height: 5f 3" Weight: 19st 10lb BMI: 48.83kg/m2	
Medication (choices available)	Terbutaline Inhaler (Inh), Symbicort 200/6 Inh, Simvastatin 20mg, Sertraline 100mg, Naproxen 250mg, Mebeverine 135mg, Metformin 500mg (PCOS), Lansoprazole 30mg, GTN Spray, Hydrocortisone (15mg am & 10mg midday, 5mg pm), Furosemide 40mg, Colecalciferol 800 units as needed, Aspirin 75mg, Co-codamol 30/50mg											

Case 7-6 Undiagnosed APS with hypoadrenalism leading to irreversible damage: Leanne Walker (née Chandy)

Leanne suffered from her early 20s with tiredness, dizziness, muscle weakness, weak grip, feeling cold, crampy pain, breathlessness, difficulty with speech, unexplained loss of weight, absent reflexes, many other gastrointestinal symptoms, and memory loss. Over the years she had received a number of diagnoses, including Polycystic Ovary Syndrome (PCOS), hirsutism, oligomenorrhagia, vitamin D deficiency, postpartum haemorrhage/hypovolaemic shock.

In 2002, an endocrinologist at a south of England hospital clinically suspected hypoadrenalism but no action was taken. In 2008, an endocrinologist at another hospital arranged a SST because of her signs and symptoms and endocrine disturbances. In January 2008, she was given a high-dose SST which showed an extremely low ACTH level of 7 ng/L at 9 am, with a low cortisol level of 70 nmol/L, results which should have raised suspicions. But as the SST showed that her adrenal cortex was able to manufacture cortisol (when stimulated to this high degree), primary hypoadrenalism was excluded. There was no follow-up of the ACTH result to investigate secondary hypoadrenalism and no steroids were given.

In our view, the tests showed that two glands (the pituitary and adrenals) were malfunctioning. Together with other glandular problems (i.e. PCOS), this should have raised suspicions of hypoadrenalism.

Chart 7-3 Short Synacthen Test - hypoadrenal

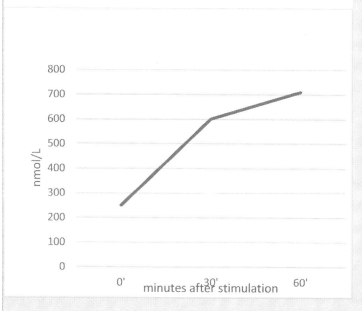

In March 2011, two GPs made home visits and observed: fatigue and lethargy; symptoms worsening; leg pains and cramps; muscle loss; difficulty standing up from sitting; reduced power in all limbs; inability to stand on left foot; speech, swallowing and breathing difficulties. Given the severity of deterioration, she was admitted to hospital.

She was given further early morning cortisol tests which showed low cortisol levels (194 nmol/L and 252 nmol/L) but the endocrinologist concluded that her symptoms were "psychologically mediated" and did not prescribe any medication.

She did her own research and decided to self medicate with hydrocortisone she purchased from the internet, 25 mg/day. Once this treatment was started, the patient began to recover. In 2013 she was officially diagnosed by a different hospital as suffering from secondary hypoadrenalism.

Higher cortisol levels from treatment were reflected in that she was not as tired, and was more able to spend time with, and enjoy her family. She was also diagnosed with subtle vitamin B12 deficiency and given vitamin B12 therapy.

The patient still suffers from weight loss, probably because of the delay in diagnosis being made. However, she is much better.

The points to note from this case are

- The patient's am/pm fasting cortisol levels were subnormal from January 2008 (70 nmol/L at 4 pm), and were dropping steadily from 56 nmol/L to 17 nmol/L from March to May 2013 despite physiological doses of steroids. This should have warranted further investigation.

- The two ACTH levels measured (7 ng/L in 2002 and 12 ng/L in November 2013) were indicative of near-adrenal crisis but no action was taken.

- The undiagnosed secondary hypoadrenalism had caused disuse atrophy of the adrenal glands, leading to progressive primary adreno-cortico failure despite steroids being administered since August 2011. The result was partial primary and partial secondary hypoadrenalism.

The "window of opportunity" at the first investigation in 2002 to preserve the patient's optimal health and wellbeing was lost forever, resulting in irreversible damage and great distress to her and her family.

Chart 7-4 Early morning cortisol with hypoadrenalism

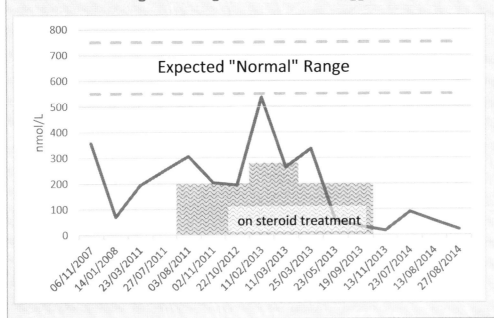

Table 7-5 Leanne Walker (née Chandy) – timeline summary

	5/12/01	16/11/07	14/01/08	23/03/11	3/08/11	22/10/12	6/11/12-7/10/13	25/10/13	21/7/14	27/8/14
Other conditions	2002 PCOS, hirsutism, oligomenorrhagia, vitamin D deficiency; 2009 Post-partum haemorrhage/hypovolaemic shock, vitamin B12 deficiency									
Signs & Symptoms	Tiredness, feels faint, dizziness, muscle wasting, weak grip, feeling cold, crampy pain, breathlessness, weakness, extreme fatigue, chest pain, difficulty with speech, loss of weight (8st7lb to 7st), absent reflexes, loss of power both legs, unsteady gait, falling back, vague stomach ache, other GI symptoms and memory loss									
Date		16/11/07	14/01/08	23/03/11	3/08/11	22/10/12	6/11/12-7/10/13	25/10/13 (Hospital 4 inpatient 13/11 – 15/11)	21/7/14	27/8/14
		Hospital 4	Hospital 1	Hospital 1	Hospital 1		Hospital 3		GP	GP
Cortisol (nmol/L)		357 fasting (hypoadrenalism suspected)	70 nmol/L fasting cortisol ACTH 7 ng/L	194 fasting	252 fasting (on HC)	195 fasting (on HC)	Fasting Cortisol and fasting ACTH not tested; 9/3/13 SHBG 46.5; TSH 0.42; T3 4.0, T4 15.6; Na 142	Cortisol 17 fasting (8:30am); 472 (11:07am); 784 (4:08pm); ACTH 12 (8:30am); <5 (2pm)	Cortisol 90 (9:27am) ACTH <5	13/8/14 cortisol day curve: 55 (8:46); 658 (11:15); 788 (13:12); 546 (14:50); 259
Medication Use					Self medicating 25mg hydrocortisone daily	Self medicating		27.5mg hydrocortisone	20mg plenadren	20mg plenadren
Other observations	5/12/01 Testosterone 3.6 nmol/L - excess		Vit D 20 nmol/L, Recommendation "it would be worth excluding hypo-adrenalism"	19/3/11 EMG nerve conduction normal Vit D 94.9 nmol/L Na 133 BP 90/48	19/8/11 Hospital 1: "symptoms psychologically mediated. Do not delay her appropriate referral to psychology, physiotherapy and CFS service"	31/3/12 Echo – normal LV function 23/3/12 Muscle biopsy – myopathic changes		Confirm secondary adrenal insufficiency; Other pituitary dysfunction excluded; Myasthenia Gravis excluded	Ferritin 46 ng/L (low), Hb 112 g/L (low)	Consider hospital admission for adrenal insufficiency

In both patients (Case 7-5 and Case 7-6), we developed the spreadsheet format for presenting the data so that a doctor could see at a glance the patterns evolving. This enabled us to recognise the same symptoms across multiple patients, and begin to understand that the likely cause was treatable rather than untreatable. It led us to recognise the link between these endocrine conditions, autoimmune disease, and vitamin B12 deficiency, and so identify that vitamin B12-replacement therapy (B12 injections) could help many of these patients previously diagnosed as incurable.

7.7.15 Management and treatment of hypoadrenalism

Identifying the cause of hypoadrenalism (whether primary, secondary or tertiary) will determine the best course of treatment.

7.7.15.1 *Importance of including vitamin B12-replacement therapy.*

If the "window of opportunity" to correct the condition has not been missed, the use of optimum replacement therapy of vitamin B12 and other nutritional support to restore the adrenal cortex will reduce or remove all symptoms and debilitating signs and the patient will regain their former health. In many cases, supplementation with oral cortisol will allow the adrenal cortex to recover, although there are risks associated with this.

7.7.15.2 *Chronic adrenal insufficiency*

Glucocorticoid should be administered at a dose that replaces the physiological daily cortisol production. This is usually achieved by the oral administration of 15-25 mg of hydrocortisone in two-to-three divided doses. Doses are determined according to the severity of the condition. A typical hydrocortisone dose would be: 10 mg at 9:00am; 10 mg 12:00midday; 5 mg 5:00pm. Doses should be adjusted following the results of an HCDC and clinical evaluation.

Note that pregnancy may require an increase in hydrocortisone dose by 50% during the last trimester.

At least half of the daily dose should be taken in the morning. Long acting glucocorticoids such as dexamethasone are not preferred as they result in increased glucocorticoid exposure **(more so with dexamethasone, than prednisolone)** due to extended glucocorticoid receptor activation at times of physiologically low secretion (Charmandari et al., 2014).

Monitoring of glucocorticoid replacement is mainly based on the patient history and signs and symptoms suggestive of glucocorticoid over- or under-replacement. Plasma ACTH, 24-hour urinary-free cortisol, or serum cortisol day curves, reflect whether hydrocortisone has been taken or not but do not convey reliable information about replacement quality.

All patients with adrenal insufficiency need to be instructed about the requirement for stress-related glucocorticoid-dose adjustment. This generally means doubling the routine oral glucocorticoid dose in the case of intercurrent illness with fever, and bed rest. Daily IV injections of 100 mg of hydrocortisone may be needed in case of prolonged vomiting, surgery or trauma (Charmandari et al., 2014).

7.7.15.3 *Mineralocorticoid replacement in primary hypoadrenalism*

Patients suffering from primary hypoadrenalism will also need a daily dose of 100-150 mcg fludrocortisone. Adequacy of treatment can be evaluated by measuring the patient's blood pressure sitting and standing.

7.7.15.4 *Adrenal androgen replacement*

This is an option in patients with lack of energy, despite optimised glucocorticoid and mineralocorticoid replacement. It may also be indicated in women with features of androgen deficiency, including loss of libido. Adrenal androgen replacement can be achieved by once-daily administration of 25-50 mg DHEA.

General advice to patients:

- Simplify your life
- Reduce the amount of carbohydrate in your diet
- Exercise moderately

Case 7-7 Rapid results from treatment – vitamin B12 deficiency and hypoadrenalism

This patient was diagnosed with vitamin B12 deficiency in another Practice in February 2011, with a blood B12 level of 176 ng/L; the Practice started her on three-monthly injections.

These did not resolve the problem, and by November 2011 her blood B12 had fallen to 132 ng/L. She was suffering fatigue, lack of energy, and joint pains.

Due to the illness, she had to move and registered at our Practice, where her vitamin B12 deficiency was re-checked during the Practice health check, since it was already recorded amongst her existing conditions.

At the Shinwell Medical Practice, daily vitamin B12 injections were prescribed and these resolved most of the problems. However, she still suffered from fatigue and lack of energy, and in May 2013 we took an early morning cortisol test and identified hypoadrenalism.

Physiological replacement of cortisol was prescribed (oral) mimicking the daily cycle, to facilitate her recovery. By August 2013 she had recovered to the extent that physiological replacement was no longer necessary.

7.7.15.5 *Monitoring the glucocorticoid replacement*

There are no easy ways to monitor the effectiveness of dosage so this must be based mainly on assessment of clinical signs and symptoms. "Thus, long-term management of patients with adrenal insufficiency remains a challenge, requiring an experienced specialist. However, all doctors should know how to diagnose and manage suspected chronic or acute adrenal failure" (Arlt & Allolio, 2003).

7.7.16 Cushing's Syndrome

Cushing's syndrome is a disorder which occurs when the body's tissues are exposed to high levels of cortisol for too long, for example by over-prescription of steroids for asthma, rheumatoid arthritis, lupus, and other inflammatory diseases (NIDDK, 2018). Other people develop Cushing's syndrome because their bodies produce too much cortisol.

Cushing's syndrome has high morbidity or mortality, but it is less common now that doctors prescribe steroid hormones appropriately. If it is not caused by over-prescription of steroid hormones, it could be caused by high levels of ACTH which over-stimulate the adrenal cortex, or by damage to either pituitary or adrenal cortex.

Box 7-3 JFK and Addison's disease

The opening of the White House medical records of former US President John F. Kennedy in 2002 revealed that he had a complex medical history, including severe back pain (Pait & Dowdy, 2017) and glandular disorders from childhood which are now understood to have been Autoimmune Polyglandular Syndrome Type II. While in London in 1947, before he became President, he collapsed and was treated in St Thomas's Hospital, London, having been admitted with nausea, vomiting and hypertension. He was diagnosed as suffering from Addison's disease. The story given to the public, however, was that he had suffered a recurrence of malaria contracted in the Pacific during the Second World War. In the 1960s' presidential campaign, his supporters denied that he had Addison's disease, basing their interpretation on a narrow definition of Addison's disease as resulting only from tuberculosis which he did not have. The most common cause by then (and the cause of his condition), however, was autoimmune adrenalitis. Medical records and other documents also show that he suffered from hypothyroidism: these two glandular conditions point to the conclusion that he suffered from APS Type II. There was also evidence of a familial connection since his sister suffered from Addison's disease and his son had Graves' disease. He also had gastrointestinal symptoms which indicate other autoimmune conditions associated with APS. One of his physicians also said publicly that he was anaemic and was treated with vitamin B12, vitamin B1 and other B-complex vitamins. The White House records show that he was given vitamin B12 injections throughout his presidency. Recent interpretations suggest that he may have been suffering from pernicious anaemia (which is consistent with a diagnosis of APS Type II) but there is no definitive confirmation of this (Mandel, 2009).

7.8   SECTION 3: Other APS component illnesses

7.8.1   Underactive thyroid (myxoedema)

As described above, hypothyroidism (myxoedema) is frequently seen in APS. Underactive thyroid is thought to occur in a similar manner to adrenal insufficiency. It takes two forms depending on whether the thyroid gland itself is damaged (primary hypothyroidism) or is simply understimulated because of reduced TSH production by the pituitary gland (secondary hypothyroidism). Both hypo- and hyper-thyroidism may be caused by autoimmune disease. In hypothyroidism this is called Hashimoto's thyroiditis and in hyperthyroidism it is known as Graves' disease.

Primary hypothyroidism presents as elevated TSH; secondary hypothyroidism will have low TSH. Secondary hypothyroidism occurs alongside autoimmune Addison's disease in a large percentage of patients. The patient and clinician should note that starting thyroxine replacement without treating the cortisol deficiency can exacerbate hypoadrenal symptoms and may precipitate adrenal crisis.

The thyroid gland produces thyroid hormones which influence the metabolic rate and protein synthesis, and have many other effects. They increase the strength of the heartbeat, the rate of breathing, intake and consumption of oxygen, and the activity of mitochondria. Combined, these factors increase blood flow and affect the body's temperature. They increase the growth rate of young people, and cells of the developing brain, and are particularly crucial for brain maturation during foetal development.

Appetite and the digestion and absorption of foods, including glucose, fats, and free fatty acids are all dependent on thyroid hormones. Thyroid hormones reduce cholesterol in the blood. They also play a role in maintaining normal sexual function, sleep, and thought patterns. Increased thyroid hormone levels are associated with increased speed of thought generation, but decreased focus. Sexual function, including libido and the maintenance of the normal menstrual cycle, are all influenced by thyroid hormones.

Patients present with trigger symptoms and family history of myxoedema. Other autoimmune conditions may be present. Blood tests should be ordered for TSH, T3, T4 and also tests to exclude other possible conditions. TSH is reported as high, T4 is low or subnormal and thyroid antibodies in most cases are absent. Diagnosis of myxoedema is made by the clinician and according to the severity, the levothyroxine dose prescribed is adjusted up or down at the recommended review dates. ***No secondary care dynamic tests are mandatory for the above diagnosis or monitoring of treatment.***

7.8.2   Diabetes mellitus

Diabetes is a disease that occurs when blood glucose, also called blood sugar, is too high because not enough insulin is being produced by the pancreas to manage sugar levels or because cells are resistant to the effects of insulin. Over time, having too much glucose in the blood can cause health problems, such as heart disease and stroke, nerve damage, poor blood flow in the feet, kidney disease and eye problems (NIDDK, 2016).

The cells in the body need sugar for energy. However, the times when cells need energy are often different from the times when there is sugar in the bloodstream (after a meal). Blood sugar after a meal needs to be stored in the liver or in longer-term storage; and sugar needs to be released from storage to reach the cells when they need energy. Insulin controls this. It stops the blood sugar level from getting too high (hyperglycaemia) or too low (hypoglycaemia). Blood sugar levels may fluctuate wildly with intake (e.g. in a meal), and the cells may not be able to absorb enough blood sugar to perform functions such as physical activity.

7.8.2.1   Type 1 Diabetes

People with Type 1 diabetes cannot make insulin (beta cells in the pancreas are damaged or destroyed by autoimmune attack). They typically need insulin injections to trigger the cells to absorb sugar from the blood, avoiding hyperglycaemia which can cause permanent damage to many body systems. Up to one-third of patients with Type 1 diabetes may develop APS (Van den Driessche et al., 2009).

Vitamin B12 deficiency due to pernicious anemia has been found to occur frequently among patients with Type 1 diabetes. Primary autoimmune hypothyroidism and coeliac disease are also frequently present in such patients, both of which affect vitamin B12 metabolism (Kibirige & Mwebaze, 2013).

7.8.2.2   Type 2 Diabetes

People with Type 2 diabetes have cells that are resistant to insulin, that is they do not respond (by absorbing blood sugar) to normal levels of insulin in the blood. Typically, they are treated with oral medications, along with diet and exercise. Diabetes is thought to be a progressive condition so it is assumed that the longer someone has Type 2 diabetes, the more likely they will require insulin injections to maintain blood sugar levels.

It is also well documented that vitamin B12 deficiency is prevalent among patients with diabetes mellitus who are taking the glucose-lowering medication metformin (Valdes-Ramos et al., 2015).

We have found that vitamin B12 therapy can help relieve symptoms of both types of diabetes if administered alongside the normal medication for diabetes. Pancreatic function appears to improve as evidenced by patients needing less insulin.

7.8.3   CFS/ME- and FM-like presentations

Conventional wisdom is that the cause of conditions labelled Chronic Fatigue Syndrome (CFS – also known as Myalgic Encephalomyelitis (ME)) and Fibromyalgia (FM) is not known. CFS may be triggered by "viral infections, such as glandular fever, bacterial infections, such as pneumonia, problems with the immune system, a hormone imbalance, mental health problems, such as stress, depression and emotional trauma" or have a genetic origin (NHS, 2017). These are conditions with a range of symptoms, including fatigue, sleep disturbances, muscle pain, cognitive dysfunction, gastrointestinal dysfunction, headaches and postexertional malaise.

However, one specialist traces the cause to HPA axis dysfunction (Holtorf, 2008). He also notes that patients suffering from these symptoms often have hypothyroidism (although it is not easily detected), and low growth hormone (again not detected by standard testing). They also have associated mitochondrial dysfunction, immune dysfunction and gastrointestinal dysfunction.

These observations confirm our experience that these conditions are also consequences of vitamin B12 deficiency plus a glandular disorder (itself caused by B12 deficiency either directly or indirectly). We are not the only medical professionals to have noticed the link with vitamin B12. Regland et al. also observed that vitamin B12 with folic acid proved helpful in providing "good and safe relief" to sufferers of these conditions (Regland et al., 2015).

With regard to treatment, Holtorf advises that physiologic doses of cortisol should be considered as part of a multisystem treatment protocol for CFS and FM, especially where there are signs or symptoms of adrenal dysfunction, low blood pressure and/or serum levels that are low or in the low-normal range (Holtorf, 2008).

7.8.4   Autoimmune skin conditions

7.8.4.1   Vitiligo

Vitiligo (white patches on the skin caused by lack of skin pigment) is often present in sufferers of autoimmune disease. In the 1970s, a researcher at the Royal Victoria Infirmary, Newcastle-on-Tyne, reported that vitiligo had been found in association with several autoimmune diseases, including thyroid disease and Addison's disease. He concluded that "vitiligo is evidently another 'skin-marker of internal disease'" and that patients should therefore be monitored for the development of other autoimmune conditions (Dawber, 1970). Classical understanding is that there is no cure although symptoms may be alleviated (NHS, 2016e).

7.8.4.2   Alopecia

Alopecia areata (hair loss) is another autoimmune skin disease for which there is considered to be "no cure". In our experience, however, alopecia can be cured with vitamin B12 therapy. We had several patients suffering from this condition who were diagnosed as vitamin B12 deficient. Conventional treatment by a dermatologist had no impact, but within seven months of commencing intensive vitamin B12 treatment, the condition was completely cured.

7.8.4.3   Urticaria

Chronic idiopathic urticaria has also been found both to have a possible autoimmune origin and to be related to vitamin B12 deficiency. In 2004 Turkish researchers found vitamin B12 levels below the normal reference range in one-third of patients with this condition although none of the patients had developed clinical signs of vitamin B12 deficiency. They also found a higher frequency of antithyroid and anti–gastric parietal cell antibodies in the patients with low vitamin B12 levels, suggesting an "autoimmune etiology in B12 deficiency" (Mete et al., 2004).

Chapter 8   Neuropsychiatric disorders, including dementia – prevention is better than cure

---

I look up to the hills, but where will my help really come from?

My help will come from the Lord, the Creator of heaven and earth.

He will not let you fall. Your Protector will not fall asleep. Israel's Protector does not get tired. He never sleeps. The Lord is your Protector. The Lord stands by your side, shading and protecting you.

The sun cannot harm you during the day, and the moon cannot harm you at night. The Lord will protect you from every danger. He will protect your soul.

The Lord will protect you as you come and go, both now and forever.

Psalms 121: 1-8 ERV

Figure 8-1 Relationships between autoimmune diseases and dementia

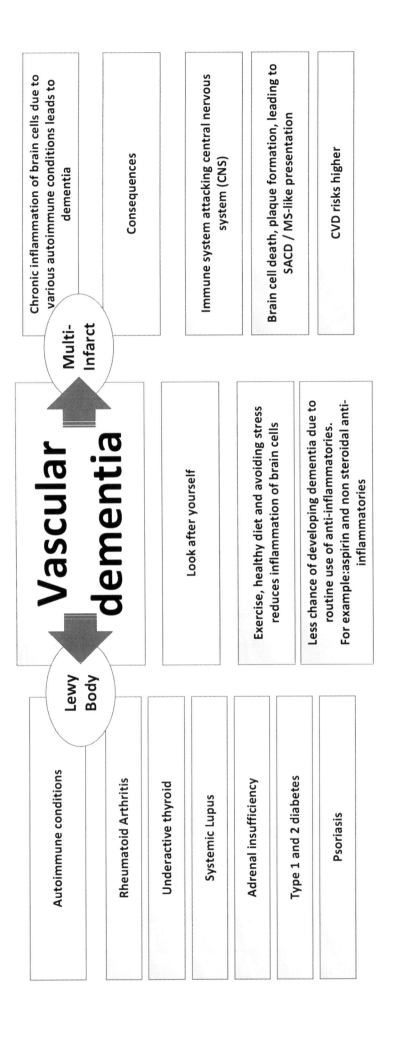

Autoimmune conditions and genetic factors can cause vascular dementia

Vascular dementia

Multi-Infarct

Lewy Body

Autoimmune conditions

Rheumatoid Arthritis

Underactive thyroid

Systemic Lupus

Adrenal insufficiency

Type 1 and 2 diabetes

Psoriasis

Chronic inflammation of brain cells due to various autoimmune conditions leads to dementia

Consequences

Immune system attacking central nervous system (CNS)

Brain cell death, plaque formation, leading to SACD / MS-like presentation

CVD risks higher

Look after yourself

Exercise, healthy diet and avoiding stress reduces inflammation of brain cells

Less chance of developing dementia due to routine use of anti-inflammatories.
For example:aspirin and non steroidal anti-inflammatories

8.1   Vitamin B12 deficiency and neuropsychiatric symptoms – an overview

Neuropsychiatric symptoms are among the most common presenting signs of vitamin B12 deficiency yet the diagnosis is often missed because of lack of awareness of this condition among clinicians (Lachner et al., 2012). In this chapter we begin by giving a brief overview of the importance of vitamin B12 for brain health and the many varied neuropsychiatric symptoms which may occur in vitamin B12-deficient patients. The remainder of the chapter focusses on the relationship of vitamin B12 to dementia, an illness of increasing worldwide concern, particularly in Western countries with ageing populations.

8.2   Historic evidence

Over sixty years ago, the neuropsychiatric effects of vitamin B12 deficiency (in the form, at that time, of pernicious anaemia) were documented in an article in the *British Medical Journal*. The author (Smith, 1960), quoting a number of authorities, stated:

> *"The occurrence of mental symptoms in association with pernicious anaemia has been known for many years and been commented upon by various authors (McAlpine, 1929; Samson et al., 1952; MacDonald Holmes, 1956; Wiener and Hope, 1959). Langdon (1905) drew attention to a group of cases in which nervous and mental symptoms preceded the onset of anaemia and described a great variety of neurotic and psychotic manifestations. Latterly (Wiener and Hope, 1959) the extreme variability of the symptoms has been stressed, and it is obvious that anything from a mild mood disorder to grossly psychotic behaviour may be encountered."*

Neuropsychiatric disturbances frequently occur in vitamin B12-deficient patients in the absence of anaemia or macrocytosis which have been considered the classic symptoms of B12 deficiency (see Chapter 4). In the 1980s, researchers showed that almost one-third of patients with the neuropsychiatric symptoms of vitamin B12 deficiency had no anaemia or macrocytosis (Lindenbaum et al., 1988).

8.3   Range of neuropsychiatric symptoms

More recently, researchers have described the neuropsychiatric symptoms of vitamin B12 deficiency as including "confusion, stupor, apathy, memory and judgment disorders or even psychoses, depressions and dementia" (Gröber et al., 2013). Others have listed: psychosis (with reported symptoms including suspiciousness, persecutory or religious delusions, auditory and visual hallucinations, tangential or incoherent speech, and disorganised thought-process); depression; mania; cognitive impairment (as in dementia) and delirium (fluctuating level of consciousness with attention deficits) (Lachner et al., 2012).

The close relationship between vitamin B12 deficiency and neuropsychiatric illness was also recently investigated in a retrospective study of patients who attended a specialised neuropsychiatric hospital in South India for a period of a year. Researchers found that of 259 patients who had vitamin B12 deficiency (defined as a B12 blood level less than 220 pmol/mL), 60 had neuropsychiatric symptoms. Twenty-one were diagnosed with Posterior dementias, 20 with frontotemporal dementia, seven with schizophrenia, four each with Parkinson's disease and alcohol-dependent syndromes (ADS), three with bipolar affective disorder, and one with Creutzfeldt-Jakob disease. Eight patients also had hypothyroidism. The presenting symptoms included behavioral disturbances in 30 (50% of those with neuropsychiatric symptoms), memory loss in 20 (33.9%), and sensorimotor and movement disorders in nine (15.3%) (Issac et al., 2015).

It has also been our experience that neuropsychiatric symptoms are among the foremost clinical signs of vitamin B12 deficiency (see, for example, Case 8-1) It can be noted that many of the patients in the cases described in this book presented with psychiatric disorders. For this reason, the presence of such symptoms should alert clinicians to the possibility of vitamin B12 deficiency. If diagnosed soon enough these conditions are treatable and the symptoms reversible, as others have also found (Lachner et al., 2012).

Case 8-1 Neuropsychiatric symptoms prominent

This patient, Eddie Rooney, presented in 2011, aged 52, with dermatitis. He was referred to a dermatologist but the treatment given did not solve the problem. He also complained of foot pain and had a number of neuropsychiatric symptoms, including longstanding depression, psychosis, hallucinations and fatigue due to lack of sleep. His condition meant that he was at risk of losing both his wife and his job. Because of these symptoms and the fact that his mother was being treated with vitamin B12, I suspected B12 deficiency. Tests indicated a very low B12 level of 145 ng/L. He was started on vitamin B12-treatment therapy and all his symptoms, including the dermatitis, foot pain and neuropsychiatric problems, disappeared within a few weeks.

8.4   Vitamin B12 deficiency and the human brain

Lachner et al. (2012) explain that vitamin B12 deficiency can cause "not only brain dysfunction, but structural damage, causing neuropsychiatric symptoms via multiple pathways" and that the possible mechanisms for this include: derangements in monoamine neurotransmitter production; derangements in DNA synthesis; vasculotoxic effects and myelin lesions associated with secondary increases in homocysteine and methylmalonic acid levels, respectively. They point out that vitamin B12 deficiency may also indirectly cause a functional folate-deficiency, resulting in high homocysteine levels, decreased monoamine production, decreased S-adenosylmethionine (SAMe) production, and abnormal methylation of phospholipids in neuronal membranes.

The medical textbook *Harrison's Principles of Internal Medicine* (2018) states:

> *"Psychiatric disturbance ... is common in both folate and cobalamin deficiencies. This, like the neuropathy, has been attributed to a failure of the synthesis of SAM [S-adenosyl methionine], which is needed in methylation of biogenic amines (e.g., dopamine) as well as that of proteins, phospholipids, and neurotransmitters in the brain. Associations between lower serum folate or cobalamin levels and higher homocysteine levels and the development of decreased cognitive function and dementia in Alzheimer's disease have been reported"* (Hoffbrand, 2018, p. 701)

Vitamin B12 deficiency is understood to cause demyelination of nerve axons (at least, vitamin B12 is required in order to facilitate the natural re-myelination of axons during the regular cycle of bodily repair). Demyelination may be related to a deficiency of SAMe (which is required for methylation of myelin phospholipids) which is a direct result of B12 deficiency, causing abnormal substrates for fatty acid synthesis in myelin.

Figure 8-2 Role of vitamin B12 in the conversion of homocysteine to SAMe

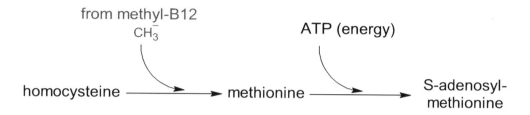

Graphic by Hugo Minney

In a discussion of the effect of B vitamins on the human brain Kennedy (2016) explains the integrated actions of B vitamins (including vitamin B12) and observes that brain concentrations of vitamin B-dependent neurochemicals are particularly high compared with amounts in the rest of the body. A deficiency is therefore likely to have a particularly strong impact on the brain which controls mood and cognition as well as most other body processes. Researchers from the US and Switzerland have found that some disorders, such as age-related cognitive and memory decline, autism and schizophrenia, could be linked to poor uptake of vitamin B12 from the blood to the brain (Zhang et al. (2016), reported in Wanjek (2016)). Further support for the effect of B vitamins on psychiatric behaviour is given in research by a team from the University of Manchester which showed that high doses (compared with low doses) of vitamins B6, B12 and biotin significantly reduced the symptoms of schizophrenia (Firth et al., 2017).

8.5   Categories of neuropsychiatric symptoms

The neuropsychiatric symptoms of vitamin B12 deficiency fall into several categories which may reflect the different functions of vitamin B12 in the human body. As described in Chapter 6, vitamin B12 is needed in both the Central Nervous System and (CNS) and Peripheral Nervous System (PNS) for the correct formation of the myelin sheath which insulates each nerve axon and ensures it sends its signal to the next neuron without "leaking" the signal to a neighbouring nerve.

Figure 8-3 nerve transmission when myelin sheath is damaged

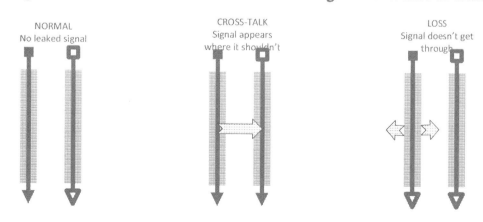

8.5.1   Headache/confusion/psychosis

In the CNS (brain and spinal cord), symptoms that might be triggered by vitamin B12 deficiency include:

- Migrainous headache
- Tension headache
- Dizziness
- Confusion, memory disturbance/forgetfulness, fogginess
- Psychosis, hallucinations, delusion (including schizophrenia (Brown & Roffman, 2014))

8.5.2   Depression and/or anxiety

Another group of symptoms relates to depression and anxiety. These are almost polar opposites in terms of how a person feels: one induces a feeling of disconnectedness and low energy; the other makes a person feel uncomfortably alert, with heightened energy but fatigue. Patients may also experience panic attacks, mood swings and mental slowness.

One cause of depression is thought to be the build-up of homocysteine (Bottiglieri et al., 2000). As described in Chapter 1, homocysteine accumulates in the absence of vitamin B12 because of lack of availability of the B12-dependent co-enzyme methionine synthase required to convert homocysteine to methionine.

8.5.3   Irritability, snappy, disturbed sleep

Other neuropsychiatric effects of vitamin B12 deficiency include irritability and disturbed sleep. One of the first changes that patients' partners and families notice following vitamin B12-replacement therapy is that these symptoms reduce, sometimes within hours of the first injection of the loading dose.

When determining the cause of mental ill-health symptoms, the physician should take into account whether there are any obvious triggers or situations. For example, depression or anxiety may be the result of recent trauma, bereavement or stress. In order to resolve symptoms, it is often useful (although not vital) to understand the cause. If no obvious cause is present, then a physician should consider diet and in particular vitamin and mineral deficiencies, and ingestion of psychoactive (whether known or unknown) compounds.

8.6   Withdrawal of vitamin-B12 therapy may lead to psychosis

It has been our experience that people on lifelong vitamin B12-replacement therapy for neuropsychiatric conditions who stop the treatment themselves, perhaps because they think they are cured, then start to exhibit behaviours that could be considered psychotic, a "risk to themselves and to others" (Mind UK, 2017).

The result is frequently that people have their liberty taken away: they are moved from their own home to hospital, under one of the sections of the Mental Health Act 1983 (Mind UK, 2017). In some cases, Dr Chandy and the B12 Deficiency Support Group charity have been involved. The Chairman of another charity, the Pernicious Anaemia Society (PAS), Martyn Hooper, has been involved in Section 136 cases (where a person is considered to be in need of immediate care or control, in which case a police officer can take him/her to a place of safety) (Hooper, 2013, 2015).

Many other Sections of the Mental Health Act 1983 may also be invoked. The two charities have participated in giving evidence that the behavioural change may be associated with the withdrawal of vitamin B12, as this vitamin is vital for the proper functioning of the nervous system, including the brain. The charities try to have treatment restored, and where they are successful, in many cases the patient resumes their independent living and enjoyment of life.

People exhibiting psychosis with no obvious psychotropic drug ingestion should be reviewed for vitamin B12 deficiency and treated accordingly. This is especially important where they have recently had vitamin B12-replacement therapy withdrawn.

8.7 What is dementia?

"Dementia: a generalised impairment of intellect, memory and personality with no impairment of consciousness" (Simon et al., 2014, p. 1012).

In the initial stages of dementia, a patient may present to their GP complaining of "being a bit forgetful", or their relatives may complain about their behaviour. For most patients suffering from dementia, the early symptoms are loss of short-term memory and inability to perform what would normally be simple tasks. If early symptoms are not identified, patients present later with failure to cope at home or self-neglect. However, for a definitive diagnosis of dementia to be made there must be a clear history of progressive impairment of memory and cognition, often accompanied by personality change.

Memory is the most common cognitive ability lost in dementia; 10% of people under the age of 70 years and 20-40% of people aged over 85 years have clinically identifiable memory loss. In addition to memory, other mental faculties may be affected; these include language, visuospatial ability and skills of calculation, judgement and problem-solving.

Neuropsychiatric and social deficits also arise in many dementia syndromes, resulting in depression, apathy, hallucinations, delusions, agitation, insomnia and disinhibition. The most common forms of dementia are progressive but some are static and unchanging or fluctuate from day to day or even minute to minute. Most patients with Alzheimer's disease (AD), the most prevalent form of dementia, suffer first from memory impairment. In other dementias, such as frontotemporal dementia, memory loss is not a presenting feature (Alzheimer's Society, 2017a).

There are several forms of dementia in addition to AD: Vascular dementia (Multi-infarct, caused by multiple strokes); Dementia with Lewy bodies; Frontotemporal dementia (FTD); Mixed dementia and Young-onset dementia (Alzheimer's Society, 2017a). The different forms may share similar outcomes for those suffering and require a similar response from their carers. The worldwide incidence of all types of dementia is estimated at 50 million, with 10 million new cases a year (WHO, 2017). This combined prevalence makes the search for causes and prevention all the more important. The World Health Organisation recognises dementia as a public health priority.

GPs have a particular duty to diagnose dementia because it is so widespread, and because specific actions can be taken to make life easier for people suffering from dementia and their carers once the diagnosis has been made. In the UK in 2018, an estimated 850,000 people were living with dementia of different types, a figure which is expected to exceed 2 million by 2051 (Alzheimer's

Society, 2017b). In the US, an estimated 5.7 million people were living with AD in 2018, expected to rise to nearly 14 million by 2050 (Alzheimer's Association, 2017).

The main factor which seems to contribute to dementia is advancing age (which we cannot "cure"). However, dementia is clearly not an inevitable consequence of age – the majority of people do not suffer from it and some centenarians have intact memory function and no evidence of clinically significant dementia.

Progression of dementia (cognitive and short-term memory decline) can also be traced through microscopic and larger changes to the brain, whether at autopsy or by CT and MRI studies, which gives hope for finding a cause and ultimately a cure.

There are generalised studies which indicate some connection with vitamin B12. For example, raised homocysteine was identified by a group of experts in 2018 as a modifiable risk factor in the development of cognitive decline, dementia and AD. The group published an International Consensus Statement declaring that the functional status of three B vitamins (folate, vitamin B12 and vitamin B6) in the body, which affects levels of homocysteine, has a significant impact on whole and regional brain atrophy and cognitive decline (Smith et al., 2018). Elsewhere, also, it has been shown that vitamin B12 deficiency can lead to cognitive decline (Clarke et al., 2007) and that across an elderly population, supplementation with vitamin B12 may delay the onset of dementia and improve the outcomes (Smith et al., 2010).

8.8   The connection between vitamin B12 deficiency and dementia

There is a close relationship between symptoms of vitamin B12 deficiency and those of dementia and some cases of vitamin B12 deficiency have been mistaken for dementia. In describing one such case, the researchers note: "Along with the other cases reported in the literature, our case also proves there are some cases of vitamin B12 deficiency that can manifest with the symptoms of frontotemporal dementia and that they are completely reversible after substitution therapy" (Blundo et al., 2011). Other clinicians have reported similarly:

> "Although in our patients, as well as in previously reported cases, the effects of vitamin B12 substitution cannot be positively distinguished from the effects of comedication, supporting therapeutic measures, and retest improvement, there is substantial evidence supporting the crucial involvement of vitamin B12 in several pathophysiological conditions affecting the CNS, reaching from myelination to transmitter function. Even though the causal relationship between cobalamin deficiency and dementia in individual patients is hard to prove and may often remain circumstantial, subclinical vitamin B12 deficiency, which today can be unambiguously identified, is a common condition in the elderly population. Considering the devastating impact of dementia on the quality of life of the individual and also the vast costs this often incurable condition causes, the proper diagnosis and inexpensive treatment of cobalamin deficiency should not be missed, especially in the early phases of cognitive decline (Goebels & Soyka, 2000).

We therefore thought it appropriate to compare the symptoms of the two conditions (Table 8-1), and consider whether dementia might be caused by vitamin B12 deficiency, either directly or indirectly, and therefore avoided by vitamin B12 supplementation.

	DEMENTIA	VITAMIN B12 DEFICIENCY
Symptoms	Generalised impairment of intellect and personality with no impairment of consciousness. Often characterised by loss of short-term memory, confusion, impairment of cognition which can result in being unable to cope with everyday life.	Loss of short-term memory. Forgetful. Irritable. Confused. Impairment of cognition. Unable to cope.
Prevalence	Increases with age, although there is an early-onset form. > 60 years: prevalence from 5% > 65 years: prevalence 20%	Increases with age: more prevalent in >75 years. Vitamin B12 deficiency can be present even as early as the embryo stage unless the pregnant vitamin B12-deficient mother is prescribed both vitamin B12 and folic acid (see Chapter 5).
How the brain is affected	<u>Vascular (Multi-infarct) dementia</u> Causes problems with the thinking and planning faculties. Often occurs after the blood supply to the brain has been interrupted e.g. in vasculitis or after a stroke (Alzheimer's Society, 2017c). <u>Dementia with Lewy bodies</u> Symptoms often include fluctuating alertness, hallucinations and problems with movement. <u>Alzheimer's disease</u> Most common form. The main cause is still being studied. Both early onset and late onset occur.	Lack of vitamin B12 appears to cause a build-up of homocysteine and brain atrophy, accompanied by loss of cognitive function and short-term memory, and vasculitis. Supplementing with vitamin B12 for a population aged 70+ has been shown to reduce the risk (Douaud et al., 2013; Smith et al., 2010).
Familial factor	The main factor is age. However, Alzheimer's is known to have a genetic component (National Institute on Ageing, 2017). For example, the apolipoprotein E (APOE) gene on chromosome 19 is thought to increase risk of late-onset. APOE comes in different forms (called alleles).The most common allele,	Predisposition to vitamin B12 deficiency can be inherited – there are at least eight different transport and metabolism proteins that may be affected by variant genes. It is possible that normal function of the genes can be restored with vitamin

Table 8-1 Comparison of characteristics of dementia and vitamin B12 deficiency

	DEMENTIA	VITAMIN B12 DEFICIENCY
	APOEε3, is thought to be neutral to Alzheimer's. However, APOEε4 increases risk and APOEε2 may be protective.	B12 supplementation over one or two generations
Reversible decline	Hard to reverse but early diagnosis and effective treatment of coexisting autoimmune conditions can slow down further deterioration of this condition.	Periodic screening in suspected cases results in early diagnosis. Commencing replacement treatment at the outset prevents further deterioration and in many cases maximum reversal can be achieved.
Central Nervous System (CNS) link	Dementia is defined by the effect on the CNS (brain and cognitive ability).	Both the CNS and the PNS are affected by vitamin B12 deficiency.
Triggers	Genetic factors are likely to be important. However, inflammation, particularly inflammation caused by autoimmune disease, may be a major trigger (Coghlan; Wotton & Goldacre, 2017). People on anti-inflammatory medication (e.g. for arthritis) have reduced levels of dementia.	Vitamin B12 deficiency may cause autoimmune conditions (see Chapter 7) and therefore resulting inflammation.
Associations	Link between autoimmune disease and heart and circulatory problems.	Vitamin B12 deficiency causes elevated homocysteine levels which are strongly associated with heart and circulatory disorders.

8.9   Links with other conditions

8.9.1   Cardiovascular Disease (CVD) and dementia

AD is more prevalent in patients suffering from conditions such as autoimmune inflammation, diabetes, other heart disease and vascular damage, and neurone/nervous-system damage (Coghlan, 2017; Wotton & Goldacre, 2017).

CVD is more prevalent in patients with autoimmune inflammation. Since vitamin B12 deficiency can cause autoimmune disorders (as described in Chapter 7) it may lead indirectly to dementia through this route. Supplementation with vitamin B12 throughout later years may play an important part in reducing the prevalence of all of these conditions (Douaud et al., 2013; Smith et al., 2010).

Vascular damage, especially of the micro blood vessels, is particularly closely related to dementia. Cerebral amyloid angiopathy (CAA)[34] is a major cause of lobar intracerebral haemorrhage (ICH) and cognitive impairment in the elderly and CAA is present in the brains of most people suffering from AD (Viswanathan & Greenberg, 2011).

Since vitamin B12 deficiency is associated with CVD, through the accumulation of homocysteine (Amer et al., 2015; Esteghamati et al., 2014; Gilfix, 2005; Harvard Health Publishing & Harvard Medical School, 2014; Mahalle et al., 2013; Ntaios et al., 2009) and its known causal effect on the cardiovascular system (Ganguly & Alam, 2015; Ueland et al., 2000), a greater role for vascular damage in causing dementia could indicate a greater importance for maintaining vitamin B12 levels in the prevention of dementia.

8.9.2   Autoimmune conditions and dementia

In Chapter 7 we showed that there is a link between many autoimmune glandular conditions and vitamin B12 deficiency. These conditions include Type I diabetes which is well known to be an autoimmune disorder, and also Type II diabetes which recent research suggests might also be an autoimmune condition (Diabetes.co.uk, 2018; Hemminki et al., 2015). It is known that people suffering from diabetes are at increased risk of developing dementia (Alzheimer Society Canada, 2018) so it is conceivable that vitamin B12 therapy, by reducing the autoimmune tendency, or by reducing the effects of diabetes, might help to reduce dementia risk through this route.

8.9.3   Neurological damage

Dementia is usually associated with some form of neurological damage in the brain. A population study of supplementation with three B vitamins (vitamin B12 in the form of cyanocobalamin, folic acid and pyridoxine), found that in elderly patients not taking the supplement, brain atrophy occurred more quickly and was associated with cognitive and memory decline (Smith et al., 2010). Images of Subtraction MRI scans included in their study report show the contrast between the brain of an elderly participant who was given active treatment with high doses of supplementary B vitamins (folic acid, and vitamins B12 and B6) over two years to lower homocysteine and that of an elderly participant in the placebo group who was given no treatment. The latter shows brain tissue changes and an atrophy rate of 2.5% per year compared with the former where there was no significant pattern of atrophy.

The study concluded: "Since accelerated brain atrophy is a characteristic of subjects with mild cognitive impairment who convert to Alzheimer's disease, trials are needed to see if the same treatment will delay the development of Alzheimer's disease" (Smith et al., 2010). The exact form of neurological damage is not well understood in dementia, possibly because "dementia" describes the symptom of cognitive decline, which may be caused by a huge number of independent mechanisms.

Many of the symptoms of vitamin B12 deficiency also relate to neurological decline in the CNS and brain. "Brain fog" is described as a feeling of being apart from people, able to hear voices but unable to understand why they might be trying to communicate with one. What better description of the early stages of cognitive decline relating to dementia?

---

[34] Cerebral amyloid angiopathy (CAA) is a condition in which proteins called amyloid build up on the walls of the arteries in the brain. CAA increases the risk for stroke caused by bleeding and dementia.

8.10 Is dementia inherited?

As described in Table 8-1, several genes play important pathogenic roles in at least some patients with AD. For example, adults with the genetic condition trisomy 21 (Down Syndrome) who survive beyond age 40 consistently show typical neuropathologic hallmarks of AD.

The role of vitamin B12 in ensuring correct gene transcription and therefore in preventing the occurrence of gene variants which might lead to illness, is described in Chapter 9.

8.11 Nutrition and lifestyle

8.11.1 Alcoholism

Dementia can accompany chronic alcoholism. This may be a result of associated malnutrition: alcohol destroys B vitamins, including thiamine (vitamin B1). Chronic alcoholism may also cause cerebral damage in other ways. For example, a rare idiopathic syndrome of dementia and seizures with degeneration of the corpus callosum (Marchiafava-Bignami Disease) has been reported in male Italian red-wine drinkers and other cases of alcoholism (Lyford et al., 2017). It is commonly treated with thiamine or B-complex vitamins (combining folate, thiamine and B12) (Nemlekar et al., 2016; Parmanand, 2016).

8.11.2 Dietary or induced B vitamin and trace mineral deficiencies

Many vitamins and trace elements are required for mental health. Thiamine (vitamin B1) deficiency is well known to cause the neuropsychiatric disorder Wernicke's encephalopathy.[35] This is particularly significant in our study because it shows the dramatic neuropsychiatric effects that one vitamin can have. Although alcoholism is a frequent cause of this condition, the clinical presentation also features patients who are malnourished because of malignant disease, gastrointestinal disease and surgery, and vomiting due to hyperemesis gravidarum. Other causes include fasting, starvation, malnutrition and the use of unbalanced diets (Galvin et al., 2010). The patient displays varied neurocognitive symptoms, typically involving mental status changes and gait and oculomotor dysfunction (BMJ Best Practice, 2018e). Prompt administration of parenteral thiamine (100 mg intravenously for three days followed by daily oral dosage) may reverse the disease if given in the first days of symptom onset. However, prolonged untreated thiamine deficiency can result in an irreversible dementia/amnestic syndrome (Korsakoff syndrome) or even death.

Vitamin B6 and niacin as well as the trace minerals zinc, copper, manganese and magnesium have also all been shown to play important roles in maintaining mental health (Cornish & Mehl-Madrona, 2008).

8.12 Treating dementia and other neuropsychiatric conditions

The main goals for dementia management are to treat correctable causes, and provide comfort and support to the patient and caregivers.

It has been shown that supplementing with vitamin B12 in an elderly population reduces the incidence of increased levels of homocysteine, brain atrophy, and cognitive decline (all characteristics of dementia). It is therefore important that this age group, in which dementia is most

---

[35] This illness is frequently combined with Korsakoff syndrome. The two illnesses together are known as Wernicke-Korsakoff syndrome or Wernicke-Korsakoff psychosis.

prevalent, receives appropriate supplements of vitamin B12 to reduce the likelihood of dementia developing (Smith et al., 2010).

Once the damage has been done, it is generally considered that damaged axons or axons with no myelin sheath are not able to recover, and therefore that the dementia will persist. However, we have observed many other instances (not including dementia) where non-functioning axons have restored their function. Others have also observed the repair of scleroids in the spinal column at the same time as restoration of motor and sensory functions (Scalabrino, 2005, 2009; Scalabrino et al., 1995).

Possible restoration of nerve function in children diagnosed with autism has also been observed. We have experienced cases where children manifesting autistic-spectrum behaviour have had all the symptoms reversed rapidly following treatment for vitamin B12 deficiency. From being highly disruptive at school, or unable to cope with schoolwork, they have become sociable pupils with good school performance. Pacholok and Stuart also comment: "doctors are finding that many autistic children improve remarkably when they receive B12 injections" (Pacholok & Stuart, 2011, p. 135).

It is also likely that vitamin B12 deficiency may cause psychosis (see Case 8-1), and that B12 supplementation may alleviate psychosis (Berger, 2004; Blundo et al., 2011; Denson, 1976; Dogan et al., 2009; Roze et al., 2003). Vitamin B12 supplements may also have a beneficial impact on the early stages of Parkinson's disease (Christine et al., 2018), epilepsy and palsies. Supporting evidence for this from our experience is provided by the fact that about 17 patients from the Shinwell Medical Group were taken off the epilepsy register following successful long-term vitamin B12-replacement therapy.

This leaves us with the hope that an appropriately balanced treatment with vitamins and hormones that are deficient may one day be available to reverse cognitive decline in people with dementia (Gröber et al., 2013).

Chapter 9   Vitamin B12 and cancer prevention

Though I speak with the tongues of men and of angels, but have not love I am only a resounding gong or clanging cymbal.

And though I have the gift of prophecy, and can understand all mysteries and all knowledge, and though I have faith, that can move mountains, but have not love, I am nothing.

And though I give all I possess to the poor, and surrender my body to the flames, but have not love, I gain nothing.

Love suffers long and is kind; love does not envy; love does not parade itself, is not puffed up; does not behave rudely, does not seek its own, is not provoked, thinks no evil; does not rejoice in iniquity, but rejoices in the truth; bears all things, believes all things, hopes all things, endures all things.

1 Corinthians 13:1-7 New King James Version

Figure 9-1 Prevention is better than cure

Prevention is better than cure (B12 and genetics)

Vitamin B12 deficiency with neuropsychiatric signs and symptoms Stages 1, 2, 3 and 4

Many, if not all, of the conditions listed below can be prevented or treated successfully by early diagnosis. Normal RNA and DNA activity are dependent on optimum B12 level

Perfect DNA transcription and copying/ genetic expression: Providing a methyl donor (B12 + folic acid) prior to and during pregnancy permanently alters the state of methylation of the offspring's DNA

Cancer / Dementia / Psychosis / Mania / Anxiety / Depression

Anaemia
Hypoferritinaemia

Vitamin D deficiency – osteomalacia (hypo/ hyper parathyroidism)

Multiple Sclerosis (MS)- like presentation

Hypothalamic-Pituitary Axis (HPA) dysfunction

Vital Hormones
All directed by pituitary:
Cortisol
Thyroxine
Parathyroid
Ovarian
Growth
Adrenal

Cells 100 Trillion
Chromosomes and DNA replication. Human Genome is divided into 23 chromosome pairs. Genetics is playing an increasing role in diagnosis, prevention and treatment of diseases.

Vital Elements
Oxygen
Water
B12/ Folic Acid
Sodium
Potassium
Iron
*
Healthy Nutrition
Daily Exercise

Hypoadrenalism (AI), Chronic Fatigue Syndrome

Myalgic encephalomyelitis (ME) like presentation

Developmental Chromosomal and Metabolic disorders

Fibromyalgia (FM)

Neural tube disorders, ADHD, Foetal Alcohol Spectrum Disorder

B12d hepatitis, B12d encephalitis, non-epileptic seizures, Parkinson-like presentation

PCOS (PolyCystic Ovary Syndrome)

Type I & II Diabetes / over/under-active thyroid

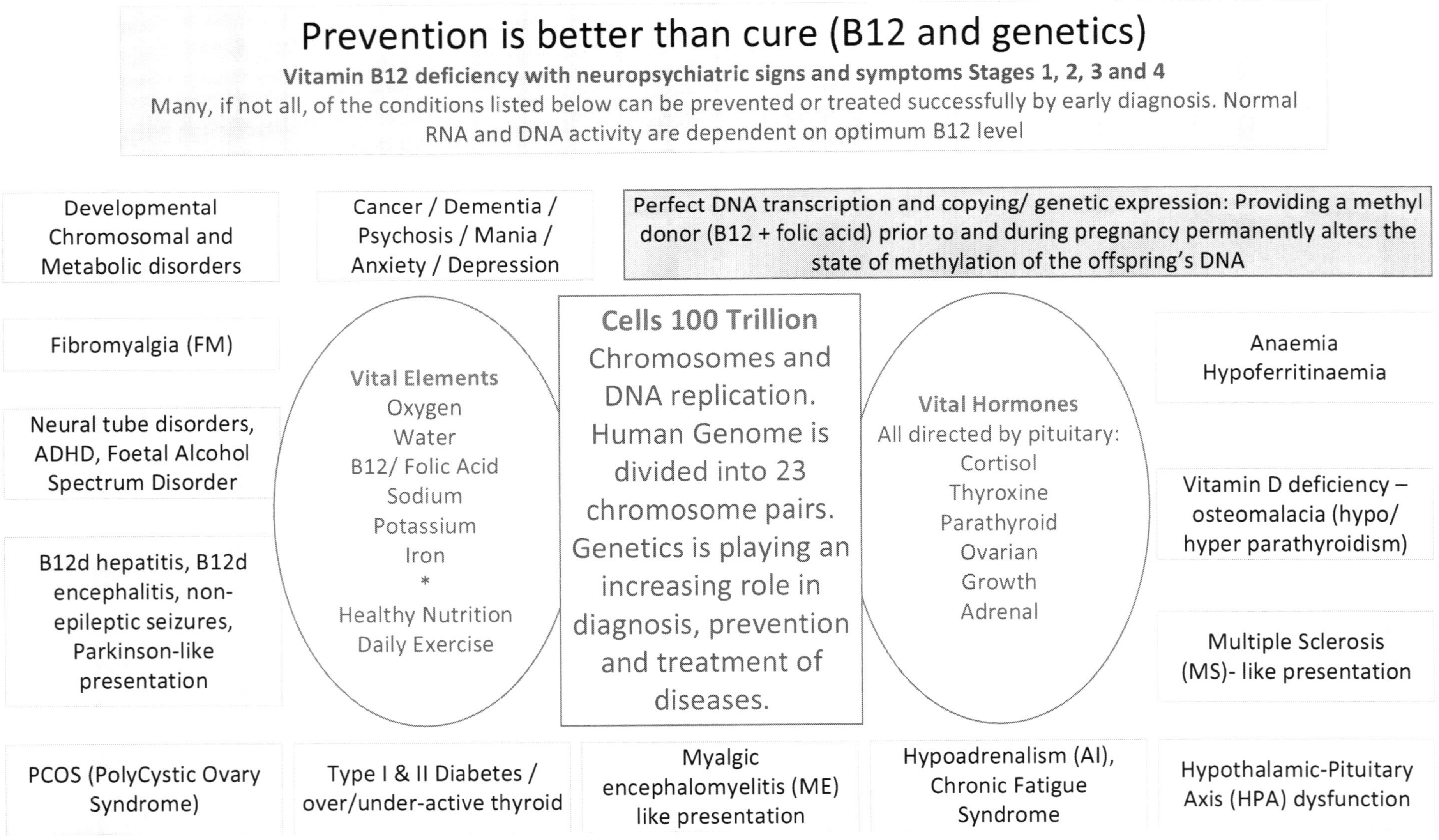

9.1 Cancer worldwide prevalence

Cancer is one of the most prevalent diseases of our time and its incidence[36] is increasing in many countries, including the UK (Jones, 2015). In the first nine months of 2018, there were 18 million new cases worldwide. The most common types of cancer (in descending order of new cases) were: lung, breast, colorectum, prostate, stomach, liver, oesophagus and cervix (IARC, 2018).

The US National Cancer Institute describes the illness thus:

> *"Cancer is the name given to a collection of related diseases. In all types of cancer, some of the body's cells begin to divide without stopping and spread into surrounding tissues. Cancer can start almost anywhere in the human body, which is made up of trillions of cells...Cancer is a genetic disease - that is, it is caused by changes to genes that control the way our cells function, especially how they grow and divide. Genetic changes that cause cancer can be inherited from our parents. They can also arise during a person's lifetime as a result of errors that occur as cells divide or because of damage to deoxyribonucleic acid (DNA) caused by certain environmental exposures."*

> *(National Cancer Institute, 2015).*

The cause of cancer is not known. It is believed to result from a number of interacting factors, including hereditary and environmental factors which cause changes to DNA. Among these is nutrition: inadequate supply of many micronutrients is now understood to play an important role in the development of some cancers. Such micronutrients include vitamin B12 which is known to be crucial for the correct formation of DNA and for the biochemical process known as DNA methylation (see below).

In this chapter we present some aspects of the relationship of vitamin B12 status to cancer as so far known. New treatments and preventive measures for cancer are constantly being researched. Having ourselves observed the widespread curative effects of vitamin B12 on body systems over many decades of clinical practice, it is our firm conviction that vitamin B12 will play an important role in both cancer treatment and prevention strategies in future. This view is reinforced by the fact that over three decades, during which we treated more than 1,000 patients for vitamin B12 deficiency at the Shinwell Medical Practice, we had *no new cases of cancer whatsoever* among these particular patients. This chapter gives evidence for why vitamin B12 may play a preventive and curative role in cancer treatment.

9.2 Some causes of cancer

The contributing factors to cancer are thought to include (in addition to inherited factors) (from the American Cancer Society (2014)):

- Lifestyle factors (nutrition, tobacco use, physical activity, etc.)
- Naturally occurring exposures (ultraviolet light, radon gas, infectious agents, etc.)
- Medical treatments (radiation and medicines, including chemotherapy which can cause secondary cancers, hormone drugs, drugs that suppress the immune system, etc.)
- Workplace exposures
- Household exposures
- Pollution

---

[36] A **cancer incidence rate** is the number of new cancers of a specific type occurring in a specified population during a year, usually expressed as the number of cancers per 100,000 population at risk.

In general, cancer-causing agents (carcinogens) are classified into three groups:

- Chemical carcinogens
- Radiation exposure
- Microbial carcinogens

Lists of carcinogens are drawn up by several agencies, including the International Agency for Research on Cancer (IARC) which is part of the World Health Organisation (WHO). Lists of *Known Human Carcinogens* can be found on the American Cancer Society website (American Cancer Society, 2014).

9.3 Cancer treatment

9.3.1 Standard treatments for cancer

One of the main types of treatment for cancer currently used is chemotherapy, the use of drugs to kill cancer cells (Cancer Research UK, 2017). There are many types of chemotherapy drugs which target cells at different stages of their cycle according to the type of cancer. Another common treatment is radiotherapy which uses high energy x-rays to damage the DNA within cancer cells (Cancer Research UK, 2018). The disadvantage of these treatments is that they damage healthy cells as well and are not always totally effective at killing cancer cells or preventing metastasis (the spread of cancer from the site where it originated to another site in the body).

9.3.2 A role for vitamin B12 in cancer treatment?

In 1997, Japanese researchers showed that large doses of methylcobalamin (an active form of vitamin B12) could inhibit the proliferation of some malignant cancer cells and suppressed tumour cells in laboratory animals. The researchers proposed that methylcobalamin could be useful in the treatment of some malignant tumours (Nishizawa et al., 1997).

To our knowledge, this important finding has not yet led to any vitamin B12-based treatment for cancer.

Ten years later, another researcher suggested that there were strong grounds for investigating vitamin B12 therapy for cancer (Volkov, 2008). He based his hypothesis on the fact that vitamin B12 is known to play an important role in many body organs and systems and that the list of these is growing, plus the fact that high levels of cobalamin have frequently been found in cancer patients. His interpretation was that these high levels were signs of the body's compensatory mechanism – in other words, the body was releasing B12 to deal with the invasion of cancer cells. He viewed vitamin B12 as a substance which "functions to keep body systems in balance, even under the stress of severe pathology".

Explaining his hypothesis, he said: "As yet I have not been able to find another explanation for high level of vitamin B12 in oncology patients other than that it is a compensatory mechanism. **Perhaps following this body's "warning sign", we should start treatment with high doses of vitamin B12 to try to help the <u>stabilization of normal function</u> of the organs and systems. Laboratory researches should be continued to substantiate <u>introduction of cobalamin as preliminary treatment of particular diseases</u>**" (Volkov, 2008).

High levels of cobalamin in the plasma of cancer patients have been found with such frequency that researchers in Denmark decided to conduct a major study to investigate whether these levels could be used as a diagnostic marker of cancer (Arendt et al., 2016). Their key population-based study used data from Danish medical registries from 1998 to 2014 and covered more than 80,000 cancer patients.

Results showed that those with "high plasma cobalamin levels prior to [cancer] diagnosis had higher mortality, indicating more advanced and aggressive cancers". Contrary to sensational news reports implying that this somehow meant that vitamin B12 caused cancer (Bird, 2013), the researchers speculated that the results reflected changes in cobalamin metabolism *caused* by cancer, not that high cobalamin levels caused cancer. They quoted the suggestion by Geissbühler et al. (2000) that hepatic metastases (cancer having spread to the liver) in particular are linked to high B12 levels. Other evidence they gave for this explanation was that haptocorrin, to which circulating cobalamin is bound, is metabolised only in the liver. Another possible explanation was that the high levels of cobalamin might reflect a "pronounced inflammatory response" to the cancer.

9.3.3 Vitamin B12 as "master key"

Volkov hypothesised that vitamin B12 has a "master key effect" on the human body. He noted that several experimental laboratory studies had indicated that use of vitamin B12 inhibited the growth of malignant cells, that there were no experimental results indicating the opposite and that there was no data indicating a toxic effect of vitamin B12. He expressed surprise that studies demonstrating these associations of vitamin B12 had not been followed up, and put forward three reasons for this:

1. Preference for treatment with vitamin B12 to modern perspective medicines does not seem appropriate for oncology patients who do not have time for such kind of experiments (an ethical question).
2. The unconvincing or unequivocal results of the research, which could be a consequence of using not high enough doses of vitamin B12, do not encourage oncologists to try vitamin B12 treatment.
3. *The paradoxical dilemma, in which the solution is so close, well-known, accessible, and cheap, makes it hard to believe that vitamin B12 may be effective in the treatment of oncology diseases* [Our italics]. (Volkov, 2008)

Vitamin B12 is not currently a "proven" anti-cancer treatment but specialists acknowledge that it is "an important nutrient for genetic stability, DNA repair, carcinogenesis, and cancer therapy" (Donaldson, 2004).

9.3.4 Vitamin B12 cancer therapy with nanotechnology?

Vitamin B12 as an anti-cancer therapy is also being investigated in other fields of science, such as nanotechnology. Interestingly, in one potential application of this technology, a team of scientists has proposed that vitamin B12, which they note has "several characteristics that make it an attractive entity for cancer treatment and possible therapeutic applications", could be used as a cancer treatment if it were delivered to cells via solid lipid nanoparticles (SLNs). These improve drug bioavailability and enable precision drug targeting (Genc et al., 2015).

Other researchers are investigating the synthesis of novel variant forms of vitamin B12 for potential use in cancer treatments (University of Kent, 2012).

9.3.5 Vitamin B12 as protection in chemotherapy

Vitamin B12 has no known toxicity, even at very high doses (see Chapter 3) and is in fact already used as a supplement to reduce toxicity in some existing chemotherapy treatments, such as Pemetrexed therapy (Singh et al., 2015; Takagi et al., 2016).

Vitamin B12 is so effective as an antioxidant that some medical scientists have suggested it should be used with caution in chemotherapy because it can counteract the effects of cytotoxic chemotherapy on tumour DNA (Eren et al., 2014). Vitamin B12 (and folic acid) are given because if levels of these vitamins are insufficient in the body, Pemetrexed may affect noncancerous as well as cancerous cells, which leads to toxic effects. One research study into the dosage of these vitamins in Pemetrexed treatment for lung cancer concluded that they did not reduce the effectiveness of the chemotherapy. The researchers noted that patients receiving these vitamins had greater tolerance for the chemotherapy treatment and improved survival prospects (Yang, Chang, et al., 2013). Further trials on the timing and dosage of these vitamins to protect patients undergoing chemotherapy are ongoing (Baldi et al., 2016).

9.4 Cancer prevention

9.4.1 The role of nutrition

It is now well established that inadequate or unbalanced nutrition plays an important role in the development of cancer. Dietary deficiencies are estimated to account for as much as one-third of preventable cancers (Ames & Wakimoto, 2002; Donaldson, 2004). Such effects can occur not only in cases of acute deficiency but also when intake is only slightly below the recommended dietary allowance (Ames & Wakimoto, 2002).

It was once thought that the only relation of diet to cancer was through exposure to carcinogens, such as alcohol or heterocyclic amines in meat (Sugimura et al., 2004), but it is now known that micronutrients play a crucial role in maintaining the integrity of DNA and correct activity of genes which help to prevent the occurrence of cancer (WCRF & AICR, 2007).

Over 40 micronutrients, including vitamin B12, play crucial roles in body metabolism and contribute to metabolic harmony. Deficiencies in one micronutrient can cause disturbances in many systems (Ames & Wakimoto, 2002). For instance, it has been shown that there is an inverse relationship[37] between the consumption of fruits and vegetables and many types of cancers. Case-control studies quoted by Ames and Wakimoto (Ames & Wakimoto, 2002 Table 2) show that a reduced consumption of fruits and vegetables can double the risk of developing most types of cancer. It should also be noted that meat, the main food source of iron, zinc and B12, is another important source of micronutrients.

9.4.2 The EPIC project

This knowledge has prompted much new research into the effects of nutrition in cancer prevention and treatment. Such research includes the ongoing extensive European Prospective Investigation into Cancer and Nutrition (EPIC) study designed to investigate the relationships between diet, nutritional status, lifestyle and environmental factors, and the incidence of cancer and other chronic diseases. Using information on diet, lifestyle characteristics, body measurements and medical history collected between 1992 and 1999 from more than half a million participants recruited across 10 European countries and followed for almost 15 years, EPIC investigators researched many aspects of the contribution of diet and lifestyle to cancer. This research is still ongoing but a summary of the significant findings by 2010 (Gonzalez & Riboli, 2010) listed the following:

- gastric cancer risk was less likely to occur with high plasma vitamin C, some carotenoids, retinol and α-tocopherol, high intake of cereal fibre and high adhesion to Mediterranean diet;

---

[37] An "inverse relationship" is a relationship between two numbers in which an increase in the value of one number results in a decrease in the value of the other number.

- red and processed meat were associated with increased gastric cancer risk;
- high intake of dietary fibre, fish, calcium, and plasma vitamin D were associated with a decreased risk of colorectal cancer;
- red and processed meat intake, alcohol intake, body mass index (BMI) and abdominal obesity were associated with an increased risk of colorectal cancer;
- high intake of fruit and vegetables in current smokers was associated with a decreased risk of lung cancer;
- an increased risk of breast cancer was associated with high saturated fat intake and alcohol intake.

The researchers noted: "These results contribute to scientific evidence for appropriate public health strategies and prevention activities aimed at reducing the global cancer burden".

9.4.3 DNA – a brief sketch

As stated above, cancer is a genetic disorder. In order to give some idea of the mechanisms by which vitamin B12 and other micronutrients may affect the activity of genes, we include this simplified sketch of the main features of DNA as so far known. Interested readers may find further detail on the US National Human Genome Research Institute website and in articles by the International Human Genome Sequencing Consortium (see bibliography in this book).

DNA is a long molecule that contains the instructions for life. It has frequently been called the "blueprint" for life but scientists see that as a limited metaphor for "something so intricate, complex, multilayered and dynamic" (Ainsworth, 2015). DNA is replicated in nearly every cell in a living organism. Most DNA is found in the nucleus of cells but a small amount is located in the mitochondria (structures within cells that convert the energy from food into a form that cells can use) (National Library of Medicine (US), 2018b).

All DNA is composed of the same chemical building blocks, called nucleotides (or bases), made of a phosphate molecule, a five-carbon sugar molecule (deoxyribose), and one of four nitrogen-based molecules: adenine, thymine, guanine and cytosine. What makes the differences between one person and another is the order in which these smaller molecules are arranged.

A person's complete set of DNA is known as the genome. Each genome contains all the information needed to build and maintain that person. A copy of the entire genome—more than 3 billion DNA base pairs — is contained in all cells that have a nucleus (National Library of Medicine (US), 2018a).

Genes are small sections of DNA that contain the instructions for building a specific molecule, usually a protein. There are estimated to be around 19-20,000 genes in humans, coding for around 120,000 proteins which are the production line which manufactures everything in the body, whether more permanent elements like bone or cartilage, or instantaneous chemicals such as noradrenaline used for a millisecond for nerve transmission.[38] Scientists trace genes by giving them names. Polymorphisms are multiple forms of genes which contribute to different outcomes in different people.

---

[38] Protein-coding sequences account for only a very small fraction of the genome (approximately 1.5%), and the rest is associated with non-coding RNA molecules, regulatory DNA sequences, LINEs, SINEs, introns, and sequences for which as yet no function has been determined (International Human Genome Sequencing Consortium, 2001).

DNA strands are extremely long in relation to the size of a cell. If unravelled, the DNA strand in just one cell would be two metres long! (Ashworth, 2011). The DNA is tightly packed and coiled into structures called chromosomes. A human chromosome can have up to 500 million base pairs (two nucleobases bound to each other by hydrogen bonds – for example, adenine-thymine) of DNA with thousands of genes.

In order to make proteins, the information stored in a gene is transferred to a similar molecule called RNA (ribonucleic acid) in the cell nucleus in a process known as *transcription*. The type of RNA that contains the information for making a protein is called messenger RNA (mRNA) because it transmits information from the nucleus into the cell's cytoplasm. The next step, known as *translation*, involves interaction between the mRNA and a ribosome, which links amino acids (the building blocks of proteins) in an order specified by mRNA. A type of RNA called transfer RNA (tRNA) assembles the protein, one amino acid at a time. This whole process is known as gene expression.

All genes do not need to be expressed all of the time so cells have mechanisms to regulate gene activity by turning genes on and off at any point in the gene expression pathway. "In multicellular organisms gene regulation defines the cell, its structure and function, and ultimately the whole organism. Aberrant gene regulation results in cancer, birth defects, and even death" (Laybourn, 2001).

Growth and development depend on cells dividing and the DNA replicating. Every time a human cell divides it has to correctly replicate the same sequence of 3 billion nucleotides. In this process, mistakes (mutations) can occur. Many of these are corrected by DNA repair processes but some are not, particularly where the DNA repair enzymes themselves are damaged. This may then lead to illness. All cancers begin when one or more genes in a cell mutate (Cancer.Net, 2018). The first mutated gene associated with cancer was discovered in 1982 and since then several hundred "cancer genes" have been identified (Pray, 2008).

9.4.4 Epigenetics: environmental influences on genes

The study of the ways in which interactions from biomolecules in the environment (including diet) affect which genes will be expressed without changing the DNA sequence is a relatively new field of science called epigenetics. All the chemicals that have been added to a person's DNA are known as the epigenome and include three inter-acting mechanisms: DNA methylation, histone modifications and non-coding microRNAs (miRNA). "The combination of these marks and miRNAs is responsible for regulating gene expression not only during cellular differentiation in embryonic and foetal development (Reik, 2007) but also throughout the life-course" (McKay & Mathers, 2011). Some researchers argue that epigenetic influences on genes are as important as the structure of genes in determining a person's characteristics and health (Ainsworth, 2015).

Research into the effects of nutrition on gene expression is a sub-field known as Nutritional Epigenetics (Landecker, 2011). Research on animal nutrition has found that changing the diet can change the animal's physical characteristics (Zhang, 2015). In humans, the micronutrients folate, vitamin B12, methionine, choline, and betaine can affect DNA methylation and histone methylation through altering one-carbon metabolism – a series of biochemical exchanges[39] (Choi & Friso, 2010). The ways in which

---

[39] One-carbon metabolism is the movement of biochemical groups containing a single carbon atom. There are three ways in which this can be done: through Tetrahydrofolate (THF) as a cofactor in enzymatic reactions; through

dietary deficiencies influence the development of cancer are highly complex but they are known to include gene mutations, DNA lesions (damaged bases or chromosome breaks), increased cell-division rates and other factors (Ames et al., 1995).

> *"Dietary exposures can have consequences for health years or decades later and this raises questions about the mechanisms through which such exposures are 'remembered' and how they result in altered disease risk. There is growing evidence that epigenetic mechanisms may mediate the effects of nutrition and may be causal for the development of common complex (or chronic) diseases" (McKay & Mathers, 2011).*

This has led to the *developmental origins of health and disease (DOHAD)* hypothesis which suggests that "environmental exposures during development increase susceptibility to cancer in adulthood, not by inducing genetic mutations, but by reprogramming the epigenome" (Walker & Ho, 2012).

Here it should be noted that the results of research into the effects of diet on cancer are often mixed or contradictory. One reason for this is that studies of dietary effects are extremely difficult to conduct. Because of the interactions of many nutrients, it is often difficult to separate the effects of one from another. Researchers must also decide over what length of time to conduct the research and at what dosages. There are also many variables (such as the lifestyle and ethnicity of participants) which have to be taken into account.

9.5   Vitamin B12, folate and correct formation of DNA

DNA damage is known to be an important risk factor for cancer (Basu, 2018; Esteller, 2003). Although much research remains to be done, there is significant evidence that several vitamins and minerals play essential roles in correct formation of DNA (Zhang, 2015). By implication, deficiencies of such micronutrients become a cancer risk. "Micronutrient deficiency can mimic radiation in damaging DNA by causing single- and double-strand breaks, oxidative lesions, or both. Those micronutrients whose deficiency appears to mimic radiation are folic acid, B12, B6, niacin, C, E, iron and zinc, with the laboratory evidence ranging from likely to compelling" (Ames, 1979).

Much of the research into the relationship of nutrition to cancer has focused on folate (and folic acid, the synthetic form used in supplements). This is partly because of the known importance of folate in preventing birth defects, and debates about folic acid fortification of food.

Low folate has been associated with chromosome breaks, a disorder which researchers explain as resulting from excessive uracil incorporation into DNA instead of thymine. "Both in vitro and in vivo studies with human cells clearly show that folate deficiency causes expression of chromosomal fragile sites, chromosome breaks, excessive uracil in DNA, micronucleus formation, DNA hypomethylation and mitochondrial DNA deletions" (Fenech, 2012). Vitamin B12 deficiency is expected to have the same effect because of the synergy between the two vitamins: "Vitamin B12 deficiency would be expected to cause chromosome breaks by the same uracil-misincorporation mechanism that is found with folate deficiency" (Ames & Wakimoto, 2002).

S-adenosylmethionine (SAM) as a methyl (-CH$_3$) donor and through Vitamin B12 (cobalamin) as a co-enzyme in methylation and rearrangement reactions.

Less research appears to have been done on the role of vitamin B12 in cancer prevention, perhaps because until recently it was assumed that vitamin B12 deficiency was less prevalent in the general population (Choi et al., 2004). However, folate cannot perform its functions in the human body correctly without vitamin B12 which is essential for many biochemical reactions. Findings which implicate low folate status with cancer development would therefore also apply in cases of vitamin B12 deficiency. This has been shown to be true in laboratory experiments (Choi et al., 2004).

The mechanism of uracil misincorporation into DNA is understood to result from abnormalities in the folate cycle which lead to low levels of methylene-THF (the folate cofactor for thymidylate synthase). This in turn decreases synthesis of thymidylate which is required for methylation of deoxyuridine monophosphate (dUMP) to deoxythymidine monophosphate (dTMP). The proportion of dUMP increases, leading to excessive uracil accumulation in DNA (Ames & Wakimoto, 2002; Blount et al., 1997; Wickramasinghe & Fida, 1994).

The result is disordered composition of DNA and chromosome breaks. The effects are described thus: "Excessive amounts [of uracil] are incorporated when thymidylate synthesis is inadequate to meet the cellular requirements for DNA synthesis and repair, leading to inappropriate nucleotide sequences, and the increased likelihood of chromosomal breakage, deletions and mutations" (Choi et al., 2004). Such damage, which can occur with either folate or vitamin B12 deficiency, could "contribute to the increased risk of cancer and cognitive defects" in humans (Blount et al., 1997). The same researchers note that folate *therapy* can reduce high uracil levels and chromosome breaks.

Abnormalities in the folate cycle may result from deficient folate intake from diet or from disruption of folate metabolism by lack of vitamin B12. As described in Chapter 1, vitamin B12 is required for the cofactor methionine synthase (MS) which is necessary for biochemical reactions in both the folate and methionine cycles. If there is not enough vitamin B12, 5-methyl tetrahydrofolate cannot be converted to tetrahydrofolate which is necessary for the next series of biochemical reactions. It is effectively "trapped" in cells as 5-MTHF which the body cannot use.

9.6 Aberrant DNA methylation in cancer

The vitamin B12-dependent cofactor MS also affects DNA methylation (the addition of one-carbon groups to DNA which affects gene expression) through the methionine cycle. When MS activity is reduced, methionine cannot be adequately metabolised to S-Adenosylmethionine (SAMe) (Zhang, 2015) which acts as the methyl donor in >80 reactions, including the methylation of DNA, histones and other proteins, neurotransmitters, and phospholipids and the synthesis of creatine – reactions which play important roles in development, gene expression, and genomic stability" (Choi et al., 2004; Shane, 2008).

DNA methylation is a "crucial epigenetic modification of the genome that is involved in regulating many cellular processes. These include embryonic development, transcription, chromatin structure, X chromosome inactivation, genomic imprinting and chromosome stability". It has been found that errors in DNA methylation processes are linked to many human diseases, including cancer (Robertson, 2005).

9.7 Dual role of folate and folic acid in cancer development

There is considerable evidence that healthy folate status plays a significant role in cancer prevention. Research has shown links between higher intakes of dietary folate and a reduced risk of cancer of the colon, of other parts of the gastrointestinal tract, and also of the pancreas (Ulrich, 2007). The picture is more complex than first thought, however, and the role of synthetic folic acid taken as a supplement and as used in food fortification may be different from that of dietary folate. Folate may "play a dual role in cancer development: it may provide protection early in carcinogenesis and in individuals with a low folate status, yet it may promote carcinogenesis if administered later and potentially at very high intakes" (Ulrich, 2007). (The difference between folate and folic acid and the issues this raises are discussed by Kresser (2012)).

The debate centres largely around the role of folate and folic acid in DNA methylation and the question of whether high intakes promote growth and replication of all cells, including cancer cells. In an article concerning the European reluctance to fortify flour with folic acid (compared with the US where this has been practised since the 1990s) because of an assumed possible cancer risk, one specialist has pointed out that folate/folic acid is only _one_ of the components of the methylation cycle so "linking only folate intakes / status to DNA methylation is a considerable simplification, as folate is just one of several actors supplying C1 [one-carbon] groups to the SAM pool" (Jägerstad, 2012).

The relationship of folate deficiency to the development of cancer is thus controversial and research has produced conflicting results. A recent review of research on the relationship of folate status to colorectal carcinogenosis concluded that the balance of evidence was that there is an inverse relationship between folate status and colorectal cancer risk (i.e. higher folate means less risk). However, it was noted that the relationship is complex and folate appears to have a dual role, depending on the timing and dose of folate intervention and whether the cancer is already established (Kim, 2007). Similar effects were found in relation to breast cancer: adverse effects were related to supplementation with folic acid rather than high intake of natural-source folate (Kim, 2006).

Others have similarly found that higher folate intake reduces the risk of colorectal and breast cancer, but they emphasise that the "optimal dose, duration and stage of carcinogenesis" for folate intervention are not yet known. They also state that the protective effects of folate may be due to other protective factors in fruits and vegetables not yet known (Eichholzer et al., 2001).

In contrast, a study conducted in Norway (Ebbing et al., 2009) from 1998 to 2005 (and followed up to December 2007), in the context of debates about food fortification with folic acid, found that folic acid and vitamin B12 taken together raised cancer incidence. The study concluded that the higher incidence of cancer was likely to have resulted from the folic acid supplementation, not the B12: "However, the observed associations between the primary end points and vitamin concentration measured during study treatment were confined to serum folate, suggesting that the adverse effects were mediated by folic acid." The suggestion is that excess folic acid, or unmetabolized folic acid, may "impair cancer immune defence".

From the above it is evident that more research is needed to establish the exact mechanisms by which folate, folic acid and vitamin B12 may impact on cancer prevention or development.

9.8   Tissue-specific cancers and vitamin B12

Less research appears to have been done specifically on the relationship of vitamin B12 deficiency to cancer. Much is not known about this relationship and research, particularly where it looks at vitamin B12 and folate together, has produced mixed results. The inconsistent results can be attributed partly to the dual roles of folate and folic acid in carcigenosis described above. Another reason may be misinterpretation of high levels of plasma cobalamin as a cause of cancer rather than as the body's response and attempt to restore balance which we described in the opening paragraphs of this chapter.

DNA methylation is known to be tissue-specific so the effects of specific micronutrients are likely to differ depending on the part of the body affected. This might explain why some types of cancer are specifically associated with B12 deficiency or with variations in the body's ability to metabolise B12.

9.8.1 Gastric cancer

The strongest known link of vitamin B12 deficiency with specific cancers is with gastric cancer and has been known for decades (Chanarin, 1990, p. 86) Patients suffering from pernicious anaemia (PA), which causes vitamin B12 deficiency (and may also be a consequence of this deficiency – see Chapter 4), have an increased risk of developing gastric cancer. Some researchers have found the relative risk rate to be seven times higher than in the general population (Vannella et al., 2013).

The link between PA and cancer is apparent when it is understood that both involve DNA damage. For example, Shane notes that megaloblastic anaemia is a "condition reflecting deranged DNA synthesis in erythropoietic cells" and that in this condition megaloblastic changes occur in all fast-growing tissues, such as the marrow and gut epithelia. He continues, "Megaloblastic cells contain close to twice the normal DNA content and the DNA is partially fragmented...The defect in DNA synthesis has been ascribed to defective thymidylate synthesis under these conditions with a resulting increase in uracil misincorporation into DNA. Removal of uracil by the repair enzyme uracil DNA glycosylase, and a decreased repair of the gaps produced by this enzyme, would lead to an increase in double-stranded DNA breaks under these conditions (Blount et al., 1997)" (Shane, 2008).

The authors of a study conducted in 1993 observed that there was not only an increased incidence of stomach cancer among PA patients but that these patients also had a high incidence of other cancers of the digestive tract and process, such as esophageal, pancreatic and rectal cancer. They also observed increases in myeloid leukaemia and multiple myeloma among PA patients (Hsing et al., 1993).

More recently, Chinese scientists noted a direct link between vitamin B12 metabolism and the occurrence of gastric cancer. In contrast to many studies which have concentrated on the one-carbon pathway described above, their study investigated possible links between gene variants which affect the uptake of B12 in the body and the incidence of gastric cancer. Their study group included 492 patients with gastric cancer and a control group of 550 non-sufferers. The results showed that a significant number of patients with gastric cancer were carriers of a risky variant of the TCN1 gene (which affects how B12 is bound to haptocorrin) or of a CUBN haplotype (which encodes the intrinsic factor (IF)-vitamin B12 receptor, cubilin). They concluded: "The circulating vitamin B12 concentration-related variants were associated with the occurrence of gastric cancer. This finding shed light on the unexpected role of vitamin B12 metabolism genes in gastric carcinogenesis and highlighted the interplay of diet, genetics, and human cancers" (Zhao et al., 2016).

9.8.2 Colon cancer

Other parts of the digestive tract also appear to be particularly affected by vitamin B12 status. For instance, recent research has shown a connection between vitamin B12 intake and colorectal cancer (CRC) risk (Sun et al., 2016). Noting the importance of diet in CRC risk, and that previous research on the relationship between vitamin B12 and/or folate and colon cancer was controversial, the researchers aimed to "quantitatively and comprehensively summarize whether vitamin B12 intake or blood vitamin B12 level is related to CRC risk". They extracted data from 14 studies involving 9,693 patients. The results showed that there was no reduction of cancer risk where only small amounts of B12 (dietary intake of <7 mcg/day) were taken, but when larger amounts were ingested (>12 mcg/day) the risk was significantly reduced. They did not find any correlation between blood B12 levels and risk, however. They suggested that further research was needed on the interaction of dietary and supplemental B12 intakes and the differing effects of the active and inactive forms of B12.

9.8.3   Pancreatic cancer

Less research has been done into the effects of micronutrients on pancreatic cancer risk. The results of one major recent research project, for example, were inconclusive. The researchers found no overall association between plasma concentrations of vitamin B12, vitamin B6, folate and homocysteine and pancreatic cancer risk, but did find a possible inverse relationship between circulating levels of vitamins B12, B6 and folate in those who obtained these micronutrients exclusively from diet (Schernhammer et al., 2007).

9.8.4   Lung cancer

Lung cancer (mostly caused by cigarette smoking) is the leading cause of cancer deaths worldwide (Lu, 2011). It is clinically divided into two broad groups, that is, small cell lung cancer (SCLC) and nonsmall cell lung cancer (NSCLC). Researchers have found close links between faulty DNA methylation and the development of lung cancer (Lu & Zhang, 2011; Piyathilake et al., 2000). Some have proposed that DNA methylation markers could be used in early diagnosis of this illness, and expressed the hope that new methylation-based therapies "will clinically cure lung cancer one day" (Lu & Zhang, 2011).

Piyathilake et al. specifically investigated the relationship between DNA hypomethylation and deficiencies of folate and vitamin B12 in patients suffering from squamous cell lung cancer. They found lower concentrations of both vitamins in SCCs than in uninvolved tissues. However, other results from this research suggested that folate, rather than vitamin B12, might be the "limiting vitamin for proper DNA methylation".

Other research has linked changes in DNA methylation to pollutants, such as tobacco smoke and chemicals in air pollution, both of which contribute to lung cancer (Jiang et al., 2017; Lee & Pausova, 2013).

9.8.5   Breast cancer

Research into the relationship of vitamin B12 intake to the occurrence of breast cancer has had mixed results. Data from the Shanghai Breast Cancer Study showed that women who consumed high levels of folate had reduced breast cancer risk and an even smaller risk if they also consumed high levels of folate cofactor nutrients such as vitamin B12, methionine and vitamin B6 (Shrubsole et al., 2001). Similarly, Yang et al. (2013) found that higher intake of folate, vitamin B12 and methionine were marginally associated with a lower risk of breast cancer. In contrast, Bassett et al. (2013) found no connection between vitamin B12 status and breast cancer, which again highlights the difficulties connected with these kinds of study.

9.8.6   Prostate cancer

A number of studies have been undertaken on the association of vitamin B12, folate or folic acid, and prostate cancer. These have also had mixed results. Some have indicated that high plasma levels of vitamin B12 and folate appear to be linked to increased prostate cancer risk (Hultdin et al., 2005) although they stress that further research is needed to confirm this relation. Collin et al. (2010), for example, noted that although their results might suggest a "possible causal relationship" between folic acid, vitamin B12 and prostate cancer risk, the limitations of research based on food frequency questionnaires are well known. A few years later, Collin suggested that the higher levels of B12 circulating in the blood of prostate cancer patients could be explained by "reverse causality" (i.e. the cancer had caused the high levels) (Collin, 2013). This would be in accordance with Volkov's hypothesis described at the beginning of this chapter – that the body is somehow compensating for the proliferation of cancer cells by releasing B12 into the bloodstream.

A major recent pooled data study (Price et al., 2016) investigated the associations between circulating folate and vitamin B12 concentrations and risk of prostate cancer overall and by disease stage and grade. This study found some weak evidence of a link between higher folate and vitamin B12 levels and risk of prostate cancer. They also found that higher folate concentration was associated with high-grade disease risk but suggested that this might be due to folic acid supplementation rather than dietary folate intake. A response by others (Obeid & Pietrzik, 2016) discussed the limitations of this study which highlighted some of the difficulties of conducting research on individual nutrients and cancer.

9.9   Critical time-windows in cancer prevention

Research has shown that there appear to be critical time-windows when diet and other epigenetic influences have a particularly significant impact on predisposition to disease. It is well known that poor nutrition in a pregnant mother affects the child but the discoveries in epigenetics suggest that these effects may be more far-reaching than previously thought. McKay and Mathers (2011) comment: "dietary exposures can have long-term consequences for health and raise questions about the mechanisms through which early life exposures are 'remembered' over long-time periods and how they result in altered disease risk. Poor nutrition in utero may result in inadequate development of specific cells and tissues."

According to Neitzel and Trimborn: "Chromosomal disorders (gene mutations) occur in an estimated 10-25% of all pregnancies. They are the leading cause of fetal loss and, among pregnancies surviving to term, the leading known cause of birth defects and mental retardation" (Neitzel & Trimborn, 2007).

Studies of the effects of restricting the amounts of vitamin B12, folate and methionine in the diets of animals prior to pregnancy resulted in adult offspring with altered immune responses, insulin-resistance, and elevated blood pressure (Sinclair et al., 2007). The researchers concluded: "The data provide the first evidence that clinically relevant reductions in specific dietary inputs to the methionine/folate cycles during the periconceptional period can lead to widespread epigenetic alterations to DNA methylation in offspring, and modify adult health-related phenotypes".

These findings have been further supported by research showing the importance of vitamin B12 status for one-carbon metabolism, influencing patterns of DNA methylation at birth which may have lifelong effects (McKay et al., 2012). Other research into maternal nutrition in humans has shown that maternal concentration of vitamin B12, vitamin B6 and homocysteine may play a significant role in the three-year weight gain of infants (McCullough et al., 2016).

However, the subject is controversial and others have pointed out that nutritional effects are complex. As it is not possible to target a single gene through this method, "indiscriminate and potentially irreversible methylation changes in a broader range of biomolecules and cells/tissues may result from such dietary treatment" (O'Neill et al., 2014). Many other factors need to be considered such as foetal sex, maternal/foetal genetic background, other maternal factors, as well as tissue/cell specificity and concentration and duration of exposure to these nutritional supplements.

Scientists agree that there is much more to be learnt from epigenetics-based studies concerning how diet affects human health over long time periods, which may lead to new ways of preventing and treating cancer. Specific research priorities include identifying the life stages during which particular epigenetic loci are affected by diet.

"'Tuning-up' human metabolism, which varies with genetic constitution and changes with age, could prove to be a simple and inexpensive way to minimize DNA damage, prevent cancer, improve health and prolong a healthy lifespan" (Ames & Wakimoto, 2002).

In the light of these new findings on the importance of diet in cancer prevention, together with the effects of other preventable causes (such as tobacco smoke), we strongly advocate ensuring healthy vitamin B12 levels throughout life, starting with the disease prevention programme for mother and child given in Figure 5-1, as a way of ensuring good health throughout life.

Documents Cited

AARDA. American Autoimmune Related Disease Association. (2018). Autoimmune Disease List. Available from: https://www.aarda.org/diseaselist/

Abdu, T. A., Elhadd, T. A., Neary, R., & Clayton, R. N. (1999). Comparison of the low dose short synacthen test (1 microg), the conventional dose short synacthen test (250 microg), and the insulin tolerance test for assessment of the hypothalamo-pituitary-adrenal axis in patients with pituitary disease. *Journal of Clinical Endocrinology and Metabolism, 84*(3), 838-843. doi:10.1210/jcem.84.3.5535. Available from: https://www.ncbi.nlm.nih.gov/pubmed/10084558

Abraham, J. (2007). Obituaries 204: Jacob Chandy 1910 - 23 June 2007. *The National Medical Journal of India, 20*(4 (July/Aug)). Available from: https://web.archive.org/web/20080503103429/http://www.nmji.in/archives/Volume_20/Number_4/Obituaries/Obituaries_Jacob.htm

Adams, J. F., Tankel, H. I., & MacEwan, F. (1970). Estimation of the total body vitamin B12 in the live subject. *Clinical Science, 39*(1), 107-113. Available from: https://www.ncbi.nlm.nih.gov/pubmed/4915181; http://www.clinsci.org/content/39/1/107.long

Addison, T. (1849). Anaemia: disease of the supra-renal capsules. *London Medical Gazette 43*, 517-518.

Addison, T. (1855). *On the Constitutional and Local Effects of Disease of the Supra-renal Capsule*. London: S. Highley.

Ainsworth, C. (2015). DNA is life's blueprint? No, there's far more to it than that. *New Scientist, 3025*. Available from: https://www.newscientist.com/article/mg22630251-000-dna-is-lifes-blueprint-no-theres-far-more-to-it-than-that/

Allen, L. H. (2002). Impact of Vitamin B-12 Deficiency During Lactation on Maternal and Infant Health. In M. K. Davis, C. E. Isaacs, L. Å. Hanson, & A. L. Wright (Eds.), *Integrating Population Outcomes, Biological Mechanisms and Research Methods in the Study of Human Milk and Lactation* (10.1007/978-1-4615-0559-4_6pp. 57-67). Boston, MA: Springer US.

Allen, L. H. (2009). How common is vitamin B-12 deficiency? *American Journal of Clinical Nutrition, 89*(2), 6935-6965. Available from: http://www.ajcn.org/content/89/2/693S.full

Alzheimer's Association. (2017). 2017 Alzheimer's Disease Facts and Figures. Available from: http://www.alz.org/facts/

Alzheimer's Society. (2017a). Alzheimer's Disease. Available from: https://www.alzheimers.org.uk/info/20007/types_of_dementia/2/alzheimers_disease

Alzheimer's Society. (2017b). Facts for the Media. Available from: https://www.alzheimers.org.uk/info/20027/news_and_media/541/facts_for_the_media

Alzheimer's Society. (2017c). Types of Dementia. Available from: https://www.alzheimers.org.uk/info/20007/types_of_dementia

Alzheimer Society Canada. (2018, Aug 24). Diabetes and dementia - is there a connection? Available from: https://alzheimer.ca/en/Home/About-dementia/Alzheimer-s-disease/Risk-factors/Diabetes-dementia-connection

Amer, M. S., Ali-Labib, R., Farid, T. M., Rasheedy, D., & Tolba, M. F. (2015). Link between vitamin B12, type 2 diabetes mellitus, and bone mineral density in elderly patients. *Journal of Clinical Gerontology & Geriatrics, 6*, 120-124.

American Cancer Society. (2014, 2 Oct 2014). Known and Probable Human Carcinogens. Available from: https://www.cancer.org/cancer/cancer-causes/general-info/known-and-probable-human-carcinogens.html

American Society of Hematology. (2011). False normal vitamin B12 levels caused by assay error. *Blood, 118*(3), 492-492. doi:10.1182/blood-2010-11-315564. Available from: http://www.bloodjournal.org/content/bloodjournal/118/3/492.full.pdf

American Society of Hematology. (2018). Anemia. Available from: http://www.hematology.org/Patients/Anemia/

Ames, B. N. (1979). Identifying environmental chemicals causing mutations and cancer. *Science, 204*(4393), 587-593. doi:10.1126/science.373122. Available from: http://science.sciencemag.org/content/204/4393/587

Ames, B. N., Gold, L. S., & Willett, W. C. (1995). The causes and prevention of cancer. *Proceedings of the National Academy of Sciences of the United States of America, 92*(12), 5258-5265. Available from: https://www.ncbi.nlm.nih.gov/pubmed/7777494; http://www.pnas.org/content/pnas/92/12/5258.full.pdf

Ames, B. N., & Wakimoto, P. (2002). Are vitamin and mineral deficiencies a major cancer risk? *Nature Reviews: Cancer, 2*(9), 694-704. doi:10.1038/nrc886. Available from: https://www.ncbi.nlm.nih.gov/pubmed/12209158

Andres, E., Federici, L., Affenberger, S., Vidal-Alaball, J., Loukili, N. H., Zimmer, J., & Kaltenbach, G. (2007). B12 deficiency: a look beyond pernicious anemia. *Journal of Family Practice, 56*(7), 537-542. Available from: https://www.ncbi.nlm.nih.gov/pubmed/17605945; https://www.mdedge.com/sites/default/files/Document/September-2017/5607JFP_Article1.pdf

Andrès, E., Loukili, N. H., Noel, E., Kaltenbach, G., Abdelgheni, M. B., Perrin, A. E., Noblet-Dick, M., Maloisel, F., Schlienger, J.-L., & Blicklé, J.-F. (2004). Vitamin B12 (cobalamin) deficiency in elderly patients. *CMAJ: Canadian Medical Association Journal, 171*(3), 251-259. Available from: http://www.ncbi.nlm.nih.gov/pubmed/15289425; http://www.cmaj.ca/content/171/3/251.full.pdf

Andrès, E., & Serraj, K. (2012). Optimal management of pernicious anemia. *Journal of Blood Medicine, 3*, 97-103. doi:10.2147/JBM.S25620. Available from: https://www.ncbi.nlm.nih.gov/pubmed/23028239; https://www.dovepress.com/getfile.php?fileID=13911

Arendt, J. F. H., Farkas, D. K., Pedersen, L., Nexo, E., & Sorensen, H. T. (2016). Elevated plasma vitamin B12 levels and cancer prognosis: A population-based cohort study. *Cancer Epidemiology, 40*, 158-165. doi:10.1016/j.canep.2015.12.007. Available from: https://www.ncbi.nlm.nih.gov/pubmed/26724465; http://www.cancerepidemiology.net/article/S1877-7821(15)00285-4/pdf

Arlt, W. (2012). Chapter 342 Disorders of the Adrenal Cortex. In D. L. Longo, A. S. Fauci, D. L. Kasper, S. L. Hauser, J. L. Jameson, & J. Loscalzo (Eds.), *Harrison's Principles of Internal Medicine* (18 ed., Vol. 2, pp. 2940-2961). New York: McGraw Hill Medical.

Arlt, W. (2018). Chapter 379 Disorders of the Adrenal Cortex. In J. L. Jameson, A. S. Fauci, D. L. Kasper, S. L. Hauser, D. L. Longo, & J. Loscalzo (Eds.), *Harrison's Principles of Internal Medicine* (20 ed., Vol. 2, pp. 2719-2739). New York: McGraw Hill Education.

Arlt, W., & Allolio, B. (2003). Adrenal insufficiency. *Lancet, 361*(9372), 1881-1893. doi:10.1016/S0140-6736(03)13492-7. Available from: http://www.ncbi.nlm.nih.gov/pubmed/12788587

Ashworth, H. (2011, 18 July 2011). How long is your DNA? *Science Focus in BBC Focus Magazine, 2018*. Available from: http://www.sciencefocus.com/qa/how-long-your-dna

Aslinia, F., Mazza, J. J., & Yale, S. H. (2006). Megaloblastic anemia and other causes of macrocytosis. *Clinical Medicine & Research, 4*(3), 236-241. Available from: https://www.ncbi.nlm.nih.gov/pubmed/16988104; https://www.ncbi.nlm.nih.gov/pmc/articles/PMC1570488/pdf/0040236.pdf

Babior, B. M., & Bunn, H. F. (2005). Chapter 92 Megaloblastic Anemias. In D. L. Kasper, A. S. Fauci, D. L. Longo, E. Braunwald, S. L. Hauser, & J. L. Jameson (Eds.), *Harrison's Principles of Internal Medicine* (16 ed., Vol. I, pp. 601-607).

Baldi, M., Behera, D., Kaur, J., Kapoor, R., & Singh, N. (2016). Rationale and Design of PEMVITASTART-An Open-label Randomized Trial Comparing Simultaneous Versus Standard Initiation of Vitamin B12 and Folate Supplementation in Nonsquamous, Non-Small-cell Lung Cancer Patients Undergoing First-line Pemetrexed-based Chemotherapy. *Clinical Lung Cancer,* 10.1016/j.cllc.2016.11.017. doi:10.1016/j.cllc.2016.11.017. Available from: https://www.ncbi.nlm.nih.gov/pubmed/28073680; http://www.clinical-lung-cancer.com/article/S1525-7304(16)30371-0/abstract; https://www.clinical-lung-cancer.com/article/S1525-7304(16)30371-0/fulltext

Bancos, I., Wass, J., & Arlt, W. (2014). How not to miss - Addison's disease. *Pulse Today, 2014*. Available from: http://www.pulsetoday.co.uk/clinical/how-not-to-miss-addisons-disease/20007578.article

Banerjee, R., & Ragsdale, S. W. (2003). The Many Faces of Vitamin B12: Catalysis by Cobalamin-Dependent Enzymes. *Annual Review of Biochemistry, 72*(1), 209-247. doi:10.1146/annurev.biochem.72.121801.161828. Available from: https://www.annualreviews.org/doi/abs/10.1146/annurev.biochem.72.121801.161828

Barclay, A. W. (1851). Death from anaemia (two cases) (unseen). *Medical Times and Gazette, 23*, 480.

Bassett, J. K., Baglietto, L., Hodge, A. M., Severi, G., Hopper, J. L., English, D. R., & Giles, G. G. (2013). Dietary intake of B vitamins and methionine and breast cancer risk. *Cancer Causes and Control, 24*(8), 1555-1563. doi:10.1007/s10552-013-0232-y. Available from: https://www.ncbi.nlm.nih.gov/pubmed?cmd=historysearch&querykey=18; http://link.springer.com/article/10.1007%2Fs10552-013-0232-y; https://link.springer.com/article/10.1007%2Fs10552-013-0232-y

Basu, A. K. (2018). DNA Damage, Mutagenesis and Cancer. *International Journal of Molecular Sciences, 19*(4). doi:10.3390/ijms19040970. Available from: https://www.ncbi.nlm.nih.gov/pubmed/29570697; https://res.mdpi.com/ijms/ijms-19-00970/article_deploy/ijms-19-00970.pdf?filename=&attachment=1

Batmanghelidj, F. (2008). *Your Body's Many Cries for Water: You're not sick; you're thirsty Don't treat thirst with medication* (3 ed.): Global Health Solutions, Inc.

Beech, C. M., Liyanarachchi, S., Shah, N. P., Sturm, A. C., Sadiq, M. F., de la Chapelle, A., & Tanner, S. M. (2011). Ancient founder mutation is responsible for Imerslund-Grasbeck Syndrome among diverse ethnicities. *Orphanet Journal of Rare Diseases, 6*, 74. doi:10.1186/1750-1172-6-74. Available from: http://www.ojrd.com/content/pdf/1750-1172-6-74.pdf

Bender, D. A. (2003). Megaloblastic anaemia in vitamin B12 deficiency. *British Journal of Nutrition, 89*(4), 439-441. doi:10.1079/BJN2002828. Available from: https://www.ncbi.nlm.nih.gov/pubmed/12654160

Bennett, M. (2001). Vitamin B12 deficiency, infertility and recurrent fetal loss. *Journal of Reproductive Medicine, 46*(3), 209-212. Available from: https://www.ncbi.nlm.nih.gov/pubmed/11304860

de Benoist, B. (2008). Conclusions of a WHO Technical Consultation on folate and vitamin B12 deficiencies. *Food and Nutrition Bulletin, 29*(2 Suppl), S238-244. doi:10.1177/15648265080292S129. Available from: https://www.ncbi.nlm.nih.gov/pubmed/18709899

Berger, J. R. (2004). The Neurological Complications of Bariatric Surgery. *Archives of Neurology, 61*(8), 1185-1189. doi:10.1001/archneur.61.8.1185. Available from: https://jamanetwork.com/journals/jamaneurology/fullarticle/786290

Betterle, C., Dal Pra, C., Mantero, F., & Zanchetta, R. (2002). Autoimmune adrenal insufficiency and autoimmune polyendocrine syndromes: autoantibodies, autoantigens, and their applicability in diagnosis and disease prediction. *Endocrine Reviews, 23*(3), 327-364. doi:10.1210/edrv.23.3.0466. Available from: https://www.ncbi.nlm.nih.gov/pubmed/12050123

Bevan, A. (1948). A message to the medical profession from the minister of health. *BMJ*. Available from: http://www.nhshistory.net/bevanmessage.pdf

Biermer, A. (1872). Über eine Form von progressiver perniciöser Anämie. *Correspondenz-Blatt für schweizer Aerzte, 2*, 15-17.

Bird, J. (2013, Nov). Vitamin B12 and Cancer: The Canary in the Coal Mine? Available from: https://www.dsm.com/campaigns/talkingnutrition/en_US/talkingnutrition-dsm-com/2013/11/vitamin_B12_cobalamin_cancer_risk.html

Blount, B. C., Mack, M. M., Wehr, C. M., MacGregor, J. T., Hiatt, R. A., Wang, G., Wickramasinghe, S. N., Everson, R. B., & Ames, B. N. (1997). Folate deficiency causes uracil misincorporation into human DNA and chromosome breakage: implications for cancer and neuronal damage. *Proceedings of the National Academy of Sciences of the United States of America, 94*(7), 3290-3295. Available from: http://www.ncbi.nlm.nih.gov/entrez/query.fcgi?cmd=Retrieve&db=PubMed&dopt=Citation&list_uids=9096386; http://www.pubmedcentral.nih.gov/picrender.fcgi?artid=20362&blobtype=pdf

Blundo, C., Marin, D., & Ricci, M. (2011). Vitamin B12 deficiency associated with symptoms of frontotemporal dementia. *Neurological sciences : official journal of the Italian Neurological Society and of the Italian Society of Clinical Neurophysiology, 32*(1), 101-105. doi:10.1007/s10072-010-0419-x. Available from: http://www.ncbi.nlm.nih.gov/pubmed/20927562

BMJ Best Practice. (2018a). Addison's disease: Investigations. Available from: https://bestpractice.bmj.com/topics/en-gb/56/investigations

BMJ Best Practice. (2018b). Adrenal suppression: Investigations. Available from: https://bestpractice.bmj.com/topics/en-gb/863/investigations#referencePop56

BMJ Best Practice. (2018c, Apr 2018). Evaluation of Anemia. Available from: https://bestpractice.bmj.com/topics/en-us/93

BMJ Best Practice. (2018d, 22 June 2018). Vitamin B12 deficiency. Available from: bestpractice.bmj.com/best-practice/monograph/822/highlights/summary.html

BMJ Best Practice. (2018e, March 2018). Wernicke's encephalopathy. *BMJ Best Practice.* Available from: https://bestpractice.bmj.com/topics/en-gb/405?q=Wernicke's encephalopathy&c=suggested

BNF. British National Formulary. (2009). *British National Formulary.* London, UK: British Medical Association & Royal Pharmaceutical Society of Great Britain.

BNF. British National Formulary. (2017, 20 July 2017). Cyanocobalamin. *British National Formulary.* Available from: https://www.medicinescomplete.com/#/content/bnf/_872171900

BNF. British National Formulary. (2018, 14 Aug 2018). Anaemia, Megaloblastic. *British National Formulary.* Available from: https://www.medicinescomplete.com/#/content/bnf/_286183421?hspl=B12

BNF. (2019). Anaemia, megaloblastic. *BNF.* Available from: https://bnf.nice.org.uk/treatment-summary/anaemia-megaloblastic.html

BNFC. British National Formulary for Children. (2008). *British National Formulary for Children.* London, UK: British Medical Association, Royal Pharmaceutical Society, the Royal College of Paediatrics and Child Health, and the Neonatal and Paediatric Pharmacists Group.

Bolon, B. (2012). Cellular and molecular mechanisms of autoimmune disease. *Toxicologic Pathology, 40*(2), 216-229. doi:10.1177/0192623311428481. Available from: https://www.ncbi.nlm.nih.gov/pubmed/22105648

Bor, M. V., von Castel-Roberts, K. M., Kauwell, G. P., Stabler, S. P., Allen, R. H., Maneval, D. R., Bailey, L. B., & Nexo, E. (2010). Daily intake of 4 to 7 microg dietary vitamin B-12 is associated with steady concentrations of vitamin B-12-related biomarkers in a healthy young population. *The American Journal of Clinical Nutrition, 91*(3), 571-577. Available from: https://www.ncbi.nlm.nih.gov/pubmed/20071646

Bottiglieri, T. (2002). S-Adenosyl-l-methionine (SAMe): from the bench to the bedside—molecular basis of a pleiotrophic molecule. *The American Journal of Clinical Nutrition, 76*(5), 1151S-1157S. doi:10.1093/ajcn/76.5.1151S %J The American Journal of Clinical Nutrition. Available from: https://dx.doi.org/10.1093/ajcn/76.5.1151S

Bottiglieri, T., Laundy, M., Crellin, R., Toone, B. K., Carney, M. W., & Reynolds, E. H. (2000). Homocysteine, folate, methylation, and monoamine metabolism in depression. *Journal of Neurology, Neurosurgery and Psychiatry, 69*(2), 228-232. Available from: https://www.ncbi.nlm.nih.gov/pubmed/10896698; https://www.ncbi.nlm.nih.gov/pmc/articles/PMC1737050/pdf/v069p00228.pdf

Boucher, J. L. (2017). The cause of multiple sclerosis is autoimmune attack of adenosyltransferase thereby limiting adenosylcobalamin production. *Medical Hypotheses, 109*, 29-37. doi:10.1016/j.mehy.2017.08.011. Available from: http://www.sciencedirect.com/science/article/pii/S030698771730275X

Bozian, R. C., Ferguson, J. L., Heyssel, R. M., Meneely, G. R., & Darby, W. J. (1963). Evidence concerning the human requirement for vitamin B12. Use of the whole body counter for determination of absorption of vitamin B12. *American Journal of Clinical Nutrition, 12*, 117-129. doi:10.1093/ajcn/12.2.117. Available from: https://www.ncbi.nlm.nih.gov/pubmed/14014759; https://academic.oup.com/ajcn/article-abstract/12/2/117/4729025?redirectedFrom=fulltext

Briani, C., Dalla Torre, C., Citton, V., Manara, R., Pompanin, S., Binotto, G., & Adami, F. (2013). Cobalamin deficiency: clinical picture and radiological findings. *Nutrients, 5*(11), 4521-4539. doi:10.3390/nu5114521. Available from: https://res.mdpi.com/def502002b51661fbfb06fec92bdfcab52fde6b130127929a61f0e29ad4bf95 59e87fe83e07550bdf223bcb1ce3b6dbb466ccf69064bbaa1fbbd325f33172a1a30a7d7a4b608f2e 0d45b10a56b7c4731804628521ebda018590ab9de7a5e5fee80aeec632813d9fa11a17f8577a6ba 33e74347ac7ccdfa64c54af3c72307b1cc1c0a8d47bca5016ace102ea13b1821c3d69d5e229ef3?fil ename=&attachment=1

Brown, H. E., & Roffman, J. L. (2014). Vitamin Supplementation in the Treatment of Schizophrenia. *CNS drugs, 28*(7), 611-622. doi:10.1007/s40263-014-0172-4. Available from: http://www.ncbi.nlm.nih.gov/pmc/articles/PMC4083629/; https://www.ncbi.nlm.nih.gov/pmc/articles/PMC4083629/pdf/nihms-597561.pdf

Cabot, R. C. (1910). Pernicious and secondary anaemia, chlorosis, and leukemia (unseen). In W. Osler & T. McGrae (Eds.), *A System of Medicine*. Oxford: Frowde.

Cancer Research UK. (2017, 15 Nov). Chemotherapy. *General cancer information: Treatment for cancer*. Available from: https://www.cancerresearchuk.org/about-cancer/cancer-in-general/treatment/chemotherapy

Cancer Research UK. (2018, 14 Dec). Radiotherapy. *General cancer information: Treatment for cancer*. Available from: https://www.cancerresearchuk.org/about-cancer/cancer-in-general/treatment/radiotherapy

Cancer.Net. (2018, Mar 2018). The Genetics of Cancer. Available from: https://www.cancer.net/navigating-cancer-care/cancer-basics/genetics/genetics-cancer

Carmel, R. (2008). How I treat cobalamin (vitamin B12) deficiency. *Blood, 112*(6), 2214-2221. doi:10.1182/blood-2008-03-040253. Available from: https://www.ncbi.nlm.nih.gov/pubmed/18606874; http://www.bloodjournal.org/content/bloodjournal/112/6/2214.full.pdf

Carmel, R. (2011). Biomarkers of cobalamin (vitamin B-12) status in the epidemiologic setting: a critical overview of context, applications, and performance characteristics of cobalamin, methylmalonic acid, and holotranscobalamin II. *American Journal of Clinical Nutrition, 94*(1), 348S-358S. doi:10.3945/ajcn.111.013441. Available from: https://www.ncbi.nlm.nih.gov/pubmed/21593511; https://www.ncbi.nlm.nih.gov/pmc/articles/PMC3174853/pdf/ajcn9410348S.pdf

Carmel, R., & Agrawal, Y. P. (2012). Failures of Cobalamin Assays in Pernicious Anemia. *New England Journal of Medicine, 367*(4), 385-386. Available from: http://home.kpn.nl/koudum-2/B12/NEJM-2012.pdf

Carmel, R., Brar, S., Agrawal, A., & Penha, P. D. (2000). Failure of Assay to Identify Low Cobalamin Concentrations. *Clinical Chemistry, 46*(12), 2017-2018. Available from: http://clinchem.aaccjnls.org/content/clinchem/46/12/2017.full.pdf

Carmel, R., Green, R., Jacobsen, D. W., & Qian, G. D. (1996). Neutrophil nuclear segmentation in mild cobalamin deficiency: relation to metabolic tests of cobalamin status and observations on ethnic differences in neutrophil segmentation. *American Journal of Clinical Pathology, 106*(1), 57-63. Available from: https://www.ncbi.nlm.nih.gov/pubmed/8701933

Carrazana, E. (2002). The neurological manifestations of vitamin B12 deficiency. In V. Herbert (Ed.), *Vitamin B12 deficiency, Proceedings of a Round Table Discussion, Florida* (pp. 21-26). Key West, Florida: Royal Society of Medicine Press.

Casella, E. B., Valente, M., de Navarro, J. M., & Kok, F. (2005). Vitamin B12 deficiency in infancy as a cause of developmental regression. *Brain and Development, 27*(8), 592-594. doi:10.1016/j.braindev.2005.02.005. Available from: http://www.sciencedirect.com/science/article/pii/S0387760405000458; https://www.brainanddevelopment.com/article/S0387-7604(05)00045-8/fulltext

Chanarin, I. (1969). *The Megaloblastic Anaemias*. Oxford: Blackwell Scientific.

Chanarin, I. (1979). *The Megaloblastic Anaemias* (2nd ed.). Oxford: Blackwell Scientific.

Chanarin, I. (1980). *Blood and its diseases* (2nd ed.). Edinburgh; New York: Churchill Livingstone.

Chanarin, I. (1982). Disorders of vitamin absorption. *Clinics in Gastroenterology, 11*(1), 73-85.

Chanarin, I. (1990). *The Megaloblastic Anaemias* (3rd ed.). Oxford: Blackwell Scientific.

Chanarin, I. (2000). Historical review: a history of pernicious anaemia. *British Journal of Haematology, 111*(2), 407-415. Available from: https://www.ncbi.nlm.nih.gov/pubmed/11122079; https://onlinelibrary.wiley.com/doi/pdf/10.1111/j.1365-2141.2000.02238.x

Chandy, J. K. (2006a). *A forgotten illness - Vitamin B12 Deficiency with Neuro Psychiatric signs and symptoms with or without Anaemia or Macrocytosis (Paper presented at University Hospital of North Durham Consultants and GPs postgraduate meeting).*

Chandy, J. K. (2006b). *Vitamin B12 deficiency with neuro-psychiatric symptoms, serum B12 level below 300ng/L with or without anaemia or macrocytosis (Paper presented at University Hospital of Hartlepool Consultants and GPs postgraduate meeting).*

Chandy, J. K. (2015, 24 April 2015). *B12 deficiency and APS with a causal link to hypothyroidism, adrenal insufficiency.* Paper presented at the Thyroid Patient Advocacy Conference, Crown Hotel, Harrogate, North Yorkshire, UK. Available from: http://www.tpauk.com/main/article/tpa-conference-friday-24-april-2015-crown-hotel-harrogate/

Chandy, J. K., & Minney, H. (2014). *Vitamin B12 deficiency, a common but forgotten illness.* Paper presented at the International Forum on Quality and Safety in Healthcare, Palais des Congrès, Paris, France.

Charcot, J. (1868). Histologie de la sclérose en plaques. *Gazette des Hopitaux, Paris, 41*, 554-555.

Charmandari, E., Nicolaides, N. C., & Chrousos, G. P. (2014). Adrenal insufficiency. *Lancet, 383*(9935), 2152-2167. doi:10.1016/S0140-6736(13)61684-0. Available from: https://www.ncbi.nlm.nih.gov/pubmed/24503135; https://www.thelancet.com/journals/lancet/article/PIIS0140-6736(13)61684-0/fulltext

Choi, S.-W., Friso, S., Ghandour, H., Bagley, P. J., Selhub, J., & Mason, J. B. (2004). Vitamin B-12 deficiency induces anomalies of base substitution and methylation in the DNA of rat colonic epithelium. *Journal of Nutrition, 134*(4), 750-755. doi:10.1093/jn/134.4.750. Available from: https://www.ncbi.nlm.nih.gov/pubmed/15051821

Choi, S. W., & Friso, S. (2010). Epigenetics: A New Bridge between Nutrition and Health. *Advances in Nutrition, 1*(1), 8-16. doi:10.3945/an.110.1004. Available from: https://www.ncbi.nlm.nih.gov/pubmed/22043447; https://www.ncbi.nlm.nih.gov/pmc/articles/PMC3042783/pdf/8.pdf

Christine, C. W., Auinger, P., Joslin, A., Yelpaala, Y., & Green, R. on behalf of the Parkinson Study Group-DATATOP Investigators. (2018). Vitamin B12 and Homocysteine Levels Predict Different Outcomes in Early Parkinson's Disease. *Movement Disorders, 33*(5), 762-770. doi:10.1002/mds.27301. Available from: https://www.ncbi.nlm.nih.gov/pubmed/29508904; https://onlinelibrary.wiley.com/doi/pdf/10.1002/mds.27301

Chui, C. H., Lau, F. Y., Wong, R., Soo, O. Y., Lam, C. K., Lee, P. W., Leung, H. K., So, C. K., Tsoi, W. C., Tang, N., Lam, W. K., & Cheng, G. (2001). Vitamin B12 deficiency--need for a new guideline. *Nutrition, 17*(11-12), 917-920. Available from: http://www.ncbi.nlm.nih.gov/pubmed/11744340

Clarke, R., Birks, J., Nexo, E., Ueland, P. M., Schneede, J., Scott, J., Molloy, A., & Evans, J. G. (2007). Low vitamin B-12 status and risk of cognitive decline in older adults. *American Journal of Clinical Nutrition, 86*(5), 1384-1391. doi:10.1093/ajcn/86.5.1384. Available from: https://www.ncbi.nlm.nih.gov/pubmed/17991650

Clarke, R., Grimley Evans, J., Schneede, J., Nexo, E., Bates, C., Fletcher, A., Prentice, A., Johnston, C., Ueland, P. M., Refsum, H., Sherliker, P., Birks, J., Whitlock, G., Breeze, E., & Scott, J. M. (2004). Vitamin B12 and folate deficiency in later life. *Age and Ageing, 33*(1), 34-41. Available from: https://www.ncbi.nlm.nih.gov/pubmed/14695861

Clemens, T. L. (2014). Vitamin B12 deficiency and bone health. *New England Journal of Medicine, 371*(10), 963-964. doi:10.1056/NEJMcibr1407247. Available from: https://www.ncbi.nlm.nih.gov/pubmed/25184870; https://www.nejm.org/doi/full/10.1056/NEJMcibr1407247?url_ver=Z39.88-2003&rfr_id=ori%3Arid%3Acrossref.org&rfr_dat=cr_pub%3Dpubmed

Coghlan, A. (2017). Autoimmune disorders linked to an increased risk of dementia. *New Scientist, 1 March 2017*. Available from: https://www.newscientist.com/article/2123274-autoimmune-disorders-linked-to-an-increased-risk-of-dementia/

Cohn, E. J., & Surgenor, D. M. (1949). The state in nature of the active principle in pernicious anemia of catalase, and of other components of liver. *Science, 109*(2835), 443. Available from: http://www.ncbi.nlm.nih.gov/entrez/query.fcgi?cmd=Retrieve&db=PubMed&dopt=Citation&list_uids=18224965

Collin, S. M. (2013). Folate and B12 in prostate cancer. *Advances in Clinical Chemistry, 60*, 1-63. Available from: https://www.ncbi.nlm.nih.gov/pubmed/23724740

Colombo, B., Franzini, P., & Mannucci, B. (1955). [Biliary, intestinal and urinary excretion of bile pigments; considerations in relation to entero-hepatic circulation.]. *Ospedale Maggiore, 43*(7), 307-312. Available from: http://www.ncbi.nlm.nih.gov/pubmed/13289099

Combe, J. S. (1824). History of a case of anaemia. *Transactions of the Medico-Chirurgical Society of Edinburgh, 1*, 193-204. Available from: https://www.ncbi.nlm.nih.gov/pmc/articles/PMC5405303

Cornish, S., & Mehl-Madrona, L. (2008). The role of vitamins and minerals in psychiatry. *Integrative Medicine Insights, 3*, 33-42. Available from: https://www.ncbi.nlm.nih.gov/pubmed/21614157; https://www.ncbi.nlm.nih.gov/pmc/articles/PMC3046018/pdf/imi-2008-033.pdf

Cree, B. A. C., & Hauser, S. L. (2018). Chapter 436. Multiple Sclerosis. In J. L. Jameson, A. S. Fauci, D. L. Kasper, S. L. Hauser, D. L. Longo, & J. Loscalzo (Eds.), *Harrison's Principles of Internal Medicine* (20 ed., Vol. 2, pp. 3188-3201). New York: McGraw Hill Education.

Datapharm. (2017). Synacthen Ampoules 250 micrograms per ml - Summary of Product Characteristics. In Datapharm (Ed.): electronic Medicines Compendium (eMC). Available from: https://www.medicines.org.uk/emc/product/1751/smpc

Dawber, R. P. (1970). Clinical associations of vitiligo. *Postgraduate Medical Journal, 46*(535), 276-277. Available from: https://www.ncbi.nlm.nih.gov/pubmed/5448375; https://pmj.bmj.com/content/postgradmedj/46/535/276.full.pdf

Dawson, E. B., Evans, D. R., & Van_Hook, J. W. (1998). Amniotic Fluid B12 and Folate Levels Associated with Neural Tube Defects. *American Journal of Perinatology, 15*(9), 511-514. doi:10.1055/s-2007-993975. Available from: https://www.thieme-connect.com/products/ejournals/abstract/10.1055/s-2007-993975; https://www.thieme-connect.com/DOI/DOI?10.1055/s-2007-993975

Debono, M., Ghobadi, C., Rostami-Hodjegan, A., Huatan, H., Campbell, M. J., Newell-Price, J., Darzy, K., Merke, D. P., Arlt, W., & Ross, R. J. (2009). Modified-release hydrocortisone to provide circadian cortisol profiles. *The Journal of clinical endocrinology and metabolism, 94*(5), 1548-1554. doi:10.1210/jc.2008-2380. Available from: https://www.ncbi.nlm.nih.gov/pubmed/19223520; https://www.ncbi.nlm.nih.gov/pmc/PMC2684472/

Denson, R. (1976). Letter: Vitamin B12 in late-onset psychosis of childhood. *Canadian Medical Association Journal, 114*(2), 113. Available from: https://www.ncbi.nlm.nih.gov/pmc/articles/PMC1956802/pdf/canmedaj01550-0029a.pdf

Devalia, V. (2006). Diagnosing vitamin B-12 deficiency on the basis of serum B-12 assay. *BMJ, 333*(7564), 385-386. doi:10.1136/bmj.333.7564.385. Available from: http://www.bmj.com/cgi/content/full/333/7564/385; ; http://www.bmj.com/cgi/content/extract/333/7564/385; https://www.ncbi.nlm.nih.gov/pubmed/16916826; https://www.ncbi.nlm.nih.gov/pmc/articles/PMC1550477/pdf/bmj33300385.pdf

Devalia, V., Hamilton, M. S., & Molloy, Anne M. on behalf of the British Committee for Standards in Haematology. (2014). Guidelines for the diagnosis and treatment of cobalamin and folate disorders. *British Journal of Haematology, 166*(4), 496-513. doi:10.1111/bjh.12959. Available from: http://dx.doi.org/10.1111/bjh.12959

Dhillo, W. S., Kong, W. M., Le Roux, C. W., Alaghband-Zadeh, J., Jones, J., Carter, G., Mendoza, N., Meeran, K., & O'Shea, D. (2002). Cortisol-binding globulin is important in the interpretation of dynamic tests of the hypothalamic--pituitary--adrenal axis. *European Journal of Endocrinology of the European Federation of Endocrine Societies, 146*(2), 231-235. Available from: https://www.ncbi.nlm.nih.gov/pubmed/11834433

Diabetes.co.uk. (2018). What is an autoimmune disease? Available from: https://www.diabetes.co.uk/autoimmune-diseases.html

Doets, E. L., Cavelaars, A. E., Dhonukshe-Rutten, R. A., van 't Veer, P., & de Groot, L. C. (2012). Explaining the variability in recommended intakes of folate, vitamin B12, iron and zinc for adults and elderly people. *Public Health Nutrition, 15*(5), 906-915. doi:10.1017/S1368980011002643. Available from: https://www.ncbi.nlm.nih.gov/pubmed/22035597; https://www.cambridge.org/core/services/aop-cambridge-core/content/view/B6A69932BEEAD4ECD260893D34E3248B/S1368980011002643a.pdf/div-class-title-explaining-the-variability-in-recommended-intakes-of-folate-vitamin-b-span-class-sub-12-span-iron-and-zinc-for-adults-and-elderly-people-div.pdf

Doets, E. L., In 't Veld, P. H., Szczecinska, A., Dhonukshe-Rutten, R. A. M., Cavelaars, A. E. J. M., van 't Veer, P., Brzozowska, A., & de Groot, L. C. P. G. M. (2013). Systematic review on daily vitamin B12 losses and bioavailability for deriving recommendations on vitamin B12 intake with the factorial approach. *Annals of Nutrition and Metabolism, 62*(4), 311-322. doi:10.1159/000346968. Available from: https://www.ncbi.nlm.nih.gov/pubmed/23796635; https://www.karger.com/Article/Pdf/346968

Dogan, Ozdemir, Sal, Cesur, & Caksen. (2009). Psychotic Disorder and Extrapyramidal Symptoms Associated with Vitamin B12 and Folate Deficiency. *Journal of Tropical Pediatrics, 55*(3), 205. Available from: https://academic.oup.com/tropej/article/55/3/205/1658519

Donaldson, M. S. (2004). Nutrition and cancer: a review of the evidence for an anti-cancer diet. *Nutrition Journal, 3*, 19. doi:10.1186/1475-2891-3-19. Available from: https://www.ncbi.nlm.nih.gov/pubmed/15496224; https://www.ncbi.nlm.nih.gov/pmc/articles/PMC526387/pdf/1475-2891-3-19.pdf

Douaud, G., Refsum, H., de Jager, C. A., Jacoby, R., Nichols, T. E., Smith, S. M., & Smith, A. D. (2013). Preventing Alzheimer's disease-related gray matter atrophy by B-vitamin treatment. *Proceedings of the National Academy of Sciences of the United States of America, 110*(23), 9523-9528. doi:10.1073/pnas.1301816110. Available from: http://www.ncbi.nlm.nih.gov/pubmed/23690582; http://www.ncbi.nlm.nih.gov/pmc/articles/PMC3677457/pdf/pnas.201301816.pdf

Dowling, D. P., Miles, Z. D., Köhrer, C., Maiocco, S. J., Elliott, S. J., Bandarian, V., & Drennan, C. L. (2016). Molecular basis of cobalamin-dependent RNA modification. *Nucleic Acids Research, 44*(20), 9965-9976. doi:10.1093/nar/gkw806. Available from: https://www.ncbi.nlm.nih.gov/pubmed/27638883; https://www.ncbi.nlm.nih.gov/pmc/PMC5175355/

Duggan, C., Srinivasan, K., Thomas, T., Samuel, T., Rajendran, R., Muthayya, S., Finkelstein, J. L., Lukose, A., Fawzi, W., Allen, L. H., Bosch, R. J., & Kurpad, A. V. (2014). Vitamin B-12 supplementation during pregnancy and early lactation increases maternal, breast milk, and infant measures of vitamin B-12 status. *Journal of Nutrition, 144*(5), 758-764. doi:10.3945/jn.113.187278. Available from: https://www.ncbi.nlm.nih.gov/pubmed/24598885; https://www.ncbi.nlm.nih.gov/pmc/articles/PMC3985831/pdf/nut144758.pdf

Ebbing, M., Bønaa, K. H., Nygård, O., Arnesen, E., Ueland, P. M., Nordrehaug, J. E., Rasmussen, K., Njølstad, I., Refsum, H., Nilsen, D. W., Tverdal, A., Meyer, K., & Vollset, S. E. (2009). Cancer Incidence and Mortality After Treatment With Folic Acid and Vitamin B12. *JAMA, 302*(19), 2119-2126. doi:10.1001/jama.2009.1622. Available from: https://www.ncbi.nlm.nih.gov/pubmed/19920236;

http://jama.jamanetwork.com/pdfaccess.ashx?url=/data/journals/jama/4488/joc90128_2119_2126.pdf

EFSA. European Food Safety Authority. (2008). 5'-deoxyadenosylcobalamin and methylcobalamin as sources for Vitamin B12 added as a nutritional substance in food supplements. *EFSA Journal, 815*, 1-21. Available from: https://efsa.onlinelibrary.wiley.com/doi/epdf/10.2903/j.efsa.2008.815

Ehrlich, P. (1880). Beobachtungen über einen Fall von perniciöser, progressiver Anämie mit Sarcombildung. Beiträge zur Lehre von der acuten Herzinsufficienz (unseen). *Verhandl. Gesellsch. Charité Arzte.*(June 10, Dec 9). Available from: https://www.pei.de/EN/institute/paul-ehrlich/publications/publications-of-paul-ehrlich-node.html

Eichholzer, M., Lüthy, J., Moser, U., & Fowler, B. (2001). Folate and the risk of colorectal, breast and cervix cancer: the epidemiological evidence. *Swiss Medical Weekly, 131*(37-38), 539-549. doi:2001/37/smw-09779. Available from: https://www.ncbi.nlm.nih.gov/pubmed/11759174; https://www.zora.uzh.ch/id/eprint/109538/1/smw-09779.pdf

Elrod, J. M., & Karnad, A. B. (2003). William Bosworth Castle: pioneer of haematological clinical investigation. *British Journal of Haematology, 121*(3), 390-395. Available from: https://www.ncbi.nlm.nih.gov/pubmed/12716360; https://onlinelibrary.wiley.com/doi/pdf/10.1046/j.1365-2141.2003.04242.x

Eren, O. O., Ozturk, M. A., Sonmez, O. U., & Oyan, B. (2014). Should we be more cautious about replacement of vitamin B12 in patients with cancer receiving cytotoxic chemotherapy? *Medical Hypotheses, 83*(6), 726-729. doi:10.1016/j.mehy.2014.09.027. Available from: https://www.ncbi.nlm.nih.gov/pubmed/25459143; http://www.medical-hypotheses.com/article/S0306-9877(14)00353-3/abstract

Erkurt, M. A., Aydogdu, I., Dikilitas, M., Kuku, I., Kaya, E., Bayraktar, N., Ozhan, O., Ozkan, I., & Sonmez, A. (2008). Effects of cyanocobalamin on immunity in patients with pernicious anemia. *Medical Principles and Practice, 17*(2), 131-135. doi:10.1159/000112967. Available from: https://www.ncbi.nlm.nih.gov/pubmed/18287797; https://www.karger.com/Article/Pdf/112967

Erturk, E., Jaffe, C. A., & Barkan, A. L. (1998). Evaluation of the Integrity of the Hypothalamic-Pituitary-Adrenal Axis by Insulin Hypoglycemia Test1. *The Journal of Clinical Endocrinology & Metabolism, 83*(7), 2350-2354. doi:10.1210/jcem.83.7.4980 %J The Journal of Clinical Endocrinology & Metabolism. Available from: https://dx.doi.org/10.1210/jcem.83.7.4980

Esteghamati, A., Hafezi-Nejad, N., Zandieh, A., Sheikhbahaei, S., Ebadi, M., & Nakhjavani, M. (2014). Homocysteine and metabolic syndrome: From clustering to additional utility in prediction of coronary heart disease. *Journal of Cardiology, 64*, 290-296. Available from: https://www.sciencedirect.com/science/article/pii/S0914508714000471

Esteller, M. (2003). Relevance of DNA methylation in the management of cancer. *Lancet Oncology, 4*(6), 351-358. Available from: https://www.ncbi.nlm.nih.gov/pubmed/12788407; https://www.thelancet.com/journals/lanonc/article/PIIS1470-2045(03)01115-X/fulltext

FAO & WHO. Food and Agriculture Organisation of the United Nations and World Health Organisation. (2001). *Human Vitamin and Mineral Requirements: Report of a joint FAO/WHO expert consultation, Bangkok, Thailand*: Food and Agriculture Organisation of the United Nations; World Health Organisation.

FAO & WHO. Food and Agriculture Organisation of the United Nations and World Health Organisation. (2004). *Vitamin and Mineral Requirements in Human Nutrition*: FAO/WHO Bangkok, Thailand.

Fenech, M. (2012). Folate (vitamin B9) and vitamin B12 and their function in the maintenance of nuclear and mitochondrial genome integrity. *Mutation Research, 733*(1-2), 21-33. doi:10.1016/j.mrfmmm.2011.11.003. Available from: http://www.sciencedirect.com/science/article/pii/S0027510711002934

Fenwick, S. (1870). On atrophy of the stomach (unseen). *Lancet, ii*, 78.

Ferrante, E., Morelli, V., Giavoli, C., Mantovani, G., Verrua, E., Sala, E., Malcmiodi, E., Bergamaschi, S., Profka, E., Cairoli, E., Palmieri, S., Chiodini, I., Lania, A. G., Spada, A., & Peccoz, P. B. (2012). Is the 250 µg ACTH test a useful tool for the diagnosis of central hypoadrenalism in adult patients with pituitary disorders? *Hormones (Athens), 11*(4), 428-435. Available from: https://www.ncbi.nlm.nih.gov/pubmed/23422765

Firth, J., Stubbs, B., Sarris, J., Rosenbaum, S., Teasdale, S., Berk, M., & Yung, A. R. (2017). The effects of vitamin and mineral supplementation on symptoms of schizophrenia: a systematic review and meta-analysis. *Psychological Medicine, 47*(9), 1515-1527. doi:10.1017/S0033291717000022. Available from: https://www.ncbi.nlm.nih.gov/pubmed/28202095; https://www.cambridge.org/core/journals/psychological-medicine/article/effects-of-vitamin-and-mineral-supplementation-on-symptoms-of-schizophrenia-a-systematic-review-and-metaanalysis/3CFE6C3B0FED2ED04B9968AD2660EA08

Flint, A. (1860). A clinical lecture on anaemia, delivered at Long Island Cottage Hospital. *American Medical Times, 1*, 181.

Froese, D. S., & Gravel, R. A. (2010). Genetic disorders of vitamin B12 metabolism: eight complementation groups--eight genes. *Expert Reviews in Molecular Medicine, 12*, e37. doi:10.1017/S1462399410001651. Available from: https://www.ncbi.nlm.nih.gov/pubmed/21114891

Galloway, M., & Hamilton, M. (2007). Macrocytosis: pitfalls in testing and summary of guidance. *BMJ, 335*(7625), 884-886. doi:10.1136/bmj.39325.689641.471. Available from: https://www.ncbi.nlm.nih.gov/pubmed/17962289; https://www.ncbi.nlm.nih.gov/pmc/articles/PMC2043457/pdf/bmj-335-7625-prac-00884.pdf

Galvin, R., Brathen, G., Ivashynka, A., Hillbom, M., Tanasescu, R., Leone, M. A., & Efns. (2010). EFNS guidelines for diagnosis, therapy and prevention of Wernicke encephalopathy. *European Journal of Neurology, 17*(12), 1408-1418. doi:10.1111/j.1468-1331.2010.03153.x. Available from: https://www.ncbi.nlm.nih.gov/pubmed/20642790; https://onlinelibrary.wiley.com/doi/pdf/10.1111/j.1468-1331.2010.03153.x

Ganguly, P., & Alam, S. F. (2015). Role of homocysteine in the development of cardiovascular disease. *Nutrition Journal, 14*(6). doi:10.1186/1475-2891-14-6. Available from: https://www.ncbi.nlm.nih.gov/pmc/articles/PMC4326479/

Geissbühler, P., Mermillod, B., & Rapin, C. H. (2000). Elevated serum vitamin B12 levels associated with CRP as a predictive factor of mortality in palliative care cancer patients: a prospective study over five years. *Journal of Pain and Symptom Management, 20*(2), 93-103. Available from: https://www.ncbi.nlm.nih.gov/pubmed/10989247; http://www.jpsmjournal.com/article/S0885-3924(00)00169-X/pdf

Genc, L., Kutlu, H. M., & Guney, G. (2015). Vitamin B12-loaded solid lipid nanoparticles as a drug carrier in cancer therapy. *Pharmaceutical Development and Technology, 20*(3), 337-344. doi:10.3109/10837450.2013.867447. Available from: https://www.ncbi.nlm.nih.gov/pubmed/24344935

Gilfix, B. M. (2005). Vitamin B12 and homocysteine. *CMAJ: Canadian Medical Association Journal, 173*(11), 1360. doi: 10.1503/cmaj.1050170. Available from: https://www.ncbi.nlm.nih.gov/pmc/articles/PMC1283514/

Glaser, K., Girschick, H. J., Schropp, C., & Speer, C. P. (2015). Psychomotor development following early treatment of severe infantile vitamin B12 deficiency and West syndrome--is everything fine? A case report and review of literature. *Brain and Development, 37*(3), 347-351. doi:10.1016/j.braindev.2014.05.006. Available from: https://www.ncbi.nlm.nih.gov/pubmed/24938481; https://www.brainanddevelopment.com/article/S0387-7604(14)00133-8/fulltext

Godman, H. (2017, March 31, 2017). Before an MS Diagnosis, Rule Out These Conditions First. Available from: https://health.usnews.com/wellness/articles/2017-03-31/before-an-ms-diagnosis-rule-out-these-conditions-first

Goebels, N., & Soyka, M. (2000). Dementia Associated With Vitamin B12 Deficiency. *The Journal of Neuropsychiatry and Clinical Neurosciences, 12*(3), 389-394. doi:10.1176/jnp.12.3.389. Available from: https://neuro.psychiatryonline.org/doi/full/10.1176/jnp.12.3.389

Golding, P. H. (2016). Holotranscobalamin (HoloTC, Active-B12) and Herbert's model for the development of vitamin B12 deficiency: a review and alternative hypothesis. *Springerplus, 5*(1), 668. doi:10.1186/s40064-016-2252-z. Available from: https://www.ncbi.nlm.nih.gov/pubmed/27350907; https://www.ncbi.nlm.nih.gov/pmc/articles/PMC4899389/pdf/40064_2016_Article_2252.pdf

Gonzalez, C. A., & Riboli, E. (2010). Diet and cancer prevention: Contributions from the European Prospective Investigation into Cancer and Nutrition (EPIC) study. *European Journal of Cancer, 46*(14), 2555-2562. doi:10.1016/j.ejca.2010.07.025. Available from: https://www.ncbi.nlm.nih.gov/pubmed/20843485; https://www.ejcancer.com/article/S0959-8049(10)00703-3/fulltext

Graner, J. L. (1985). Addison, pernicious anemia and adrenal insufficiency. *CMAJ: Canadian Medical Association Journal, 133*(9), 855-857, 880. Available from: https://www.ncbi.nlm.nih.gov/pubmed/3902186

Green, R. (2017). Vitamin B12 deficiency from the perspective of a practicing hematologist. *Blood, 129*(19), 2603-2611. doi:10.1182/blood-2016-10-569186. Available from: https://www.ncbi.nlm.nih.gov/pubmed/28360040; http://www.bloodjournal.org/content/bloodjournal/129/19/2603.full.pdf

Gröber, U., Kisters, K., & Schmidt, J. (2013). Neuroenhancement with vitamin B12-underestimated neurological significance. *Nutrients, 5*(12), 5031-5045. doi:10.3390/nu5125031. Available from: http://www.ncbi.nlm.nih.gov/pubmed/24352086; http://www.ncbi.nlm.nih.gov/pmc/articles/PMC3875920/pdf/nutrients-05-05031.pdf

Hamilton, M. S., Blackmore, S., & Lee, A. (2006). Possible cause of false normal B-12 assays. *BMJ, 333*(7569), 654-655. doi:10.1136/bmj.333.7569.654-c. Available from: http://www.ncbi.nlm.nih.gov/entrez/query.fcgi?cmd=Retrieve&db=PubMed&dopt=Citation&list_uids=16990334

Hannibal, L., Lysne, V., Bjorke-Monsen, A. L., Behringer, S., Grunert, S. C., Spiekerkoetter, U., Jacobsen, D. W., & Blom, H. J. (2016). Biomarkers and Algorithms for the Diagnosis of Vitamin B12 Deficiency. *Frontiers in Molecular Biosciences, 3*, 27. doi:10.3389/fmolb.2016.00027. Available from: https://www.ncbi.nlm.nih.gov/pubmed/27446930; https://www.ncbi.nlm.nih.gov/pmc/articles/PMC4921487/pdf/fmolb-03-00027.pdf

Haq, M. O., Rusoff, L. L., & Gelpi, A. J., Jr. (1952). Antibiotic feed and vitamin B12 supplements for lactating dairy cows. *Science, 115*(2982), 215-216.

Harvard Health Publishing, & Harvard Medical School. (2014, March). In brief: B vitamins and homocysteine. *Harvard Health Publishing.* Available from: https://www.health.harvard.edu/staying-healthy/in_brief_b_vitamins_and_homocysteine

Hathcock, J. N. (2014). Vitamin B12. In D. MacKay, A. Wong, & H. Nguyen (Eds.), *Vitamin and Mineral Safety* (3 ed., pp. 94-97): Council for Responsible Nutrition.

Hauser, S. L. (2018). Chapter 434. Diseases of the Spinal Cord. In J. L. Jameson, A. S. Fauci, D. L. Kasper, S. L. Hauser, D. L. Longo, & J. Loscalzo (Eds.), *Harrison's Principles of Internal Medicine* (20 ed., Vol. 1, pp. 3172-3183). New York: McGraw Hill Education.

Hauser, S. L., & Goodin, D. S. (2005). Chapter 359 Multiple Sclerosis and other Demyelinating Diseases. In D. L. Kasper, A. S. Fauci, D. L. Longo, E. Braunwald, S. L. Hauser, & J. L. Jameson (Eds.), *Harrison's Principles of Internal Medicine* (16 ed., Vol. II, pp. 2461-2471). New York: McGraw-Hill.

Hauser, S. L., & Goodin, D. S. (2008). Chapter 375 Multiple Sclerosis and Other Demyelinating Diseases. In A. S. Fauci, E. Braunwald, D. L. Klasper, S. L. Hauser, D. L. Longo, J. L. Jameson, & J. Loscalzo (Eds.), *Harrison's Principles of Internal Medicine* (17 ed., Vol. II, pp. 2611-2621). New York: McGraw Hill Medical.

Hauser, S. L., & Goodin, D. S. (2012). Chapter 380 Multiple Sclerosis and other Demyelinating Disorders. In D. L. Longo, A. S. Fauci, D. L. Kasper, S. L. Hauser, J. L. Jameson, & J. Loscalzo (Eds.), *Harrison's Principles of Internal Medicine* (18 ed., Vol. 2, pp. 3395-3409). New York: McGraw Hill Medical.

Hemmer, B., Glocker, F. X., Schumacher, M., Deuschl, G., & Lucking, C. H. (1998). Subacute combined degeneration: clinical, electrophysiological, and magnetic resonance imaging findings. *Journal of Neurology, Neurosurgery and Psychiatry, 65*(6), 822-827. Available from: http://www.ncbi.nlm.nih.gov/entrez/query.fcgi?cmd=Retrieve&db=PubMed&dopt=Citation&list_uids=9854956; http://www.pubmedcentral.nih.gov/picrender.fcgi?artid=2170379&blobtype=pdf

Hemminki, K., Liu, X., Forsti, A., Sundquist, J., Sundquist, K., & Ji, J. (2015). Subsequent Type 2 Diabetes in Patients with Autoimmune Disease. *Scientific Reports, 5*, 13871. doi:10.1038/srep13871. Available from: https://www.ncbi.nlm.nih.gov/pubmed/26350756; https://www.ncbi.nlm.nih.gov/pmc/articles/PMC4563366/pdf/srep13871.pdf

Herbert, V. (1987). The 1986 Herman award lecture. Nutrition science as a continually unfolding story: the folate and vitamin B-12 paradigm. *American Journal of Clinical Nutrition, 46*(3), 387-402. doi:10.1093/ajcn/46.3.387. Available from: https://academic.oup.com/ajcn/article-abstract/46/3/387/4694497?redirectedFrom=fulltext

Herbert, V. (2002). Vitamin B12 - an overview. In V. Herbert (Ed.), *Vitamin B12 deficiency* (pp. 1-8). Key West, Florida: Royal Society of Medicine Press. (Reprinted from: 1999).

Herbert, V., & Zalusky, R. (1962). Interrelations of vitamin B12 and folic acid metabolism: folic acid clearance studies. *Journal of Clinical Investigation, 41*, 1263-1276. doi:10.1172/JCI104589. Available from: https://www.ncbi.nlm.nih.gov/pubmed/13906634; https://www.ncbi.nlm.nih.gov/pmc/articles/PMC291041/pdf/jcinvest00315-0081.pdf

Hodgkin, D. C. (1958). X-ray analysis and the structure of vitamin B12. *Fortschritte der Chemie Organischer Naturstoffe, 15*, 167-220. Available from: http://www.ncbi.nlm.nih.gov/entrez/query.fcgi?cmd=Retrieve&db=PubMed&dopt=Citation&list_uids=13597976

Hodgkin, D. C., Kamper, J., Mackay, M., Pickworth, J., Trueblood, K. N., & White, J. G. (1956). Structure of vitamin B12. *Nature, 178*(4524), 64-66. Available from: http://www.ncbi.nlm.nih.gov/entrez/query.fcgi?cmd=Retrieve&db=PubMed&dopt=Citation&list_uids=13348621

Hodgkin, D. G., Pickworth, J., Robertson, J. H., Trueblood, K. N., Prosen, R. J., & White, J. G. (1955). The crystal structure of the hexacarboxylic acid derived from B12 and the molecular structure of the vitamin. *Nature, 176*(4477), 325-328. Available from: http://www.ncbi.nlm.nih.gov/pubmed/13253565

Hoffbrand, A. V. (2008). Chapter 100 Megaloblastic Anemias. In A. S. Fauci, E. Braunwald, D. L. Klasper, S. L. Hauser, D. L. Longo, J. L. Jameson, & J. Loscalzo (Eds.), *Harrison's Principles of Internal Medicine* (17 ed., Vol. 2, pp. 643-651). New York: McGraw-Hill Medical.

Hoffbrand, A. V. (2012). Chapter 105. Megaloblastic Anemias. In D. L. Longo, A. S. Fauci, D. L. Kasper, S. L. Hauser, J. L. Jameson, & J. Loscalzo (Eds.), *Harrison's Principles of Internal Medicine* (18 ed., Vol. 1, pp. 862-872). New York: McGraw Hill Medical.

Hoffbrand, A. V. (2018). Chapter 95 Megaloblastic Anemias. In J. L. Jameson, A. S. Fauci, D. L. Kasper, S. L. Hauser, D. L. Longo, & J. Loscalzo (Eds.), *Harrison's Principles of Internal Medicine* (20 ed., Vol. 1, pp. 698-708). New York: McGraw Hill Education.

Hoffbrand, A. V., & Provan, D. (1997). ABC of clinical haematology. Macrocytic anaemias. *BMJ, 314*(7078), 430-433. Available from: https://www.ncbi.nlm.nih.gov/pubmed/9040391

Hoffbrand, A. V., & Weir, D. G. (2001). The history of folic acid. *British Journal of Haematology, 113*(3), 579-589. Available from: https://www.ncbi.nlm.nih.gov/pubmed/11380441

Holtorf, K. (2008). Diagnosis and Treatment of Hypothalamic-Pituitary-Adrenal (HPA) Axis Dysfunction in Patients with Chronic Fatigue Syndrome (CFS) and Fibromyalgia (FM). *Journal of Chronic Fatigue Syndrome, 14*(3). doi:10.1300/J092v14no3_06. Available from: https://www.holtorfmed.com/dr-pdf/Diagnosis%20Treatment%20CFS%20FM.pdf

Honzik, T., Adamovicova, M., Smolka, V., Magner, M., Hruba, E., & Zeman, J. (2010). Clinical presentation and metabolic consequences in 40 breastfed infants with nutritional vitamin B12 deficiency-- what have we learned? *European Journal of Paediatric Neurology, 14*(6), 488-495. doi:10.1016/j.ejpn.2009.12.003. Available from: https://www.ncbi.nlm.nih.gov/pubmed/20089427

Hooper, M. (2013). *Living with Pernicious Anaemia and Vitamin B12 Deficiency*. London: Hammersmith Health Books.

Hooper, M. (2015). *What you need to know about Pernicious Anaemia and Vitamin B12 Deficiency*. London: Hammersmith Health Books.

Hooper, M., Hudson, P., Porter, F., & McCaddon, A. (2014). Patient journeys: diagnosis and treatment of pernicious anaemia. *British Journal of Nursing, 23*(7), 376-381. Available from: http://www.ncbi.nlm.nih.gov/pubmed/24732991

Hsing, A. W., Hansson, L. E., McLaughlin, J. K., Nyren, O., Blot, W. J., Ekbom, A., & Fraumeni, J. F., Jr. (1993). Pernicious anemia and subsequent cancer. A population-based cohort study. *Cancer, 71*(3), 745-750. Available from: https://www.ncbi.nlm.nih.gov/pubmed/8431855

Hultdin, J., Van Guelpen, B., Bergh, A., Hallmans, G., & Stattin, P. (2005). Plasma folate, vitamin B12, and homocysteine and prostate cancer risk: a prospective study. *International Journal of Cancer, 113*(5), 819-824. doi:10.1002/ijc.20646. Available from: https://www.ncbi.nlm.nih.gov/pubmed/15499634; http://onlinelibrary.wiley.com/store/10.1002/ijc.20646/asset/20646_ftp.pdf?v=1&t=j1mo1xhm&s=b0e974b510c322e06513fceadb423f49abae05c5

Hunt, A., Harrington, D., & Robinson, S. (2014). Vitamin B12 deficiency. *BMJ, 349*, g5226. doi:10.1136/bmj.g5226. Available from: https://www.ncbi.nlm.nih.gov/pubmed/25189324; https://www.bmj.com/content/349/bmj.g5226.long

Huser, H.-J. (1966). A note on Biermer's anemia (unseen). *Medical Clinics of North America, 50*, 1611.

Hvas, A. M., & Nexo, E. (2006). Diagnosis and treatment of vitamin B12 deficiency--an update. *Haematologica, 91*(11), 1506-1512. Available from: https://www.ncbi.nlm.nih.gov/pubmed/17043022; http://www.haematologica.org/content/haematol/91/11/1506.full.pdf;

IARC. World Health Organisation: International Agency for Research on Cancer. (2018). *All Cancers*. Available from: http://gco.iarc.fr/today/data/factsheets/cancers/39-All-cancers-fact-sheet.pdf

Ihara, H., Hashizume, N., Totani, M., Inage, H., Kimura, S., Nagamura, Y., Sudo, K., Aoki, Y., Saeki, H., Sagawa, N., Kamioka, K., Shimizu, K., Watanabe, R., Watanabe, M., Hirayama, K., Nakamori, M., Takenami, K., Yoshida, M., Kawasaki, Y., Ogiwara, T., Kawai, T., & Watanabe, T. (2008). Traditional reference values for serum vitamin B12 and folate are not applicable to automated serum vitamin B12 and folate assays: comparison of value from three automated serum vitamin B12 and folate assays. *Journal of Analytical Bio-Science, 31*(4), 291-298. Available from: http://plaza.umin.ac.jp/j-jabs/31/ft.31.291.pdf

Independent. (1999, 23 Nov). The mother of all miracles, Indy/Life. *Independent Indy/Life*. Available from: https://www.independent.co.uk/life-style/health-and-families/health-news/the-mother-of-all-miracles-742046.html

International Human Genome Sequencing Consortium. (2001). Initial sequencing and analysis of the human genome. *Nature, 409*, 860. doi:10.1038/35057062. Available from: http://dx.doi.org/10.1038/35057062; https://www.nature.com/articles/35057062.pdf

IoM. Institute of Medicine. (1998a). Appendix N: Estimation of the period covered by Vitamin B12 stores. In *Dietary Reference Intakes for Thiamin, Riboflavin, Niacin, Vitamin B6, Folate, Vitamin B12, Pantothenic Acid, Biotin, and Choline* (10.17226/6015pp. 527-530). Washington (DC): National Academies Press (US); Institute of Medicine; National Academies of Science.

IoM. Institute of Medicine. (1998b). *Dietary Reference Intakes for Thiamin, Riboflavin, Niacin, Vitamin B6, Folate, Vitamin B12, Pantothenic Acid, Biotin, and Choline*. Available from: https://www.nap.edu/catalog/6015/dietary-reference-intakes-for-thiamin-riboflavin-niacin-vitamin-b6-folate-vitamin-b12-pantothenic-acid-biotin-and-choline

IoM. Institute of Medicine. (1998c). *Vitamin B12*. Available from: https://www.nap.edu/catalog/6015/dietary-reference-intakes-for-thiamin-riboflavin-niacin-vitamin-b6-folate-vitamin-b12-pantothenic-acid-biotin-and-choline

Issac, T. G., Soundarya, S., Christopher, R., & Chandra, S. R. (2015). Vitamin B12 deficiency: an important reversible co-morbidity in neuropsychiatric manifestations. *Indian Journal of Psychological Medicine, 37*(1), 26-29. doi:10.4103/0253-7176.150809 Available from: https://www.ncbi.nlm.nih.gov/pubmed/25722508; http://www.ijpm.info/article.asp?issn=0253-7176;year=2015;volume=37;issue=1;spage=26;epage=29;aulast=Issac

Jackson, C. (Writer) & C. Jackson (Director). (2006). Inside Out - B12 Deficiency [BBC TV North East]. In C. Jackson (Producer), *Inside Out*. UK: BBC. Available from: http://www.youtube.com/watch?v=IXx7uIYBcXk

Jägerstad, M. (2012). Folic acid fortification prevents neural tube defects and may also reduce cancer risks. *Acta Paediatrica, 101*(10), 1007-1012. doi:10.1111/j.1651-2227.2012.02781.x. Available from: https://www.ncbi.nlm.nih.gov/pubmed/22783992; https://onlinelibrary.wiley.com/doi/pdf/10.1111/j.1651-2227.2012.02781.x

Jewells, V., Horsley, L. C., Markovic-Plese, S., & Troiani, L. (2015). Completing the Differential: A Comprehensive Discussion of Multiple Sclerosis Mimics. *Neurographics, 5*, 148-166. doi:10.3174/ng.4150120.

Jiang, C.-L., He, S.-W., Zhang, Y.-D., Duan, H.-X., Huang, T., Huang, Y.-C., Li, G.-F., Wang, P., Ma, L.-J., Zhou, G.-B., & Cao, Y. (2017). Air pollution and DNA methylation alterations in lung cancer: A systematic and comparative study. *Oncotarget, 8*(1), 1369-1391. doi:10.18632/oncotarget.13622. Available from: https://www.ncbi.nlm.nih.gov/pubmed/27901495

Jones, G. (2015, 4 Feb 2015). Why are cancer rates increasing? Available from: https://scienceblog.cancerresearchuk.org/2015/02/04/why-are-cancer-rates-increasing/

Juno Pharmaceuticals. (2015). SYNACTHEN® New Zealand Data Sheet. In Juno Pharmaceuticals NZ Ltd (Ed.). Manukau, Auckland, New Zealand: Medsafe New Zealand Medicines and Medical Devices Safety Authority. Available from: http://www.medsafe.govt.nz/profs/Datasheet/s/synactheninj.pdf

JustVitamins. (2014, 4 Mar 2014). What are Fat-Soluble Vitamins? Available from: https://www.justvitamins.co.uk/blog/what-are-fat-soluble-vitamins/#.Wb7RiciGMuU

JustVitamins. (2016, May 5). Is RDA the same as NRV? Available from: https://www.justvitamins.co.uk/blog/rda-or-nrv/#.W8jc32hKjD5

Kamath, A., & Pemminati, S. (2017). Methylcobalamin in Vitamin B12 Deficiency: To Give or not to Give? *Journal of Pharmacology & Pharmacotherapeutics, 8*(1), 33-34. doi:10.4103/jpp.JPP_173_16. Available from: https://www.ncbi.nlm.nih.gov/pubmed/28405134; http://www.jpharmacol.com/article.asp?issn=0976-500X;year=2017;volume=8;issue=1;spage=33;epage=34;aulast=Kamath

Kamper, M. J., & Hodgkin, D. C. (1955). Some observations on the crystal structure of a chlorine-substituted vitamin B12. *Nature, 176*(4481), 551-553. Available from: http://www.ncbi.nlm.nih.gov/pubmed/13265771

Kasperlik-Zaluska, A. A., Czarnocka, B., Czech, W., Walecki, J., Makowska, A. M., Brzezinski, J., & Aniszewski, J. (1998). Secondary adrenal insufficiency associated with autoimmune disorders: a report of twenty-five cases. *Clinical Endocrinology, 49*(6), 779-783. Available from: https://www.ncbi.nlm.nih.gov/pubmed/10209566; https://onlinelibrary.wiley.com/doi/abs/10.1046/j.1365-2265.1998.00611.x

Kassebaum, N. J., Jasrasaria, R., Naghavi, M., Wulf, S. K., Johns, N., Lozano, R., Regan, M., Weatherall, D., Chou, D. P., Eisele, T. P., Flaxman, S. R., Pullan, R. L., Brooker, S. J., & Murray, C. J. L. (2014). A systematic analysis of global anemia burden from 1990 to 2010. *Blood, 123*(5), 615-624. doi:10.1182/blood-2013-06-508325. Available from: https://www.ncbi.nlm.nih.gov/pubmed/24297872; http://www.bloodjournal.org/content/bloodjournal/123/5/615.full.pdf

Kennedy, D. O. (2016). B Vitamins and the Brain: Mechanisms, Dose and Efficacy--A Review. *Nutrients, 8*(2), 68. doi:10.3390/nu8020068. Available from: https://www.ncbi.nlm.nih.gov/pubmed/26828517; https://res.mdpi.com/nutrients/nutrients-08-00068/article_deploy/nutrients-08-00068.pdf?filename=&attachment=1

Khalil, R., Naqvi, S., & Chastain, V. (2012). Vitamin B12 deficiency as a cause of hemolytic anemia. *Journal of Hospital Medicine, 7*(2). Available from: https://www.shmabstracts.com/abstract/vitamin-b12-deficiency-as-a-cause-of-hemolytic-anemia/

Khan, S., Del-Duca, C., Fenton, E., Holding, S., Hirst, J., Dore, P. C., & Sewell, W. A. (2009). Limited value of testing for intrinsic factor antibodies with negative gastric parietal cell antibodies in pernicious anaemia. *Journal of Clinical Pathology, 62*(5), 439-441. doi:10.1136/jcp.2008.060509. Available from: https://www.ncbi.nlm.nih.gov/pubmed/19398595; http://jcp.bmj.com/content/62/5/439.long

Kibirige, D., & Mwebaze, R. (2013). Vitamin B12 deficiency among patients with diabetes mellitus: is routine screening and supplementation justified? *J Diabetes Metab Disord, 12*(1), 17. doi:10.1186/2251-6581-12-17. Available from: https://www.ncbi.nlm.nih.gov/pubmed/23651730; https://www.ncbi.nlm.nih.gov/pmc/articles/PMC3649932/pdf/2251-6581-12-17.pdf

Kim, S., Thiessen, P. A., Bolton, E. E., Chen, J., Fu, G., Gindulyte, A., Han, L., He, J., He, S., Shoemaker, B. A., Wang, J., Yu, B., Zhang, J., & Bryant, S. H. (2016). PubChem Substance and Compound databases. *Nucleic Acids Research, 44*(D1), D1202-1213. doi:10.1093/nar/gkv951. Available from: https://www.ncbi.nlm.nih.gov/pmc/articles/PMC4702940/pdf/gkv951.pdf

Kim, Y.-I. (2006). Does a high folate intake increase the risk of breast cancer? *Nutrition Reviews, 64*(10 Pt 1), 468-475. Available from: https://www.ncbi.nlm.nih.gov/pubmed/17063929

Kim, Y.-I. (2007). Folate and colorectal cancer: an evidence-based critical review. *Molecular Nutrition & Food Research, 51*(3), 267-292. doi:10.1002/mnfr.200600191. Available from: https://www.ncbi.nlm.nih.gov/pubmed/17295418; https://onlinelibrary.wiley.com/doi/abs/10.1002/mnfr.200600191

Kira, J., Tobimatsu, S., & Goto, I. (1994). Vitamin B12 metabolism and massive-dose methyl vitamin B12 therapy in Japanese patients with multiple sclerosis. *Internal Medicine, 33*(2), 82-86. Available from: http://www.ncbi.nlm.nih.gov/entrez/query.fcgi?cmd=Retrieve&db=PubMed&dopt=Citation&list_uids=8019047

Kocer, B., Engur, S., Ak, F., & Yilmaz, M. (2009). Serum vitamin B12, folate, and homocysteine levels and their association with clinical and electrophysiological parameters in multiple sclerosis. *Journal of Clinical Neuroscience, 16*(3), 399-403. doi:10.1016/j.jocn.2008.05.015. Available from: http://www.ncbi.nlm.nih.gov/entrez/query.fcgi?cmd=Retrieve&db=PubMed&dopt=Citation&list_uids=19153046

Koury, M. J., & Ponka, P. (2004). NEW INSIGHTS INTO ERYTHROPOIESIS: The Roles of Folate, Vitamin B12, and Iron. *Annual Review of Nutrition, 24*(1), 105-131. doi:10.1146/annurev.nutr.24.012003.132306. Available from: https://doi.org/10.1146/annurev.nutr.24.012003.132306

Kresser, C. (2012, 9 Mar 2012). The little known (but crucial) difference between folate and folic acid. Available from: https://chriskresser.com/folate-vs-folic-acid/

Kumarappa, B. (Ed.) (1951). *Basic Education (Mahatma Gandhi sayings on Education vol. 1)* (1 ed. Vol. 1). Ahmedabad: Navajivan Publishing House.

Kurkowska-Jastrzębska, I., Wicha, W., & Członkowska, A. (2006). Vitamin B12 deficiency can mimic multiple sclerosis – report of two cases. *Case Reports and Clinical Practice Review, 7*, 64-68. Available from: https://www.amjcaserep.com/download/index/idArt/449522

Lachner, C., Steinle, N. I., & Regenold, W. T. (2012). The neuropsychiatry of vitamin B12 deficiency in elderly patients. *Journal of Neuropsychiatry and Clinical Neurosciences, 24*(1), 5-15. doi:10.1176/appi.neuropsych.11020052. Available from: http://www.ncbi.nlm.nih.gov/pubmed/22450609; http://psychiatryonline.org/data/Journals/NP/20365/jnp00112000005.pdf

Landecker, H. (2011). Food as exposure: Nutritional epigenetics and the new metabolism. *Biosocieties, 6*(2), 167-194. doi:10.1057/biosoc.2011.1. Available from: https://www.ncbi.nlm.nih.gov/pubmed/23227106; https://www.ncbi.nlm.nih.gov/pmc/articles/PMC3500842/pdf/biosoc20111a.pdf

Laureti, S., Vecchi, L., Santeusanio, F., & Falorni, A. (1999). Is the Prevalence of Addison's Disease Underestimated? *The Journal of Clinical Endocrinology & Metabolism, 84*(5), 1762-1762. doi:10.1210/jcem.84.5.5677-7. Available from: http://dx.doi.org/10.1210/jcem.84.5.5677-7

Laybourn, P. (2001). Gene Regulation. In S. Brenner & J. H. Miller (Eds.), *Encyclopedia of Genetics* (10.1006/rwgn.2001.0520pp. 803-813). San Diego: Academic Press.

Lee, K. W. K., & Pausova, Z. (2013). Cigarette smoking and DNA methylation. *Frontiers in Genetics, 4*, 132. doi:10.3389/fgene.2013.00132. Available from: https://www.ncbi.nlm.nih.gov/pubmed/23882278; https://www.ncbi.nlm.nih.gov/pmc/articles/PMC3713237/pdf/fgene-04-00132.pdf

Leelarathna, L., Powrie, J. K., & Carroll, P. V. (2009). Thomas Addison's disease after 154 years: modern diagnostic perspectives on an old condition. *QJM, 102*(8), 569-573. doi:10.1093/qjmed/hcp053. Available from: https://www.ncbi.nlm.nih.gov/pubmed/19420117

Leichtenstern, O. M. (1884). Progressive perniciöse anämie bei tabeskranken. *Deutsche Medizinische Wochenschrift, 10*, 849-850.

Li, X., Hao, L., Yang, Y., Lu, W., & Xu, M. (2017). The association of serum folate, vitamin B12, homocysteine levels with pregnancy complications and newborn health in pregnant women.

International Journal of Clinical and Experimental Medicine, 10(7), 11213-11219. Available from: http://www.ijcem.com/files/ijcem0052364.pdf

Lichtheim, L. (1887). Zur kenntniss der perniciösen anämie. *Munchener Medizinische Wochenschrift, 34*, 301-306.

Lieutaud, J. (1816). *Synopsis of the Universal Practice of Medicine: Exhibiting a Concise View of All Diseases, Both Internal and External: Illustrated with Complete Commentaries* (edited and translated by): Edward and Richard Parker, Philadelphia.

Lindenbaum, J., Healton, E. B., Savage, D. G., Brust, J. C., Garrett, T. J., Podell, E. R., Marcell, P. D., Stabler, S. P., & Allen, R. H. (1988). Neuropsychiatric disorders caused by cobalamin deficiency in the absence of anemia or macrocytosis. *New England Journal of Medicine, 318*(26), 1720-1728. doi:10.1056/NEJM198806303182604. Available from: http://www.ncbi.nlm.nih.gov/pubmed/3374544

Lorber, S. H., & Shay, H. (1950). Entero-hepatic circulation of bromsulphalein. *Journal of Clinical Investigation, 29*(6), 831. Available from: http://www.ncbi.nlm.nih.gov/pubmed/15436781

Lorber, S. H., & Shay, H. (1952). Entero-hepatic circulation of bromsulphalein. I. Studies on man with special reference to the clinical BSP test. *Gastroenterology, 20*(2), 262-271. Available from: http://www.ncbi.nlm.nih.gov/pubmed/14906620

Lu, F., & Zhang, H. T. (2011). DNA Methylation and Nonsmall Cell Lung Cancer. *The Anatomical Record, 294*(11), 1787-1795. doi:10.1002/ar.21471. Available from: https://onlinelibrary.wiley.com/doi/full/10.1002/ar.21471

Lyford, C., Dinnerstein, E., & Ramachandran, T. S. (2017, 27 Jul 2017). Marchiafava-Bignami Disease. Available from: http://emedicine.medscape.com/article/1146086-overview

Mahalle, N., Kulkarni, M. V., Garg, M. K., & Naik, S. S. (2013). Vitamin B12 deficiency and hyperhomocysteinemia as correlates of cardiovascular risk factors in Indian subjects with coronary artery disease. *Journal of Cardiology, 61*(4), 289-294. Available from: https://www.sciencedirect.com/science/article/pii/S0914508713000427

Mandel, L. R. (2009). Endocrine and autoimmune aspects of the health history of John F. Kennedy. *Annals of Internal Medicine, 151*(5), 350-354. Available from: https://www.ncbi.nlm.nih.gov/pubmed/19721023

McBride, J. (2000, 2 Aug). B12 Deficiency May Be More Widespread Than Thought. *Agricultural Research Service.* Available from: http://www.ars.usda.gov/is/pr/2000/000802.htm

McCullough, L. E., Miller, E. E., Mendez, M. A., Murtha, A. P., Murphy, S. K., & Hoyo, C. (2016). Maternal B vitamins: effects on offspring weight and DNA methylation at genomically imprinted domains. *Clinical Epigenetics, 8*, 8. doi:10.1186/s13148-016-0174-9. Available from: https://www.ncbi.nlm.nih.gov/pubmed/26807160; https://www.ncbi.nlm.nih.gov/pmc/articles/PMC4722751/pdf/13148_2016_Article_174.pdf

McKay, J. A., Groom, A., Potter, C., Coneyworth, L. J., Ford, D., Mathers, J. C., & Relton, C. L. (2012). Genetic and non-genetic influences during pregnancy on infant global and site specific DNA methylation: role for folate gene variants and vitamin B12. *PloS One, 7*(3), e33290. doi:10.1371/journal.pone.0033290. Available from: http://www.ncbi.nlm.nih.gov/pmc/articles/PMC3316565/pdf/pone.0033290.pdf

McKay, J. A., & Mathers, J. C. (2011). Diet induced epigenetic changes and their implications for health. *Acta Physiologica (Oxford, England), 202*(2), 103-118. doi:10.1111/j.1748-1716.2011.02278.x. Available from: https://www.ncbi.nlm.nih.gov/pubmed/21401888; https://onlinelibrary.wiley.com/doi/abs/10.1111/j.1748-1716.2011.02278.x

McLean, E., de Benoist, B., & Allen, L. H. (2008). Review of the magnitude of folate and vitamin B12 deficiencies worldwide. *Food and Nutrition Bulletin, 29*(2 Suppl), S38-51. doi:10.1177/15648265080292S107. Available from: https://www.ncbi.nlm.nih.gov/pubmed/18709880

Merck & Co. (1958). *Vitamin B12* (Merck & Co Inc Ed., 10.1002/jps.3030471131). Rahway, New Jersey: Merck & Co Inc Chemical Division.

MeSH. Medical Subject Headings. Vitamin B12 MeSH unique ID D014805. *Medical Subject Headings, National Center for Biotechnology Information.* Available from: https://www.ncbi.nlm.nih.gov/mesh/68014805

Mete, N., Gulbahar, O., Aydin, A., Sin, A. Z., Kokuludag, A., & Sebik, F. (2004). Low B12 levels in chronic idiopathic urticaria. *Journal of Investigational Allergology and Clinical Immunology, 14*(4), 292-299. Available from: https://www.ncbi.nlm.nih.gov/pubmed/15736714

Miller, A., Korem, M., Almog, R., & Galboiz, Y. (2005). Vitamin B12, demyelination, remyelination and repair in multiple sclerosis. *Journal of the Neurological Sciences, 233*(1-2), 93-97. doi:10.1016/j.jns.2005.03.009. Available from: http://www.ncbi.nlm.nih.gov/pubmed/15896807, http://www.jns-journal.com/article/S0022-510X(05)00087-0/pdf

Miller, D. R., & Hayes, K. C. (1982). Vitamin Excess and Toxicity. In J. N. Hathcock (Ed.), *Nutritional Toxicology* (Vol. 1, pp. 81-133). New York; London: Academic Press.

Mills, J. L., Carter, T. C., Kay, D. M., Browne, M. L., Brody, L. C., Liu, A., Romitti, P. A., Caggana, M., & Druschel, C. M. (2012). Folate and vitamin B12-related genes and risk for omphalocele. *Human Genetics, 131*(5), 739-746. doi:10.1007/s00439-011-1117-3. Available from: http://www.ncbi.nlm.nih.gov/pmc/articles/PMC3374579/pdf/nihms379362.pdf

Minalyan, A., Benhammou, J. N., Artashesyan, A., Lewis, M. S., & Pisegna, J. R. (2017). Autoimmune atrophic gastritis: current perspectives. *Clinical and Experimental Gastroenterology, 10*, 19-27. doi:10.2147/CEG.S109123. Available from: https://www.ncbi.nlm.nih.gov/pubmed/28223833; https://www.dovepress.com/getfile.php?fileID=34757

Mind UK. (2017, Sept 2017). Sectioning (Mental Health Act 1983). Available from: https://www.mind.org.uk/information-support/legal-rights/sectioning/about-sectioning/

Minnet, C., Koc, A., Aycicek, A., & Kocyigit, A. (2011). Vitamin B12 treatment reduces mononuclear DNA damage. *Pediatrics International, 53*(6), 1023-1027. doi:10.1111/j.1442-200X.2011.03448.x. Available from: http://onlinelibrary.wiley.com/doi/10.1111/j.1442-200X.2011.03448.x/abstract; https://onlinelibrary.wiley.com/doi/abs/10.1111/j.1442-200X.2011.03448.x

Minney, H. (2010, 23-8-2010). B12 deficiency - cost of mis-diagnosis. Available from: http://www.b12d.org/misdiagnosis

Minot, G. R., & Murphy, W. P. (1926). Treatment of pernicious anemia by a special diet [1926 article] reproduced in *Yale Journal of Biology and Medicine*, 74(5): pp. 341-353. *Journal of the American Medical Association, 87*, 470-476. Available from:

http://www.ncbi.nlm.nih.gov/entrez/query.fcgi?cmd=Retrieve&db=PubMed&dopt=Citation&list_uids=11769340;
http://www.pubmedcentral.nih.gov/picrender.fcgi?artid=2588744&blobtype=pdf

Minot, G. R., & Murphy, W. P. (1983). Landmark article (JAMA 1926). Treatment of pernicious anemia by a special diet. By George R. Minot and William P. Murphy. *JAMA, 250*(24), 3328-3335. Available from:
http://www.ncbi.nlm.nih.gov/entrez/query.fcgi?cmd=Retrieve&db=PubMed&dopt=Citation&list_uids=6358569

Molloy, A. M. (2018). Should vitamin B12 status be considered in assessing risk of neural tube defects? *Annals of the New York Academy of Sciences, 1414*(1), 109-125. doi:10.1111/nyas.13574. Available from: https://www.ncbi.nlm.nih.gov/pubmed/29377209; https://www.ncbi.nlm.nih.gov/pmc/articles/PMC5887889/pdf/NYAS-1414-109.pdf

Molloy, A. M., Kirke, P. N., Brody, L. C., Scott, J. M., & Mills, J. L. (2008). Effects of folate and vitamin B12 deficiencies during pregnancy on fetal, infant, and child development. *Food and Nutrition Bulletin, 29*(2 Suppl), S101-111; discussion S112-105. doi:10.1177/15648265080292S114. Available from: https://www.ncbi.nlm.nih.gov/pubmed/18709885

Molloy, A. M., Kirke, P. N., Troendle, J. F., Burke, H., Sutton, M., Brody, L. C., Scott, J. M., & Mills, J. L. (2009). Maternal vitamin B12 status and risk of neural tube defects in a population with high neural tube defect prevalence and no folic Acid fortification. *Pediatrics, 123*(3), 917-923. doi:10.1542/peds.2008-1173. Available from:
http://pediatrics.aappublications.org/content/123/3/917.full.pdf

Molloy, A. M., Mills, J. L., McPartlin, J., Kirke, P. N., Scott, J. M., & Daly, S. (2002). Maternal and fetal plasma homocysteine concentrations at birth: the influence of folate, vitamin B12, and the 5,10-methylenetetrahydrofolate reductase 677C-->T variant. *American Journal of Obstetrics and Gynecology, 186*(3), 499-503. Available from:
https://www.ncbi.nlm.nih.gov/pubmed/11904614; https://www.ajog.org/article/S0002-9378(02)47284-5/fulltext

Morel, S., Georges, A., Bordenave, L., & Corcuff, J. B. (2009). Thyroid and gastric autoimmune diseases. *Annales d'Endocrinologie, 70*(1), 55-58. doi:10.1016/j.ando.2008.11.003. Available from:
http://www.sciencedirect.com/science/article/pii/S0003426608002540

Murphy, M. M., Molloy, A. M., Ueland, P. M., Fernandez-Ballart, J. D., Schneede, J., Arija, V., & Scott, J. M. (2007). Longitudinal study of the effect of pregnancy on maternal and fetal cobalamin status in healthy women and their offspring. *Journal of Nutrition, 137*(8), 1863-1867. doi:10.1093/jn/137.8.1863. Available from: https://www.ncbi.nlm.nih.gov/pubmed/17634256

Nagao, T., & Hirokawa, M. (2017). Diagnosis and treatment of macrocytic anemias in adults. *J Gen Fam Med, 18*(5), 200-204. doi:10.1002/jgf2.31. Available from:
https://www.ncbi.nlm.nih.gov/pubmed/29264027;
https://www.ncbi.nlm.nih.gov/pmc/articles/PMC5689413/pdf/JGF2-18-200.pdf

National Cancer Institute. (2015, Feb 15 2015). What is Cancer? Available from:
https://www.cancer.gov/about-cancer/understanding/what-is-cancer

National Institute on Ageing. (2017, 2017-07-24). Alzheimer's Disease Genetics Fact Sheet. Available from: https://www.nia.nih.gov/health/alzheimers-disease-genetics-fact-sheet

National Library of Medicine (US). (2018a, Oct 2 2018). What is a genome? *Genetics Home Reference.* Available from: https://ghr.nlm.nih.gov/primer/hgp/genome

National Library of Medicine (US). (2018b, Oct 2 2018). What is DNA? *Genetics Home Reference.* Available from: https://ghr.nlm.nih.gov/primer/basics/dna

Neitzel, H., & Trimborn, M. (2007). Human Chromosomes: Structural and Functional Aspects. In G. Obe & Vijayalaxmi (Eds.), *Chromosomal Alterations: Methods, Results and Importance in Human Health* (pp. 1-20). Berlin and Heidelberg: Springer Science & Business Media.

Nemlekar, S. S., Mehta, R. Y., Dave, K. R., & Shah, N. D. (2016). Marchiafava: Bignami Disease Treated with Parenteral Thiamine. *Indian Journal of Psychological Medicine, 38*(2), 147-149. doi:10.4103/0253-7176.178810. Available from: https://www.ncbi.nlm.nih.gov/pubmed/27114628; http://www.ijpm.info/article.asp?issn=0253-7176;year=2016;volume=38;issue=2;spage=147;epage=149;aulast=Nemlekar

NEQAS. UK National Quality Assessment Scheme for Haematinic Assays. (2014, 18 Feb 2014). B12 ALERT: False normal B12 results and the risk of neurological damage. *United Kingdom National Quality Assessment Scheme for Haematinic Assays.* Available from: http://archive.is/hbPHE#selection-73.1-72.2

Ness-Abramof, R., Nabriski, D. A., Braverman, L. E., Shilo, L., Weiss, E., Reshef, T., Shapiro, M. S., & Shenkman, L. (2006). Prevalence and evaluation of B12 deficiency in patients with autoimmune thyroid disease. *American Journal of the Medical Sciences, 332*(3), 119-122. Available from: https://www.ncbi.nlm.nih.gov/pubmed/16969140; https://www.amjmedsci.org/article/S0002-9629(15)32718-X/fulltext

Neufeld, M., & Blizzard, R. M. (1980). Polyglandular autoimmune diseases. In A. Pinchera, D. Doniach, G. Fenzi, & L. Baschieri (Eds.), *Autoimmune aspects of endocrine disorders: Symposium Proceedings (Serono Symposia International Foundation symposium held in Pisa, Italy)* (Vol. 33, pp. 357-365). London, New York: Academic Press.

Neufeld, M., Maclaren, N., & Blizzard, R. (1980). Autoimmune polyglandular syndromes. *Pediatric Annals, 9*(4), 154-162. Available from: https://www.ncbi.nlm.nih.gov/pubmed/6990358

Nexo, E., & Hoffmann-Lücke, E. (2011). Holotranscobalamin, a marker of vitamin B-12 status: analytical aspects and clinical utility. *American Journal of Clinical Nutrition, 94*(1), 359S-365S. doi:10.3945/ajcn.111.013458. Available from: http://ajcn.nutrition.org/content/94/1/359S.full.pdf

NHS. (2016a, 16 May 2016). Complications: vitamin B12 or folate deficiency anaemia. Available from: https://www.nhs.uk/conditions/vitamin-b12-or-folate-deficiency-anaemia/complications/

NHS. (2016b, 17 Feb 2016). Multiple Sclerosis. *Health A-Z.* Available from: https://www.nhs.uk/conditions/multiple-sclerosis/

NHS. (2016c, 16 May 2016). Overview: Vitamin B12 or folate deficiency anaemia. Available from: https://www.nhs.uk/conditions/vitamin-b12-or-folate-deficiency-anaemia/

NHS. (2016d, 16 May 2016). Treatment: Vitamin B12 or folate deficiency anaemia. *Health A-Z.* Available from: https://www.nhs.uk/conditions/vitamin-b12-or-folate-deficiency-anaemia/treatment/

NHS. (2016e, 17 Oct 2016). Vitiligo. *Health A-Z.* Available from: https://www.nhs.uk/conditions/vitiligo/

NHS. (2017, 16 May 2017). Overview: Chronic Fatigue Syndrome (CFS/ME). *Health A-Z.* Available from: https://www.nhs.uk/conditions/chronic-fatigue-syndrome-cfs/

NHS. (2018, 8 Aug 2018). Vegetarian and vegan mums-to-be. *Eat Well:.* Available from: https://www.nhs.uk/live-well/eat-well/vegetarian-and-vegan-mums-to-be/

NICE. National Institute for Health and Care Excellence. (2015, 30 Sep 2015). Active B12 assay for diagnosing vitamin B12 deficiency: Medtech Innovation Briefing. Available from: https://www.nice.org.uk/advice/mib40/resources/active-b12-assay-for-diagnosing-vitamin-b12-deficiency-pdf-63499159342789

NICE CKS. National Institute for Health and Care Excellence Clinical Knowledge Summaries. (2018a, March). Anaemia - B12 and folate deficiency. Available from: https://cks.nice.org.uk/anaemia-b12-and-folate-deficiency#!topicsummary

NICE CKS. National Institute for Health and Care Excellence Clinical Knowledge Summaries. (2018b, Feb). Multiple Sclerosis. Available from: https://cks.nice.org.uk/multiple-sclerosis

Nicolaides, N. C., Chrousos, G. P., & Charmandari, E. (2017, October 14 2017). Adrenal Insufficiency. Available from: https://www.ncbi.nlm.nih.gov/books/NBK279083/

NIDDK. National Institute of Diabetes and Digestive and Kidney Diseases. (2016, Nov 2016). What is Diabetes? Available from: https://www.niddk.nih.gov/health-information/diabetes/overview/what-is-diabetes

NIDDK. National Institute of Diabetes and Digestive and Kidney Diseases. (2018, May 2018). Cushing's Syndrome. Available from: https://www.niddk.nih.gov/health-information/endocrine-diseases/cushings-syndrome

Nielsen, M. J., Rasmussen, M. R., Andersen, C. B., Nexo, E., & Moestrup, S. K. (2012). Vitamin B12 transport from food to the body's cells--a sophisticated, multistep pathway. *Nature Reviews: Gastroenterology & Hepatology, 9*(6), 345-354. doi:10.1038/nrgastro.2012.76. Available from: https://www.ncbi.nlm.nih.gov/pubmed/22547309; http://www.nature.com/articles/nrgastro.2012.76

NIH. National Institutes of Health. (2017). *PubChem Open Chemistry Database.* Available from: https://pubchem.ncbi.nlm.nih.gov/

NIH ODS. National Institutes of Health Office of Dietary Supplements. (2011a). Vitamin B6: Dietary Supplement Fact Sheet. Available from: https://ods.od.nih.gov/factsheets/VitaminB6-HealthProfessional/

NIH ODS. National Institutes of Health Office of Dietary Supplements. (2011b). *Vitamin B12: Fact Sheet for Consumers.* Available from: https://ods.od.nih.gov/factsheets/VitaminB12-Consumer/

NIH ODS. National Institutes of Health Office of Dietary Supplements. (2018a). Dietary Supplement Fact Sheets. Available from: https://ods.od.nih.gov/factsheets/list-all/

NIH ODS. National Institutes of Health Office of Dietary Supplements. (2018b). *Vitamin B12: Fact Sheet for Health Professionals.* Available from: https://ods.od.nih.gov/factsheets/VitaminB12-HealthProfessional/

NIH ODS. National Institutes of Health Office of Dietary Supplements. (2019, 15 Jan). Niacin: Fact Sheet for Health Professionals. Available from: https://ods.od.nih.gov/factsheets/Niacin-HealthProfessional/

Nilsson, M., Norberg, B., Hultdin, J., Sandstrom, H., Westman, G., & Lokk, J. (2005). Medical intelligence in Sweden. Vitamin B12: oral compared with parenteral? *Postgraduate Medical Journal, 81*(953), 191-193. doi:10.1136/pgmj.2004.020057. Available from: http://www.ncbi.nlm.nih.gov/pmc/articles/PMC1743228/pdf/v081p00191.pdf

Nilsson, S. E., Read, S., Berg, S., & Johansson, B. (2009). Heritabilities for fifteen routine biochemical values: findings in 215 Swedish twin pairs 82 years of age or older. *Scandinavian Journal of Clinical and Laboratory Investigation, 69*(5), 562-569. doi:10.1080/00365510902814646. Available from: http://informahealthcare.com/doi/abs/10.1080/00365510902814646

Nishimoto, S., Tanaka, H., Okamoto, M., Okada, K., Murase, T., & Yoshikawa, H. (2015). Methylcobalamin promotes the differentiation of Schwann cells and remyelination in lysophosphatidylcholine-induced demyelination of the rat sciatic nerve. *Frontiers in Cellular Neuroscience, 9*, 298. doi:10.3389/fncel.2015.00298. Available from: https://www.ncbi.nlm.nih.gov/pubmed/26300733; https://www.ncbi.nlm.nih.gov/pmc/articles/PMC4523890/pdf/fncel-09-00298.pdf

Nishizawa, Y., Yamamoto, T., Terada, N., Fushiki, S., & Matsumoto, K. (1997). Effects of methylcobalamin on the proliferation of androgen-sensitive or estrogen-sensitive malignant cells in culture and in vivo. *International Journal for Vitamin and Nutrition Research, 67*(3), 164-170. Available from: http://www.ncbi.nlm.nih.gov/pubmed/9202976

NobelPrize.org. (2016). The Nobel Prize in Physiology or Medicine 1934. Available from: https://www.nobelprize.org/nobel_prizes/medicine/laureates/1934/

Ntaios, G., Savopoulos, C., Grekas, D., & Hatzitolios, A. (2009). The controversial role of B-vitamins in cardiovascular risk: An update. *Archives of Cardiovascular Diseases, 102*, 847-854. Available from: https://www.sciencedirect.com/science/article/pii/S1875213609002411?via%3Dihub

Nurk, E., Refsum, H., Drevon, C. A., Tell, G. S., Nygaard, H. A., Engedal, K., & Smith, A. D. (2010). Cognitive performance among the elderly in relation to the intake of plant foods. The Hordaland Health Study. *British Journal of Nutrition, 104*(8), 1190-1201. doi:10.1017/S0007114510001807. Available from: https://www.ncbi.nlm.nih.gov/pubmed/20550741

O'Leary, F., & Samman, S. (2010). Vitamin B12 in health and disease. *Nutrients, 2*(3), 299-316. doi:10.3390/nu2030299. Available from: https://www.ncbi.nlm.nih.gov/pubmed/22254022; https://www.ncbi.nlm.nih.gov/pmc/PMC3257642/

O'Neill, R. J., Vrana, P. B., & Rosenfeld, C. S. (2014). Maternal methyl supplemented diets and effects on offspring health. *Frontiers in Genetics, 5*, 289. doi:10.3389/fgene.2014.00289. Available from: https://www.ncbi.nlm.nih.gov/pubmed/25206362; https://www.ncbi.nlm.nih.gov/pmc/articles/PMC4143751/pdf/fgene-05-00289.pdf

Obeid, R., Murphy, M., Sole-Navais, P., & Yajnik, C. (2017). Cobalamin Status from Pregnancy to Early Childhood: Lessons from Global Experience. *Advances in Nutrition, 8*(6), 971-979. doi:10.3945/an.117.015628. Available from: https://www.ncbi.nlm.nih.gov/pubmed/29141978; https://www.ncbi.nlm.nih.gov/pmc/articles/PMC5683008/pdf/an015628.pdf

Obeid, R., & Pietrzik, K. (2016). Re: Alison J. Price, Ruth C. Travis, Paul N. Appleby, et al. Circulating Folate and Vitamin B12 and Risk of Prostate Cancer: A Collaborative Analysis of Individual Participant

Data from Six Cohorts Including 6875 Cases and 8104 Controls. In press. http://dx.doi.org/10.1016/j.eururo.2016.03.029: Serum Concentrations of Folate and Vitamin B12 and the Risk of Prostate Cancer According to Pooled Data: The Devil Is in the Detail. *European Urology, 70*(5), e133-e134. doi:10.1016/j.eururo.2016.05.024. Available from: https://www.ncbi.nlm.nih.gov/pubmed/27236495; http://www.europeanurology.com/article/S0302-2838(16)30188-9/pdf

Olson, S. R., Deloughery, T. G., & Taylor, J. A. (2016). Time to Abandon the Serum Cobalamin Level for Diagnosing Vitamin B12 Deficiency. *Blood, 128*(22), 2447-2447. Available from: http://www.bloodjournal.org/content/128/22/2447

Oster, H., Challet, E., Ott, V., Arvat, E., Kloet, E. R. d., Dijk, D.-J., Lightman, S., Vgontzas, A., & Cauter, E. V. (2017). The Functional and Clinical Significance of the 24-Hour Rhythm of Circulating Glucocorticoids. *Endocrine Reviews, 38*(3-45). doi:10.1210/er.2015-1080. Available from: https://www.ncbi.nlm.nih.gov/pubmed/27749086

Ott, W. H., Rickes, E. L., & Wood, T. R. (1948). Activity of crystalline vitamin B12 for chick growth. *Journal of Biological Chemistry, 174*(3), 1047. Available from: http://www.ncbi.nlm.nih.gov/pubmed/18871266

Pacholok, S. M., & Stuart, J. J. (2011). *Could it be B12? : an epidemic of misdiagnoses* (2nd ed.). Fresno, Calif.: Quill Driver Books.

Pait, T. G., & Dowdy, J. T. (2017). John F. Kennedy's back: chronic pain, failed surgeries, and the story of its effects on his life and death. *Journal of Neurosurgery: Spine, 27*(3), 247-255. doi:10.3171/2017.2.SPINE151524. Available from: https://www.ncbi.nlm.nih.gov/pubmed/28693374

Papierska, L., & Rabijewski, M. (2013). Delay in diagnosis of adrenal insufficiency is a frequent cause of adrenal crisis. *International Journal of Endocrinology, 2013*, 482370. doi:10.1155/2013/482370. Available from: https://www.ncbi.nlm.nih.gov/pubmed/23864857; https://www.ncbi.nlm.nih.gov/pmc/articles/PMC3707239/pdf/IJE2013-482370.pdf

Parmanand, H. T. (2016). Marchiafava–Bignami disease in chronic alcoholic patient. *Radiology Case Reports, 11*(3), 234-237. doi:10.1016/j.radcr.2016.05.015. Available from: https://www.ncbi.nlm.nih.gov/pmc/articles/PMC4996925/

Parr, B. (1819). *The London Medical Dictionary: Including, Under Distinct Heads, Every Branch of Medicine; Viz. Anatomy, Physiology, and Pathology, the Practice of Physic and Surgery, Therapeutics, and Materia Medica; with Whatever Relates to Medicine in Natural Philosophy, Chemistry, and Natural History* (Vol. II). London: Mitchell, Ames and White.

PAS. Pernicious Anaemia Society. (2018a). Diagnosing Vitamin B12 Deficiency and Pernicious Anaemia. Available from: https://pernicious-anaemia-society.org/diagnosis/

PAS. Pernicious Anaemia Society. (2018b). Patients FAQ. Available from: https://pernicious-anaemia-society.org/faq/patients-faq/

PAS. Pernicious Anaemia Society. (2018c). Pernicious Anaemia. Available from: https://pernicious-anaemia-society.org/pernicious-anaemia/

Pearce, J. M. (2004). Thomas Addison (1793-1860). *Journal of the Royal Society of Medicine, 97*(6), 297-300. Available from: http://www.ncbi.nlm.nih.gov/pubmed/15173338; http://www.ncbi.nlm.nih.gov/pmc/articles/PMC1079500/pdf/0970297.pdf

Pearce, J. M. (2008). Subacute combined degeneration of the cord: Putnam-Dana syndrome. *European Neurology, 60*(1), 53-56. doi:10.1159/000131715. Available from: https://www.ncbi.nlm.nih.gov/pubmed/18520150; https://www.karger.com/Article/Pdf/131715

Pender, M. P. (2012). CD8+ T-Cell Deficiency, Epstein-Barr Virus Infection, Vitamin D Deficiency, and Steps to Autoimmunity: A Unifying Hypothesis. *Autoimmune Diseases, 2012*, 189096. doi:10.1155/2012/189096. Available from: https://www.ncbi.nlm.nih.gov/pubmed/22312480; https://www.ncbi.nlm.nih.gov/pmc/articles/PMC3270541/pdf/AD2012-189096.pdf

Piyathilake, C. J., Johanning, G. L., Macaluso, M., Whiteside, M., Oelschlager, D. K., Heimburger, D. C., & Grizzle, W. E. (2000). Localized folate and vitamin B-12 deficiency in squamous cell lung cancer is associated with global DNA hypomethylation. *Nutrition and Cancer, 37*(1), 99-107. Available from: http://www.ncbi.nlm.nih.gov/entrez/query.fcgi?cmd=Retrieve&db=PubMed&dopt=Citation&list_uids=10965526

Pray, L. A. (2008). DNA Replication and Causes of Mutation. *Nature Education, 1*(1), 214. Available from: https://www.nature.com/scitable/topicpage/DNA-Replication-and-Causes-of-Mutation-409

Price, A. J., Travis, R. C., Appleby, P. N., Albanes, D., Barricarte Gurrea, A., Bjorge, T., Bueno-de-Mesquita, H. B., Chen, C., Donovan, J., Gislefoss, R., Goodman, G., Gunter, M., Hamdy, F. C., Johansson, M., King, I. B., Kuhn, T., Mannisto, S., Martin, R. M., Meyer, K., Neal, D. E., Neuhouser, M. L., Nygard, O., Stattin, P., Tell, G. S., Trichopoulou, A., Tumino, R., Ueland, P. M., Ulvik, A., de Vogel, S., Vollset, S. E., Weinstein, S. J., Key, T. J., & Allen, N. E. (2016). Circulating Folate and Vitamin B12 and Risk of Prostate Cancer: A Collaborative Analysis of Individual Participant Data from Six Cohorts Including 6875 Cases and 8104 Controls. *European Urology, 70*(6), 941-951. doi:10.1016/j.eururo.2016.03.029. Available from: https://www.ncbi.nlm.nih.gov/pubmed/27061263; http://www.europeanurology.com/article/S0302-2838(16)00379-1/pdf

Priestley, A., & Cummings, A. (2016). "Can you stop my multiple sclerosis?" [Television series episode] Panorama. London: British Broadcasting Corporation.

PubChem Compound Database. Cobalamin CID=6438156, and Cobalamin CID=56840966. Available from: https://pubchem.ncbi.nlm.nih.gov/compound/6438156 https://pubchem.ncbi.nlm.nih.gov/compound/56840966

Public Health England. (2016). *Government Dietary Recommendations: Government recommendations for energy and nutrients for males and females aged 1 – 18 years and 19+ years.* Available from: https://assets.publishing.service.gov.uk/government/uploads/system/uploads/attachment_data/file/618167/government_dietary_recommendations.pdf

Radowitz, J. v. (2016, 10 Jun 2016). Breakthrough treatment for Multiple Sclerosis found to reverse symptoms. *Independent*. Available from: http://www.independent.co.uk/life-style/health-and-families/health-news/multiple-sclerosis-breakthrough-treatment-found-to-reverse-symptoms-a7073706.html

Ray, J. G., & Blom, H. J. (2003). Vitamin B12 insufficiency and the risk of fetal neural tube defects. *QJM, 96*(4), 289-295. Available from: https://www.ncbi.nlm.nih.gov/pubmed/12651973

Refsum, H. (2001). Folate, vitamin B12 and homocysteine in relation to birth defects and pregnancy outcome. *British Journal of Nutrition, 85 Suppl 2*, S109-113. Available from: https://www.ncbi.nlm.nih.gov/pubmed/11509098

Regland, B., Forsmark, S., Halaouate, L., Matousek, M., Peilot, B., Zachrisson, O., & Gottfries, C. G. (2015). Response to vitamin B12 and folic acid in myalgic encephalomyelitis and fibromyalgia. *PloS One, 10*(4), e0124648. doi:10.1371/journal.pone.0124648. Available from: https://www.ncbi.nlm.nih.gov/pubmed/25902009; https://www.ncbi.nlm.nih.gov/pmc/articles/PMC4406448/pdf/pone.0124648.pdf

Reik, W. (2007). Stability and flexibility of epigenetic gene regulation in mammalian development. *Nature, 447*(7143), 425-432. doi:10.1038/nature05918. Available from: https://www.ncbi.nlm.nih.gov/pubmed/17522676

Reynolds, E. (2006). Vitamin B12, folic acid, and the nervous system. *Lancet Neurology, 5*(11), 949-960. doi:10.1016/S1474-4422(06)70598-1. Available from: http://www.ncbi.nlm.nih.gov/pubmed/17052662; http://www.sciencedirect.com/science/article/pii/S1474442206705981

Rickes, E. L., Brink, N. G., Koniuszy, F. R., Wood, T. R., & Folkers, K. (1948a). Comparative Data on Vitamin B12 From Liver and From a New Source, Streptomyces griseus. *Science, 108*(2814), 634-635. doi:108/2814/634-a [pii]; 10.1126/science.108.2814.634-a. Available from: http://www.ncbi.nlm.nih.gov/entrez/query.fcgi?cmd=Retrieve&db=PubMed&dopt=Citation&list_uids=17783357

Rickes, E. L., Brink, N. G., Koniuszy, F. R., Wood, T. R., & Folkers, K. (1948b). Crystalline Vitamin B12. *Science, 107*(2781), 396-397. doi:10.1126/science.107.2781.396. Available from: http://www.ncbi.nlm.nih.gov/pubmed/17783930; http://www.sciencemag.org/content/107/2781/396

Rietsema, W. J. (2014). Active form of vitamin B12. *BMJ, 349*, g5226. doi:10.1136/bmj.g5226. Available from: https://www.bmj.com/content/349/bmj.g5226/rr/764190

Rizzo, G., Lagana, A. S., Rapisarda, A. M., La Ferrera, G. M., Buscema, M., Rossetti, P., Nigro, A., Muscia, V., Valenti, G., Sapia, F., Sarpietro, G., Zigarelli, M., & Vitale, S. G. (2016). Vitamin B12 among Vegetarians: Status, Assessment and Supplementation. *Nutrients, 8*(12). doi:10.3390/nu8120767. Available from: https://www.ncbi.nlm.nih.gov/pubmed/27916823; https://res.mdpi.com/nutrients/nutrients-08-00767/article_deploy/nutrients-08-00767.pdf?filename=&attachment=1

Robertson, K. D. (2005). DNA methylation and human disease. *Nature Reviews Genetics, 6*(8), 597-610. doi:10.1038/nrg1655. Available from: https://www.ncbi.nlm.nih.gov/pubmed/16136652; http://www.nature.com/articles/nrg1655

Roessler, F. C., & Wolff, S. (2017). Rapid healing of a patient with dramatic subacute combined degeneration of spinal cord: a case report. *BMC Research Notes, 10*(1), 18. doi:10.1186/s13104-016-2344-4. Available from: https://www.ncbi.nlm.nih.gov/pubmed/28057043; https://www.ncbi.nlm.nih.gov/pmc/articles/PMC5216536/pdf/13104_2016_Article_2344.pdf

Rosenblatt, D. S., & Fowler, B. (2006). Disorders of Cobalamin and Folate Transport and Metabolism. In J. Fernandes, J.-M. Saudubray, G. v. d. Berghe, & J. H. Walter (Eds.), *Inborn Metabolic Diseases: Diagnosis and Treatment* (4 ed., pp. 341-356). Berlin, Heidelberg: Springer.

Rothwell, P. M., & Charlton, D. (1998). High incidence and prevalence of multiple sclerosis in south east Scotland: evidence of a genetic predisposition. *Journal of Neurology, Neurosurgery and Psychiatry, 64*(6), 730-735. Available from: http://www.ncbi.nlm.nih.gov/entrez/query.fcgi?cmd=Retrieve&db=PubMed&dopt=Citation&list

uids=9647300;
http://www.pubmedcentral.nih.gov/picrender.fcgi?artid=2170112&blobtype=pdf

Rotter, D. (2005). Homocysteine and Vitamin B12. Available from: https://www.b12-vitamin.com/homocysteine/

Roze, E., Gervais, D., Demeret, S., Ogier de Baulny, H., Zittoun, J., Benoist, J.-F., Said, G., Pierrot-Deseilligny, C., & Bolgert, F. (2003). Neuropsychiatric Disturbances in Presumed Late-Onset Cobalamin C Disease. *Archives of Neurology, 60*(10), 1457-1462. doi:10.1001/archneur.60.10.1457. Available from: https://jamanetwork.com/journals/jamaneurology/fullarticle/784788

Russell, J. S. R., Batten, F. E., & Collier, J. (1900). Subacute Combined Degeneration of the Spinal Cord. *Brain, 23*, 39-110.

Sands, K. (2017, 28 Sept 2017). A 12-year-old boy died from Addison's disease after the chance of lifesaving treatment was 'missed'. *Wales Online*. Available from: https://www.walesonline.co.uk/news/wales-news/boy-died-addisons-disease-after-13687355

Santarelli, L., Gabrielli, M., Cremonini, F., Santoliquido, A., Candelli, M., Nista, E. C., Pola, P., Gasbarrini, G., & Gasbarrini, A. (2004). Atrophic gastritis as a cause of hyperhomocysteinaemia. *Alimentary Pharmacology and Therapeutics, 19*(1), 107-111. Available from: https://www.ncbi.nlm.nih.gov/pubmed/14687172

Sargis, R. M. (2015, 8 Apr 2015). An Overview of the Hypothalamus. Available from: https://www.endocrineweb.com/endocrinology/overview-hypothalamus

Scalabrino, G. (2001). Subacute combined degeneration one century later. The neurotrophic action of cobalamin (vitamin B12) revisited. *Journal of Neuropathology and Experimental Neurology, 60*(2), 109-120. Available from: https://academic.oup.com/jnen/article/60/2/109/2609890

Scalabrino, G. (2005). Cobalamin (vitamin B(12)) in subacute combined degeneration and beyond: traditional interpretations and novel theories. *Experimental Neurology, 192*(2), 463-479. doi:10.1016/j.expneurol.2004.12.020. Available from: http://www.sciencedirect.com/science/article/pii/S0014488604005382

Scalabrino, G. (2009). The multi-faceted basis of vitamin B12 (cobalamin) neurotrophism in adult central nervous system: Lessons learned from its deficiency. *Progress in Neurobiology, 88*(3), 203-220. doi:S0301-0082(09)00058-6 [pii]; 10.1016/j.pneurobio.2009.04.004. Available from: http://www.ncbi.nlm.nih.gov/entrez/query.fcgi?cmd=Retrieve&db=PubMed&dopt=Citation&list_uids=19394404

Scalabrino, G., Lorenzini, E. C., Monzio-Compagnoni, B., Colombi, R. P., Chiodini, E., & Buccellato, F. R. (1995). Subacute combined degeneration in the spinal cords of totally gastrectomized rats. Ornithine decarboxylase induction, cobalamin status, and astroglial reaction. *Laboratory Investigation, 72*(1), 114-123. Available from: http://www.ncbi.nlm.nih.gov/entrez/query.fcgi?cmd=Retrieve&db=PubMed&dopt=Citation&list_uids=7837784

Scalabrino, G., Mutti, E., Veber, D., Aloe, L., Corsi, M. M., Galbiati, S., & Tredici, G. (2006). Increased spinal cord NGF levels in rats with cobalamin (vitamin B12) deficiency. *Neuroscience Letters, 396*(2), 153-158. doi:S0304-3940(05)01314-5 [pii], 10.1016/j.neulet.2005.11.029. Available from:

http://www.ncbi.nlm.nih.gov/entrez/query.fcgi?cmd=Retrieve&db=PubMed&dopt=Citation&list
   uids=16352395

Scalabrino, G., Veber, D., & Mutti, E. (2007). New pathogenesis of the cobalamin-deficient neuropathy.
   Medicina Nei Secoli, 19(1), 9-18. Available from:
   http://www.ncbi.nlm.nih.gov/entrez/query.fcgi?cmd=Retrieve&db=PubMed&dopt=Citation&list
   uids=18447164

Schernhammer, E., Wolpin, B., Rifai, N., Cochrane, B., Manson, J. A., Ma, J., Giovannucci, E., Thomson, C.,
   Stampfer, M. J., & Fuchs, C. (2007). Plasma folate, vitamin B6, vitamin B12, and homocysteine
   and pancreatic cancer risk in four large cohorts. *Cancer Research, 67*(11), 5553-5560.
   doi:10.1158/0008-5472.CAN-06-4463. Available from:
   https://www.ncbi.nlm.nih.gov/pubmed/17545639;
   http://cancerres.aacrjournals.org/content/canres/67/11/5553.full.pdf

Schlaghecke, R., Kornely, E., Santen, R. T., & Ridderskamp, P. (1992). The Effect of Long-Term
   Glucocorticoid Therapy on Pituitary–Adrenal Responses to Exogenous Corticotropin-Releasing
   Hormone. *New England Journal of Medicine, 326*(4), 226-230.
   doi:10.1056/NEJM199201233260403. Available from:
   https://doi.org/10.1056/NEJM199201233260403

Scott, J. M. (1999). Folate and vitamin B12. *Proceedings of the Nutrition Society, 58*(2), 441-448.
   doi:10.1017/S0029665199000580. Available from:
   https://www.cambridge.org/core/article/folate-and-vitamin-
   b12/93748DEBFA8ADFA72FAAE2DAF7C34AAA

Scott, J. M., & Molloy, A. M. (2012). The discovery of vitamin B(12). *Annals of Nutrition and Metabolism,
   61*(3), 239-245. doi:10.1159/000343114. Available from:
   https://www.ncbi.nlm.nih.gov/pubmed/23183296;
   https://www.karger.com/Article/Abstract/343114

Senmaru, T., Fukui, M., Tanaka, M., Kuroda, M., Yamazaki, M., Oda, Y., Naito, Y., Hasegawa, G., Toda, H.,
   Yoshikawa, T., & Nakamura, N. (2012). Atrophic gastritis is associated with coronary artery
   disease. *Journal of Clinical Biochemistry and Nutrition, 51*(1), 39-41. doi:10.3164/jcbn.11-106.
   Available from: https://www.ncbi.nlm.nih.gov/pubmed/22798711;
   https://www.ncbi.nlm.nih.gov/pmc/articles/PMC3391861/pdf/jcbn-51-39.pdf

Shane, B. (2008). Folate and vitamin B12 metabolism: overview and interaction with riboflavin, vitamin
   B6, and polymorphisms. *Food and Nutrition Bulletin, 29*(2 Suppl), S5-16; discussion S17-19.
   doi:10.1177/15648265080292S103. Available from:
   https://www.ncbi.nlm.nih.gov/pubmed/18709878

Sharma, A., Gerbarg, P., Bottiglieri, T., Massoumi, L., Carpenter, L. L., Lavretsky, H., Muskin, P. R., Brown,
   R. P., Mischoulon, D., & as Work Group of the American Psychiatric Association Council on
   Research. (2017). S-Adenosylmethionine (SAMe) for Neuropsychiatric Disorders: A Clinician-
   Oriented Review of Research. *Journal of Clinical Psychiatry, 78*(6), e656-e667.
   doi:10.4088/JCP.16r11113. Available from: https://www.ncbi.nlm.nih.gov/pubmed/28682528;
   https://www.ncbi.nlm.nih.gov/pmc/articles/PMC5501081/pdf/nihms822867.pdf

Sherman, S. I., & Gagel, R. F. (2005). Disorders affecting multiple endocrine systems. In D. L. Kasper, A. S.
   Fauci, D. L. Longo, E. Braunwald, S. L. Hauser, & J. L. Jameson (Eds.), *Harrison's Principles of
   Internal Medicine* (16 ed., Vol. I, pp. 2231-2238). New York: McGraw-Hill Medical.

Shrubsole, M. J., Jin, F., Dai, Q., Shu, X. O., Potter, J. D., Hebert, J. R., Gao, Y. T., & Zheng, W. (2001). Dietary folate intake and breast cancer risk: results from the Shanghai Breast Cancer Study. *Cancer Research, 61*(19), 7136-7141. Available from: https://www.ncbi.nlm.nih.gov/pubmed/11585746; http://cancerres.aacrjournals.org/content/canres/61/19/7136.full.pdf

Simon, C., Everitt, H., Dorp, F. v., & Burkes, M. (2014). *Oxford Handbook of General Practice* (4 ed.): Oxford Medical Handbooks.

Simson, G., Herfort, A., Krim, M., & Meyer, L. M. (1950). Effects of vitamin B12 in multiple sclerosis. *Proceedings of the Society for Experimental Biology and Medicine, 75*(3), 721. Available from: http://www.ncbi.nlm.nih.gov/entrez/query.fcgi?cmd=Retrieve&db=PubMed&dopt=Citation&list_uids=14808380

Sinclair, K. D., Allegrucci, C., Singh, R., Gardner, D. S., Sebastian, S., Bispham, J., Thurston, A., Huntley, J. F., Rees, W. D., Maloney, C. A., Lea, R. G., Craigon, J., McEvoy, T. G., & Young, L. E. (2007). DNA methylation, insulin resistance, and blood pressure in offspring determined by maternal periconceptional B vitamin and methionine status. *Proceedings of the National Academy of Sciences of the United States of America, 104*(49), 19351-19356. doi:10.1073/pnas.0707258104. Available from: http://www.pnas.org/content/104/49/19351.full.pdf

Singh, N., Maturu, V. N., & Behera, D. (2015). Total Plasma Homocysteine Level Assessment and Timing of Folate/B12 Supplementation Prior to Initiation of Pemetrexed-Based Chemotherapy for Nonsquamous Non-Small Cell Lung Cancer Patients: An Irrelevant Investigation, an Unnecessary Delay, or Both? *Oncologist, 20*(7), e21. doi:10.1634/theoncologist.2015-0040. Available from: https://www.ncbi.nlm.nih.gov/pubmed/26069280; https://www.ncbi.nlm.nih.gov/pmc/articles/PMC4492244/pdf/theoncologist_1540.pdf

Singhal, D., & Berger, J. R. (2012). Detecting Multiple Sclerosis Mimics Early. *Future Neurology, 7*(5), 547-555. Available from: https://www.medscape.com/viewarticle/770971_1

Smith, A. D. (1960). Megaloblastic Madness. *British Medical Journal, 2*(5216), 1840-1845. Available from: https://www.ncbi.nlm.nih.gov/pubmed/20789014; https://www.ncbi.nlm.nih.gov/pmc/articles/PMC2098604/pdf/brmedj03056-0030.pdf

Smith, A. D., de Jager, C. A., Refsum, H., & Rosenberg, I. H. (2015). Homocysteine lowering, B vitamins, and cognitive aging. *American Journal of Clinical Nutrition, 101*(2), 415-416. doi:10.3945/ajcn.114.098467. Available from: https://www.ncbi.nlm.nih.gov/pubmed/25646343

Smith, A. D., Kim, Y. I., & Refsum, H. (2008). Is folic acid good for everyone? *American Journal of Clinical Nutrition, 87*(3), 517-533. doi:10.1093/ajcn/87.3.517. Available from: http://ajcn.nutrition.org/content/87/3/517.pdf; https://www.ncbi.nlm.nih.gov/pubmed/18326588

Smith, A. D., Refsum, H., Bottiglieri, T., Fenech, M., Hooshmand, B., McCaddon, A., Miller, J. W., Rosenberg, I. H., & Obeid, R. (2018). Homocysteine and Dementia: An International Consensus Statement. *Journal of Alzheimer's Disease, 62*(2), 561-570. doi:10.3233/JAD-171042. Available from: https://www.ncbi.nlm.nih.gov/pubmed/29480200; https://www.ncbi.nlm.nih.gov/pmc/articles/PMC5836397/pdf/jad-62-jad171042.pdf; https://www.ncbi.nlm.nih.gov/pmc/articles/PMC5836397/pdf/jad-62-jad171042.pdf

Smith, A. D., Refsum, H., & Jacoby, R. (2016). Evidence-based prevention and treatment of dementia. *Lancet Neurology, 15*(10), 1005-1006. doi:10.1016/S1474-4422(16)30074-6. Available from: https://www.ncbi.nlm.nih.gov/pubmed/27450472

Smith, A. D., Smith, S. M., Jager, C. A. d., Whitbread, P., Johnston, C., Agacinski, G., Oulhaj, A., Bradley, K. M., Jacoby, R., & Refsum, H. (2010). Homocysteine-Lowering by B Vitamins Slows the Rate of Accelerated Brain Atrophy in Mild Cognitive Impairment: A Randomized Controlled Trial. *PloS One, 5*(9), 10. doi:10.1371/journal.pone.0012244. Available from: http://www.plosone.org/article/info:doi%2F10.1371%2Fjournal.pone.0012244

Smith, D. A., & Refsum, H. (2011). Do we need to reconsider the desirable blood level of vitamin b12? *Journal of Internal Medicine, epub.* doi:10.1111/j.1365-2796.2011.02485.x. .

Smith, E. L. (1948). Purification of anti-pernicious anaemia factors from liver. *Nature, 161*(4095), 638. Available from: http://www.ncbi.nlm.nih.gov/pubmed/18856623

Smith, J., & Coman, D. (2014). Vitamin B12 Deficiency: an Update for the General Paediatrician. *Pediatrics & Therapeutics, 4*(1), 188-193. doi:10.4172/2161-0665.1000188. Available from: https://pdfs.semanticscholar.org/338a/a8885db50cb2ae59af8448cda929faa3b947.pdf

Smulders, Y. M., Smith, D. E., Kok, R. M., Teerlink, T., Swinkels, D. W., Stehouwer, C. D., & Jakobs, C. (2006). Cellular folate vitamer distribution during and after correction of vitamin B12 deficiency: a case for the methylfolate trap. *British Journal of Haematology, 132*(5), 623-629. doi:10.1111/j.1365-2141.2005.05913.x. Available from: https://www.ncbi.nlm.nih.gov/pubmed/16445837; https://onlinelibrary.wiley.com/doi/pdf/10.1111/j.1365-2141.2005.05913.x

Sobotka, H., Christoff, N., & Baker, H. (1958). Elevated vitamin levels in cerebrospinal fluid in multiple sclerosis. *Proceedings of the Society for Experimental Biology and Medicine, 98*(3), 534-536. Available from: http://www.ncbi.nlm.nih.gov/entrez/query.fcgi?cmd=Retrieve&db=PubMed&dopt=Citation&list_uids=13567762

Society for Endocrinology. (2018, January 2018). You and your Hormones: Adrenal glands. Available from: http://www.yourhormones.info/glands/adrenal-glands/

Solomon, L. R. (2007). Disorders of cobalamin (vitamin B12) metabolism: emerging concepts in pathophysiology, diagnosis and treatment. *Blood Reviews, 21*(3), 113-130. doi:S0268-960X(06)00039-7 [pii];10.1016/j.blre.2006.05.001. Available from: http://www.ncbi.nlm.nih.gov/entrez/query.fcgi?cmd=Retrieve&db=PubMed&dopt=Citation&list_uids=16814909; https://www.bloodreviews.com/article/S0268-960X(06)00039-7/fulltext; http://home.kpn.nl/hindrikdejong/Solomon-B12-2006.pdf

Specker, B. L., Black, A., Allen, L., & Morrow, F. (1990). Vitamin B-12: low milk concentrations are related to low serum concentrations in vegetarian women and to methylmalonic aciduria in their infants. *American Journal of Clinical Nutrition, 52*(6), 1073-1076.

Stichting Tekort. (2018). Treatment with high dose vitamin B12 been shown to be safe for more than 50 years. Available from: https://stichtingb12tekort.nl/wetenschap/stichting-b12-tekort-artikelen/english/treatment-with-high-dose-vitamin-b12-been-shown-to-be-safe-for-more-than-50-years/

Stubbe, J. (1994). Binding site revealed of nature's most beautiful cofactor. *Science, 266*, 1663+. Available from:

http://link.galegroup.com/apps/doc/A15948819/AONE?u=googlescholar&sid=AONE&xid=10317 fd6

Sugimura, T., Wakabayashi, K., Nakagama, H., & Nagao, M. (2004). Heterocyclic amines: Mutagens/carcinogens produced during cooking of meat and fish. *Cancer Science, 95*(4), 290-299. Available from: https://onlinelibrary.wiley.com/doi/pdf/10.1111/j.1349-7006.2004.tb03205.x

Sukla, K. K., & Raman, R. (2012). Association of MTHFR and RFC1 gene polymorphism with hyperhomocysteinemia and its modulation by vitamin B12 and folic acid in an Indian population. *European Journal of Clinical Nutrition, 66*(1), 111-118. doi:10.1038/ejcn.2011.152. Available from: http://www.nature.com/ejcn/journal/v66/n1/pdf/ejcn2011152a.pdf

Sun, N.-H., Huang, X.-Z., Wang, S.-B., Li, Y., Wang, L.-Y., Wang, H.-C., Zhang, C.-W., Zhang, C., Liu, H.-P., & Wang, Z.-N. (2016). A dose-response meta-analysis reveals an association between vitamin B12 and colorectal cancer risk. *Public Health Nutrition, 19*(8), 1446-1456. doi:10.1017/S136898001500261X. Available from: https://www.ncbi.nlm.nih.gov/pubmed/26373257

Surendran, S., Adaikalakoteswari, A., Saravanan, P., Shatwaan, I. A., Lovegrove, J. A., & Vimaleswaran, K. S. (2018). An update on vitamin B12-related gene polymorphisms and B12 status. *Genes & Nutrition, 13*, 2. doi:10.1186/s12263-018-0591-9. Available from: https://www.ncbi.nlm.nih.gov/pubmed/29445423; https://www.ncbi.nlm.nih.gov/pmc/articles/PMC5801754/pdf/12263_2018_Article_591.pdf

Takagi, Y., Hosomi, Y., Nagamata, M., Watanabe, K., Takahashi, S., Nakahara, Y., Yomota, M., Sunami, K., Okuma, Y., Shimokawa, T., & Okamura, T. (2016). Phase II study of oral vitamin B12 supplementation as an alternative to intramuscular injection for patients with non-small cell lung cancer undergoing pemetrexed therapy. *Cancer Chemotherapy and Pharmacology, 77*(3), 559-564. doi:10.1007/s00280-015-2954-x. Available from: https://www.ncbi.nlm.nih.gov/pubmed/26821156; http://link.springer.com/article/10.1007%2Fs00280-015-2954-x

Tamura, J., Kubota, K., Murakami, H., Sawamura, M., Matsushima, T., Tamura, T., Saitoh, T., Kurabayshi, H., & Naruse, T. (1999). Immunomodulation by vitamin B12: augmentation of CD8+ T lymphocytes and natural killer (NK) cell activity in vitamin B12-deficient patients by methyl-B12 treatment. *Clinical and Experimental Immunology, 116*(1), 28-32. Available from: https://www.ncbi.nlm.nih.gov/pubmed/10209501; https://www.ncbi.nlm.nih.gov/pmc/articles/PMC1905232/pdf/cei0116-0028.pdf

Tanaka, T., Scheet, P., Giusti, B., Bandinelli, S., Piras, M. G., Usala, G., Lai, S., Mulas, A., Corsi, A. M., Vestrini, A., Sofi, F., Gori, A. M., Abbate, R., Guralnik, J., Singleton, A., Abecasis, G. R., Schlessinger, D., Uda, M., & Ferrucci, L. (2009). Genome-wide association study of vitamin B6, vitamin B12, folate, and homocysteine blood concentrations. *American Journal of Human Genetics, 84*(4), 477-482. doi:10.1016/j.ajhg.2009.02.011. Available from: http://pdn.sciencedirect.com/science?_ob=MiamiImageURL&_cid=276895&_user=10&_pii=S0029929709000974&_check=y&_coverDate=2009-04-10&view=c&_gw=y&wchp=dGLbVBA-zSkWz&md5=46489d2ddf8ebad41d7e9e2140fa11b2/1-s2.0-S0002929709000974-main.pdf

Taşkesen, M., Yaramiş, A., Katar, S., Gözü_Pirinççioğlu, A., & Söker, M. (2011). Neurological presentations of nutritional vitamin B12 defi ciency in 42 breastfed infants in Southeast Turkey. *Turkish Journal of Medical Sciences, 41*(6), 1091-1096. doi:10.3906/sag-1009-1137. Available from: https://journals.tubitak.gov.tr/medical/issues/sag-11-41-6/sag-41-6-20-1009-1137.pdf

Thompson, E. (2017). [Email to Dr Chandy: B12 pregnancy levels in each trimester].

Thompson, M. D., Cole, D. E. C., & Ray, J. G. (2009). Vitamin B-12 and neural tube defects: the Canadian experience. *American Journal of Clinical Nutrition, 89*(2), 697S-701S. doi:10.3945/ajcn.2008.26947B. Available from: https://www.ncbi.nlm.nih.gov/pubmed/19116334

Tincani, A., Ceribelli, A., Cavazzana, I., Franceschini, F., Sulli, A., & Cutolo, M. (2008). Autoimmune Polyendocrine Syndromes. In Y. Shoenfeld, R. Cervera, & M. E. Gershwin (Eds.), *Diagnostic Criteria in Autoimmune Diseases* (10.1007/978-1-60327-285-8_50pp. 265-269): Humana Press.

Toft, D. J., & Spinasanta, S. (2016). Addison's Disease and Adrenal Insufficiency Overview: What is Addision's disease? What are the symptoms? *EndocrineWeb.* Available from: https://www.endocrineweb.com/conditions/addisons-disease/addison-disease-adrenal-insufficiency-overview

Tsiminis, G., Schartner, E. P., Brooks, J. L., & Hutchinson, M. R. (2016). Measuring and tracking vitamin B12: A review of current methods with a focus on optical spectroscopy. *Applied Spectroscopy Reviews, 52*(5). doi:10.1080/05704928.2016.1229325. Available from: https://www.tandfonline.com/doi/full/10.1080/05704928.2016.1229325

Tucker, K. L., Rich, S., Rosenberg, I., Jacques, P., Dallal, G., Wilson, P. W. F., & Selhub, J. (2000). Plasma vitamin B-12 concentrations relate to intake source in the Framingham Offspring Study. *American Journal of Clinical Nutrition, 71*(2), 514-522. doi:10.1093/ajcn/71.2.514. Available from: https://academic.oup.com/ajcn/article/71/2/514/4729184

Turner, M. R., & Talbot, K. (2009). Functional vitamin B12 deficiency. *Practical Neurology, 9*(1), 37-41. doi:9/1/37 [pii]; 10.1136/jnnp.2008.161968. Available from: http://www.ncbi.nlm.nih.gov/entrez/query.fcgi?cmd=Retrieve&db=PubMed&dopt=Citation&list_uids=19151237

Ueland, P. M., Refsum, H., Beresford, S. A., & Vollset, S. E. (2000). The controversy over homocysteine and cardiovascular risk. *American Journal of Clinical Nutrition, 72*, 324-332. doi:10.1093/ajcn/72.2.324. Available from: https://academic.oup.com/ajcn/article/72/2/324/4729375

Ulrich, A., Muller, D., Linnebank, M., & Tarnutzer, A. A. (2015). Pitfalls in the diagnostic evaluation of subacute combined degeneration. *BMJ Case Reports, 2015.* doi:10.1136/bcr-2014-208622. Available from: https://www.ncbi.nlm.nih.gov/pubmed/25976195; https://www.ncbi.nlm.nih.gov/pmc/articles/PMC4434358/pdf/bcr-2014-208622.pdf

Ulrich, C. M. (2007). Folate and cancer prevention: a closer look at a complex picture. *American Journal of Clinical Nutrition, 86*(2), 271-273. doi:10.1093/ajcn/86.2.271. Available from: https://www.ncbi.nlm.nih.gov/pubmed/17684194

University of Kent. (2012). Vitamin variants could combat cancer as scientists unravel B12 secrets. *Phys.org [online].* Oct 8 2012. Available from: https://phys.org/news/2012-10-vitamin-variants-combat-cancer-scientists.html#nRlv

Vaidya, B., Chakera, A. J., & Dick, C. (2009). Addison's disease. *BMJ, 339*, b2385. doi:10.1136/bmj.b2385. Available from: http://www.ncbi.nlm.nih.gov/pubmed/19574315

Valdes-Ramos, R., Guadarrama-Lopez, A. L., Martinez-Carrillo, B. E., & Benitez-Arciniega, A. D. (2015). Vitamins and type 2 diabetes mellitus. *Endocrine, Metabolic & Immune Disorders Drug Targets,*

15(1), 54-63. Available from: https://www.ncbi.nlm.nih.gov/pubmed/25388747; https://www.ncbi.nlm.nih.gov/pmc/articles/PMC4435229/pdf/EMIDDT-15-54.pdf

Van den Driessche, A., Eenkhoorn, V., Van Gaal, L., & De Block, C. (2009). Type 1 diabetes and autoimmune polyglandular syndrome: a clinical review. *Netherlands Journal of Medicine, 67*(11), 376-387. Available from: https://www.ncbi.nlm.nih.gov/pubmed/20009114

Vannella, L., Lahner, E., Osborn, J., & Annibale, B. (2013). Systematic review: gastric cancer incidence in pernicious anaemia. *Alimentary Pharmacology and Therapeutics, 37*(4), 375-382. doi:10.1111/apt.12177. Available from: https://www.ncbi.nlm.nih.gov/pubmed/23216458; https://onlinelibrary.wiley.com/doi/pdf/10.1111/apt.12177

Varela-Moreiras, G., Murphy, M. M., & Scott, J. M. (2009). Cobalamin, folic acid, and homocysteine. *Nutrition Reviews, 67*, S69-72. doi:10.1111/j.1753-4887.2009.00163.x. Available from: https://www.ncbi.nlm.nih.gov/pubmed/19453682; https://academic.oup.com/nutritionreviews/article-abstract/67/suppl_1/S69/1873436?redirectedFrom=fulltext; https://academic.oup.com/nutritionreviews/article-abstract/67/suppl_1/S69/1873436?redirectedFrom=fulltext

Varela-Rey, M., Iruarrizaga-Lejarreta, M., Lozano, J. J., Aransay, A. M., Fernandez, A. F., Lavin, J. L., Mosen-Ansorena, D., Berdasco, M., Turmaine, M., Luka, Z., Wagner, C., Lu, S. C., Esteller, M., Mirsky, R., Jessen, K. R., Fraga, M. F., Martinez-Chantar, M. L., Mato, J. M., & Woodhoo, A. (2014). S-adenosylmethionine levels regulate the schwann cell DNA methylome. *Neuron, 81*(5), 1024-1039. doi:10.1016/j.neuron.2014.01.037. Available from: https://www.ncbi.nlm.nih.gov/pubmed/24607226; https://www.cell.com/neuron/pdf/S0896-6273(14)00068-3.pdf

Veit, K. (2017). Pseudothrombotic microangiopathy and vitamin B12 deficiency in pernicious anemia. *Proceedings (Baylor University. Medical Center), 30*(3), 346-347. Available from: https://www.ncbi.nlm.nih.gov/pubmed/28670082; https://www.ncbi.nlm.nih.gov/pmc/articles/PMC5468040/pdf/bumc0030-0346.pdf

Verkleij-Hagoort, A. C., Verlinde, M., Ursem, N. T., Lindemans, J., Helbing, W. A., Ottenkamp, J., Siebel, F. M., Gittenberger-de Groot, A. C., de Jonge, R., Bartelings, M. M., Steegers, E. A., & Steegers-Theunissen, R. P. (2006). Maternal hyperhomocysteinaemia is a risk factor for congenital heart disease. *BJOG: An International Journal of Obstetrics and Gynaecology, 113*(12), 1412-1418. doi:10.1111/j.1471-0528.2006.01109.x. Available from: http://onlinelibrary.wiley.com/store/10.1111/j.1471-0528.2006.01109.x/asset/j.1471-0528.2006.01109.x.pdf?v=1&t=hhhg1i3v&s=7bdcc053118082ba87fe306aa02b7eb83c0c324d

Viswanathan, A., & Greenberg, S. M. (2011). Cerebral Amyloid Angiopathy in the Elderly. *Annals of Neurology, 70*(6), 871-880. doi:10.1002/ana.22516. Available from: http://onlinelibrary.wiley.com/store/10.1002/ana.22516/asset/22516_ftp.pdf?v=1&t=j5rysjua&s=38d556f7406aa186d81db9476202d1b1707431e4

Volkov, I. (2008). The master key effect of vitamin B12 in treatment of malignancy--a potential therapy? *Medical Hypotheses, 70*(2), 324-328. doi:10.1016/j.mehy.2007.05.029. Available from: https://www.ncbi.nlm.nih.gov/pubmed/17640826

Wailoo, K. (1997). The Corporate "Conquest" of Pernicious Anemia: technology, blood researchers, and the consumer. In M. D. Baltimore (Ed.), *Drawing blood technology and disease identity in twentieth-century America* (pp. 99-133). Baltimore & London: Johns Hopkins University Press.

Walker, C. L., & Ho, S.-m. (2012). Developmental reprogramming of cancer susceptibility. *Nature Reviews: Cancer, 12*(7), 479-486. doi:10.1038/nrc3220. Available from: https://www.ncbi.nlm.nih.gov/pubmed/22695395; https://www.ncbi.nlm.nih.gov/pmc/articles/PMC3820510/pdf/nihms481534.pdf

Wanjek, C. (2016, 10 Feb 2016). Low B12 Seen in Aging, Autism and Schizophrenia. *Live Science, Health.* Available from: https://www.livescience.com/53675-vitamin-b12-aging-autism-schizophrenia.html

Wass, J. (2012). How to avoid precipitating an acute adrenal crisis. *BMJ, 345*, e6333. doi:10.1136/bmj.e6333. Available from: http://www.bmj.com/content/345/bmj.e6333.full; http://www.bmj.com/content/345/bmj.e6333.long

Watanabe, F., Yabuta, Y., Bito, T., & Teng, F. (2014). Vitamin B12-containing plant food sources for vegetarians. *Nutrients, 6*(5), 1861-1873. doi:10.3390/nu6051861. Available from: https://www.ncbi.nlm.nih.gov/pubmed/24803097; https://res.mdpi.com/nutrients/nutrients-06-01861/article_deploy/nutrients-06-01861.pdf?filename=&attachment=1

WCRF, & AICR. World Cancer Research Fund and American Institute for Cancer Research. (2007). *Food, Nutrition, Physical Activity, and the Prevention of Cancer: a Global Perspective.* Available from: http://www.aicr.org/assets/docs/pdf/reports/Second_Expert_Report.pdf

Welch, M. (2006, 14 Feb 2006). New Discovery?: High Cortisol Binding Globuli as cause of Addison's? Available from: http://www.addisons-network.co.uk/high_cbg_ad.html

Welch, R. G. (1957). Addison's disease in a nine-year-old girl. *British Medical Journal, 1*(5025), 980-982. Available from: http://www.ncbi.nlm.nih.gov/pubmed/13413266; http://www.ncbi.nlm.nih.gov/pmc/articles/PMC1973322/pdf/brmedj03152-0036.pdf

WHO. World Health Organisation. (2017, 17 Dec). Dementia: Key Facts. Available from: http://www.who.int/news-room/fact-sheets/detail/dementia

Wickramasinghe, S. N., & Fida, S. (1994). Bone marrow cells from vitamin B12- and folate-deficient patients misincorporate uracil into DNA. *Blood, 83*(6), 1656-1661. Available from: https://www.ncbi.nlm.nih.gov/pubmed/8123857; http://www.bloodjournal.org/content/bloodjournal/83/6/1656.full.pdf

Wong, C. W. (2015). Vitamin B12 deficiency in the elderly: is it worth screening? *Hong Kong Medical Journal. Xianggang Yi Xue Za Zhi, 21*, 155-164. doi:10.12809/hkmj144383. Available from: https://www.hkmj.org/abstracts/v21n2/155.htm

Wotton, C. J., & Goldacre, M. J. (2017). Associations between specific autoimmune diseases and subsequent dementia: retrospective record-linkage cohort study, UK. *Journal of Epidemiology and Community Health, 71*(6), 576-583. doi:10.1136/jech-2016-207809. Available from: http://jech.bmj.com/content/71/6/576.long

Wu, G., Bazer, F. W., Cudd, T. A., Meininger, C. J., & Spencer, T. E. (2004). Maternal nutrition and fetal development. *Journal of Nutrition, 134*(9), 2169-2172. doi:10.1093/jn/134.9.2169. Available from: https://www.ncbi.nlm.nih.gov/pubmed/15333699

Yang, D., Baumgartner, R. N., Slattery, M. L., Wang, C., Giuliano, A. R., Murtaugh, M. A., Risendal, B. C., Byers, T., & Baumgartner, K. B. (2013). Dietary intake of folate, B-vitamins and methionine and breast cancer risk among Hispanic and non-Hispanic white women. *PloS One, 8*(2), e54495.

doi:10.1371/journal.pone.0054495. Available from: https://www.ncbi.nlm.nih.gov/pmc/articles/PMC3569453/pdf/pone.0054495.pdf

Yang, T.-Y., Chang, G.-C., Hsu, S.-L., Huang, Y.-R., Chiu, L.-Y., & Sheu, G.-T. (2013). Effect of folic acid and vitamin B12 on pemetrexed antifolate chemotherapy in nutrient lung cancer cells. *BioMed Research International, 2013*, 389046. doi:10.1155/2013/389046. Available from: https://www.ncbi.nlm.nih.gov/pubmed/23984356; https://www.ncbi.nlm.nih.gov/pmc/articles/PMC3747471/pdf/BMRI2013-389046.pdf

Zhang, N. (2015). Epigenetic modulation of DNA methylation by nutrition and its mechanisms in animals. *Animal Nutrition, 1*(3), 144-151. doi:10.1016/j.aninu.2015.09.002. Available from: https://www.ncbi.nlm.nih.gov/pubmed/29767106; https://www.ncbi.nlm.nih.gov/pmc/articles/PMC5945948/pdf/main.pdf

Zhang, Y., Hodgson, N. W., Trivedi, M. S., Abdolmaleky, H. M., Fournier, M., Cuenod, M., Do, K. Q., & Deth, R. C. (2016). Decreased Brain Levels of Vitamin B12 in Aging, Autism and Schizophrenia. *PloS One, 11*(1), e0146797. doi:10.1371/journal.pone.0146797. Available from: https://www.ncbi.nlm.nih.gov/pubmed/26799654; https://www.ncbi.nlm.nih.gov/pmc/articles/PMC4723262/pdf/pone.0146797.pdf

Zhao, L., Wei, Y., Song, A., & Li, Y. (2016). Association study between genome-wide significant variants of vitamin B12 metabolism and gastric cancer in a han Chinese population. *IUBMB Life (International Union of Biochemistry and Molecular Biology), 68*(4), 303-310. doi:10.1002/iub.1485. Available from: https://www.ncbi.nlm.nih.gov/pubmed/26959381; http://onlinelibrary.wiley.com/store/10.1002/iub.1485/asset/iub1485.pdf?v=1&t=j1mo562y&s= 48f376a0bd67d16f67f33e9cfac99f0358389d06

Zittan, E., Preis, M., Asmir, I., Cassel, A., Lindenfeld, N., Alroy, S., Halon, D. A., Lewis, B. S., Shiran, A., Schliamser, J. E., & Flugelman, M. Y. (2007). High frequency of vitamin B12 deficiency in asymptomatic individuals homozygous to MTHFR C677T mutation is associated with endothelial dysfunction and homocysteinemia. *American Journal of Physiology: Heart and Circulatory Physiology, 293*(1), H860-865. doi:10.1152/ajpheart.01189.2006. Available from: http://ajpheart.physiology.org/content/293/1/H860.full.pdf

Zulfiqar, A. A., & Andrès, E. (2017). Association pernicious anemia and autoimmune polyendocrinopathy: a retrospective study. *Journal of Medicine and Life, 10*(4), 250-253. Available from: https://www.ncbi.nlm.nih.gov/pubmed/29362601

Index

Note: if you can't find what you are looking for, it may be under a heading,eg Atrophic gastritis is under the section Immune.

Prevention · 16, 37, 123, 197, 203, 207, 211, 212, 213, 216,
   217, 220, 221, 225, 268, 277
   Prophylaxis · 60, 83, 267, 268, 269
Pringle, Professor Mike · 11, 12, 13, 21, 83
Protocol · xvi, 1, 2, 9, 15, 17, 21, 22, 45, 55, 56, 69, 95, 136,
   140, 160, 173, 178, 179, 182, 267, 276
Psychiatric · 58, 109, 148, 200, 271, 274
Psychosis · 13, 58, 202, 271, 274

R

Ramsey Hunt Syndrome · 61, 83, 268
Recovery · 81
Red Blood Cell, RBC, erythrocytes · 37, 89, 90, 99
Restless legs syndrome (RLS) · 39
Rheumatoid arthritis · 39, 55, 110, 167, 168, 191

S

SAMe, S-adenosylmethionine · 27, 35, 36, 38, 100, 105,
   126, 128, 135, 200, 201, 220
Schilling test · 50, 88
Serum B12 · 56, 93
Shinwell Medical Centre · 12, 17, 20, 21, 35, 53, 54, 76, 77,
   78, 81, 83, 84, 150, 151, 155, 161, 165, 176, 191, 209,
   213
Short Synacthen Test, SST · 178, 181, 183, 184, 186, 187
Signs and Symptoms · 1, 5, 14, 17, 21, 44, 45, 46, 47, 49,
   53, 55, 56, 57, 58, 59, 60, 73, 83, 86, 90, 95, 97, 98, 100,
   118, 119, 122, 130, 131, 135, 137, 139, 146, 147, 151,
   153, 156, 160, 168, 174, 180, 182, 183, 187, 190, 191,
   267, 268, 269, 270, 271, 273, 276, 277, 278,279, 280,
   282
Single limb paralysis · 60, 83, 142, 146, 268, 274
Skin · 28, 200, 274
Smith, Professor David · 4, 48, 49, 62
Smoke inhalation · 26, 51, 270
Smoking · 51, 58, 223, 271
Subacute Combined Degeneration (SACD) · 14, 16, 31, 38,
   41, 46, 60, 81, 83, 109, 133, 135, 136, 137, 138, 139,
   140, 141, 142, 144, 146, 147, 153, 156, 158, 160, 161,
   274
Subclinical B12d · 17, 55, 109, 155, 204, 270
Symptoms · 31, 56, 81, 124, 130, 135, 156, 179, 186, 189,
   205, 267, 273, 276, 282, 283

Dementia · 207
Macrocytosis · 5
Multiple Sclerosis (MS) · 139

T

tHcy – total plasma homocysteine · 49, 50
Therapeutic Trial · 17, 45, 47, 60, 64, 73, 95, 109, 139, 151,
   160, 182, 267, 269, 270, 277
Tinnitus · 58, 271, 274
Transcobalamin II, see also Holotranscobalamin II · 49, 52,
   88

U

Ulcerative colitis · 39
UTI · 58, 271, 274

V

Vertigo · 159, 274
Viral · 156, 274
Vitamin
   Vitamin B1 · 208
   Vitamin B3 Niacin · 28, 29
   Vitamin B9 Folic Acid · xvi, 6, 7, 14, 16, 25, 26, 27, 28,
      29, 34, 35, 36, 37, 38, 41, 46, 47, 49, 51, 53, 54, 57,
      70, 71, 75, 83, 89, 90, 91, 94, 95, 98, 99, 100, 101,
      104, 105, 106, 107, 109, 110, 111, 112, 113, 114,
      116, 117, 118, 122, 123, 124, 125, 126, 127, 128,
      129, 140, 149, 154, 180, 194, 200, 204, 205, 207,
      208, 216, 218, 219, 220, 221, 222, 223, 224, 267,
      268, 269, 276, 282
   Vitamin D · 26, 57, 82, 95, 104, 122, 123, 161, 169, 180,
      184, 186, 187, 189, 217, 267, 276, 277, 278, 281
Vitiligo · 5, 17, 51, 58, 102, 165, 167, 177, 179, 194, 271,
   274, 282

W

Waardenburg Syndrome · 5
Weariness · 58, 271

Appendix 1: Protocol for excluding B12 deficiency (Megaloblastic anaemia/Pernicious anaemia) from adult and child patient presentation

Relevance

This protocol is relevant to all diagnosing clinicians, i.e. GPs and Nurses. HCAs and other staff should be aware of the possible 'presenting symptoms' and suggest that patients see a diagnosing clinician for further investigation.

Presenting Symptoms

If a patient presents with **Tiredness, depression, hair loss, pins and needles, numbness in hands or feet, tremors and palsies, palpitations, recurrent headache or dizziness**, B12 deficiency should be considered.

Beginning a diagnosis – presenting to GP/ Nurse

Using the **One Minute Health Check on page 271**

If B12 deficiency is suspected order a blood test for FBC, Serum vitamin B12, Folic Acid, TSH, U+Es, LFT, Serum ferritin, Glucose, 8-9am cortisol, Vitamin D to confirm/ exclude the most common conditions found alongside Vitamin B12 deficiency. Other appropriate diagnostic tests at this point include parathyroid, adrenal and ovarian hormone tests.

Refer to Appendix B for diagnosis and treatment and await blood results if appropriate. Note that for patients with severe Signs and Symptoms, treatment may need to be initiated without waiting for the results of blood tests.

Once blood results are available: if the serum B12 level is below 180ng/L (or local laboratory threshold) then staff should make a 15 minute appointment with the GP or nurse who requested the blood test.

Results of other blood tests: many conditions are commonly found alongside Vitamin B12 deficiency, and should be treated in the normal manner at the same time as administering B12 replacement therapy. See also the hypoadrenalism (Addison's disease or adrenal insufficiency) treatment protocol.

Confirming B12 deficiency

Blood tests are categorised as follows when combined with signs and symptoms indicative of B12 deficiency.

Table A1-1 Confirming B12 deficiency

Blood serum B12 ng/L	B12 nmol/ml	classification
Less than 200 ng/L	< 148 nmol/ml	Clinically significant/ severe B12 deficiency
200-350 ng/L	148 – 259 nmol/ml	Moderate deficiency
>350 ng/L	> 259 nmol/L	"Subtle" (subnormal/low normal blood serum B12 but with signs & symptoms)

This information is based on BMJ Best Practice 2012 and Harrison's Internal Medicine (starting with 16th Edition 2004)

In addition to these classifications, patients can be assigned to a therapeutic trial (to confirm a suspected diagnosis) or prophylaxis (where the clinician has evidence to suggest this is needed to prevent symptoms developing or getting worse). For example, if the patient is diagnosed as moderate or subtle deficiency (>180ng/L or >200ng/L with signs and symptoms, other autoimmune condition or family history) then they should be clinically reviewed every 4 weeks until you reach a clinical decision whether to commence treatment – even when the B12 level does not drop below 180-200ng/L. A deterioration of condition demonstrated by signs and symptoms is sufficient to commence a **therapeutic trial**.

Prophylaxis of vitamin B12 deficiency

In the following instances B12 replacement therapy should be instituted as a prophylactic measure (to prevent further deterioration or even development of symptoms) regardless of blood serum B12 concentration: Prophylaxis is expected to continue for life.

1- **Specific medical history** renal imbalance, diabetes, >65 years old, or following GI surgery, Crohn's colitis, early onset dementia

2- **Moderate/ subtle B12 deficiency with mild signs & symptoms**

3- **Moderate/ subtle B12 deficiency with severe signs & symptoms:** patient presenting with strong family history, presence of other auto-immune conditions, major signs and symptoms which could become irreversible if treatment is not commenced urgently eg optic neuritis/ neuropathy, sudden onset blindness, subacute combined degeneration, ME, CFS, MS-like presentation, single limb paralysis, sudden loss of muscle mass (Motor Neurone Disease-like presentation), non-epileptic seizures, dysphagia, Bell's Palsy/ Ramsey Hunt syndrome, Parkinson's like presentation, dementia, total alopecia, migrainous headache, temporal arteritis, recurrent miscarriages, dysfunctional uterine bleeding, or psychosis

Other Actions to Take

- If clinical depression is suspected – complete PHQ9 and treat/refer as appropriate
- Neurological manifestation – neurological examination and refer to neurologist for further investigation
- Provisional diagnosis of any other condition – refer to appropriate speciality.

Mother & Foetus, Neonate, Child - B12 deficiency: prevention, early diagnosis and treatment

An undiagnosed, untreated B12 deficient mother receiving only folic acid supplement could deliver her child with neuromuscular damage, sub-acute combined degeneration of the spinal cord, congenital abnormalities, tumours including brain damage and spina bifida. This can be avoided with B12 replacement before and during pregnancy (treat as for B12 deficiency (PA[40]) with neurological signs and symptoms).

The neonate 0 – 1 month born to an untreated B12 deficient mother should receive intensive IV B12 replacement treatment in the hospital neonatal department. Folate deficiency frequently accompanies B12 deficiency and folate may be offered in combination.

See treatment for B12 deficiency (PA) with neurological signs & symptoms.

Child 1 month – 13 years

If an untreated B12 deficient mother opts to breast feed, mother and infant will require B12 replacement and regular monitoring as per BNF guidelines. Please note, baby milk powder fortified with vitamin B12 may not be sufficient to correct the moderate to severe deficiency in a new-born.

A child, whether born to a known B12 deficient mother or not, who presents with delayed development, hyper activity, behavioural problems, dyspraxia, learning disability, autistic spectrum disorder like presentation, should initially be screened by blood test, to exclude B12 deficiency, underactive thyroid, inborn errors of metabolism, and any other condition suspected.

---

[40] PA – Pernicious Anaemia

Treatment as per BNF guidelines for children. Review the signs and symptoms and vary the frequency according to the child's needs (following the loading doses of alternate day injections); 1mg weekly, fortnightly, monthly, 2 monthly or 3 monthly.

When required, refer to appropriate paediatric speciality.

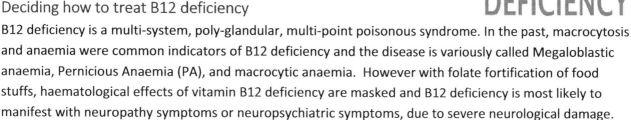

Deciding how to treat B12 deficiency

B12 deficiency is a multi-system, poly-glandular, multi-point poisonous syndrome. In the past, macrocytosis and anaemia were common indicators of B12 deficiency and the disease is variously called Megaloblastic anaemia, Pernicious Anaemia (PA), and macrocytic anaemia. However with folate fortification of food stuffs, haematological effects of vitamin B12 deficiency are masked and B12 deficiency is most likely to manifest with neuropathy symptoms or neuropsychiatric symptoms, due to severe neurological damage.

Before treatment starts, patients should agree to B12 replacement therapy by signing and dating the appropriate consent form.

Where 1-3 body systems are affected (see Appendix A – symptoms) and blood serum B12 is below the local lab threshold (200ng/L usually) then treat as for B12 deficiency (PA) without neurological involvement.

Where 1-3 body systems are affected and blood serum is above the local lab threshold, then monitor the patient and review. Following specific medical history, prophylaxis may be initiated.

4-6 body systems affected, blood serum more than 350ng/L (subtle deficiency) then offer a therapeutic trial to confirm diagnosis. Blood serum less than 350ng/L (moderate and severe deficiency), follow treatment for B12 deficiency (PA) with neurological signs & symptoms.

If more than 6 body systems are affected, commence treatment immediately without waiting for blood tests. Treat as B12 deficiency (PA) with neurological signs & symptoms.

Treatment regimes:

B12 deficiency (PA) and other macrocytic anaemias without neurological involvement. A small number of people have B12 deficiency and do not exhibit neurological signs and symptoms: hydroxocobalamin[41] by intramuscular injection Initially 1mg 3 times a week for 2 weeks then 1mg every 2-3 months. *Clinically review every 3 months with or without serum B12 test and if clinically indicated increase the frequency according to patient's clinical requirements (to minimise symptoms)

B12 deficiency (PA) without macrocytosis with neurological signs and symptoms. Initially hydroxocobalamin (or methylcobalamin) 1mg on alternate days until no further improvement (maximum reversal of neuro-psychiatric signs and symptoms are achieved), then 1mg every 1 or 2 months. *Clinically review every 2 months with or without serum B12 and if clinically indicated increase the frequency to every month or more frequently

Note: treatment should be tailored to patient need; some people need injections more frequently than once per month for short periods.

Prophylaxis of B12 deficiency for specific medical history and patients presenting with moderate or severe symptoms but may not have low blood serum B12 ('subtle' B12 deficiency): 1mg hydroxocobalamin or

---

[41] methylcobalamin is used in USA, Canada, India, Japan and other countries. Pharmacists in Wales also report that they can prescribe methylcobalamin. Methylcobalamin is considered superior to hydroxocobalamin by many people because it is one of the natural body forms of B12

methylcobalamin IM or SC alternate days for 6 doses (2 weeks), then 1mg IM or SC every 1-2 months: review and increase frequency to minimise the development of symptoms

Oral B12 treatment may also be offered for mild deficiency, and where a B12 deficiency has been demonstrated through a therapeutic trial but absorption of B12 from the gut is normal (ie no autoimmune conditions, no GI tract surgery or disorders, no IF or parietal cell antibodies) and dietary deficiency is suspected (vegetarian or vegan, or limited intake of red meat). Oral (OC[42]) B12 1mg/ 3mg/ 5mg per day. The patient's blood serum B12 should rise rapidly. If the patient's signs and symptoms do not improve then review and consider treatment for B12 deficiency (PA) without neurological signs.

Therapeutic Trial should be used where B12 deficiency is suspected because of signs and symptoms, but B12 deficiency is subtle or subclinical on the basis of blood serum results. 1mg IM or SC (hydroxocobalamin or methylcobalamin) should be given alternate days for 2 – 3 weeks (6 to 9 doses) followed by 1mg IM or SC[43] per week for 3 months. Signs and symptoms should be monitored, and frequency varied if required. If there is no improvement in signs and symptoms after 3 months (13 weeks) then B12 deficiency can be excluded. A therapeutic trial will not interact with other medication given and other treatment can be started at the same time.

Cyanide poisoning (victims of smoke inhalation who show signs of significant cyanide poisoning) hydroxocobalamin (or methylcobalamin in some countries) the usual dose is 5g (or 70mg/kg in children) by intravenous infusion, given once or twice according to severity.

NOTE THAT cyanocobalamin is licensed for 1mg IM injection monthly; because of reduced retention in the body in comparison to hydroxocobalamin and methyl-cobalamin (not licensed). Cyanocobalamin is excreted by the kidney preferentially which is why Cobalamin is used to treat cyanide poisoning. Current guidelines suggest that cyanocobalamin should NOT be used for treating B12 deficiency.

Nitrous oxide anaesthesia. Nitrous oxide inactivates Vitamin B12 in the body including brain cells. Therefore a B12 deficient patient (or his or her GP) should alert the surgeon and anaesthetist so that an alternative anaesthetic agent will be used during surgery. A full blown megaloblastic state can develop over the course of just a few days following nitrous oxide anaesthesia.

Cessation of treatment

In most cases, treatment should continue for life. Treatment should be varied as follows:

- If the patient shows signs of improvement or is stable for 2 years, then the frequency of injections can be extended from monthly to every 2 months.

- If the patient suffers symptoms before the next scheduled injection, then the GP should consider injections closer together to minimise suffering

- Blood serum B12 is not considered a good measure of the effectiveness of injections; relief from signs and symptoms is the best measure. It should be noted that the majority of B12 in blood serum is in the inactive form, and that the serum B12 test measures all forms of Cobalamin including the less biologically active cyanocobalamin form.

---

[42] OC – Over the Counter. B12 can be purchased as oral lozenges or spray from health food shops and the internet. Use methylcobalamin for preference
[43] Injections Intra-Muscular (IM, into the muscle of the shoulder or thigh) or Sub Cutaneous (SC, stomach, buttock etc). IM injections will be released into the blood more quickly giving faster effects but lasting less time, whereas injections into fatty tissue will be released more gradually

One Minute Health Check – B12 Deficiency signs and symptoms

A quick score will reveal if B12 deficiency, underactive thyroid or iron deficiency anaemia are possible diagnoses, and if the physician should order further tests. **This should be completed by the patient – it is sometimes helpful to circle the actual symptom experienced.**

Name _____ DOB _____ Date _____

Where will you grade these symptoms 1-10? 1 indicates that this symptom is mild and infrequent. 10 indicates the patient has it all the time and it is severe and debilitating. A score of 5 indicates that the patient has the symptom and it affects their daily life to a moderate extent.

Table A1-2 One Minute Health Check symptoms

Signs and Symptoms	Score 1-10
Energy/ haemopoetic	
Weariness, Lethargy, tiredness, fatigue, faints	
Sleepy, tired in the afternoon	
Nervous system	
Tremor, foot drop	
¥ Loss of balance (ataxia), seizures, falls	
¥ Tingling or numbness in hands and/or feet, burning sensation	
Restless leg syndrome	
Facial Palsy	
Spastic movements, Crampy pain in limbs	
¥ Stiffness of limbs, muscle wasting	
¥ Weakness or loss of sensation in limbs, shooting pain in back/ limbs, paralysis	
Migrainous headache	
Psychiatric	
Irritable, snappy, disturbed sleep	
Confused, Memory disturbance/ forgetful, fogginess	
Tension Headaches	
* Mental slowness, Mood swings, Anxiety/ Panic Attacks, depression	
* Psychosis, hallucinations, delusion	
Eye Ear Throat	
Blurred vision/ double vision/ drooping of eyelid (lid lag), orbital pain	
Dizziness, tinnitus	
Difficulty swallowing, persistent cough	
Immune System	
Prone to recurrent URTI, UTI, Respiratory infections	
Other auto-immune conditions	
Hypoadrenalism, myxodema/ underactive thyroid	

Signs and Symptoms	Score 1-10
Cardiovascular/ Respiratory	
Shortness of breath, wheeziness	
Palpitations, chest pain	
Pallor, lemon yellow complexion	
Bruising, Vasculitis	
Gastro-Intestinal (GI)	
Sore tongue, bleeding gums	
Red beefy tongue	
Cracking the angles of mouth	
Metallic taste, unusual taste, loss of appetite, loss of weight	
Gastric symptoms-acidity, heartburn	
Intermittent diarrhoea, IBS	
Skin hair nail skeletal	
Premature greying	
Alopecia, Unexplained hair loss	
Joint inflammation, swelling, pain	
Dry skin, brittle nails	
Genito-Urinary (GU)	
Heavy painful periods, irregular periods, infertility & frequent miscarriages	
Polycystic ovarian disease	
Loss of libido	
Shooting pain from groin to perineum	
Incontinence	
Personal & Family History	
Family history of B12 deficiency (Pernicious Anaemia), underactive thyroid, diabetes, vitiligo, depression	
Vegetarian, vegan, poor diet	
Alcoholism, Smoking	

* PHQ9 Patient Health Questionnaire to be completed
¥ Neurological examination and appropriate referral if indicated

Physician should also order routine blood tests including serum B12 in the following cases:
- ME, CFS, Fibromyalgia, Hypoadrenalism, MS-like presentation
- Children born to B12-deficient mothers, presenting with behavioural problems, learning disability, dyspraxia, dyslexia and autistic spectrum disorders

Before making a provisional diagnosis of B12 deficiency, exclude all other possible diagnoses, with appropriate additional blood tests as clinically indicated.

Decision Tree to diagnose / exclude B12 deficiency
Record the MAXIMUM score of any single symptom within a body system, in the yellow header bar of the body system (on the Signs and Symptoms form on page 271).

Count scores of severity 5 or above in the yellow Signs and Symptoms bars (ie count body systems).

1. **B12 deficiency (Pernicious Anaemia) and other macrocytic anaemias without neurological involvement**[44]. Hydroxocobalamin or methylcobalamin initially 1mg 3 times per week for 2 weeks, then 1mg every 2 – 3 months

2. **B12 deficiency (Pernicious Anaemia) with neurological signs and symptoms**[44]. Initially 1mg on alternate days until no further improvement (maximum reversal of neuro-psychiatric signs and symptoms are achieved), then 1mg every 1 – 2 months.

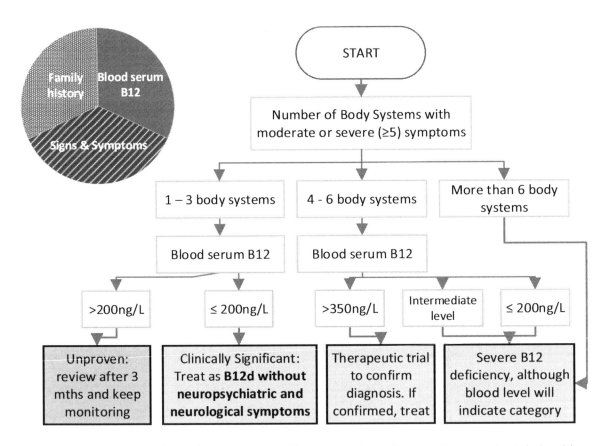

3. **Prophylaxis or Therapeutic Trial**. 1mg IM or SC (hydroxocobalamin or methylcobalamin) should be given alternate days for 2 – 3 weeks (6 to 9 doses) followed by 1mg IM or SC[45] per week for 3 months. If there is no improvement in signs and symptoms after 3 months (13 weeks) then B12 deficiency can be excluded. A therapeutic trial will not interact with medication given and any other treatment can be started at the same time. Review treatment pathway after 3 months.

---

[44] Clinically review every 1 or 2 months with or without serum B12 and if clinically indicated increase the frequency to every 2 months, every month or more frequently
[45] Injections Intra-Muscular (IM, into the muscle of the shoulder or thigh) or Sub Cutaneous (SC, stomach, buttock etc) of hydroxocobalamin or methylcobalamin 1mg/ml or 5mg/ml

B12 Consent Form

Dear patient

Your blood test shows that you have low levels of Vitamin B12 in the body, and your signs and symptoms indicate that you have a deficiency of Vitamin B12.

Vitamin B12 is essential for life. Vitamin B12 deficiency can result in damage to every system and gland in the body

- it is needed to make new cells in the body, including red blood cells, and for enabling genes (DNA) to switch on and off

- it is needed for maintenance of the myelin sheath around nerve cells, and deficiency can result in numbness, paralysis, or shooting pains, as well as confusion and memory loss

- it is a vital catalyst in the body's energy pathways, so without it you may suffer lethargy and tiredness, and at the same time disturbed sleep

- It helps maintain cell membranes, which means it is important for a normal immune system, for hormone production, and for the production of digestive juices.

Vitamin B12 is found in meat, fish, eggs and milk but not in fruit or vegetables. The medical view is that a normal balanced diet contains enough B12. However, failure to absorb Vitamin B12 from food will cause B12 deficiency resulting in many forms of illnesses and disabilities.

Treatment – Vitamin B12 can be administered by either injection or taken by mouth. This is an ongoing treatment and your Doctor will advise you on how this will be given. You will be monitored and have further blood tests, to check on progress.

Risks – Although injectable B12 is completely non-toxic, some people report a little local discomfort after injection.

The practice has explained:-

    About the condition

    Treatment required and ongoing monitoring

I fully understand and I accept the above:

Signature: ....

Date: ....

For Surgery Information:

Diagnosis

Clinically significant B12 def less than 200 (lab threshold) (with signs & symptoms) ....[ ]

Subclinical / subtle B12 Def (above lab threshold) (WITH signs & symptoms) ....[ ]

Additional Requirements

Signs & Symptoms sheet completed..[ ]

Consent form signed ....[ ]

Patient Information Leaflets given..[ ]

Vitamin B12 deficiency and direct or indirect causation of disease

Deficiency of vitamin B12 is a multi-system, polyglandular, multipoint poisonous syndrome. B12 is required for proper function of most of the body's systems, so deficiency leads to disease in these systems.

This appendix lists some of the common conditions that can be treated successfully by using Vitamin B12 replacement therapy, and a causative mechanism can be described.

Haematological
Unexplained recurrent anaemia
Myelodysplasia
Pancytopaenia / bruising

Psychiatric
Depression
Memory loss / confusion
Anxiety
Psychosis
Angry / moody / snappy

Gastro-intestinal
Recurrent gastritis
Mouth ulcers, bleeding gums
Pernicious anaemia
IBS / diverticulosis
Unexplained diarrhoea
Crohn's Colitis

Cardio-Vascular / Respiratory Systems
Cardiac failure – arthrosclerosis, stroke
Temporal arteritis
Vasculitis
Exacerbation of angina – palpitations, breathlessness
Asthma exacerbation

ENT (Ear, nose & throat)
Tinnitus / vertigo
Glossopharyngeal neuropathy (swallowing difficulties)
Persistent cough
Dizziness / falls

Endocrine / Immune systems
Post Viral Immune Deficiency Fatigue Syndrome (ME)
Poor wound healing/ susceptibility to infection
Auto-immune conditions such as vitiligo, myxodema, hypoadrenal diabetes coexisting with B12 deficiency

Neurological
Dementia
Alzheimers'
Optic Atrophy / blindness
Doublevision, Ptosis
Loss of sensation in limbs, trunk, face, genitalia
Pseudo seizures, non-epileptic seizures
Blackouts and faints
SubAcute Combined Degeneration (SACD)
Single limb paralysis
Multiple-sclerosis like B12 deficiency syndrome
Neuropathic pain / myopathy
Cramps / crampy pain
Babies with neuromuscular damage may be born to mothers who are B12 deficient during pregnancy
Tension / migraine headaches
Parkinson's like presentation
Motorneurone like presentation with limb muscle atrophy
Bell's palsy
Ramsay Hunt syndrome

Bone
Osteoporosis, suppressed activity of osteoblasts
Inflammatory polyarthritis

Dermatology
Alopecia
Dry scaly skin/ dermatitis
Brittle nails

Genito-Urinary
Dysfunctional Uterine Bleeding
Repeated miscarriages
Polycystic ovarian disease
Dysmenorrhoea, menorrhagia
Recurrent UTI
Loss of libido
Double-incontinence

If treatment is delayed, this may cause irreversible damage, or fatality. Always exclude vitamin B12 deficiency before making a final diagnosis and deciding treatment options.

If vitamin B12 deficiency co-exists with other causes, B12 therapy compliments other treatments rather than interferes

Exclusion Criteria

Conditions which, if diagnosed, will exclude a diagnosis of B12 deficiency unless the patient meets above criteria for diagnosis:

- Depressive illness
- Phobic anxiety state
- Neurosis
- Bulimia
- Anorexic nervosa
- Vasovagal attacks
- Partial seizure
- Epileptic seizure
- Brain tumour
- Cranio pharyngeoma
- Temporal arteritis
- Gastric colon and renal cancers
- Cerebral aneurism

Appendix 2 Protocol for Diagnosing
Hypoadrenalism/Addison's Disease

Relevance

This protocol is relevant to all diagnosing clinicians, i.e. GPs and Nurses. HCAs and other staff should be aware of the possible 'presenting symptoms' and suggest that patients see a diagnosing clinician for further investigation.

Presenting symptoms

Adrenal insufficiency is caused by either primary adrenal failure (mostly due to autoimmune adrenalitis) or by hypothalamic-pituitary impairment of the corticotropic axis (predominantly due to pituitary disease). It is a rare disease, but is life-threatening when overlooked.

Beginning a diagnosis

Main presenting symptoms such as fatigue, anorexia, and weight loss are nonspecific, thus diagnosis is often delayed. The diagnostic workup is well established but some pitfalls remain, particularly in the identification of secondary and tertiary adrenal insufficiency.

Patients may also present with critical or emergency symptoms of hypoadrenalism. The Physician should immediately arrange emergency admission to hospital.

When patients present with mild to moderate symptoms of possible hypoadrenalism, the GP should order early morning cortisol levels (8am – 9am fasting cortisol) along with FBC, B12, Folic Acid, Ferritin, TSH, T3, T4, Parathyroid hormone, Vitamin D, U&Es, Liver Function, blood glucose etc; in order to differentially or concurrently diagnose ME, CFS, fibromyalgia, MS-like presentation, depression, psychosis, B12 deficiency, myxodema etc.

Symptoms to consider when making a diagnosis are listed in the table on page 282. The table can be used to complete a work-up of symptoms, which with the cortisol level estimation, allows the clinician to make a provisional diagnosis. More detail for each stage is given in this protocol to assist diagnosis and treatment. A 'consent to treatment' form is included.

The most important/ frequent symptoms are:

- Feels faint, dizzy, headache
- Weakness, fatigue
- Anorexia, weight loss
- Abdominal pain, salt craving
- Loss of muscle mass
- Breathlessness

Table A2-1 Diagnosis using results of symptoms table – please circle condition and cortisol level to diagnose stage

	Stage 1 Preclinical	Stage 2 Preclinical	Stage 3 Subtle/ subclinical	Stage 4 Clinically significant	Stage 5 Clinically Critical	Stage 6 Clinical Emergency
Signs and Symptoms	Mild	Mild to Moderate	Moderate	Significant	Critical	Emergency (adrenal crisis)
Cortisol (blood level)	400-500 nmol/L	300-400 nmol/L	150-300 nmol/L	50-150 nmol/L	25-50 nmol/L	0-25 mol/L

8-9 AM cortisol 400-500nmols/L ≈20% adrenal cortical damage[46]	a) Signs and Symptoms mild. b) Patient has a history of vitamin B12 deficiency and/or presence of other autoimmune polyendocrine conditions (APS).
Clinically review with 8-9 AM serum cortisol 6 monthly	c) Family history of vitamin B12 deficiency and presence of other autoimmune conditions.

Treatment

No replacement treatment offered.

Clinically review with 8-9am cortisol level 6 to 12 monthly.

Continue to treat appropriately and adequately other co-existing autoimmune conditions (myxoedema, vitamin B12 deficiency, diabetes etc).

If vitamin D deficient, provide appropriate vitamin D replacement therapy.

Stage 2 Pre-clinical and Primary Prevention

8-9 AM cortisol 300-400nmols/L ≈20-40% adrenal cortical damage	a) Signs and Symptoms mild to moderate b) Patient has a history of vitamin B12 deficiency and/or presence of other autoimmune polyendocrine conditions (APS).
Clinically review with 8-9 AM serum cortisol 2 monthly	c) Family history of vitamin B12 deficiency and presence of other autoimmune conditions. d) Cortisol level dropping, signs and symptoms worsening

Treatment

3 months therapeutic trial of physiological doses of:-

Hydrocortisone - 10mg 7am, 5mg 12 noon, 2.5mg 5pm (17.5mg per day) OR

Prednisolone - 2mg 7am, 1mg 12 noon, 1mg 5pm (4mg per day) Equivalent to 16mg of Hydrocortisone per day.

After the therapeutic trial, adjust the daily dose between 15-25mg as per clinical requirement:-

- Check the early morning cortisol level prior to the 7am oral Hydrocortisone or Prednisolone dose. On the day of early morning cortisol blood testing, the first treatment dose has to be delayed according to the timing of the appointment
- Check cortisol level the same day, 3 hours after taking the first dose of Hydrocortisone/ Prednisolone.
  Half life of Hydrocortisone 3 hours.
  Half life of Prednisolone up to 6 hours.
  If the level has risen well above 400-500nmols/L AND if signs and symptoms improve:-
  Reduce the doses to half in 3 months then to nil by 6 months.

---

[46] The level of adrenal cortical damage is an estimate based on symptoms. Actual damage is not easy to measure

Clinically follow up with 8-9 am cortisol level 6 monthly or yearly, all in consultation with the patient.

If the normal circadian levels (hydrocortisone day curve) are maintained, no further replacement will be required.

- Continue to treat appropriately or adequately other co-existing autoimmune conditions (hypo/hyper thyroidism, vitamin B12 deficiency, diabetes, hypo/hyper-parathyroidism, polycystic ovarian disease etc. Replace vitamin D if vitamin D deficient.

Stage 3 Subtle/subclinical manifestation of hypoadrenalism

8-9 AM cortisol 150-300nmols/L ≈40-60% adrenal cortical damage	a) Signs and Symptoms moderate. b) Patient has a history of vitamin B12 deficiency and/or presence of other autoimmune p9lyendocrine disorders (APS).
ACTH - low/normal/high Aldosterone – normal/low DHEA – low/normal	c) Strong family history of vitamin B12 deficiency and presence of other autoimmune conditions.

Treatment

Appropriate replacement treatment prescribed. Repeat bloods and 8-9 am cortisol each month and clinically review.

If the cortisol level is steadily declining and sign and symptoms worsening -

Option 1) Refer to Endocrinologist.

Option 2) If the patient declines specialist referral and request primary care intervention: commence **physiological** doses of Hydrocortisone or Prednisolone.

Option 3) Shared care – refer to Endocrinologist and commence physiological doses of steroids and closely monitor the response by carrying out HCDC.

Table A2-2 Stage 3 dose of hydrocortisone

	7 am	12 noon	5 pm
Hydrocortisone	10mg	10mg	5mg
OR Prednisolone	2mg/3mg	2mg/3mg	1mg

Hydrocortisone is the generally preferred replacement treatment. 1mg of Prednisolone is equivalent to 4mg of Hydrocortisone.

Hydrocortisone - Peak blood level in 3 hours. Prednisolone has a longer half-life.

Hydrocortisone day curve (HCDC) in primary care setting

HCDC can be useful to assess the level of serum cortisol during the day (wakeful hours)

Within 30 minutes of waking, cortisol level should be at its highest (500-700 nmols/L)

- Initially measure cortisol level before the first daily dose (usually 7am) (no steroids taken since 5pm the previous day)
- Second sample is taken 3 hours after the 1st dose (10am)

- The third sample can be taken at 3pm (3 hours following the midday dose).
- A fourth sample can be taken at 8pm if desired.

If all the four levels are close to, or just below, the Circadian Rhythm Values, the patient's cortisol replacement dosing will be the optimum physiological dosing. As it is physiological dosing, any possibility of adrenal suppression is reassuringly prevented from ever taking place. Other adverse side effects for e.g. gastric ulcer, osteoporosis, iatrogenic cushionoid syndrome, etc. are also avoided.

Review and repeat the above 3 monthly.

If the levels are beginning to rise above the Circadian Curve, reduce the doses accordingly. There are occasions when cortical cells can regenerate and return to normal function. If this happens, gradually reduce and eventually stop the steroid-replacement therapy.

Clinically follow up these patients biannually or annually by recording absence or re-emergence of signs and symptoms and normal or diminishing cortisol levels, in close relation to the state of functioning of their adrenal glands.

Please note –

The very first day the patient presents to a clinician is most critical - because that day is the "Window of opportunity" to diagnose, treat and prevent impending irreversible damage.

Stage 4 Clinically significant hypoadrenalism

8-9 AM cortisol 50-150nmols/L ≈60-80% adrenal cortical damage ACTH - normal/low/high Aldosterone - normal/low DHEA – normal/low	a) Signs and Symptoms severe b) Patient has a history of B12 Deficiency and/or presence of other Auto Immune Poly-endocrine disorders (APS). c) Strong family history of B12 Deficiency and presence of other Auto Immune conditions.

Treatment

Correct Aldosterone and DHEA deficiency appropriately

Clinically review 1 weekly – if early morning cortisol level is low (50-150nmol/L) even though signs and symptoms are only moderate repeat early morning serum cortisol weekly.

IF cortisol level continues to be low:

Either choose **Option 1** – refer to Endocrinologist. **OR**

Option 2 – Commence oral physiological doses of Hydrocortisone or Prednisolone. Also provide parenteral Hydrocortisone 100mg for self-administration in an emergency. Steroid card and information leaflet etc. are provided.

Prior to hospital investigations patient will be advised to stay off oral steroids for 24, 48, or 72 hours. Please note Insulin tolerance test is not recommended for a strongly suspected Hypoadrenal patient.

Option 3 - If the patient prefers primary/secondary care (shared care) management, follow Option 3 in Stage 3 of this condition

  a) Commence physiological dose of hydrocortisone OR prednisolone. Also carryout HCDC assessment in the Primary Care setting in order to achieve optimum replacement levels.

b)   Refer to Endocrinologist the same time

Stage 5 Clinically critical hypoadrenalism

8-9 AM cortisol 25-50nmol/L ~80 95% cortical damage	Signs and symptoms severe. Patient not critically ill – however, requires immediate intervention by the GP.

Treatment

Refer to Endocrinologist under 2-week rule.

Administer 100 mg hydrocortisone IV. Commence physiological doses of oral hydrocortisone/prednisolone

Table A2-3 Stage 5 dose of hydrocortisone

	7 am	12 noon	5 pm
Hydrocortisone	20mg	20mg	5-10mg *
OR Prednisolone	5mg	5mg	2.5mg *

   * Adjusting up or down according to response

Stage 6 Clinical emergency (adrenal crisis)

8-9 AM cortisol 0-25 nmols/L ≈80-95% cortical damage	Signs and symptoms: • patient collapse, semiconscious/unconscious; • unable to self-inject emergency hydrocortisone; • patient critically ill.

Treatment

Administer 100 mg of Hydrocortisone IV or 100mg Efcortisol IV.

999 ambulance admission blue light.

Alert the crew/hospital. Provide ambulance crew with emergency guidelines re: adrenal crisis management, IV fluids (saline) and IV Hydrocortisone administration etc.

On hospital discharge continue therapeutic/ physiological doses of hydrocortisone as recommended by the endocrinologist.

Table A2-4 Stage 6 dose of hydrocortisone

	7 am	**12 noon**	**5 pm**
Hydrocortisone	10mg - 20mg	10mg - 20mg	2.5 - 10mg
Prednisolone	3mg - 5mg	3mg - 5mg	1 - 2.5mg

1) Prescribe IM/IV Hydrocortisone 100mg (5 amples) for self-administration or by a relative or friend. Syringes and needles provided.
2) Steroid card completed and given to patient.
3) Medic alert Hypoadrenalism/Addison's bracelet (patient to obtain (www.medicalert.org.uk or www.addisons.org.uk).
4) Patient information leaflet.
5) Patient, partner, friend shown how to administer the injection.

Review

- Clinically review – 1 to 3 monthly with AM cortisol level and HCDC values.
- Continue to treat appropriately and adequately other co-existing Auto-Immune conditions (Hypo / Hyper Thyroidism, B12 Deficiency, Diabetes, Hypo-Hyper Parathyroidism etc.

If vitamin D deficient, provide appropriate vitamin D therapy.

Hypoadrenalism (Addison's Disease) signs and symptoms - check

A quick score will reveal if hypoadrenalism is a possible diagnoses, and if the physician should order further tests.

This should be completed by the patient – it is sometimes helpful to circle the actual symptom experienced.

Name _____ DOB _____ Date _____

Where will you grade these symptoms 1-10 and circle most relevant symptoms? 1 indicates that this symptom is mild and infrequent. 10 indicates the patient has it all the time and it is severe and debilitating. A score of 5 indicates that the patient has the symptom and it affects their daily life to a moderate extent.

Joint & muscle pain/weakness	
Increased pigmentation of the skin – due to raised ACTH level (not in all cases) pigmentation may be accompanied by vitiligo	
Intermittent abdominal pain and salt craving	
Vague stomach ache or other gut symptoms, diarrhoea & nausea	
Experiences weakness, fatigue, anorexia and weight loss	
Feels faint, dizzy & headache	
Signs & Symptoms Usually subtle	
Depression/Anger/Difficulty concentrating	
Decrease in axillary and pubic hair – common in women – Alopecia	
Loss of muscle mass	
Neuropathy, Myopathy	
Dizziness, Unsteadiness, Falls, Syncope	
Breathlessness, Difficulty with speech, Chest pain	
Postural hypotension, Hyponatremia (low sodium)	
Impotence & Amenorrhoea	
Hypoglycaemia	

Diagnosis.

- Before making a provisional diagnosis of Hypoadrenalism, excluding all other possible diagnosis with appropriate blood test and investigations as clinically indicated.
- Physician should also order blood tests including FBC, B12, Folic Acid, Ferritin, TSH, T3, T4, Vit D in the following cases (ME, CFS, fibromyalgia, MS like presentation, depression, psychosis, B12 Deficiency & Myxoedema Etc).

Diagnosis (circle)

	Stage 1 Preclinical	Stage 2 Preclinical	Stage 3 Subtle	Stage 4 Clinically significant	Stage 5 Clinically Critical	Stage 6 Clinical Emergency
Signs and Symptoms	Mild	Mild to Moderate	Moderate	Significant	Critical	Emergency (adrenal crisis)
Cortisol (blood level)	400-500 nmol/L	300-400 nmol/L	150-300 nmol/L	50-150 nmol/L	25-50 nmol/L	0-25 nmol/L

Hypoadrenalism (Addison's Disease) Consent Form

Dear Patient

Your blood test shows that you have low levels of Cortisol in your body. Cortisol is most essential for life. Cortisol is produced by the adrenal glands. Under activity of the adrenal gland is called HYPOADRENALISM. Many of the symptoms of hypoadrenalism are due to a deficiency of the steroid hormone cortisol.

The deficiency can be corrected effectively in all stages of its presentation.

Treatment

Usually the treatment will be oral steroid tablets for some patients, we may offer an Emergency Pack including an injection for use by family member or friends. In this case training will be given.

It is most beneficial and safe for the patient, if the deficiency is corrected promptly in the very early stages of its presentations.

Treatment:

Oral steroid tablets are taken by mouth. In emergencies; injection form has to be used by self or by a family member or a friend.

Side effects:

You are given safe physiological doses of cortisol just to correct the deficiency. The dose will be adjusted following periodic blood tests so that the level of cortisol is kept just below the normal cortisol day curve level. Therefore you will not experience any side effects from the replacement therapy.

The Practice has explained

About the condition

Treatment required and ongoing monitoring

I fully understand and I accept the above:

Signature:..

Date: ....

For Surgery Information:

Additional Requirements

Signs & Symptoms sheet completed .... [ ]
Consent form signed.. [ ]
Steroid card given.. [ ]
Patient Information Leaflets given .... [ ]
IM/IV hydrocortisone 100ng or efcortisol prescribed .... [ ]
Syringes/needles etc provided .... [ ]
Self injecting training given .... [ ]

      e-mail info@addisons.org.uk Website www.addisons.org.uk

      www.medicalert.org.uk – to obtain Addison's/hypoadrenalism bracelet

Printed in Great Britain
by Amazon

46819136R00165